INSIDERS' GUIDE® TO GRAND CANYON
AND NORTHERN ARIZONA

HELP US KEEP THIS GUIDE UP TO DATE

Every effort has been made by the authors and editors to make this guide as accurate and useful as possible. However, many things can change after a guide is published—phone numbers change, facilities come under new management, etc.

We would love to hear from you concerning your experiences with this guide and how you feel it could be improved and be kept up to date. While we may not be able to respond to all comments and suggestions, we'll take them to heart and we'll also make certain to share them with the authors. Please send your comments and suggestions to the following address:

The Globe Pequot Press
Reader Response/Editorial Department
P. O. Box 480
Guilford, CT 06437

Or you may e-mail us at:

editorial@GlobePequot.com

Thanks for your input, and happy travels!

INSIDERS'GUIDE®

INSIDERS' GUIDE® SERIES

INSIDERS' GUIDE® TO
GRAND CANYON
AND NORTHERN ARIZONA

SECOND EDITION

TODD R. BERGER, TANYA H. LEE, AND KERRI QUINN

INSIDERS'GUIDE®

GUILFORD, CONNECTICUT
AN IMPRINT OF THE GLOBE PEQUOT PRESS

The prices and rates in this guidebook were confirmed at press time. We recommend, however, that you call establishments before traveling to obtain current information.

Publications from the Insiders' Guide® series are available at special discounts for bulk purchases for sales promotions, premiums, or fund-raisings. Special editions, including personalized covers, can be created in large quantities for special needs. For more information, please contact The Globe Pequot Press at (800) 962–0973.

INSIDERS'GUIDE®

Text design by LeAnna Weller Smith

Maps created by XNR Productions Inc. © The Globe Pequot Press

ISSN 1547-6790
ISBN 0-7627-3002-1

Manufactured in the United States of America
Second Edition/First Printing

CONTENTS

DIRECTORY OF MAPS

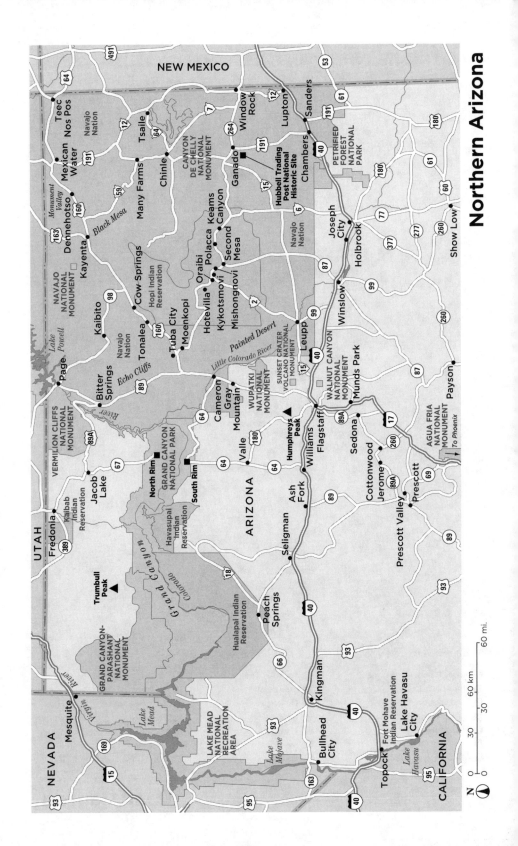

Northern Arizona

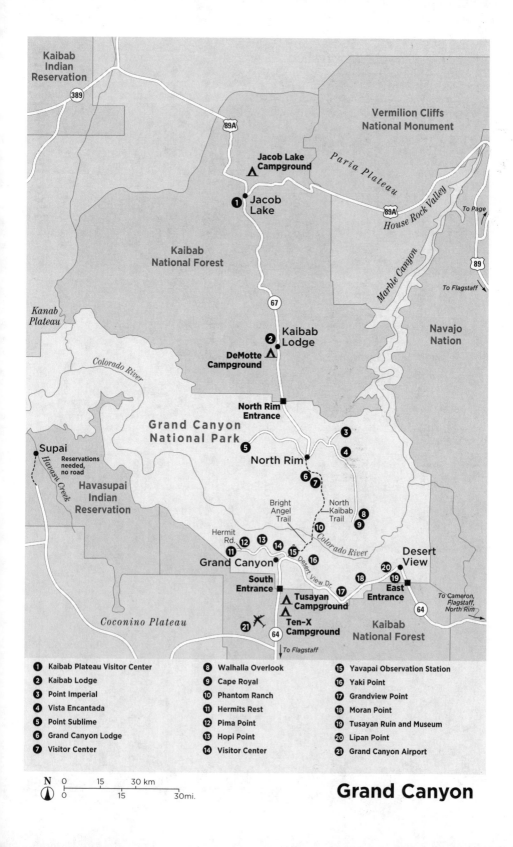

Kaibab
Indian
Reservation

389

89A

Vermilion Cliffs
National Monument

Paria Plateau

Jacob Lake
Campground

To Page

89A

House Rock Valley

1 Jacob
Lake

Kaibab
National Forest

89

To Flagstaff

*Kanab
Plateau*

Marble Canyon

Colorado River

67

Navajo
Nation

2 Kaibab
Lodge

DeMotte
Campground

Supai

Reservations
needed,
no road

North Rim
Entrance

Grand Canyon
National Park

3

Havasu Creek

Havasupai
Indian
Reservation

5

North Rim

4

6

7

Bright
Angel
Trail

North
Kaibab
Trail

8

9

Hermit
Rd.

12 13

11

14

15

10

Colorado River

16

Desert
View

Grand Canyon

South
Entrance

Tusayan
Campground

Desert View Dr.

18

17

20

19

East
Entrance

To Cameron,
Flagstaff,
North Rim

Ten-X
Campground

Coconino Plateau

21

64

Kaibab
National Forest

64

To Flagstaff

1 Kaibab Plateau Visitor Center
2 Kaibab Lodge
3 Point Imperial
4 Vista Encantada
5 Point Sublime
6 Grand Canyon Lodge
7 Visitor Center

8 Walhalla Overlook
9 Cape Royal
10 Phantom Ranch
11 Hermits Rest
12 Pima Point
13 Hopi Point
14 Visitor Center

15 Yavapai Observation Station
16 Yaki Point
17 Grandview Point
18 Moran Point
19 Tusayan Ruin and Museum
20 Lipan Point
21 Grand Canyon Airport

N
0   15   30 km
0   15   30mi.

Grand Canyon

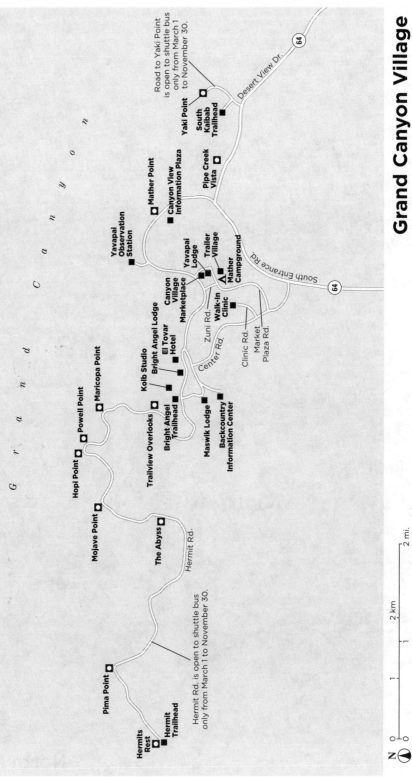

Grand Canyon Village

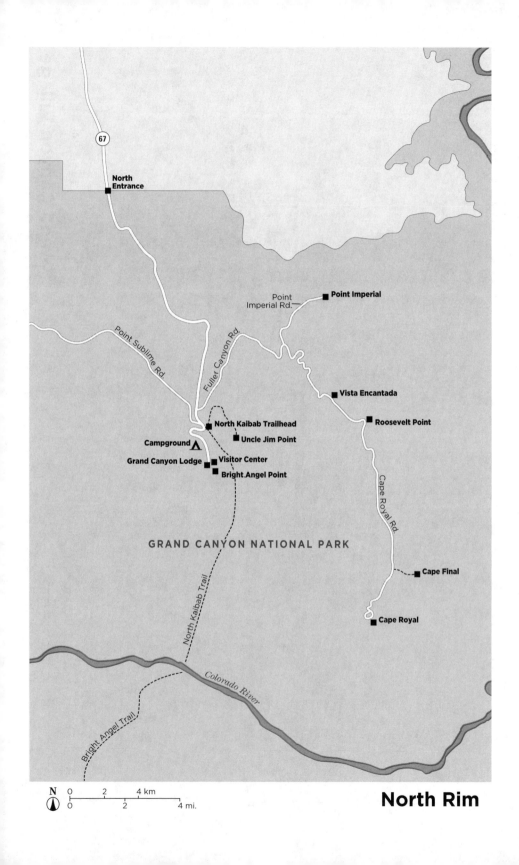

North Rim

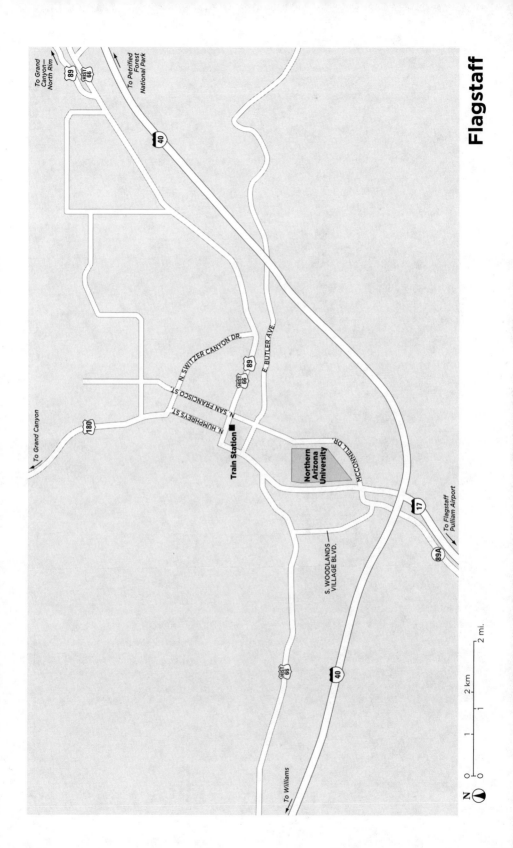

Flagstaff

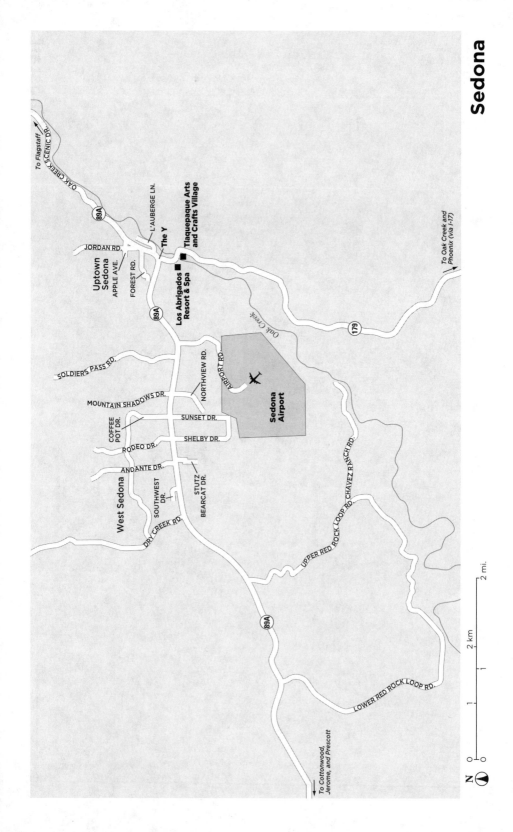

Sedona

PREFACE

As I sit here along the South Rim of Grand Canyon and feel the warm autumn breeze flow over me in wave after wave, I understand why I live here and have chosen to write about this remarkable place. This land cleanses my soul. Wilderness. There's nothing like it—particularly this wilderness, with its weird rock formations, forested rims and desert bottom, knee-jarring trails, endless switchbacks, and native-only-to-here wildlife. This place is ready-made to cleanse the soul.

Looking out over the canyon, I can see two forest fires burning on the North Rim, one rather large. Fires burned in these areas earlier this summer, and now that the monsoon has passed, the fires have flared up again. They don't threaten any structures or people, so park rangers are letting them burn out—although the rangers are keeping a close eye on the flames. The fire crew knows it, and so do I: The fires are part of the wilderness.

I walk back from the rim through the pinyon-juniper forest (with its smattering of ponderosa pine) and hear the now familiar sound of a bull elk bugling—really more of a whistle than a trumpet blast—in the distance. It is the sound of the rut, the bulls sounding out their plaintive cries for cows. It is elegant, this noise, part of the wilderness, and I immediately chastise myself for lacking such elegance in human interactions. But just as quickly, my mind slips back into the present, as I notice an Abert squirrel, with its tasseled ears, on top of a log. A pinyon jay squawks nearby, cementing me in the present, a happier place. Once again, for the thousandth time, this place has cleansed my soul.

But this book is not about me or how Grand Canyon and the rest of northern Arizona make me feel. It's about you, the reader, the visitor. By providing a few details, sharing a few choice spots, describing a fabulous meal, or warning of something in the woods that might make your leg swell up like a hockey goalie's pad, this book aims to steer you into this wilderness and gently set you down without incident to explore wherever your soul dictates. Or at least to help you find a suitably greasy cheeseburger.

—Todd R. Berger

The view of Marble Canyon, the section of Grand Canyon National Park where the Colorado River swings due north, is long and spectacular from Desert View. TODD R. BERGER

ACKNOWLEDGMENTS

A work of this magnitude requires the help of numerous people, and I thank all who lent a helping hand or answered a rather thick-headed question with good cheer. First and foremost, I would like to thank Tanya Lee and Kerri Quinn, authors of the first edition of this book. I remain awestruck by their thorough research, attention to detail, and wonderful finds in northern Arizona. Their work is the foundation on which this second edition is built, and I felt comfortable further recommending many sites first brought to my attention by Tanya and Kerri. In some sections of the book, much of the wording, although updated as needed, remains as originally worded. In my opinion, it could not be improved upon.

I would also like to thank my girl-friend, Bonnie Platt, who endured not only late nights of writing but a general moodiness that lingered until I sent in the final draft to Globe Pequot. A ballet and modern dance teacher by trade, she gamely donned a backpack and escorted me into the canyon, once on a rim-to-rim hike of 24 miles through the canyon. I know she enjoyed herself and would go again, but it's not her true passion, and I thank her for humoring me.

I would also like to thank my two knee surgeons, Drs. Laurie Koch and Owen O'Neill, who apparently did a very nice job removing all that torn cartilage suffered during the process of writing a previous book. I thought I was hobbled for life, but I've been all over Grand Canyon and northern Arizona since with no ill effects. I hope a sea of knees comes their way, though not mine—again.

I would like to thank others who had a role, however large or small, in what follows, including: Arnie Alanen, Maija Alanen, Richard Berger, Paula Brisco, Professor Irene Clepper, Pam Frazier, Ronald Guelzow, Molly Harding, Don and Midge Harris, Kate Kjorlien, my Montrail hiking boots, Motel 6, the entire Navajo Nation, Abigail Platt-Berger, Becky Post, the staff of El Tovar, Jeff Serena, Bonnie Taylor, Liz Taylor, and my Volkswagen Jetta. Without the help of each of these people (and things), I wouldn't have gotten any-where near this far. Thank you.

—Todd R. Berger

HOW TO USE THIS BOOK

This is a guidebook, although it is also a history book, geology book, natural history essay, and hiking book. By necessity, the myriad subjects you will find in this guidebook barely scratch the surface—you will have to consult more in-depth sources for detailed information about desert hiking, Grand Canyon rock layers, Navajo rugs, aspen trees, or tarantulas. But here you will find an introduction to all of these subjects, essentially enough information for you to judge whether you would enjoy traveling to a spot, enough information to find your way around if you're already there, or enough information to whet your appetite to learn more.

The book is organized logically rather than strictly geographically, with the most popular location (i.e., Grand Canyon National Park) discussed first and the rest of northern Arizona following. Sections of the book are grouped geographically: You will find information about Navajoland before the Hopi Reservation chapter, and the Sedona chapter is next to the Coconino National Forest chapter. You may need to use the book on a trip across northern Arizona to see the value in this organization, but that's what this book is for, so hop to it. However, don't rely only on this book to get you there and back. Bring along a good road map, and if you're headed for wilderness areas, make sure you have a detailed topographical map of the region and a compass or a GPS unit.

If you had a copy of the first edition of this book, you will see in this new edition many changes, including two chapters on Grand Canyon (Grand Canyon—South Rim and Backcountry and Grand Canyon—North Rim); a combined Navajoland chapter featuring all of the major sites on the reservation; a new chapter on Petrified Forest National Park; and a new Getting Here, Getting Around chapter to help you make sense of the multiple ways to travel to this rural land, all of which are challenging. The chapters also appear in a radically different order.

You'll also find greatly expanded information in several chapters, including many more lodging options in Flagstaff; more detailed information on lodging, restaurants, and sites to see on the South Rim of Grand Canyon; expanded detail on visiting the North Rim; discussions of new stores to visit in Flagstaff, Sedona, and Grand Canyon; and lodging and camping options near Petrified Forest National Park.

Almost all of the area chapters have information on how to get there, accommodations, restaurants, what to do, and shopping, and some discuss the arts, annual events, nightlife, geology, wildlife, history, hiking, camping, and kidstuff, the latter a listing of kid-friendly places and activities. Look for the **i** symbol which flags helpful Insider tips.

When in doubt, consult the table of contents or index. This book isn't meant to be read cover to cover. It is meant to be opened, read briefly, dog-eared, and tossed down in the foot well of the passenger seat until it is needed again. It is meant to be *used*.

[Facing page] *The inner canyon of Grand Canyon has numerous side canyons to explore; here, a hiker moves along Transept Creek, upriver from the North Kaibab Trail.* TODD R. BERGER

AREA OVERVIEW

Northern Arizona is an odd place. Covering a bit more than one-third of the state, the region has characteristics that tie it to the southern deserts of Arizona, the mountains of Colorado, and the canyonlands of Utah. It is of course home to Grand Canyon, perhaps America's most celebrated national park. But northern Arizona is also home to the largest American Indian reservation in the country, the only reservation completely surrounded by another reservation in the United States, arguably the best rafting water in the nation, the largest collection of petrified wood in the world, a vibrant arts community in and around Sedona, ancestral Puebloan and Sinaguan ruins at multiple sites dating back hundreds of years, and a gigantic meteor crater gouged out of the earth 50,000 years ago.

A lot of what you see in northern Arizona is due to two factors: climate and elevation. The northern part of the state sits on the southwestern edge of the Colorado Plateau, a huge uplift of rock stretching over the Four Corners region of the southwestern United States and covering large swaths of the states of Utah, Colorado, New Mexico, and Arizona. In Arizona, the plateau extends south to the Mogollon Rim area in central Arizona and west to the Grand Wash Cliffs. With the exception of the Kingman area northwest to Lake Mead, all of northern Arizona sits on the Colorado Plateau.

The plateau, really a group of plateaus accentuated by mesas, buttes, spires, and pinnacles for which the area is justly famous, is part of the Rocky Mountain system. The gorgeous red, purple, pink, white, and yellow rock layers that make up the plateau extend more than 130,000 square miles at elevations ranging from 2,000 feet at the end of Grand Canyon to 13,000 feet in the LaSal Mountains of Utah (Arizona's highest peak, Humphreys Peak,

rises to 12,633 feet just north of Flagstaff). This is a land of sky-high mountains, deep river canyons, dry gullies, potentially treacherous washes, thousands of streams with their own canyons, high desert scrubland, pinyon-juniper forests, ponderosa pine and aspen forests, and lush, green valleys.

The main geological force at work in northern Arizona and the rest of the plateau is the erosive power of the Colorado River. It seems strange that this great river, confronted with a plateau rising to 7,000 feet at its tamer elevations, chose to go *through* the plateau rather than *around* it. Scientists espouse various theories on why this happened, including a theory that the river once flowed in reverse. Whatever the method, the river cut through the plateau, surrounding slopes were themselves eroded by flooding and heavy snows, and over time, over an unfathomable amount of time, the spectacular features of northern Arizona began to take shape, most notably at Grand Canyon.

CLIMATE AND ANIMAL LIFE

Winters in northern Arizona are cool to cold, and the climate is semiarid, averaging 10 to 25 inches of annual precipitation, much of it in the form of snow at higher elevations, including Flagstaff and Grand Canyon (particularly on the North Rim).

Ponderosa pine forests dominate above 6,500 feet, with pinyon-juniper forests nudging out the tall, straight, cinnamon-barked pines below that elevation, and Douglas firs, aspen, and spruce joining the ponderosas above that elevation. Given that Flagstaff sits at about 7,000 feet and is surrounded by ponderosas, it is not surprising that one of the town's earliest industries was logging.

Mammals of northern Arizona are incredibly diverse and, because so much of the area is rural and protected, relatively populous. On the road north to Grand Canyon, you are likely to see pronghorn on the open scrubland (look closely, particularly north of Valle), and if you drive U.S. Highway 180 from Flagstaff to Grand Canyon (or vice versa) at night, be alert for lots and lots of elk grazing by the side of the road. Mule deer, with their oversized ears, seem ubiquitous, even at the bottom of Grand Canyon; they are seen most commonly in the early morning and late afternoon near water sources, when temperatures on the plateau are a little more palatable and hunger strikes. Other mammals inhabiting these forests include bobcats, mountain lions, Mexican free-tailed bats, bighorn sheep, badgers, beavers, coyotes, spotted skunks, porcupines, gray foxes, desert cottontails, multiple species of squirrels, ringtail cats, long-tailed weasels, and a whole lot more.

The skies of northern Arizona are also full, with birds of hundreds of species soaring and diving and looking for supper. The most celebrated of northern Arizona's airborne denizens is the California condor, America's largest flying bird and one of the rarest birds in the world. Their presence here is the result of a historic captive breeding and reintroduction program, which saved the species. Today, more than 40 birds fly free over northern Arizona, and they can be readily seen at Grand Canyon, particularly in summertime in the Grand Canyon Village area near Bright Angel Lodge. In the summer of 2003, scientists at the park confirmed the hatching of a California condor fledgling in the canyon, the first wild hatching of a California condor in northern Arizona in at least 80 years.

Raptors are also all over the area, and multiple species can often be viewed during the spring and fall migrations. Researchers from HawkWatch International plant themselves at South Rim overlooks at Grand Canyon National Park to count and identify raptors, and it is not uncommon to spot more than a dozen species and hundreds of birds during a day's work.

Northern Arizona is filled with song-birds, including the melodic canyon wren, the squawky pinyon jay, and several species of fast-moving hummingbirds. In short, the region is a birder's paradise.

Some prefer to keep their head toward the ground looking for reptiles and amphibians. Northern Arizona does not skimp on its selection of these denizens. Here you will find such crowd-pleasers as Grand Canyon pink rattlesnakes, western diamondback rattlesnakes, kingsnakes, chuckwallas, Arizona tree frogs, western-banded geckos, tiger salamanders, collared lizards, and many more. Although some of these animals are poisonous, particularly the rattlesnakes, they are also rarely seen, due to their preferred avoidance of humans. You may see a rattler, particularly if you hike down into Grand Canyon, but it is highly unlikely you will come out of the canyon with a bite mark. If you see one, give it space and time to slither away.

GEOLOGY

The Colorado Plateau is part of the Cordilleras, the last and greatest system of mountains to rise in North America. These mountains formed primarily in post-Triassic times, less than 136 million years ago, when the continent drifting westward from the Atlantic met the floor of the Pacific, which was moving eastward. These movements created pressure on the west rim of the Laurentian Shield, which is the basic structure of the continent. The shield is made up of the oldest rocks in North America, some of which can be seen at the bottom of Grand Canyon. The most ancient rocks in Grand Canyon are 1.8 billion years old, roughly half the age of the planet itself.

The plateau rose slowly in several stages. Many, many years later, the Colorado River began to cut the gorge now known as Grand Canyon. The awe-inspiring

Petroglyphs in Petrified Forest National Park below the overlook at Newspaper Rock.
TODD R. BERGER

landscape of the entire plateau, including northern Arizona, results from water and wind erosion of flat-lying or slightly dipping Mesozoic (65 to 225 million years old) sedimentary rocks, including sandstones, limestones, and shales. Mesas, buttes, and pinnacles are created by erosion when a relatively resistant rock unit (such as sandstone) caps relatively weaker rock, such as shale. The semi-arid climate of the plateau means many areas have little vegetative cover, and this factor also influences erosion patterns.

The sedimentary sandstone, shale, and limestone in Grand Canyon and elsewhere on the plateau formed during the Paleozoic era when what is now northern Arizona was immersed in a shallow sea that advanced and retreated.

The rocks hold vast supplies of the region's wealth: fuel and water. The land here holds considerable deposits of uranium, colossal fields of oil shale, and high-quality low-sulfur bituminous coal; most of these deposits are on Native American lands. The water is constantly percolating down through the rock layers, erupting at such places as Roaring Springs in Grand Canyon, which supplies all of the water for the North and South Rim developed areas via the Transcanyon Pipeline.

HUMAN INHABITANTS

Archaeologists estimate that Native Americans have been on this continent for at least 15,000 years, possibly as long as 60,000 years. Evidence found at Grand Canyon confirms habitation back 12,000 years, but there is very likely much more evidence to be found. Today, the Havasupai and Hualapai live on land of the Middle Colorado Highlands, including parts of western Grand Canyon. The Navajo Reservation runs to the edge of eastern Grand Canyon, and the Hopi Reservation lies roughly 100 miles east of the park. Although the Hopi trace their ancestry to the ancestral Puebloan people who occupied the dwellings seen today at places like Wupatki National Monument, the Navajo are relative newcomers to the Southwest, having arrived 500 to 700 years ago.

Europeans arrived on the scene in the late 16th century. The Spanish came first, and after 1848, Anglo-American cultures (southern, Mormon, and New Englander) immigrated to the area in large numbers.

Today, this rural land is a diverse mixture of members of five Native American tribes, residents of European ancestry, Hispanics, and growing populations of African Americans and settlers from Pacific Rim nations.

GETTING HERE, GETTING AROUND

Northern Arizona is a vast, remote region filled with national parks, national monuments, national forests, several American Indian reservations, a smattering of towns and cities, and one of the nation's major rivers. The region lies within one to five hours (depending on your destination) overland from two major metropolitan areas—Phoenix and Las Vegas—and within a day's drive from Los Angeles, San Diego, the Sierra Nevada, Salt Lake City, Albuquerque, and the Colorado Rockies.

Your choices on how to get to the region abound, and your decision on how to get here will largely depend on where you are coming from, your destination within the area, your comfort with "doing it yourself" on remote highways versus joining a tour group, and the contents of your wallet. The individual chapters for the different sites in northern Arizona contain more transportation and travel information specific to the site; this chapter contains an overview of the major ways to travel to the region and some of the ways to get around the area, so you can make an informed choice before getting on a plane, getting behind the wheel, boarding a train, or hopping on a bus.

GETTING HERE

By Air

If you're flying to northern Arizona, you will pass through at least one of the five commercial airports in the region. As flights are cheapest to major cities, most visitors to northern Arizona fly into Phoenix or Las Vegas and drive to north-ern Arizona. Flights into Las Vegas can be particularly inexpensive. Others prefer to fly into Flagstaff, which is only 80 miles from the South Rim but requires a connection in Phoenix and quite a bit of extra expense. Still others choose to catch a flight at the North Las Vegas Airport and fly directly to the Grand Canyon Airport, just a few miles south of the park. Whatever you decide, you can navigate your way through the skies to northern Arizona using the following information.

PHOENIX SKY HARBOR INTERNATIONAL AIRPORT

To get to Flagstaff by air, the city with the only major commercial airport in northern Arizona and the principal hub for most sites throughout northern Arizona, visitors must travel through Phoenix Sky Harbor International Airport (602-273-3300, http://phoenix.gov/AVIATION/index.html). Phoenix is the hub for America West Airlines, which operates daily flights from Phoenix to Flagstaff via America West Express, and a hub for Southwest Airlines, which means travelers can fly on direct flights to Phoenix from dozens of locations around the country.

Many travelers bound for northern Arizona choose to fly to Phoenix, rent a car, and make the beautiful two-hour drive to Flagstaff (see the By Car section later in this chapter). By car, the Phoenix Airport is just under four hours from the South Rim of Grand Canyon.

AIRLINES SERVING SKY HARBOR INTERNATIONAL AIRPORT

Twenty-one domestic and international airlines fly into Sky Harbor.

Domestic

Alaska Airlines
(800) 426-0333, www.alaskaair.com

Aloha Airlines
(800) 367-5250, www.alohaairlines.com

America West Airlines
(800) 235-9292, www.americawest.com

American Airlines
(800) 433-7300, www.aa.com

American Trans Air
(800) 225-2995, www.ata.com

Arizona Express
(866) 435-9872, www.azexpress.com

Continental Airlines
(800) 525-0280,
www.flycontinental.com

Delta Airlines
(800) 221-1212, www.delta-air.com

Frontier Airlines
(800) 432-1359,
www.frontierairlines.com

Great Lakes Aviation
(800) 367-5320, www.greatlakesav.com

Hawaiian Airlines
(800) 367-5320, www.hawaiianair.com

Midwest Express Airlines
(800) 452-2022,
www1.midwestexpress.com

Northwest Airlines
(800) 225-2525, www.nwa.com

Southwest Airlines
(800) 435-9792, www.southwest.com

Sun Country Airlines
(800) 359-6786, www.suncountry.com

United Airlines
(800) 241-6522, www.ual.com

US Airways
(800) 428-4322, www.usairways.com

International

Aeromexico
(800) 237-6639, www.aeromexico.com

Air Canada
(888) 247-2262, www.aircanada.ca

British Airways
(800) 247-9297,
www.british-airways.com

Lufthansa German Airlines
(800) 645-3880, www.lufthansa.com

NAVIGATING SKY HARBOR

Phoenix Sky Harbor International Airport has three passenger terminals—referred to as Terminal 2, Terminal 3, and Terminal 4 (Terminal 1 no longer stands). They are connected by a free interterminal bus system that loops around the airport. All America West, America West Express, and Southwest flights utilize Terminal 4, as do flights on Aeromexico, British Airways, Hawaiian Airlines, and Lufthansa German Airlines.

To get to the check-in counter and all gates for America West Express (again, the only airline flying into Flagstaff) from other terminals, ride the interterminal bus. From Terminal 2, catch the eastbound or westbound bus from the center island outside the front doors. Either bus will get you to Terminal 4 in roughly the same amount of time. From Terminal 3, catch the eastbound bus on the north side of the building at Level A, or the westbound bus on the south side of the building on the same level. The bus stops at the center island. The buses arrive and depart every 7 to 10 minutes between 6:00 A.M. and midnight, and somewhat less frequently between midnight and 6:00 A.M. You will arrive at Terminal 4 on Level 1, the same level that houses baggage claim and the rental car counters. The ticketing and check-in counters are upstairs on Level 2. All gates are on Level 3.

The concourses on Level 3 are connected by moving walkways. America West flights leave from Concourses A and B, on the north side of the terminal. Level 3 also has food courts, shops, currency exchange, pubs, airline clubs, passenger assistance counters, coffeehouses, and newsstands.

If you lose something at the airport, contact the Sky Harbor Lost and Found office at (602) 273-3307. The office is open Monday through Friday 8:00 A.M. to 5:00 P.M.

Phoenix Sky Harbor International Airport has short-term parking in garages at all three passenger terminals, and economy parking in a garage and surface lot east of Terminal 4 and in a surface lot west of Terminal 2. Parking in the terminal garages runs $1.00 per half hour, with a daily maximum of $16.00. Parking in both the western and eastern economy surface lots runs $1.00 per half hour, with a daily maximum of $5.00. In the eastern economy garage, parking is $1.00 per half hour, with a daily maximum of $7.00.

The interterminal shuttle bus stops at both economy lots. When boarding a shuttle bus at one of the terminals, make sure you are on the bus heading for the economy lot you parked in (either East or West).

For more information about parking at Sky Harbor, call ACE Parking Management at (602) 273-4545.

CAR RENTAL AT SKY HARBOR

Several rental car companies operate out of Sky Harbor. The following have counters at all three passenger terminals, in the baggage claim areas. In Terminal 4, the rental car counters are on Level 1. All of the following have additional locations throughout Phoenix.

Advantage
(800) 777-5500 or (602) 244-0450,
www.arac.com

Alamo
(800) 327-9633 or (602) 244-0897,
www.goalamo.com

Avis
(800) 831-2847 or (602) 273-3222,
www.avis.com

Budget
(800) 527-0700 or (602) 267-1717,
www.budgetrentacar.com

Courtesy
(800) 368-5145 or (602) 273-7503,
www.courtesyleasing.com

Dollar
(800) 800-4000 or (602) 224-2323,
www.dollarcar.com

Enterprise
(800) 736-8222 or (602) 225-0588,
www.enterprise.com

Hertz
(800) 654-3131 or (602) 267-8822,
www.hertz.com

National
(800) 227-7368 or (602) 275-4771,
www.nationalcar.com

Thrifty
(800) 847-4389 or (602) 244-0311,
www.thrifty.com

BUS TRAVEL FROM SKY HARBOR

Greyhound has a limited-service stop at Phoenix Sky Harbor International Airport, located at the southwestern corner of Level A in Terminal 4, with buses departing four times daily for Flagstaff. No ticketing is available at the airport, but you can buy tickets and get schedules in advance by calling (800) 229-9424 or by accessing Greyhound's Web site at www.greyhound.com.

LAS VEGAS MCCARRAN INTERNATIONAL AIRPORT

Many visitors to northern Arizona decide to fly into Las Vegas's McCarran International Airport (702-261-5211, www.mccarran.com), particularly travelers bound for northwestern Arizona, including Lake Mead National Recreation Area, the Arizona Strip, the Hualapai and Havasupai Indian Reservations, and the North and South Rims of Grand Canyon. There are no direct connections to northern Arizona airports from McCarran, but two airlines offer flights to Grand Canyon Airport from the North Las Vegas Airport (see the following section on the North Las Vegas Airport). By car, McCarran Airport is about four hours from the South Rim of Grand Canyon, five hours from the North Rim of Grand Canyon, and about three hours from Flagstaff.

AIRLINES SERVING LAS VEGAS MCCARRAN INTERNATIONAL AIRPORT

Some 31 domestic, international, and charter airlines serve Las Vegas McCarran International Airport, with direct service to destinations throughout the country and around the world.

Domestic

AirTran Airways
(800) 247-8726, www.airtran.com

Alaska Airlines
(800) 426-0333, www.alaskaair.com

Aloha Airlines
(800) 367-5250, www.alohaairlines.com

America West Airlines
(800) 235-9292, www.americawest.com

American Airlines
(800) 433-7300, www.aa.com

American Trans Air
(800) 225-2995, www.ata.com

Arizona Express
(866) 435-9872, www.azexpress.com

Continental Airlines
(800) 525-0280,
www.flycontinental.com

Delta Airlines
(800) 221-1212, www.delta-air.com

Frontier Airlines
(800) 432-1359,
www.frontierairlines.com

Hawaiian Airlines
(800) 367-5320, www.hawaiianair.com

JetBlue Airways
(800) JET-BLUE, www.jetblue.com

Midwest Express Airlines
(800) 452-2022,
www.midwestexpress.com

Northwest Airlines
(800) 225-2525, www.nwa.com

Southwest Airlines
(800) 435-9792, www.southwest.com

Spirit Airlines
(800) 772-7117, www.spiritair.com

Sun Country Airlines
(800) 359-6786, www.suncountry.com

United Airlines
(800) 241-6522, www.ual.com

United Express/Skywest Airlines
(800) 453-9417, www.ual.com

US Airways
(800) 428-4322, www.usairways.com

International

Aeromexico
(800) 237-6639, www.aeromexico.com

Air Canada
(888) 247-2262, www.aircanada.ca

Allegiant Air
(877) 202-6444, www.allegiant-air.com

Allegro Airlines
(877) 443-7585, www.allegroair.com

Aviacsa
188-85-28-42-27

Japan Airlines
(800) JAL-FONE, www.jal.co.jp/en

Mexicana
(800) 531-7921

Virgin Atlantic Airways
(800) 862-8621, www.virgin-atlantic.com

Charter

Champion Air
(800) 387-6951, www.championair.com

Omni Air International
(800) 718-8901, www.omniairintl.com

Skyservice Airlines
(877) 485-6060

PARKING AT LAS VEGAS MCCARRAN

Short-term parking is available in the ramp in front of Terminal 1. Follow the signs saying PARKING as you enter the airport from I-215, Russell Road, or Paradise Road, then follow the *yellow* triangles to short-term parking. Short-term parking runs 25 cents per 10 minutes up to a three-hour maximum ($4.50).

Valet parking is available in the ramp in front of Terminal 1. Follow the signs saying PARKING as you enter the airport from I-215, Russell Road, or Paradise Road, then follow the *red* triangles to valet parking. Valet parking has a $4.00 minimum charge, then $1.00 per additional hour up to a $14.00 maximum for each 24-hour period.

Long-term parking is a third option in the ramp in front of Terminal 1. Follow the signs saying PARKING as you enter the airport from I-215, Russell Road, or Paradise Road, then follow the *green* triangles to long-term parking. Long-term parking in the ramp runs $3.00 for the first hour and $1.00 per additional hour. The daily maximum charge is $10.00 for each 24-hour period.

Remote parking is another option, available at the surface lot just north of Russell Road. When entering the airport via I-215, get in the right-hand lane and exit at Russell Road. Turn left onto Russell Road and then turn left again into the lot. From Paradise Road southbound, get into one of the two left-hand lanes and exit at Russell Road/Air Cargo. Turn left onto Russell Road and then left again into the lot. From Russell Road westbound, follow Russell toward the airport and turn right into the lot just before reaching I-215. Remote parking runs $2.00 for the first hour and $1.00 each additional hour up to a daily maximum of $8.00.

You can also park in the surface lot at Terminal 2, on the left-hand side of the road across from the terminal. Follow the signs to Terminal 2. Parking fees at the Terminal 2 lot are $1.00 for the first hour and $1.00 for each additional hour, up to a daily maximum of $8.00.

For parking questions, call the Parking Office at (702) 261-5122. The office is open 7:00 A.M. to 5:00 P.M. Monday through Friday.

CAR RENTAL AT LAS VEGAS MCCARRAN

The rental car counters at McCarran are in the center of the baggage claim area in Terminal 1. The cars are parked away from the terminal, and the individual car rental companies will direct you to their courtesy shuttle for the short ride to the lots.

Alamo/National
(702) 261-5391, www.alamo.com or www.nationalcar.com

Avis
(800) 831-2847 or (702) 261-5591, www.avis.com

Budget
(800) 527-0700 or (702) 736-1212, www.budgetrentacar.com

Dollar
(800) 800-4000 or (702) 739-9507, www.dollarcar.com

Enterprise
(800) 736-8222 or (702) 261-4435, www.enterprise.com

Hertz
(800) 654-3131 or (702) 736-4900, www.hertz.com

Payless
(702) 736-6147, www.paylesscarrental.com

SavMor
(800) 634-6779 or (702) 736-1234

Thrifty
(800) 847-4389 or (702) 896-7600, www.thrifty.com

NORTH LAS VEGAS AIRPORT

North Las Vegas Airport (702-261-3806, www.mccarran.com/ga_nlv.asp) is the only airport in the Las Vegas area with scenic tours and scheduled flights to northern Arizona. Two airlines, **Air Vegas** (702-736-6599, www.airvegas.com) and **Scenic Airlines** (702-638-3200, www. scenic.com) offer service from North Las Vegas to Grand Canyon Airport, near Tusayan a few miles south of Grand Canyon Village on the South Rim. Scenic Airlines offers multiple scheduled flights daily to/from Grand Canyon Airport, as well as several different scenic tours (flights to Grand Canyon Airport and tours on the ground by motor coach). For more information about scenic tours offered by Scenic Airlines and Air Vegas, see the Grand Canyon—South Rim and Backcountry chapter.

The North Las Vegas Airport offers a courtesy shuttle service to/from downtown and Strip hotels. The shuttles run between 9:00 A.M. and 6:30 P.M. It is strongly advised that you call ahead (702-261-3806) to make reservations to ride the shuttle.

FLAGSTAFF PULLIAM MUNICIPAL AIRPORT

Flagstaff's Pulliam Municipal Airport (928-556-1234) is the gateway airport to northern Arizona. Founded in 1949, the airport, which sits at an elevation of 7,014 feet 4 miles south of the city, is one of the loftiest commercial airports in the United States. Flagstaff and its airport are centrally located on the southern edge of northern Arizona, within a three-hour drive of most of the northern region of the state, with the exception of the remote Arizona Strip.

America West Express (800-235-9292, www.americawest.com) is the only airline flying into Flagstaff Pulliam Municipal Airport, with service to/from Phoenix's Sky Harbor International Airport.

The airport lies south of Flagstaff along I-17. A surface parking lot in front of the terminal building has 400 spaces. To get to town from the airport, follow the signs to I-17 and head north on the

The terminal of Flagstaff's Pulliam Airport is comfortable, modern, and distinctly southwestern. TODD R. BERGER

interstate. Interstate 17 turns into Milton Road as you enter Flagstaff, and Milton will carry you to historic downtown Flagstaff and U.S. Highway 180, which heads northwest toward Grand Canyon.

Pulliam Airport's terminal building, opened in 1993, is a beautiful structure with a distinctly southwestern yet functional design. When entering the terminal building, the America West Express counter will be to your right, while the rental car counters and baggage claim are to your left. The airport has a restaurant, game room, and gift shop, all located in the main terminal area.

CAR RENTAL AT FLAGSTAFF PULLIAM

Several rental car companies operate out of Pulliam. The counters for the following are all located directly opposite the baggage claim area in the main terminal area.

Avis
(800) 831-2847, www.avis.com

Budget
(800) 527-0700,
www.budgetrentacar.com

Hertz
(800) 654-3131 or (602) 267-8822,
www.hertz.com

National/Alamo
(800) 227-7368 or (800) 327-9633,
www.nationalcar.com or
www.alamo.com

GRAND CANYON AIRPORT

Grand Canyon Airport (928-638-2463, 866-235-9422) lies about 3 miles south of Grand Canyon National Park's South Entrance, just south of the town of Tusayan along Arizona Highway 64. The airport is the starting point for all scenic air tours of the canyon, whether by helicopter or airplane. The airport is also the destination of Grand Canyon tours originating in Las Vegas, including those of **Air Vegas** (702-736-6599, www.airvegas.com) and **Scenic Airlines** (702-638-3200, www.scenic.com). Scenic Airlines also offers regularly scheduled flights between Grand Canyon Airport and North Las Vegas Airport. In addition, **Grand Canyon Airlines** (800-528-2407 or 928-638-2407, www.grandcanyonairlines.com) and **Air Grand Canyon** (800-247-4726 or 928-638-2686, www.airgrandcanyon.com) fly out of the airport and have several scenic packages. (See the Air Tours section of the Grand Canyon—South Rim and Backcountry chapter for more information on air tours.)

The main terminal can be reached from either North or South Airport Roads, which make a big U through the airport and unite at the main terminal. The main terminal is on the west side of the road beyond the Papillon Helicopter terminal (the large building with the built-in control tower) if you enter the airport on North Airport Road, and beyond the AirStar and Kenai Helicopter terminals if you enter the airport on South Airport Road. Counters for all of the airlines are located in the main terminal. Free parking is available on the other side of Airport Road in front of the main terminal.

Enterprise Rent-a-Car (928-638-2871 or 800-736-8222, www.enterprise.com) has a desk at Grand Canyon Airport. The counter is open seasonally April 1 to October 31, and pickup service is available. Rental car returns are in the parking lot in front of the terminal.

Grand Canyon Coaches (928-638-0821) operates a shuttle service from the airport to Tusayan and into the park. A ride to the rim lodges in Grand Canyon Village runs $5.00 per person ($10.00 minimum) plus $8.00 per person for the park entrance fee if you do not have an annual pass.

Several companies operate helicopter tours out of Grand Canyon Airport, including **AirStar Helicopters** (928-638-2622 or 800-962-3869, www.airstar.com), **Kenai Helicopters** (928-638-2764 or 800-541-4537, www.flykenai.com), and **Papillon Grand Canyon Helicopters** (928-638-2419 or 800-528-2418, www.papillon.com). The

AirStar and Kenai terminals are next to each other near the south entrance to the airport. The Papillon terminal is between the north entrance and the main terminal. (See the Air Tours section of the Grand Canyon—South Rim and Backcountry chapter for more information on helicopter tours.)

GETTING AROUND

If you plan to travel all or part of the way to northern Arizona without leaving the ground, options abound, although your choices will be limited if you plan to travel to remote areas. You can take a train or a shuttle bus to the South Rim of Grand Canyon, but for the North Rim, the Navajo and Hopi Reservations, and much of the Coconino National Forest, a car is required. One of the best ways to explore the region is on foot, allowing a much more intimate view of the high desert. In fact, much of the region can only be explored on foot. For information on hiking in wilderness areas, see the individual chapters.

By Bus

Greyhound (800–229–9424, www. greyhound.com) stops in some four dozen locations across Arizona, including Phoenix, Phoenix Sky Harbor Airport, Tucson, Williams, Flagstaff, and Winslow, as well as thousands of destinations farther afield.

By Car

Northern Arizona is rural, wide-open land. And due to the presence of Grand Canyon, roads often travel long distances to get to places that are only a few miles apart by air. If you're driving, be prepared for long stretches between towns and services; steep elevation changes; travel on narrow, remote two-lane highways; and wildlife grazing by the side of the road (and some-

times strolling across the blacktop). The national forests and parts of northern Arizona's several American Indian reservations are crisscrossed by dirt roads best attacked with a high-clearance vehicle. Some roads, such as the backcountry roads through the Kaibab National Forest to remote western Grand Canyon trailheads, become quagmires after storms and simply close during the wintertime. Call ahead to your destination if bad weather threatens.

Two major interstate highways, I–17 and I–40, reach northern Arizona, uniting at Flagstaff. Interstate 17 begins in Phoenix and ends 137 miles later at Flagstaff, while I–40 in Arizona runs from the New Mexico border just east of Lupton on the Navajo Reservation to Topock on the Colorado River at the California border. The four-lane roads are the safest highways in the region and efficiently carry visitors to Williams, Flagstaff, Winslow, Holbrook, and Petrified Forest National Park.

U.S. Highway 180 runs northwest out of Flagstaff, rising to a little more than 8,000 feet in the San Francisco Peaks as it travels the 52 miles to Valle and the intersection with Arizona Highway 64. The South Rim of the Grand Canyon lies 28 miles north. U.S. Highway 180 sometimes closes in wintertime.

Arizona Highway 64 runs due north 56 miles from Williams (on I–40) to the South Rim of Grand Canyon National Park. The highway then turns east, following the park's Desert View Drive to Desert View and the East Entrance, and then winds down to Cameron on U.S. Highway 89, a total distance of 53 miles.

U.S. Highway 89 runs north from Flagstaff 85 miles to the Utah border. Along the way, it intersects with Arizona Highway 64 at Cameron (which runs west to the South Rim of Grand Canyon National Park), U.S. Highway 160 (which runs northeast across the northern part of the Navajo Reservation), U.S. Highway 89A (which runs west to Arizona Highway 67 at Jacob Lake and on to Kanab,

Two interstate highways, I-17 and I-40, intersect at Flagstaff. Here, a lone driver heads westbound on I-40. TODD R. BERGER

Utah), and the town of Page. U.S. Highway 89 is the principal north-south highway in northern Arizona and is the only expedient way to reach the North Rim of Grand Canyon and the Arizona Strip by car.

Arizona Highway 67 begins at Jacob Lake and the intersection with U.S. 89A, and runs 41 miles due south to the North Rim of Grand Canyon National Park. This highway closes from late fall to late spring, generally mid-October to mid-May, as does the North Rim of the park.

U.S. Highway 160 runs from its intersection with U.S. 89 10 miles west of Tuba City, past Navajo National Monument, through Kayenta, and on to the Four Corners Tribal Monument. At Kayenta, the highway intersects U.S. 163, which runs north to Monument Valley Tribal Park and on into Utah.

Back in Flagstaff, Arizona Highway 89A runs south through Oak Creek Canyon to Sedona, about 25 miles away. The sudden elevation change and the incredible winding nature of this highway

make it one of the most spectacular drives in the Southwest.

Las Vegas, Nevada, lies 75 miles northwest of Kingman via U.S. Highway 93, which crosses the Colorado River over Hoover Dam. From Kingman, all of northern Arizona opens up to the east, with Flagstaff 144 miles distant.

By Train

Traveling from Chicago to Los Angeles, **Amtrak**'s Southwest Chief stops at four stations in northern Arizona: Winslow, Flagstaff, Williams, and Kingman. The train runs once daily in each direction. For more information, contact Amtrak at (800) USA-RAIL or www.amtrak.com.

Grand Canyon Railway (800-843-8724, www.thetrain.com) operates daily trains between Williams and the South Rim of Grand Canyon National Park. For more information about service and fares, see the Grand Canyon—South Rim and Backcountry and Williams chapters.

GRAND CANYON—SOUTH RIM AND BACKCOUNTRY

When Spanish explorers first saw Grand Canyon, probably from somewhere between Moran and Lipan Points on the South Rim, they estimated the river was only 6 feet across. Since their Hopi guides "didn't know" the way down into the canyon, the Spanish sent three explorers to bushwhack their way to the river on their own. They only made it a third of the way down, discovering as they went that boulders that appeared from the rim to be only 5 or 6 feet high were in fact almost 200 feet tall.

Fast forward 400 years, and not much has changed. Looking into the canyon from the South Rim today, it is hard to appreciate its true vastness: The Grand Canyon is 277 river miles long, 8 to 14 miles wide, and 5,300 feet deep. It is rightly considered one of the seven natural wonders of the world, a place to be cherished and protected for future generations.

GEOLOGY AND WILDLIFE

Scientists differ on the specifics of how Grand Canyon was formed, but there is agreement that the primary culprit was, and is, erosion. Many geologists believe the Colorado River cut the Inner Gorge of Grand Canyon as the lands around the river on the Colorado Plateau rose, but others advocate the theory that the river cut through the plateau after, or near the end of, the plateau's uplift. Although you can see at the bottom of the canyon rocks half as old as the planet, the canyon was created only over the last 5 to 6 million years. Each layer or group of layers of rock in the canyon has its own color, and these are the muted pastel horizontal "stripes" you see.

The oldest rocks can be seen near the river at the eastern end of the canyon. These are the Vishnu schist and Zoroaster granite, formed 1.7 billion years ago during Precambrian times when layers of sandstone, shale, and limestone interspersed with ancient lava flows were laid down. These rocks were overlaid by 12 vertical miles of new rocks. Heat and pressure crushed, folded, and melted the older rocks before the overlying rock eroded away at the end of the Precambrian era. The resulting gap in the geological record between the oldest rocks in the Inner Gorge and the much younger Paleozoic rocks directly above them is called the Great Unconformity. Other, smaller unconformities, probably also caused by erosion, can also be seen in Grand Canyon.

After the Precambrian erosion ended, the land was covered by an ancient tropical sea. Sandstone, shale, and limestone layers of rock were laid down. When the sea retreated, erosion began again, followed by another period of sedimentary rock formation. Later, a Permian desert covered the region and winds deposited sand dunes. Twice more, the area was covered by shallow seas that laid down layers of limestone. At the end of Permian times, the most recent sea retreated. The sedimentary rock that had been deposited since the end of the Paleozoic era eroded away on the Kaibab and Coconino Plateaus, but those rocks are the ones you see in the Painted Desert and other areas east, southeast, and north of Grand Canyon.

The river cut the canyon to a depth of almost a mile. What widened it was erosion from rain and snow, which flowed over the rims, "melting" the soft sandstone and limestone layers and causing major rockfalls.

Erosion by the Colorado has been slowed by the building of the Glen Canyon Dam, but horizontal rain and snow erosion continue unabated. Just a few summers ago, a huge rockfall closed some of the hiking trails and broke the water pipeline that crosses the canyon.

The geological record in the canyon is only part of the historical story. The layers of rocks also contain a fossil record, from primitive algae in the lowest Precambrian layers to various sea creatures in upper layers.

Today, the flora and fauna of Grand Canyon are representative of three "life zones." On the rim is the Transition Zone. Here you will see pinyon pine, juniper, ponderosa pine, and gambel oak. Abert squirrels, mule deer, elk, and coyotes roam the forests. Overhead, look for red-tailed hawks, golden eagles, and jet black ravens.

The middle zone is called the Upper Sonoran. Cliff rose, mountain mahogany, and prickly pear cactus (long a food source for the indigenous peoples of this area and available to visitors as jam in most gift shops) inhabit this zone. Here you may be lucky enough to see bighorn sheep and California condors (and to avoid seeing rattlesnakes!).

The lowest zone, through which the river flows, is the Lower Sonoran Zone (below 3,500 feet). This is essentially a desert zone, and here you will see banana yucca and mesquite.

Before the Glen Canyon Dam was built in the early 1960s, rushing floods scoured the riverbanks clean every spring and created sandbars along the river's shores. The river was high and muddy during these floods, warm in the summer and low, muddy, and cold during the winter. When the river was dammed, these natural cycles were interrupted; the river flowed cold and clear all year long. Changing the river's flow changed the habitat for fish, wildlife, and plants that once lived here. Four native species of fish have been lost from the river, and nonnative vegetation such as salt cedar has invaded the river's beaches. In 1996, the Bureau of Reclamation instituted major releases of water from the dam to simulate the historic floods, but since the amount of water released was much less than what flowed during a normal flood, the effects on the ecosystem of the river were minimal, and the goal of restoring habitat for the fish and plants that once thrived in and near the river was not achieved.

HISTORY

Hundreds of ancient American Indian ruins have been found within Grand Canyon. The recent discovery of a Folsom point preform (the first step in flaking an arrowhead) dates the earliest known human habitation of Grand Canyon at roughly 10,000 B.C.

Artifacts made by the people of the Desert Culture indicate that the canyon was inhabited by humans at least 4,000 years ago. Among these artifacts are split twig figurines of animals. Today, jewelers and other artists create modern interpretations of these distinctive sculptures in silver, gold, bronze, and paint.

The ancestral Puebloan people also left their mark here by building numerous small villages including Tusayan Ruins on the South Rim, a village of approximately 30 people that dates from the late 1100s. Walhalla Glades on the North Rim was built between A.D. 1050 and 1150. The inhabitants of these 100 farm sites built structures and terraced gardens where they grew squash, beans, and corn, the staples of the diet of the indigenous peoples of the Southwest. Unkar Delta along the Colorado River was occupied from about A.D. 850 to 1100. The fertile delta was an excellent spot for an agricultural people to settle, but eventually, some scientists believe, drought and deforestation drove them out. The ancestral Puebloan people are called the *Hisatsinom* by today's Hopi, who live in villages on Black

Mesa, east of Grand Canyon. The Hopi are among the descendants of the ancestral Puebloan people, and they identify a site in Grand Canyon as the *sipapu* from which the people emerged into this, the Fourth World. Hopis still make pilgrimages to their shrines within the canyon. The Navajo word that identifies the ancestral Puebloan people is *Anasazi,* which means "ancient enemy." Because the descendants of the ancestral Puebloan people, such as the Hopi and Navajos have intermarried, some Navajo also claim descent from people of the ancestral Puebloan culture.

Today the Hualapai and the Havasupai Indians live on reservations within the canyon and on its South Rim.

The first Europeans to see the South Rim of Grand Canyon were part of the Coronado expedition of 1540 that set out in search of the Seven Cities of Cibola. The expedition, led by García Lopez de Cárdenas, was guided by Hopis.

For the next two centuries, European explorers pretty much ignored the impassable chasm. In 1776, the Spanish priest who had been appointed to oversee San Xavier Mission south of Tucson began to explore the canyon from the west. On June 20, 1776, Francisco Tómas Garcés reached Cataract Creek, a tributary of the Colorado and home to the Havasupai. Five days later, he left to follow the river east, crossing the Little Colorado and going on to Moencopi and then to the Hopi pueblos.

The "discovery" of the North Rim is credited to two Franciscan priests, Francisco Atanasio Domínguez and Silvestre Vélez de Escalante in 1776.

From 1821 to 1848, Grand Canyon belonged to independent Mexico and no record remains of any Mexican exploration of the canyon, although American trappers, including Bill Williams, explored the canyon in search of beaver in the early 1800s. In 1825 fur trader William Henry Ashley (of the Rocky Mountain Fur Company) and six others attempted to run the river in two canoes. They started down the Green River in Wyoming and found the beginning of the trip so arduous that they never actually made it to Grand Canyon.

Grand Canyon became part of the United States in 1848, ceded by Mexico in the Treaty of Guadalupe Hidalgo. Two years later, the Territory of New Mexico, including Grand Canyon, was created. The federal government began to map the new territory, sending soldiers to find routes across it and to build military strongholds.

Grand Canyon was wrested away from New Mexico when President Abraham Lincoln established the Arizona Territory in 1863. During the roundup of Navajos for the Long Walk to Bosque Redondo, some may have escaped capture by hiding in remote parts of Grand Canyon. The Treaty of 1868 established a Navajo Reservation to which those who survived the incarceration were allowed to return. The reservation was expanded in 1884, 1900, and 1930 to include the eastern rim of Grand Canyon and Marble Canyon north of the Little Colorado.

The man credited with the first successful trip down the Colorado River is Maj. John Wesley Powell, who, beginning at the end of May 1869, descended Green River in Wyoming and traveled with 10 companions in four wooden boats the length of the canyon, arriving at the mouth of the Virgin River (today within Lake Mead National Recreation Area) three months later. Powell was a veteran explorer and a geologist, and this was the first scientific exploration of the canyon. The men were forced to portage their boats frequently, their provisions often ran low, and the rapids presented a formidable challenge. By the end of the trip, only two boats and six men remained. The other boats had been destroyed, and three men had left the expedition along the way. In May 1871, better prepared, Powell led a second Colorado River expedition, this time taking with him amateur scientists, an artist, and a photographer. This expedition made winter camp at Kanab Creek in October and started down the river again in August 1872, leaving the

Almost a mile below the South Rim, the Colorado River flows through the Inner Gorge. The area is accessible by camping overnight in the backcountry. TODD R. BERGER

river at Kanab Creek in early September. One of the people with Powell on the North Rim in the early 1870s was Thomas Moran, a young artist, whose paintings of Grand Canyon helped make it known worldwide. His illustrations accompanied Powell's 1875 report, "The Exploration of the Colorado River." Moran Point on the South Rim is named for him.

Between 1870 and 1880, the non–Native American population of the Arizona Territory quadrupled as ranchers, settlers, and colonists arrived on the new frontier. The population increase, along with cattle grazing, mining, and lumbering, put pressure on the Native peoples already here, and conflict often ensued. A reservation for the Hualapai Indians was set up on the Lower Colorado in 1874 after they were defeated in a three-year war with the U.S. military. They escaped from the reservation and returned to their traditional lands near Kingman and Peach Springs. In 1883, President Chester A. Arthur ordered that a

reservation of one million acres south of the southern bend of the Colorado be established for the Hualapai, and this is the reservation that exists today. In 1880, President Rutherford B. Hayes created the Havasupai Indian Reservation, which two years later was reduced to just over 500 acres of land encompassing only the village and fields.

In 1871, Mormon John Doyle Lee established a ferry that crossed the Colorado River near the mouth of the Paria River. Lee was something of an outcast, having had a part in a massacre of pioneers by Mormons and Paiutes several years earlier. Lee was arrested in 1874 and executed in 1877 for his part in the atrocity. No one else was ever tried. After Lee was arrested, his wife, Emma, took over the ferry until it was purchased by the Latter Day Saints in 1879. The Grand Canyon Cattle Company owned it briefly, and then sold it to Coconino County. The ferry was in operation until an accident killed three men in 1928. The ferry did not reopen after the accident, and Navajo Bridge replaced it as the river crossing. Lees Ferry is the place from which distances on the Colorado River within Grand Canyon are measured.

The late 19th century saw an invasion of prospectors in Grand Canyon. Most mining claims did not pay off and some of the prospectors turned into tourist guides. Seth B. Tanner was one such. He used an old American Indian trail to get to his claims, and the trail eventually became known as the Tanner Trail. Legend has it that John D. Lee buried his gold somewhere below the Tanner Trail. It became part of the trail used by horse thieves and later the site where bootlegged liquor was made and then sold in Grand Canyon Village during Prohibition.

As the railroad came through northern Arizona, more people came to know about the wonders of Grand Canyon. In 1901, the Santa Fe Railroad reached Grand Canyon's South Rim, saving tourists an arduous stagecoach or horseback ride. Grand Canyon Village soon spread out from the train depot.

The first-class, quarter-million-dollar El Tovar Hotel opened in 1905 to accommodate visitors. All the water needed at the El Tovar and at Grand Canyon Village was brought by train 120 miles from Del Rio near Prescott.

Hermits Rest is named for Louis Boucher, who arrived in the canyon in 1891 and stayed for 21 years tending his mining claims in Boucher Canyon and living at Dripping Springs. He planted an orchard and a garden, and he too took advantage of the growing popular interest in the canyon by renting out cabins to tourists.

The first automobile arrived on the South Rim on January 12, 1902. It had been driven from Flagstaff and, because the car broke down frequently, the trip had taken five days. By the early 1920s, the automobile was the preferred way for tourists to come to the canyon.

In 1904 Ellsworth and Emery Kolb built Kolb Studio for photographing travelers as they started down the Bright Angel Trail. In 1911 the Kolb brothers made the first moving picture of a river trip on the Green and Colorado Rivers.

President Benjamin Harrison set aside Grand Canyon as a forest reserve in 1893, and President Theodore Roosevelt proclaimed the canyon a game reserve in 1906. Under the Antiquities Act of 1906, Roosevelt then declared the creation of Grand Canyon National Monument in 1908. In 1912 Arizona became a state, and in 1917 bills were introduced in the House and Senate to make Grand Canyon a national park. President Woodrow Wilson signed the bill into law in 1919. The newly formed National Park Service, headed by Stephen Mather, for whom Mather Point is named, had the challenging task of administering the park and managing and preserving the natural and cultural resources there. In 1927 Congress added 51 square miles to the park, and in 1932 President Herbert Hoover created a new Grand Canyon National Monument (wholly outside the boundaries of the original national monument declared by President Roosevelt in 1908), including 300 square miles to the west of the national park, an area that includes Toroweap Viewpoint and Vulcans Throne.

From the beginning of the 20th century, water used at Grand Canyon was brought by rail to the South Rim. In 1926, when the demand for water had increased dramatically because more tourists were visiting the canyon, M. R. Tillotson, a park engineer, built a plant to recycle wastewater for use in steam locomotives, in boilers, to flush toilets, and to irrigate landscaping. In 1931 construction began on a pipeline for pumping water from Indian Garden, 3,200 feet down in the canyon, up to the rim. By 1932 the water train was no longer in operation. In 1960 the available water supply was inadequate. A pipeline was built from Roaring Springs below the North Rim down Bright Angel Canyon, across the suspension bridge, and up to the pumping station at Indian Garden. The pipeline was operational in 1970.

The Fred Harvey Company was given the contract as the principal concessionaire at the South Rim of Grand Canyon in 1920, although the company had been operating tourist services there for many years prior. In 1922 it built Phantom Ranch as an overnight stopping place for tourists on mule trips down Bright Angel Trail. The ranch, like Desert View Watchtower and Hermits Rest, was designed by Mary Elizabeth Jane Colter.

The first dam on the Colorado was Hoover Dam, built at the west end of the canyon in 1936, forming Lake Mead. As the Big Buildup to provide power to the new urban centers of the Southwest continued, more dams and power plants were built on the Colorado Plateau. The last dam to be constructed was Glen Canyon Dam in 1964. The reservoir behind the dam, Lake Powell, flooded many historic and prehistoric cultural sites, as well as geological wonders. Other dams were proposed for the Colorado River within Grand Canyon, but pressure from the public and environmentalists kept the proposed dams at Marble Canyon and Bridge Canyon from being built. These areas were later incorporated into the national park.

Today, Lake Powell is a major Arizona and Utah water recreation site. A proposal to drain the lake has been on the table for several years, as has been a proposal to build a pipeline from Lake Powell to supply water to the Navajo and Hopi Reservations as well as the cities of Flagstaff and Williams.

GETTING TO THE SOUTH RIM

Today, about five million visitors a year come to see Grand Canyon. They come by car and bus from the gateway communities of Flagstaff and Williams, as well as by train from Williams and by plane from Las Vegas.

Open Road Tours operates a shuttle service between Flagstaff and the South Rim. Two daily shuttles leave from Flagstaff's Amtrak station, with two shuttles daily returning to Flagstaff from the South Rim. For more information call (928) 226–8060 or (800) 766–7117, or log on to www.openroadtours.com.

If you want a more exotic trip to the canyon, take the train. Grand Canyon Railway runs a round-trip service once a day from Williams. Call (800) THE–TRAIN for reservations. For more information about the train, see the By Train section in this chapter or the Williams chapter.

Airplanes from North Las Vegas land at Grand Canyon Airport. Grand Canyon Coaches operates a shuttle between the airport and the park, with stops in Tusayan and at Maswik Transportation Center on the western end of Grand Canyon Village. The shuttle runs every half hour. Call (928) 638–0821 for more information.

Twenty-four hour taxi service is also available; call (928) 638–2822 or 2631. You can rent a car from April through October. from Enterprise at the airport terminal. To reserve a car, call (928) 638–2871 or (800) 736–8222.

By Air

The Grand Canyon Airport (928–628–2446) is just south of Tusayan off AZ 64. **Scenic Airlines** (702-638-3200, www.scenic.com) offers regularly scheduled air service between North Las Vegas Airport and Grand Canyon Airport. Scenic Airlines and **Air Vegas** (702-736-6599, www.airvegas.com) offer tour packages from North Las Vegas Airport to Grand Canyon Airport. In addition, several airplane and helicopter tour companies operate out of Grand Canyon Airport. See the Air Tours section later in this chapter for more information about these companies, and see the Grand Canyon Airport listing in the Getting Here, Getting Around chapter for more information about the airport and its amenities.

By Car

Most people drive to the South Rim of Grand Canyon from Williams or Flagstaff.

Your drive north on U.S. Highway 180 and Arizona Highway 64 from Flagstaff to the South Rim of Grand Canyon will take you through part of the San Francisco Volcanic Field. Some of the small cinder cones you see still have craters, and there are several lava caves in this area. Farther north the highway passes just north of Red Mountain, Slate Mountain, and Kendricks Peak, mountains formed by volcanic activity. U.S. Highway 180 climbs to 8,046 feet through ponderosa pine and aspen forest, then descends into a pinyon, juniper, and sagebrush landscape. The highway joins Arizona Highway 64 at Valle, and here you begin a thousand-foot climb to the South Rim.

There is one gas station in Tusayan and one gas station (open seasonally) near the East Entrance to Grand Canyon National Park. Given the scarcity of stations, gasoline prices are high. Be sure to fill up before leaving Williams or Flagstaff.

From Interstate 40 in Williams, exit at Arizona Highway 64 (exit 165), and follow AZ 64 the 56 miles to the park. This route is an excellent choice when approaching the park from the west or when weather conditions are not good. Arizona Highway 64 does not rise as high into the San Francisco Mountains as U.S. 180 and rarely closes in the wintertime.

By Train

Grand Canyon Railway operates between the Amtrak station at 233 North Grand Canyon Boulevard in Williams and the Grand Canyon Depot below El Tovar Hotel on the South Rim. The train departs Williams daily (except December 24 and 25) at 10:00 A.M. and arrives at the South Rim at 12:15 P.M. It then makes the return trip from Grand Canyon, leaving at 3:30 P.M. and arriving back in Williams at 5:45 P.M. The train cars are pulled by a century-old steam engine during the summer months (a diesel locomotive pulls the train the remainder of the year). Hardly a standard sit-for-hours-and-stare-out-the-window railroad, Grand Canyon Railway will keep you entertained with cowboys strolling the aisles, wandering musicians, and a mock train robbery. The railway has five different classes of service, from Coach Class to Luxury Parlor Class. One-way fares range from $58 per adult ($25 per child) Coach Class to $147 per adult ($114 per child) Luxury Parlor Class. The railway also offers several tour packages, including motor-coach tours along the rim, train and lodging combinations, and air and rail packages from Las Vegas. For information call (800) 843–8724 or log on to www.thetrain.com.

By Transcanyon Shuttle

Transportation between the South and North Rims of Grand Canyon is available seasonally through Transcanyon Shuttle. The shuttle runs when the North Rim is open, generally mid-May through mid-October, leaving once daily from the North Rim and once daily from the South Rim. Call (928) 638–2820 for more information.

STARTING YOUR VISIT

Okay, so you've finally reached Grand Canyon National Park and paid your $20 per vehicle entrance fee (Golden Eagle, Golden Access, and Golden Age Passports are also sold and accepted, as is an Annual Grand Canyon Passport for $40 and a National Parks Pass for $50). You

South Rim Weather Considerations

Summer temperatures on the South Rim average in the mid 80s during the day and in the low 50s at night. Winter temperatures average in the mid 50s during the day and in the mid 20s at night.

Temperatures in the inner canyon are much higher than on the rims, and in the summer you can expect temperatures of 110 degrees or more.

Plan to dress in layers, and pack a heavy sweater or fleece jacket even for summer trips—you'll need it at night on the rims.

Grand Canyon is subject to heavy thunderstorms during the monsoon season (roughly July through September), and hikers need to be aware that extremely dangerous flash flooding and lightning storms can occur. Heavy rain or snow may also loosen boulders and cause rock slides in the canyon.

---

have your sunscreen, plenty of water, snacks for the kids, and a camera with several rolls of film. What now?

Begin your visit by stopping at Canyon View Information Plaza, opened in 2000 as the first step in the implementation of the 1995 General Management Plan, which will eventually include a public transportation system and many additional changes.

To get to Canyon View Information Plaza, continue past the entrance station and follow South Entrance Road to the Mather Point parking lot. Park here and walk the short, paved trail to the plaza. You can also reach Canyon View Information Plaza aboard the eastbound Village Route shuttle bus, which stops at multiple locations throughout Grand Canyon Village. (The westbound bus will also get you there, but it will take longer as the bus must first loop around the western end of the village.) Village Route shuttle stops with parking include Market Plaza, Maswik Transportation Center, on the south side of Village Loop Road near the intersection with Center Road, and at park headquarters on South Entrance Road at Zuni Road. Stop at Canyon View Information Plaza to get oriented before you decide what to do first. The complex also has rest rooms and a bookstore in separate buildings. Canyon View Information Plaza is open daily.

If you can't wait another minute to see the canyon, Mather Point is just a few hundred feet from the information plaza, or board the Village Loop or Kaibab Trail Loop shuttle bus to take you to other viewpoints (see below for shuttle bus routes).

The National Park Service offers ranger-led activities, including geology and fossil walks, condor talks, discussions on ancestral Puebloan culture, and evening programs on a variety of topics. Consult the *Guide,* the free newspaper handed out to visitors entering the park, for current topics, times, and meeting places.

Grand Canyon Village

Grand Canyon Village, as well as nearby Market Plaza, Mather Campground, Trailer Village, and Canyon View Information Plaza, are the primary destinations of most visitors to the South Rim of Grand Canyon. All of the South Rim lodges inside the park are in this area, as are all of the restaurants (except for snack bars at Desert View and Hermits Rest), the post office and bank,

Smoke from a North Rim forest fire spreads haze across Grand Canyon at sunset.
TODD R. BERGER

the train depot, a grocery and camping-gear store, a one-hour photo lab, several Grand Canyon Association bookstores, the Backcountry Information Center, and the Bright Angel Trailhead.

Most of the village is accessible on foot or by riding the Village Route shuttle bus, which loops around the village between the beginning of Hermit Road and Canyon View Information Plaza. Save yourself a headache by parking your car in a main lot in the village at Center Road, Maswik Transportation Center, park headquarters, or Market Plaza, and setting out on foot or aboard a shuttle bus. There are also limited parking facilities at Maswik Lodge, at Yavapai Lodge, behind Hopi House, and at Bright Angel Lodge, but all of these facilities are small and fill early.

You can reach the village in your car by following South Entrance Road. If you're staying at Yavapai Lodge, turn left at the second intersection, after Mather Point. Yavapai Lodge is just ahead on your right. If you're staying at any of the rim lodges or at Maswik Lodge, continue on South Entrance Road another 2 miles to the intersection with Village Loop Drive. At Village Loop Drive, veer right for the rim lodges (El Tovar, Kachina, Thunderbird, and Bright Angel). Turn left for the parking areas at Center Road and Maswik Transportation Center, Maswik Lodge, and the Backcountry Information Center.

The street (Village Loop Drive) that runs along the rim lodges and restaurants is one-way, headed west. The road loops around (hence the road's name) and turns back into a two-way road by Maswik Lodge. If you take a left at the stop sign just past Maswik, you will drive past the mule barns, the intersection with Center Road, and loop back around to South Entrance Road and the rim lodges.

Shuttle Buses

Hermits Rest Route: The round-trip to Hermits Rest and back takes 75 minutes if you don't get off the bus. Bus service may be stopped during thunderstorms. Pets, except for service animals, are not allowed on any of the shuttles. The only place to get water is at Hermits Rest, the last stop on the 8-mile road.

The Hermits Rest shuttle stops at Trailview Overlooks, Maricopa Point, Powell Point and Memorial, Hopi Point (rest rooms available), Mohave Point, the Abyss, Pima Point, and Hermits Rest, where there are rest rooms and water available. You may get off the shuttle at any stop and walk along the Rim Trail to another stop and get on another bus. West of Maricopa Point, the trail is unpaved.

Village Route: The Village Route shuttle bus takes you (beginning at Canyon View Information Plaza) to Yavapai Rooms, Market Plaza, and Yavapai Lodge (parking lot B), Yavapai Point, Shrine of the Ages (parking lot A), Train Depot (which is the stop for El Tovar, Hopi House, and Verkamp's), Bright Angel Lodge (the stop for Lookout Studio and Kolb Studio), Hermits Rest Transfer, Maswik Lodge, Backcountry Information Center (parking lot E), Center Road (parking lots C and D), Village East (auto repair), Shrine of the Ages, Mather Campground, Trailer Village, Market Plaza (Yavapai Lodge), and back to Canyon View Information Plaza.

Kaibab Trail Route: The Kaibab Trail (green) shuttle bus loop stops at Canyon View Information Plaza, Pipe Creek Vista, the South Kaibab Trailhead, and Yaki Point, and then heads back to the information plaza. This is the only way to access Yaki Point and the South Kaibab Trailhead between March 1 and November 30. Private vehicles are allowed on Yaki Point from December 1 through February.

Most shuttle buses are not wheelchair accessible. Accessible shuttles are available with 24 hours' notice, or you may get an accessibility permit at the visitor center to allow your private vehicle into shuttle-only areas.

Shuttle schedules vary widely throughout the year, depending on when sunset and sunrise occur, and on park visitation.

Accessibility

Some programs and facilities on the South Rim are wheelchair accessible with assistance, and wheelchair-accessible tours can be arranged with prior notice. Check at the lodges' transportation desks or call (928) 638-2631. The National Park Service provides wheelchairs for temporary day use at no fee. You can usually find a wheelchair at the visitor center at Canyon View Information Plaza. Inquire there to get a temporary parking permit for designated parking. TDD phones are available at hotels. You may obtain the *Grand Canyon National Park Accessibility Guide* at the visitor center, Yavapai Observation Station, Kolb Studio, Tusayan Museum, and Desert View Information Center.

Check your copy of the park's *Guide* for current schedules for all three routes.

SERVICES AT GRAND CANYON NATIONAL PARK

Grand Canyon National Park has a walk-in medical clinic, located just off Center Road on Clinic Road about 2 miles south of Village Loop Drive. The **Grand Canyon Walk-In Clinic** is open every day except Sunday and can be reached at (928) 638-2551; in an emergency, dial 911 (9-911 from all in-park lodge rooms). A dentist is also available at the clinic by appointment. Call (928) 638-2395 for information.

The **post office** for Grand Canyon Village is next to Canyon Village Marketplace, 2 miles east of Village Loop Drive.

It's open Monday through Saturday (closed on federal holidays). Call (928) 638-2512 for information.

Bank One (928-638-2437) operates a branch Monday through Friday at Grand Canyon, next to the post office in Canyon Village Marketplace. The bank offers full teller services, cash advances, and an ATM. The ATM is accessible 24 hours.

Pets are allowed on the rim trails but cannot stay in in-park lodge rooms or walk with you on hikes below the rim. **Grand Canyon Kennels** (928-638-0534), open daily, is near Maswik Lodge in Grand Canyon Village, with boarding services for dogs and cats.

The **Grand Canyon Garage,** located just east of the intersection of South Entrance Road and Village Loop Drive, can perform minor or major vehicle repairs seven days a week. Call (928) 638-2631 for 24-hour emergency towing.

There are two **lost and found** offices within the park. If you lose something at one of the park lodges or restaurants, call Xanterra at (928) 638-2631. If you lose something anywhere else in the park, call the National Park Service at (928) 638-7798.

If you or your clothes get a little rank, **laundry and showers** are available next to Mather Campground.

The Books & More store, across from the visitor center at Canyon View Information Plaza, is the largest bookstore in the park, with dozens of publications on Grand Canyon and the surrounding wilderness. The store also sells posters, videos, maps, T-shirts, and puzzles, with all profits donated to Grand Canyon National Park.

Cell Phones

Most cell phones work on the South Rim of Grand Canyon (especially in the vicinity of Grand Canyon Village), although you will have to pay roaming charges unless your connection is through Alltel. Cell phones do not work in the inner canyon, or in other wilderness areas of northern Arizona, such as the Kaibab National Forest, Coconino National Forest, and the North Rim of Grand Canyon. Service is spotty on the Hopi and Navajo Reservations. Along major trails in Grand Canyon, emergency telephones are available that, in a true emergency, can connect you to park dispatch. The only other way to "stay in touch" while hiking in the wilderness areas of northern Arizona is to carry a satellite phone.

ACCOMMODATIONS

Accommodations on or near the South Rim fall into two categories: those inside the park, which are run by Xanterra, and those outside the park in Tusayan (7 miles south of the park entrance) or in Valle (27 miles south). To reserve rooms ahead of time inside the park, call Xanterra at (888) 297-2757, write to them at Xanterra Parks & Resorts, 14001 East Iliff Street, Suite 600, Denver, CO 80014, or log on to their Web site, www.grand canyonlodges.com. The local number for Xanterra is (928) 638-2631. For all accommodations outside the park, call the individual hotel directly or log on to the hotel's Web site.

PRICE CODE

The following price code is for two adults during the high season, generally between Memorial Day and Labor Day. The codes do not include taxes and other fees. Rates at Grand Canyon lodges drop precipitously during the off-season, particularly during the winter months. Rates are generally higher for hotels on the rim.

$	Less than $75
$$	$76 to $125
$$$	$126 to $175
$$$$	$176 to $225
$$$$$	More than $225

In-Park Accommodations

Xanterra operates a variety of lodges inside the park, both on the rim and back from the rim, as well as one facility (Phantom Ranch) at the bottom of the canyon. All in-park South Rim hotel rooms and cabins have phones and televisions. The hotels offer smoking and nonsmoking rooms and some wheelchair-accessible rooms. No pets are allowed in the lodges or on the trails below the rim, but you can board your pet at the kennel in Grand Canyon Village near Maswik Lodge. Call (928) 638-0534 for more information. Children under 16 can stay free with their parents. During the high season, rooms inside the park are scooped up quickly. You may be able to get a room due to a cancellation when arriving at the park (call 928-638-2631 to check), but you also may find yourself driving back to Flagstaff if you rely too heavily on this strategy. Unless it is unavoidable, call ahead and secure lodging before your arrival.

El Tovar Hotel $$$$$
**On the South Rim in Grand Canyon Village
(888) 297-2757 (Xanterra reservations)
www.grandcanyonlodges.com**
El Tovar, set to celebrate its centennial in 2005, is the oldest hotel in the park—and the most opulent. This National Historic Landmark is where the rich and famous stay, including presidents, movie stars, and business moguls. If you don't fit into one of those categories but have a weakness for living the good life, El Tovar is the place for you. Opened in 1905 to accommodate the influx of tourists arriving at the canyon aboard the new rail line from Williams to the South Rim, El Tovar was

El Tovar, built in 1905 on the South Rim, is home to both the finest hotel and best restaurant in Grand Canyon National Park. TODD R. BERGER

designed in the alpine style and built for the then-exorbitant cost of $250,000. The lobby has a hunting-lodge feel, with a large fireplace, big game trophies (including, oddly, moose, which are not native to the region), comfortable sofas and chairs, a gift shop, and a sundries store. El Tovar has 78 small rooms decorated in a rustic western style. Other amenities include the best restaurant in the park (see the Restaurants section) and an elegant lounge with a veranda near the rim. The rim and Hopi House (a historic gift shop selling Native American artwork) are just outside the doors.

**Kachina Lodge and
Thunderbird Lodge $$$
On the South Rim in Grand Canyon Village
(888) 297-2757 (Xanterra reservations)
www.grandcanyonlodges.com**
The near-twin Kachina and Thunderbird Lodges, built in the late 1960s and early 1970s, lack the rustic character of El Tovar and Bright Angel Lodge, but the two-story, neighboring motels sit on the rim with easy access to the Rim Trail, El Tovar Dining Room, the Arizona Room, Kolb Studio, and the head of the Bright Angel Trail. Canyon-view rooms naturally run a little higher. Neither lodge has a check-in desk. For the Kachina Lodge, check in at the neighboring El Tovar Hotel. For the Thunderbird Lodge, check in at the neighboring Bright Angel Lodge.

**Bright Angel Lodge $$$
On the South Rim in Grand Canyon Village
(888) 297-2757 (Xanterra reservations)
www.grandcanyonlodges.com**
Bright Angel Lodge, which is also a National Historic Landmark, has 89 cabins and rooms, all within a short walk from the rim. One of the most intriguing features of this lodge, designed by architect Mary Elizabeth Jane Colter and opened in 1935, is the fireplace in the Canyon Room. The hearth is built of rock layers accurately depicting the layers of the canyon itself. Prices range widely at Bright Angel Lodge, which offers everything from rela-

tively standard motel rooms to historic cabins right on the rim. The lodge has two restaurants—the Bright Angel Restaurant and the Arizona Room—as well as a soda fountain and a lounge.

**Maswik Lodge $$
In Grand Canyon Village, about a quarter mile from the rim
(888) 297-2757 (Xanterra reservations)
www.grandcanyonlodges.com**
Maswik Lodge has 250 rooms, spread out in small, motel-type buildings. The rooms are spare, modern, and comfortable, with bathrooms and televisions. Despite not being directly on the rim, Maswik is close, and having a willingness to walk a short way to see the canyon can lead to significant savings. Maswik has a cafeteria and a sports pub, with pool tables, sporting events flickering on several televisions, and plenty of libations.

**Yavapai Lodge $$
In Grand Canyon Village, about a half mile from the rim near Market Plaza
(888) 297-2757 (Xanterra reservations)
www.grandcanyonlodges.com**
Yavapai Lodge is the largest lodge in the park, with 358 rooms spread out in two areas in small, two-story motel-type buildings. It is also the farthest from the rim of the in-park lodges, although it is right next to the grocery store, camping store, post office, and bank of Market Plaza, and within a mile of Canyon View Information Plaza, the park's main visitor center (accessible via the Village Route shuttle bus, which stops near the parking lot entrance to the lodge's cafeteria). Rooms are modern and comfortable, and despite the lodge's proximity to the park's commercial shopping area with the attendant traffic, the lodge's rooms are secluded in a pinyon and ponderosa pine forest.

**Phantom Ranch $$$$$
At the bottom of Grand Canyon along Bright Angel Creek
(888) 297-2757 (Xanterra reservations)
www.grandcanyonlodges.com**

Phantom Ranch is on Bright Angel Creek at the bottom of Grand Canyon, just upriver from the Colorado River. The remote outpost harbors some of the most sought-after lodging in the park. TODD R. BERGER

You can't drive to Phantom Ranch, you can't take a helicopter there, and there is no gondola ride to the bottom. But if you don't mind (or mind only a little) a 7-mile hike down the South Kaibab Trail or a 9-mile mule ride down the Bright Angel Trail (both one-way), you can enjoy an intimate view of the Grand Canyon and the Colorado River from the bottom, some 5,000 feet below the rim. Phantom Ranch has several cabins surrounding a main canteen building and restaurant, as well as a bargain-priced ($26) bunkhouse for backpackers. You can book the cabins and bunks individually through Xanterra, or buy the two- or three-day mule ride package from the concessionaire, which includes cabin accommodations. The cabins and bunkhouse fill very early, and advance reservations are an absolute must—Xanterra accepts reservations up to 23 months in advance. Do not go to Phantom Ranch without a reservation.

You do not need a backcountry camping permit to stay at Phantom Ranch. Also keep in mind that temperatures at Phantom Ranch are generally 20 to 30 degrees hotter than those on the rim; many canyon visitors avoid staying at Phantom Ranch during the summer months.

Out-of-Park Accommodations

Best Western Grand Canyon Squire Inn $$$-$$$$
On Arizona Highway 64, Tusayan
(928) 638-8410, (800) 622-6966
www.grandcanyonsquire.com
A haven for out-of-towners, the Squire, as this hotel is known, also attracts locals who live in the park or Tusayan with such creature comforts as a bowling alley and

barbershop (the only place to get a trim within 60 miles). The 250-room hotel on the southern end of the Tusayan strip also features the Coronado Room restaurant (see the Restaurants section of this chapter), a coffee shop, the Fireside Lounge and Sports Bar, a tanning booth, a fitness center, a seasonal heated pool, seasonal tennis courts, a sauna and Jacuzzi, and a game room with pool tables. The lobby features a waterfall and a gift shop. Rooms are comfortable with the standard features, and the hotel can set you up with a nonsmoking or wheelchair-accessible room on request. Children under 12 stay free (with their parents), and the hotel does not allow pets.

Grand Canyon Inn $$$
Intersection of U.S. Highway 180 and Arizona Highway 64, Valle
(928) 635-9203, (800) 635-9203
Located 27 miles south of the South Entrance to Grand Canyon National Park in the high desert burg of Valle, the Grand Canyon Inn is a good choice if you are looking to get away from the crowds at Grand Canyon. The family-owned and rather pink Grand Canyon Inn has 101 rooms, a seasonal swimming pool, a children's pool, a restaurant, and a souvenir shop. Children 12 and under stay free, and pets are not allowed. Something less than scenic, Valle is a tourist town that developed due to its location at the intersection of the two highways that get people to Grand Canyon from the south. Other than patronizing a convenience store/gas station, a few gift shops, Flintstones Bedrock City, and the Planes of Fame Air Museum, you will likely want to head for the canyon first thing rather than linger in Valle.

The Grand Hotel $$$-$$$$
On Arizona Highway 64, Tusayan
(928) 638-3333, (888) 634-7263
www.visitgrandcanyon.com
Tusayan is 7 miles south of Grand Canyon Village, and the Grand Hotel is a top-notch choice if you opt to stay in a hotel outside the park. The Grand has a huge, comfortable lobby with a central fireplace and gift shop. The hotel also has an indoor pool and a Jacuzzi, rarities in these parts. The average-size rooms have rustic furnishings; some of the more expensive rooms have balconies. Children under 19 stay free at the Grand, but pets are not allowed. The Canyon Star restaurant in the hotel serves breakfast, lunch, and dinner (see Restaurants later in this chapter). In the evenings, Navajo dancers bounce and spin in the center of the Canyon Star. The Grand also has a bar.

**Grand Canyon Quality Inn &
Suites** $$$$
On Arizona Highway 64, Tusayan
(928) 638-2673, (800) 221-2222
www.grandcanyonqualityinn.com
The Grand Canyon Quality Inn & Suites is tucked behind the Grand Canyon Experience and Wendy's on the main strip in Tusayan. The hotel has 232 rooms—176 guest rooms and 56 two-room suites—as well as a seasonal swimming pool, whirlpool, and indoor spa. Rooms are comfortably furnished with standard items most people have come to expect at mid-range hotel chains, such as coffeemaker (with complimentary coffee), hair dryer, iron, ironing board, and remote-control television. A continental breakfast comes with the room, and the Quality Inn also harbors a restaurant that features a full bar and serves breakfast, lunch, and dinner. The hotel has smoking and non-smoking rooms, as well as wheelchair-accessible rooms. The hotel will charge extra for more than two adults in a room, but children under 18 stay free. Pets are not allowed. A large souvenir shop off the lobby offers some original art and a selection of authentic Navajo jewelry, as well as the usual tourist items.

**Holiday Inn Express
Grand Canyon** $$-$$$
On Arizona Highway 64, Tusayan
(928) 638-3000, (800) HOLIDAY
www.gcanyon.com

Opened in 1995, the Holiday Inn Express hosts 166 modern rooms with one king bed or two queen beds. The motel also has a few suites. The rooms have cable television, phones with dataports and voice mail, and other standard features. Nonsmoking and handicap-accessible rooms are available. Children under age 19 stay free with a mom or dad (or both). The hotel lacks a restaurant or lounge, as well as a swimming pool, but all rooms include a free continental breakfast. The Holiday Inn Express is a good choice for those looking to save a few bucks and spend most of their time touring the canyon rather than lingering in the hotel.

Rodeway Inn—Red Feather Lodge $$-$$$
On Arizona Highway 64, Tusayan
(928) 638-2414, (800) 538-2345
www.redfeatherlodge.com
Right in the middle of the Tusayan strip, the Rodeway Inn—Red Feather Lodge offers 231 rooms with cable TV and phones with dataports and voice mail. Children under 18 stay free with a parent, and unlike most establishments in this neck of the woods, the Rodeway *does* allow pets, although they will require a $50 deposit and charge you an extra $10 per night for Fido or Socks. The motel features a restaurant, seasonal pool and Jacuzzi, and game room. Nonsmoking and wheelchair-accessible rooms are available. After a good night's sleep, you can get your metabolism back up to speed with the complimentary coffee in the lobby. The Rodeway's free continental breakfast should also help.

The best times to take pictures of the canyon are near sunrise and just before sunset. The sun is very bright at other times of day, which tends to mute the already pastel colors of the canyon.

CAMPING
South Rim Area

There are two campgrounds near the South Rim inside Grand Canyon National Park, as well as one RV campground. It is illegal to camp anywhere else in the rim areas of the park.

Mather Campground
Off Market Plaza Road, Grand Canyon Village
(800) 365-2267 (SPHERIX reservations)
www.reservations.nps.gov
Mather Campground is the largest camping area in the park and the only tent campground in Grand Canyon Village. To find the campground from the South Entrance, follow South Entrance Road (AZ 64) to the flashing overhead stoplights. Though unsigned, this is Center Road. Turn left onto Center. Drive a short distance and then turn right onto Market Plaza Road. Mather Campground is a couple of miles up on the right-hand side, just past the intersection with Zuni Road.

Mather is large, very busy, and often packed. Call SPHERIX or go on-line for advance reservations, which the National Park Service strongly recommends from April through November. From December through March, you cannot make reservations for Mather; all sites are first come, first served during the off-season. If you arrive at the park without a reservation, you can inquire at the campground entrance about site availability. It is best to do this mid-morning, about the time people are checking out.

Mather has more than 300j regular sites with a maximum of six people and two vehicles per site. The sites can accommodate tents or RVs, but Mather has no hookups (see the following Trailer Village listing). Mather also has group sites, which can accommodate up to 50 people and three vehicles. Fees are $15 per site per night for regular sites and $40 per site per night for group sites.

Amenities at Mather Campground include a dump station, laundry facilities, showers, and rest rooms, as well as a location within walking distance of the full-service grocery store, post office, and bank at Market Plaza. The campground is about a mile from the rim.

Trailer Village
Off Market Plaza Road, next to Mather Campground, Grand Canyon Village
(888) 297–2757 (Xanterra reservations)
www.grandcanyonlodges.com
Trailer Village is in between Mather Campground and Market Plaza. To get there, follow the directions to Mather Campground but drive past the campground entrance to the next right. Signs will clearly indicate that you are headed for Trailer Village. Trailer Village is the place for RVs on the South Rim. The campground offers 84 RV sites with hookups. Sites cost $25.00 per site per night for two adults, with a $2.00 additional charge per extra person over 16. As with Mather, reservations are strongly recommended.

Desert View Campground
On Arizona Highway 64, 25 miles east of Grand Canyon Village
Open only during the summer months (mid-May through mid-October), Desert View Campground is near the East Entrance to the park and the Desert View area. It is a long, though beautiful, drive from Grand Canyon Village, and the campground offers quieter sites in a smaller setting than those at Mather Campground. To get to the campground, take AZ 64 east from Grand Canyon Village to Desert View and follow the signs. If you are entering the park at the East Entrance, the turnoff to the campground and the Desert View area is about a quarter mile up the highway on the right. Desert View has 50 sites available only on a first-come, first-served basis. Sites can accommodate up to two

vehicles and six people. All sites are $10 per site per night.

Tusayan

Grand Canyon Camper Village
On Arizona Highway 64 at the northern end of Tusayan
(928) 638–2887
Grand Canyon Camper Village is a commercial campground 7 miles south of Grand Canyon Village. The large campground has more than 200 sites for RVs (hookups are available) and tents, as well as tepees available for rental. Use of the coin-operated showers will please your camp mates. The minimum charge for a site here is $22.

Ten-X Campground
On Arizona Highway 64, 2 miles south of Tusayan
(928) 638–2443 (District Ranger Office)
About 9 miles south of Grand Canyon Village, Ten-X Campground is operated by the USDA Forest Service within the Kaibab National Forest. The campground is just off the AZ 64 highway leading to the national park, tucked in a forest of ponderosa pines and gambel oaks. The campground has 70 regular sites, with a limit of six campers per site. There is also one group site able to accommodate very large groups (up to 100 campers, with site fees dependant on the number of campers). The campground does not have RV hookups or showers, but does have fire rings, picnic tables, vault toilets, and water. The campground does not take reservations, but it rarely fills. Camping at the regular sites costs $10 per vehicle per night.

Kaibab National Forest

In addition to the Ten-X Campground, the Kaibab National Forest allows free, dispersed camping within the forest south of

Camping Ethics

Whether you're camping in the Kaibab National Forest or below the rim in Grand Canyon, the phrase to keep in mind is "zero impact." By respecting the land and resources you use when camping, you help to preserve these wilderness areas for your friends, your children, and your grandchildren, as well as the descendants of all the rest of humanity. Zero impact camping in the Grand Canyon area involves the following principles. More information on outdoor ethics can be found on-line at www.lnt.org.

- Be well prepared. Know the route and area in which you're planning to hike.
- Good campsites are found, not made. Altering a campsite is prohibited.
- Stay on the main trails; do not short-cut switchbacks.

- Pack out what you bring in, including toilet paper and all other trash.
- Campfires are prohibited below the rim. Do not burn toilet paper—pack it out.
- Bury solid human waste at least 200 feet from water in a shallow cathole 4–6 inches deep and 4–6 inches in diameter.
- To wash yourself or your dishes, carry water 200 feet away from creeks and potholes. Scatter strained dishwater.
- Keep loud voices and noises to a minimum.
- Leave what you find where you found it, including all natural resources (plants, flowers, rocks, fossils, animals, etc.) and all cultural resources (pottery shards, arrowheads, mining equipment, etc.).

the park. If you choose this option, there are rules that *must* be followed, including not camping closer than a quarter mile from a water source, carrying all trash out of the forest and disposing of it properly, and obeying campfire restrictions in place during your stay (call 928–638–2443 to check on fire restrictions). The rules are meant not to be annoying or constricting of your lifestyle but to preserve wilderness areas for future generations and to keep wilderness areas wild for the animals that live in the forest. If you are messy and don't believe in zero impact wilderness ethics, do not choose this option. The forest south of the park is crisscrossed with hundreds of miles of dirt roads, allowing access to remote areas of the forest for those with high-clearance vehicles. For

more information on dispersed camping or the Kaibab National Forest in general, contact the **Tusayan District Ranger Office** at (928) 638–2443, or stop in the office just off AZ 64 north of Tusayan (between Tusayan and the South Entrance to Grand Canyon National Park). The rangers are on duty 8:00 A.M. to 4:30 P.M. Monday through Friday. The Web site address for the entire Kaibab National Forest (which has three sections north and south of Grand Canyon National Park) is www.fs.fed.us/r3/kai.

Backcountry Camping

You can camp in the backcountry of Grand Canyon National Park, which at this national park means down in the canyon. However, this requires advance planning, and it requires *extensive* advance planning if you wish to camp in areas away from the Corridor Trails (Bright Angel Trail, and the North and South Kaibab Trails). Start by requesting a *Backcountry Trip Planner* from the **Backcountry Information Center** at (928) 638-7875 (the phone is staffed between 1:00 and 5:00 P.M. MST). You *cannot* use this phone number to buy backcountry permits (those requests must be faxed, mailed, or applied for in person). Similar information is available on-line at www.nps.gov/grca/back country. Other excellent sources of information on backcountry camping at Grand Canyon include *The Official Guide to Hiking the Grand Canyon* by Scott Thybony, published by Grand Canyon Association (800-858-2808, www.grandcanyon. org) and *Hiking Grand Canyon National Park* by Ron Adkison, published by Falcon/Globe Pequot (800-243-0495, www.GlobePequot.com).

Briefly, to camp in the backcountry, you will need to hike or ride a mule or horse to get there. The backcountry of the park is divided into three administrative zones (not to be confused with the life zones discussed earlier): Corridor, Threshold, and Primitive. The different zones are a reflection of the difficulty of the trails, the facilities available, and the help available in an emergency. There are numerous campgrounds scattered throughout the backcountry in the Corridor and Threshold Zones. At-large camping is available in Primitive Zones. *You need a backcountry permit to camp anywhere in any backcountry zone, whether in an established campground or not.*

If you have not hiked in Grand Canyon before, stick to the Corridor Zones. The trails are maintained and are regularly patrolled by rangers. Do not plan trips into the backcountry during the months of June, July, and August. The inner-canyon heat is comparable to Phoenix in the summertime, and backpacking in that type of heat is extremely dangerous, especially during the strenuous ascent out of the canyon. July, August, and early September is also monsoon season at Grand Canyon, with a high danger of flash flooding in narrow canyons within the park.

Backcountry permits are available up to four months in advance. They get scooped up very, very early, so apply as soon as you finalize plans (or base the timing of your trip on availability dates). Permit fees include $10.00 per permit and $5.00 per person per night.

It is possible to get a last-minute backcountry permit when you arrive at the park by showing up at the South Rim Backcountry Information Center (located in Maswik Transportation Center near Maswik Lodge on the western end of Grand Canyon Village and open Monday through Friday). However, you will need to be flexible about your camping dates and your campground choices. Be advised you may come up empty-handed, especially during the high hiking seasons in spring and fall, so have a backup plan. You will also need to follow several rules to have any chance at a permit. (1) You should arrive *two days before* your intended first night of camping below the rim to get a number to secure your place in line for the leftover permits. It is best to do this in the afternoon. (2) You will then need to come back the next morning (one day before your trip) promptly at 8:00 A.M. and wait for the ranger to call your number. *Don't arrive late.* When your number is called, step up to the window, request your schedule, and the ranger will tell you what he/she has available. Have your itinerary planned in advance, and have a couple of backup itineraries ready.

It is possible, but extremely unlikely, to get same-day permits by showing up at the Backcountry Information Center. Unless you're the luckiest person on Earth, you won't get a permit for Corridor campgrounds the same day you plan to camp at one.

RESTAURANTS

Many will come to Grand Canyon National Park thinking that the eating establishments in and around a major tourist destination like Grand Canyon will consist of tourist fare, from heat-lamp-enhanced burgers to limp, soggy fries. Although there are some establishments that will meet those low expectations, Grand Canyon National Park and environs also host at least one first-class restaurant and several most delectable, if not quite as deluxe, alternatives. Although prices are higher than you will pay in places lacking Grand Canyon–style scenery, the prices at most of the restaurants with table service won't clean out your wallet or cause heart palpitations. In addition to the restaurants listed below, you'll find a McDonald's, Wendy's, Krispy Kreme doughnut stand, and Pizza Hut Express in Tusayan; note that although these options may be quick and familiar, you can expect prices on your Extra Value Meal or floppy slice of pizza pie to be at least 50 percent higher than similar restaurants in Raleigh, Omaha, or Sacramento.

PRICE CODE

The price codes below represent average prices for dinner for two, excluding tax, gratuity, and drinks.

$	Less than $20
$$	$21 to $35
$$$	$36 to $60
$$$$	More than $60

In-Park Restaurants

The Arizona Room $$$
Bright Angel Lodge on the South Rim, Grand Canyon Village
(928) 638-2631 (Xanterra main switchboard)
Easier to get seated at and nearly as delightful, the Arizona Room in Bright Angel Lodge is a nice alternative if you can't get into the El Tovar Dining Room or you prefer a less formal, more cozy atmosphere. The food here is top-notch, and like the El Tovar, the restaurant sits right on the Rim Trail with large windows for canyon-gawking.

The Arizona Room is open seasonally (mid-February to December) for dinner only (serving 4:30 to 10:00 P.M.), and no reservations are accepted. Enter the restaurant outside the lodge on the eastern, rim side of the building. The wait can be long during the summer months, but you can always put your name on the waiting list, get an approximate seating time, and stroll along the Rim Trail until it's time to eat.

The Arizona Room is small compared to other park restaurants, with tables tightly packed. However, the size and layout of the restaurant give it a bistrolike elegance unusual for a national park restaurant.

Appetizers at the Arizona Room run from Kaibab Bean Dip (pinto and black beans with red, blue, and yellow corn tortilla chips) to the Grilled Portobello Salad (roasted chile-and-olive-oil-marinated portobello mushrooms with organic greens, tomatoes, and a citrus vinaigrette). Entree specialties of the house include the Blackened Ribeye Steak with Cilantro-Lemon Butter; Tequila-Marinated, Grilled Pork Medallions with Lemon-Lime Salsa; and Sea Salt and Coriander Crusted Pan-Seared Salmon with Melon Salsa. Desserts include New York Style Cheesecake (with prickly pear syrup) and the Toasted Pistachio Brownie. What more can you say but "yum"?

The wine list is briefer and less extravagant than El Tovar's, but the nice selection of reds and whites from California and Washington State (most available by the glass as well as the bottle) is likely to include something of interest to diners. The restaurant also serves beer, including the local favorites Bright Angel Amber and Kaibab Pale Ale, as well as a full line of cocktails with a specialization in margaritas.

Bright Angel Restaurant   **$$**
Bright Angel Lodge on the South Rim,
Grand Canyon Village
(928) 638-2631 (Xanterra main
switchboard)

The Bright Angel Restaurant is a popular
spot for breakfast, lunch, and dinner, due
to the quality of the food, the relatively
inexpensive prices, and the location
along the Rim Trail in the middle of the
village. The restaurant is kid-friendly and
spacious with plenty of natural sunlight
and a casual atmosphere, and it's open
daily.

Reservations are not required at the
Bright Angel Restaurant, although you will
find yourself waiting during the busy seat-
ing times. You can wait in the neighboring
Bright Angel Bar, which doubles as an
espresso bar during the morning hours, or
browse the adjacent gift shop.

Breakfast favorites at the Bright Angel
include Banana French Toast, Colorado
Quiche (with eggs, ham, Swiss cheese,
and green onions), and the Desert Scram-
ble (three scrambled eggs with cream
cheese and herbs, served with a choice of
meat, breakfast potatoes, and toast). For
lunch, options include the South of the
Border Salad (lettuce, tomato, onions,
black olives, and cheddar cheese topped
with seasoned ground beef and refried
beans and served in a fried tortilla bowl),
the Adobo Chicken Sandwich, and the
Bright Angel Burger.

Dinner at the Bright Angel includes
several appetizers, stews and chilis served
in sourdough bread bowls, a selection of
meal-size salads, and several different bur-
ritos. Numerous entrees crowd the menu,
such as Santa Fe Stuffed Shells, the River
Runner (a grilled and seasoned rainbow
trout fillet), and Trailblazing Fajitas
(chicken or steak grilled with onions and
peppers, and served with tortillas, gua-
camole, sour cream, salsa, Spanish rice,
and refried beans).

Desserts include Chocolate Suicide
Cake and Warm Apple Grunt (hot apple
slices in cinnamon sugar, topped with gra-
nola and accompanied by a scoop of

vanilla ice cream). The drink list includes
limited wine selections, several beers, and
specialty drinks such as the Grand Gold
(Cuervo 1800 Reservo, sweet and sour,
lime, and a splash of Grand Marnier) and
Kaibab Coffee (house coffee with Irish
cream and Frangelico).

Canyon Café at Yavapai Lodge   **$-$$**
In Yavapai Lodge near Market Plaza,
Grand Canyon Village
(928) 638-2631 (Xanterra main
switchboard)

Set up cafeteria style just off the lobby of
Yavapai Lodge, Canyon Café serves
breakfast, lunch, and dinner to folks interested in convenience and speed. Cafeteria selections include fried chicken,
hamburgers, pizza, a salad bar, and some
traditional meat-and-potatoes entrees.
The Canyon Café serves a wide selection
of beverages (including beer and wine for
mom and dad). It's open daily.

Delicatessen at Marketplace   **$-$$**
In Market Plaza, Grand Canyon Village

The Delicatessen is a cafeteria-style
eatery inside the Canyon Village Marketplace grocery store on the eastern edge
of Grand Canyon Village. Sandwiches are
made to order, and the deli also serves
Caesar salads, calzones, pizza by the
slice, fries, and other fast options. Beverages include soda and Naked fruit/veg-
etable juices. Open daily for lunch and
dinner.

El Tovar Dining Room   **$$$-$$$$**
El Tovar Hotel on the South Rim, Grand
Canyon Village
(928) 638-2631, ext. 6432

Dining at El Tovar is nothing short of
extraordinary. Luscious entrees, impecca-
ble service, a rustic yet first-class decor,
and proximity to the grandest of canyons
all combine to make an evening at El
Tovar one that will stick in your mind for
some time after you leave Grand Canyon
National Park.

Opened within the El Tovar Hotel in
1905, the main dining room, most recently

remodeled in 1998, includes heavy wooden ceiling beams, expansive windows overlooking the Rim Trail and the canyon beyond, and colorful murals painted by Hopi artist Bruce Timeche, depicting Hopi, Navajo, Apache, and Mohave traditional life. Bowtied waitstaff swirl among the white-linen-topped tables like California condors on canyon wind currents and dote on their guests with comfortable elegance and mind-reading attentiveness.

Gawk all you want, but what really brings people to El Tovar is the food, considered by many to be some of the best in the state. The restaurant is open every day for breakfast, lunch, and dinner, and each menu shines. Breakfast patrons thrive on the Cornmeal Crusted Trout with Two Eggs, as well as the Sonoran Style Eggs with Chicken and Chorizo, the latter blending Native American and Mexican influences. If you go for a stroll along the rim and find yourself back at El Tovar at lunchtime, you might opt for the Pine Nut Chicken Salad Sandwich on a Whole Wheat Roll (served with smoked apple mayonnaise) or perhaps the Prickly Pear Grilled Chicken Breast, with jalapeño jack cheese, roasted onion confit, seasonal vegetables, and rice du jour.

All of this said, to truly behold all that El Tovar is, it is imperative you come for dinner. To get things started, consider the Marinated Roma Tomato, Country Olives and Extra Virgin Olive Oil appetizer and/or the El Tovar Black Bean Soup, with tortilla crisps, scallions, and sour cream. The Caesar Dorado salad is also an excellent choice. The portions are easily enough for two, so consider sharing with your dinner guest (you don't have to share if you don't want to). The main course menu features both pastas and entrees, including Garden Penne Rigati with Bruschetta; the colorful Salmon Tostada with Organic Greens, Lime Sour Cream, Chile Olive Oil, Corn Salsa, and Chile Lime Rice; and Braised New Zealand Lamb Shank with Rose-mary Demi-Glace and Roasted Red Pepper Asiago Polenta.

El Tovar has a nicely variated wine list, and those looking for a drink with regional flare might consider the prickly pear cactus margarita, an intriguing if somewhat sweet variation on the classic. Desserts vary day by day, and the restaurant offers a nice selection of ports, cognacs, and other dessert wines to finish off the evening.

Reservations are not necessary for breakfast and lunch, although for the midday meal, you may wish to arrive before 11:45 A.M. to avoid the crowds arriving by train. Dinner reservations are a must, and they can be made up to six months in advance if you have a room reservation at the El Tovar or up to 30 days in advance if you don't. You may be able to get in for dinner if you call for a reservation after you have arrived at the park or simply walk up to the maître d' and inquire, but you will likely have to settle for a very early or very late seating. If you know you will be at the park at a certain time, call ahead and get a more civilized seating time.

An elegant lounge abuts the El Tovar Dining Room, a nice spot for a drink after a long day touring the park or hiking the trails. In the summer, you can sit out on the lounge's veranda and watch the light fade over the canyon at sunset.

Maswik Cafeteria $–$$
In Maswik Lodge, Grand Canyon Village
(928) 638-2631 (Xanterra main
switchboard)
Very similar in menu and spirit to the Canyon Café at Yavapai Lodge, the Maswik Cafeteria off the lobby at Maswik Lodge serves up lunch and dinner family favorites like burritos, burgers, hot sandwiches, and pastas. It's also open for breakfast, so you can get a plate of scrambled eggs or a bowl of cereal with great ease. If you are in a hurry, have antsy kids, or are just too exhausted from toodling around the park to mess with dinner at one of the restaurants on the

rim, Maswik will fill you up nicely, if unremarkably. Open daily.

Phantom Ranch Canteen $$$
At the bottom of Grand Canyon along
Bright Angel Creek
(928) 638-2631 (Xanterra main
switchboard)

If you're on the rim, you can't just stop by for dinner at Phantom Ranch Canteen, but if you find yourself at the bottom of the canyon along the North Kaibab Trail, the canteen is the one and only restaurant option. There are specific seating times for breakfast and dinner, and only guests staying at Phantom Ranch and possessing meal reservations can eat during the seating times. It is strongly recommended that you make your reservations for breakfast and/or dinner at the same time you book your lodging at Phantom Ranch. If you are not staying at Phantom Ranch, you can eat at the canteen between 8:00 A.M. (8:30 A.M. from November 1 to March 31) and 4:00 P.M., and from 8:00 to 10:00 p.m. Everything you eat at the Phantom Ranch Canteen got there on the back of a mule, so the options are understandably limited. Meals include steak or vegetarian dinners, Hiker's Stew, sack lunches (available anytime), and breakfasts that will fill you up. The canteen also sells snacks, as well as a limited number of hiker supplies like Band-Aids, stamps, and T-shirts.

Also inside the park are several snack bars, including the **Hermits Rest Snack Bar** at the end of Hermit Road (8 miles west of Grand Canyon Village); the **Bright Angel Fountain** in Bright Angel Lodge (the entrance is outside on the rim side of the building), which serves ice cream, sandwiches, and other quick snacks; and the **Desert View Trading Post Snackbar** at Desert View, 25 miles east of Grand Canyon Village near the East Entrance to the park. All are open daily.

Out-of-Park Restaurants

Café Tusayan $$
On Arizona Highway 64, Tusayan
(928) 638-2151

Café Tusayan is a locally owned, somewhat Denny's-like establishment on Tusayan's main drag. Open daily and serving breakfast, lunch, and dinner, the cafe specializes in prime rib, but the menu has numerous other options, including tangy spaghetti (marinara or with meat sauce), quesadillas, meal-size salads, and beef stroganoff. The breakfast menu has many things you would expect, such as the two-egg plate, French toast, and hot oatmeal. It also has a few things you wouldn't expect, such as the Café Tusayan Omelet (green peppers, ham, red onions, mushrooms, pinyon pine nuts, and three cheeses) and muesli. The lunch menu includes several sandwiches, most notably a classic grilled cheese, and burgers in different sizes with your choice of toppings (green chilis, mushrooms, bacon, or blue cheese). The cafe has a children's menu, with numerous choices under four bucks, and a nice selection of desserts such as carrot cake and five types of pie. Café Tusayan serves wine (sold primarily by the bottle) and beer, including the local favorites Mogollon Apache Trout Stout and Oak Creek Nut Brown Ale.

Canyon Star $$$
The Grand Hotel
On Arizona Highway 64, Tusayan
(928) 638-3333

Most (but not all) of the restaurants just south of the park in Tusayan are harbored in the many hotels along the Tusayan Strip. Located in the Grand Hotel, Canyon Star has a rustic, western decor. Dinner menu items include southwestern cuisine, barbecued ribs, and steaks. The restaurant also serves a breakfast buffet and dinner buffet during the winter months, adding a lunch buffet during the busy summer season. Reservations are not required and are usually not needed in this large restaurant.

The Canyon Star hosts free nightly entertainment, including cowboy crooners and Navajo dancers.

The Coronado Room $$$-$$$$
Best Western Grand Canyon Squire Inn
On Arizona Highway 64, Tusayan
(928) 638-2681
The Coronado Room in the Best Western Grand Canyon Squire is a good choice for those seeking a somewhat formal meal (casual clothes are fine) best lingered over and savored. The Coronado's appetizers include oysters on the half shell, while entrees roll out an honor roll of local and not-so-local specialties, such as steaks, game hen, elk, lobster thermidor, and several Mexican/southwestern dishes. House specialties include Chicken Marsala and Veal Picata. The Coronado has a full bar and extensive wine list. Open daily for dinner only.

We Cook Pizza and Pasta $-$$
On Arizona Highway 64, Tusayan
(928) 638-2278
We Cook (named after the restaurant's owner, W. E. Cook) serves surprisingly tasty pizza and pasta dishes in the heart of Tusayan's commercial district. All dishes are available for in-house dining or take-out (but no delivery service). Prices might be a little higher than you are used to back home, but in this neighborhood, We Cook offers some of the best deals around. The restaurant serves specialty pizzas, from the Meaty Cook with a pile of meat toppings to the Pure Vegan, topped with, among other things, soy cheese. You can also piece together your own pizza by choosing one of four basic pizzas and adding toppings to your liking. Nonpizza options include spaghetti, Cajun Chicken Fettucine, a selection of calzones, and a salad bar. Beer, wine, and soft drinks are also available. Open daily for lunch and dinner.

Yippee-Ei-O! Steakhouse $$$
On Arizona Highway 64, Tusayan
(928) 638-2780
Tusayan's Yippee-Ei-O! Steakhouse is hard to miss. With a parking lot entrance flanked by two covered wagons, a VW van painted like a cow grazing in front of the restaurant, and an exterior straight out of Dodge City, the über–Wild West look of the establishment shouts "steaks and fun" to hungry travelers passing through. The interior doesn't drop the ball, either, with a staff sporting 10-gallon hats, belts with big buckles, and cowboy boots, and a lodgey decor complete with branding irons, steer horns, saddles, and cowboy art. With all of the effort on atmosphere in an unabashedly touristy area, you might expect mediocre food at best—and you would be wrong. Yippee-Ei-O! does a very nice job with its mainstay (steaks), all of which are cooked over an open juniper fire. The granddaddy is the 24-ounce Trail Boss, a whopper of a steak that will fill up to near-dangerous levels 95 percent of the people who try to eat the whole thing. Many smaller steaks are also available, as well as Cotton Pickin' Chicken (a chicken filet doused in barbecue sauce), Colorado River Shrimp (not *really* from the Colorado, but breaded and delicious), and Barbecued Smoked Pork Chops. The restaurant also serves several "Cowless Cookin'" dishes (such as the Vegetarian Platter and the Spaghetti Western), and lots of appetizers, including deep-fried rattlesnake meat. Yippee-Ei-O! has a full bar, and during the summer you can stab your fork into a steak at a table on the patio out front. Open daily for lunch and dinner.

HISTORIC AND SCENIC SITES ALONG THE RIM

The following listing includes the major historic and scenic sites along the South Rim, with the exception of restaurants and hotels, which are discussed separately. The site listing begins with the Rim Trail, which runs from Hermits Rest to Pipe Creek Vista, continues to discuss Hermit Road as it heads west to Hermits Rest, then returns to review sites in Grand Canyon Village and areas east all the way to Desert View.

The Rim Trail runs from Pipe Creek Vista to Hermits Rest, allowing access to dozens of overlooks and providing an easy way to walk through Grand Canyon Village. Here, strollers walk along the trail next to El Tovar. TODD R. BERGER

Rim Trail

The Rim Trail, which winds 13 miles from Pipe Creek Vista on Desert View Drive to Hermits Rest, is the easiest and most accessible hiking trail in Grand Canyon National Park. The trail can be accessed at any point along the rim in Grand Canyon Village, along Hermit Road, or at Yavapai and Mather Points, and hikers can travel any length of the trail they like.

The Rim Trail is paved between Pipe Creek Vista and Maricopa Point on Hermit Road, although the trail is open only to hikers (no bicycles allowed). The trail from Maricopa Point to Hermits Rest is unpaved and winds harrowingly close to the rim, undulating wildly with the topography. If fear of heights is not an issue, you'll find that the unpaved portion of the trail offers stunning overlooks and few people.

From many of the park's most popular overlooks, the Rim Trail offers solitude just a short stroll down the trail. The walk between Yavapai Point and Grand Canyon Village is particularly pleasing, with many stunning overlooks not accessible by car or shuttle bus, including **Grandeur Point,** with gorgeous views of the Bright Angel Trail, Grand Canyon Village (El Tovar Hotel in particular), Indian Garden, Plateau Point, and Bright Angel Canyon.

The Rim Trail follows the rim the length of Grand Canyon Village. It is the easiest and prettiest way to access different sites along the rim, including the Bright Angel Trailhead, Kolb Studio, Lookout Studio, Bright Angel Lodge, Kachina and Thunderbird Lodges, El Tovar, Hopi House, and Verkamp's. The Rim Trail in Grand Canyon Village is also one of the best spots for viewing California condors during the summer. Look for them perched on the rocky ledges below Lookout Studio and soaring above the Bright Angel Trail.

Hermit Road

Hermit Road connects Grand Canyon Village to Hermits Rest, 8 miles to the west. Although the road can be traveled by private car only from December 1 through February 28 (or 29), the Hermits Rest Route shuttle bus provides free, like-clockwork access to the overlooks along the road during the rest of the year. Heading west, the shuttle bus makes eight stops along the road: the Trailview Overlooks, Maricopa Point, Powell Point, Hopi Point, Mohave Point, the Abyss, Pima Point, and Hermits Rest. Heading east, the shuttle bus stops only at Mohave Point and Hopi Point. The Rim Trail parallels Hermit Road throughout its 8-mile journey, and many of the overlooks are only a short walk down the trail. Hermit Road is also a good biking road, as most of the year the shuttle buses are the only traffic. However, the road is narrow with no shoulder, and when a shuttle bus approaches, it is strongly advised for your own safety and to keep the shuttle buses on schedule that you pull to the side of the road and dismount your bike until the shuttle bus has passed.

After boarding the shuttle bus at the Village Route Transfer Station on the western edge of Grand Canyon Village, you will climb a couple hundred feet to the **Trailview Overlooks,** the first shuttle-bus stop along Hermit Road. Two neighboring overlook sites are here, Trailview I and Trailview II, with spectacular views of Grand Canyon Village, the Bright Angel Trail, Indian Garden, Grandeur Point, the San Francisco Peaks near Flagstaff, and Red Butte south of the park. This is the best overlook on the South Rim for viewing the Bright Angel Trail, which from here looks like angel-hair pasta tossed against the canyon's rock layers. If you have hiked up the Bright Angel Trail, these viewpoints will make it very clear

in your mind why the climb hurt so much.

Maricopa Point is the next stop along the Hermits Rest Route. Maricopa provides some of the first views of the western Grand Canyon along Hermit Road and nice overlooks of the Bright Angel Trail, Plateau Point, and Bright Angel Canyon, as well as a bird's-eye view of the **Orphan Mine,** a former uranium mine that operated on a private inholding of land within the park until 1969. The head frame of the mine still stands west of Maricopa Point. If you are walking on the Rim Trail west of Maricopa, your route will detour around the Orphan Mine site. Signs posted along the fence indicate why: Environmental testing for radiation on the site is in progress. However, there is little danger to hikers walking along the perimeter of the mine site.

West of Maricopa Point and the Orphan Mine, **Powell Point** is the home of the **Powell Memorial,** a monument erected in 1915 to commemorate the 1869 river trip of John Wesley Powell and his crew from Green River, Wyoming, through Grand Canyon, to the confluence with the Virgin River, a location submerged under Lake Mead today. Although monumental and resting on a beautiful viewpoint, the memorial seems a little funereal and out of place in this wilderness. You can also get nice views of the Orphan Mine head frame from Powell Point.

Hopi Point, the next overlook along Hermit Road, juts farther out into the canyon than any other point on the developed South Rim. The overlook is wildly popular at sunrise and sunset—and for good reason: The views east and west down the canyon are unrivaled. On clear days, you can see most of the major formations in the central canyon, from Vishnu Temple off the North Rim in the east to Mount Trumbull in the west, towering above the canyon at 8,028 feet above sea level. You can also get a nice view of the Colorado River from here. Hopi Point is one of two eastbound stops for the Hermits Rest shuttle bus.

A raven perched in front of the 3,000-foot-high Mohave Wall as seen from Pima Point.
TODD R. BERGER

Mohave Point, slightly less than a mile down Hermit Road or the Rim Trail from Hopi Point, is the other stop for the eastbound shuttle bus. Hopi Point blocks the view eastward from Mohave, but the view westward is outstanding. You can see Pima Point, several rapids on the Colorado River, and the Alligator (a below-the-rim extension of the point jutting slightly northwestward far into the canyon). Osiris Temple and Isis Temple, two towering canyon buttes that stand out among several spectacular formations, are clearly visible from here. Mohave Point is a great place to view the sunset in the western canyon.

The Abyss, the next stop along Hermit Road, is tucked back into a wide side canyon flanked by Mohave and Pima Points. The stop is not a good choice for sunset or sunrise, but what *will* make your jaw drop is the 3,000-foot-high cliff known as the Mohave Wall, clearly visible

from the viewpoint. The mammoth rock wall gives a feel for the size of this canyon, which can seem so abstract from many other overlooks, like a scale model built in someone's basement. If you got to the Abyss from Mohave Point via the Rim Trail, the view from here will also scare you to death as you realize what you just hiked along.

About 1 mile before Hermits Rest and 7 miles from Grand Canyon Village, **Pima Point,** the last stop on Hermit Road before Hermits Rest, towers 6,798 feet above sea level. The point is the former site of a tramway that carried supplies down into the canyon to Hermit Camp, a tourist camp built by the Santa Fe Railroad. The camp was in operation from 1912 to 1930, and the tramway ran from 1928 to late 1930s. Today Pima Point offers views of the Colorado River (including Granite Rapid, which can be heard from the point) and large portions of the western Grand Canyon. The point is a wonderful spot to watch sunset, but to return to Grand Canyon Village after our local star sets, you will need to ride the westbound shuttle bus to Hermits Rest and then head back eastbound to Grand Canyon Village, as the eastbound bus does not stop at Pima Point.

Hermits Rest

Hermits Rest is as far west as you can travel on South Rim paved roads within Grand Canyon National Park. The historic, Mary Colter–designed gift shop and snack bar (928-638-2351; open daily), constructed in 1909 at the end of a new (at that time) 8-mile road from Grand Canyon Village, houses a huge, amphitheater-like fireplace. The building looks like it grew out of the hillside. The name "Hermits Rest" is in honor of Louis Boucher, a soft-spoken man who lived at Dripping Springs in the canyon below Hermits Rest around the turn of the 20th century.

The Hermit Trailhead is a few hundred yards west of Hermits Rest. The steep, inner-canyon trail connects to several trails below the rim, including the Dripping Springs Trail (and, branching from the Dripping Springs Trail, the Boucher Trail), the Waldron Trail, and the Tonto Trail. The Hermit Trail is recommended for experienced Grand Canyon hikers only.

Kolb Studio

Back in Grand Canyon Village, Kolb Studio (open daily) is the westernmost and one of the most interesting historic buildings along the rim. Located just east of the head of the Bright Angel Trail and just west of Bright Angel Lodge, the studio is the former store, movie theater, darkroom, gallery, and home of photographers Ellsworth and Emery Kolb.

Ellsworth Kolb arrived at Grand Canyon in what was then the Arizona Ter-

ritory in 1901 and his brother followed him from Pittsburgh the following year. The Kolb brothers bought a photographic business based in Williams and moved the operation to Grand Canyon, where they set up shop in a tent on a private inholding of land at the head of the Bright Angel Trail. The brothers shot photographs of tourists riding mules down the Bright Angel Trail, developed them while the riders were in the canyon, and sold them to the tourists upon their return to the South Rim. The business proved profitable, and the Kolb brothers built the first part of Kolb Studio in 1904. Additions in 1915 and 1926 brought the building to its present size.

The Kolb brothers explored Grand Canyon from top to bottom, east to west, and north to south. In 1911, the brothers struck upon the idea of re-creating John Wesley Powell's 1869 river trip from Green River, Wyoming, through Grand Canyon, and of filming the trip with the new technology of moving pictures. The resulting film was shown in the Kolb Studio auditorium after its completion in 1915 and ran daily until Emery Kolb's death in 1976.

In the 1990s, the nonprofit Grand Canyon Association funded restoration of Kolb Studio and reopened the historic building as a bookstore, interpretive site, and art gallery. Revolving exhibits are shown in the gallery, ranging from the annual *Arts for the Parks* exhibition of paintings of America's national parks to spectacular photography shows featuring the canyon and other natural areas. Check the *Guide* for current exhibitions.

Lookout Studio

Lookout Studio (928-638-2631, ext. 6087; open daily) is a little farther east on the Rim Trail toward Bright Angel Lodge. Completed in 1914, the stone building seems to melt right into the canyon rim like other Mary Colter–designed buildings at Grand Canyon. The building was constructed by the Santa Fe Railroad as a gift shop, a role it still fulfills today. The selec-

Once the home and studio of pioneer photographers Ellsworth and Emery Kolb, Kolb Studio today includes a Grand Canyon Association bookstore and a gallery with rotating art and photography exhibits. TODD R. BERGER

tion of books, Native American artwork, posters, and touristy items offered was meant to rival the goods being sold at nearby Kolb Studio and at Verkamp's, a little farther east up the Rim Trail.

Today, the historic store offers a patio where you can step into the sun and look out over the canyon. This is a good spot for viewing California condors flying over the canyon or perched on the rocky out-croppings below the building.

Mule Barns

Although not open to the public, the his-toric mule barns, on Village Loop Drive on the opposite side of the train tracks from the rim lodges, are a site to see both for the architecture and the long-eared tourist haulers in the corral. The buildings and corral, built by the Fred Harvey Company (later purchased by the

company that would become Xanterra) date from around 1907. Note that if you have booked a mule ride into the canyon, you will *not* meet your wrangler and steed here. All mule trips rendezvous at the stone-and-wood-railing corral at the Bright Angel Trailhead.

Santa Fe Railroad Depot

Located below El Tovar Hotel, the Santa Fe Railroad Depot, today the destination of trains traveling on the Grand Canyon Railway tracks from Williams, was built in 1910. The historic structure is the only train station inside a national park in the United States. Although the interior of the station is not open to the public, you can watch the trains come in or depart from the plat-form. During the summer, the Grand Canyon Railway train cars are pulled by a century-old steam engine.

Grand Canyon Pioneer Cemetery

Grand Canyon Pioneer Cemetery is located just west of Grand Canyon National Park Headquarters 1.5 miles east of Village Loop Drive on South Entrance Road. It is one of only two cemeteries still being used in the National Park System. The first Grand Canyon Village resident to be buried here, John Hance, was laid to rest in 1919, and the cemetery's gravestones are a virtual who's who of Grand Canyon history. Here you will find the graves of Ada Bass, William Wallace Bass, Ralph Cameron, Ellsworth Kolb, Emery Kolb, Edwin McKee, and Gunner Widforss, as well as the United Airlines Accident Memorial, which marks the graves of unidentified victims of the 1956 collision of TWA and United airplanes over Grand Canyon.

Canyon employees and residents can still choose to make the Grand Canyon Pioneer Cemetery their final resting place, provided they have worked and lived at the park for three years. When visiting the cemetery, please stay on the gravel paths and do not touch the gravestones, as many are fragile.

Yavapai Observation Station and Yavapai Point

The road to Yavapai Observation Station (open daily) and Yavapai Point stretches out from South Entrance Road about 1 mile west of Mather Point and 2 miles east of Village Loop Drive. Yavapai Observation Station has large glass windows overlooking the canyon and is the home of a bookstore operated by the nonprofit Grand Canyon Association. The building, completed in 1928, was one of the first buildings in a national park built specifically to interpret geology, a role it still fulfills today.

There are numerous places along the Rim Trail, which runs by the observation station, for outdoor gawking at the canyon. The point offers nice views of Bright Angel Canyon, the Colorado River and the Inner Gorge, Plateau Point, and the North Rim's Cape Royal, as well as long views east and west down the canyon. Yavapai is an excellent viewing spot for both sunrise and sunset.

Mather Point

Named after Stephen T. Mather, the first director of the National Park Service, Mather Point is the most-visited viewpoint in Grand Canyon National Park, due largely to it being the first viewpoint reached as you drive into the park on South Entrance Road. Mather Point is also the closest overlook to Canyon View Information Plaza, the park's main visitor center, which is a short walk from the point down a paved trail. All of this adds up to crowds, although walking a short distance down the Rim Trail from Mather will bring a surprising amount of solitude.

Mather Point does not stick out into the canyon as far as neighboring Yavapai and Yaki Points, but the panoramic view from the overlook will take your breath away nonetheless. Mather offers views of the Colorado River, Phantom Ranch, Plateau Point, the South Kaibab Trail and Cedar Ridge, and Isis Temple.

Desert View Drive

Desert View Drive stretches 25 miles east from its intersection with South Entrance Road just east of Mather Point. The highway is the continuation of AZ 64 and carries travelers east of Grand Canyon Village to Desert View, the park's East Entrance, and on to Cameron and the intersection with U.S. 89. Although the road does not run directly along the rim throughout most of its length, it does allow access to numerous rim viewpoints.

The road to **Yaki Point** and the **South Kaibab Trailhead** will be the first intersection you come to along Desert View Drive, about 1 mile from the intersection with South Entrance Road. The road is closed to private car traffic March 1 to November 30, although the Kaibab Trail Route shuttle bus, which can be boarded at Canyon View Information Plaza, does carry passengers up the road to the trailhead and the point. This is by far the easiest way to visit the point, but if you are driving along Desert View Drive during the times of the year when the road to Yaki Point is closed, you can park your car along Desert View Drive or at the picnic area just beyond the turn to Yaki Point on the right, and walk the .75 mile to the point. The South Kaibab Trailhead is about a half mile up the road to the left. Yaki Point offers nice views of Bright Angel Canyon, Zoroaster Temple, Brahma Temple, and Clear Creek Canyon, and is a good choice for both sunrise and sunset.

Additional picnic areas are on either side of the road as you head farther east along Desert View Drive. Facilities vary, but at the very least you can find a shady spot with a picnic table and a distinct lack of tourists. There also several unmarked overlooks along the drive. If you decide to pull off to take a look, be careful pulling back onto Desert View Drive. Blindspots and fast-moving cars make getting back on the road hazardous.

About 7.5 miles beyond the turnoff to Yaki Point you will arrive at the road to **Grandview Point.** The trailhead for the Grandview Trail is here. Copper miners digging for ore on Horseshoe Mesa in the canyon below Grandview Point built the precipitous Grandview Trail in 1892–93 and used it to haul copper ore out by mule or burro. The area is also the former home of the Grand View Hotel, which operated from a site just back from the point from 1897 to 1907 and again from 1911 to 1913. The hotel did not survive the coming of the railroad in 1901 to Grand Canyon Village, 12 miles away by stagecoach. Today,

Grandview Point offers nice views of the eastern canyon, including Horseshoe Mesa (with its distinctive horseshoe shape), Cape Royal on the North Rim, Wotans Throne, and Vishnu Temple.

Just under 2 miles east of the intersection with the road to Grandview Point, Desert View Drive slides past the South Rim trailhead to the **Arizona Trail.** The first section of this length-of-Arizona trail was dedicated in 1988 on the Arizona Strip north of Grand Canyon National Park. You can walk most (or a small part, if you prefer) of the trail today; eventually the trail will run from the Utah border to Mexico, uninterrupted over some 750 miles, through Arizona's wildlands. From this point along Desert View Drive, the Arizona Trail heads south out of the national park, through the Tusayan District of the Kaibab National Forest, and into the Kachina Peaks Wilderness (within the Coconino National Forest) north of Flagstaff.

Moran Point is just under 4 miles farther east along Desert View Drive. The point is named after Thomas Moran, the 19th-century landscape painter whose work exposed America to the wonders of Grand Canyon. The point offers nice views of the Sinking Ship formation, Wotans Throne, Vishnu Temple, Red Canyon, and the Colorado River, including Hance Rapid.

Driving another 4 miles east on Desert View Drive will bring you to **Tusayan Ruin and Museum** (928–638–7968), the site of an ancestral Puebloan dwelling that stood here around A.D. 1200. The museum offers free 30-minute guided tours of the site and displays exhibits on the American Indian tribes in the Grand Canyon area and models of how the ancestral Puebloan structure looked when it was occupied. Visitors can also walk through the ruins on a self-guided trail. A Grand Canyon Association bookstore sells books and other materials about the park, with all profits donated to the National Park Service at Grand Canyon.

A scant 1 mile east on Desert View Drive takes you to **Lipan Point,** with spectacular views up the eastern canyon and long views (when the skies are clear) up the western canyon. You can also get nice views of the Colorado River from Lipan Point, and the point is a dandy spot to park yourself at sunset. The view west as the shadows lengthen across the mesas and buttes of the canyon is simply sublime. Many argue that the view from Lipan Point is the grandest on the South Rim. The trailhead for the Tanner Trail, an extremely steep backcountry trail, is also here.

Navajo Point, which offers many similar viewing angles to Lipan Point, is another 1 mile up Desert View Drive. At 7,461 feet, Navajo Point is the highest overlook on the South Rim.

Desert View

The 70-foot-high Desert View Watchtower, one of the most spectacular historic buildings in Grand Canyon National Park, keeps watch over Desert View, 25 miles east of Grand Canyon Village. The Watchtower imitates the design of stone towers found throughout the Southwest, which date from the days of the ancestral Puebloan people. Designed by Mary Colter, the tower was completed in 1932 and dedicated in 1933. From the beginning, it was designed to look like a ruin. Fact is, though, the tower is supported by steel beams, and every stone that seems to cling precariously to the structure was carefully selected and put in place under the watchful eye of the meticulous Colter. The interior of the tower features painted symbols and murals in the style of ancestral Puebloan designs. You can climb the tower for a spectacular view of the eastern canyon, including Marble Canyon and the Colorado River.

The Watchtower includes an attached gift store (928–638–2736). Nearby are Desert View Trading Post (928–638–2360), which sells snacks, souvenirs, and Native American jewelry; the Grand Canyon Association's Desert View Book-

store and Information Center; the Desert View Marketplace grocery store (928–638–2393); and rest rooms. These shops are all open daily. The Desert View Campground and the Desert View Chevron station (both open seasonally) are also nearby.

NEARBY ATTRACTIONS

Air Museum Planes of Fame
755 Mustang Way, Valle
(928) 635–1000
www.planesoffame.org/Valle.htm
The Air Museum Planes of Fame is located at the intersection of U.S. Highway 180 and Arizona Highway 64 in Valle, 27 miles south of Grand Canyon Village. The aviation museum features 22 historic airplanes, including General Douglas MacArthur's restored command plane, *Bataan,* which is kept in airworthy condition. Among the museum's other rare aircraft are a 1928 Ford Trimotor, a Cessna L-19 Bird Dog observation plane, and a Grumman F-1 Tiger supersonic navy jet fighter. The museum also features memorabilia and a pictorial history of women in aviation, from hot-air balloons to the space shuttle. The museum is open 9:00 A.M. to 5:00 P.M. daily (closed on Thanksgiving and Christmas) and charges an admission fee of $5.95 for adults and $1.95 for children 5 to 12 years old. Children under 5 get in free.

Flintstones Bedrock City
On Arizona Highway 64, Valle
(928) 638–2600
A roadside attraction if ever there was one, Flintstones Bedrock City in Valle, 27 miles south of Grand Canyon Village, includes the "houses" of Fred and Barney, several dinosaurs, and talking statues of the whole Flintstones gang. There are also several live "goatasauruses" (i.e., goats) for the kids to pet, a giant brontosaurus that has a slide for a tail, a ride for kids through an artificial volcano, and a diner that sells, among other things, Bronto-

burgers. Bedrock City also has a gift shop, a theater showing Flintstones cartoons, and a campground sleep-deprivingly close to busy AZ 64. It will cost you five bucks to get in if you're older than two, and the place is worth a stop if you have a car full of antsy kids or if you have an appreciation for all-American oddness. Open daily.

The Grand Canyon Experience
On Arizona Highway 64, Tusayan
(928) 638-2468
www.grandcanyonimaxtheater.com
The only movie theater anywhere near Grand Canyon, the Grand Canyon Experience, formerly known as the Grand Canyon IMAX Theater, is the home of the stunning IMAX film *Grand Canyon: The Hidden Secrets*. Located on the northern edge of Tusayan 2 miles south of the South Entrance to Grand Canyon National Park, the theater runs its 34-minute, 70mm film on a screen 82 feet wide and six stories high. The image area encompasses the viewer's entire field of vision, and this, combined with six-track Dolby stereo sound, will make you feel like you're right there with the first explorers of Grand Canyon. Open daily, with movies showing at the bottom of the hour. The Grand Canyon Experience complex includes a National Geographic Bookstore, a gift shop, a tour reservation desk, a National Park Service Pay Station, and several fast-food outlets.

HIKING

Hiking the South Rim

There is a hiking experience for people of all ages and skill levels at Grand Canyon—from a few minutes' walk along the Rim Trail to an arduous journey into the depths of the canyon.

The Rim Trail runs from Hermits Rest west of Grand Canyon Village to Pipe Creek Vista along Desert View Drive. You can access the trail from many points and

If you plan to hike frequently in the backcountry of Grand Canyon National Park, consider purchasing a one-year Frequent Hiker Membership. The $25 pass waves the $10 permit fee, meaning you will get your money's worth by making three trips into the canyon within 12 months. With the membership, you will still need to pay the $5.00 per hiker per night fee.

walk along the rim for as long or short a distance as you wish. The path is paved between Maricopa Point west of the village to Pipe Creek Vista on the east. Along the way, stop and visit the historic Mary Colter structure at Hermits Rest, have a look at Kolb Studio, stop for a cool drink at El Tovar, shop at Hopi House, and rest at Pipe Creek Vista while enjoying the spectacular scenery, which changes every moment. You'll even have time to enjoy part of the Rim Trail if you've come on the Grand Canyon Railway from Williams and plan on spending only a few hours at the canyon.

For longer hikes, you need to be prepared—carry water and salty foods and wear sturdy shoes or boots and sunscreen. Remember that you will spend about one-third of your time hiking down into the canyon and about two-thirds of your time getting back out.

Do not attempt to hike to the river and back in one day. You will see signs in Grand Canyon Village, notices in the *Guide,* be warned by rangers at the visitor center and on the trail, and see placards posted along the trails warning you in big, bold letters not to do this. Despite this, numerous ill-prepared and unknowledgeable hikers—lacking sufficient water and food, not taking frequent rest breaks, hiking during the hottest part of the day, and/or overextending themselves by hiking too far down—venture into the canyon daily during the summer. The *Williams–Grand Canyon News,* the local

During the monsoon months of July, August, and September, use extreme caution when hiking in the inner canyon. Narrow canyons that feed into the Colorado River are subject to flash flooding, and sometimes the storm can be miles away upcanyon—you won't know anything is wrong until the wall of mud and water comes crashing down the canyon. Avoid narrow canyons, check weather forecasts, and watch the skies when hiking below the rim in late summer.

newspaper, carries dozens of heat-related incident reports every week. Part of the problem is the ease of walking *down* the trail into the canyon. Hikers come to think that hiking in the canyon is no big deal on the hike down as they drop 5,000 feet to the river, but by the time they reach the Colorado and turn around for the trip back up, fatigue and gravity change everything. It does not matter how experienced a hiker you are or how fit you are: It is usually the experienced, fit hikers who get into the most trouble because they head down the trail with overconfidence. Hiking in Grand Canyon requires careful planning and honest reflection on your own abilities given the rugged environment. We say it again in the strongest terms: *Do not attempt to hike to the river and back in one day.*

When hiking down any of the canyon trails, step to the side (the cliff side rather than the canyon side) when hikers headed up the trail approach, particularly hikers with packs. These hikers are likely exhausted and winded from the long climb out, and your courtesy will invariably be greeted with a smile and a "thanks."

The Bright Angel Trail and the South Kaibab Trail are used not only by hikers but also by wranglers leading mule trains into the canyon. If a mule train approaches, step to the side of the trail and follow the head wrangler's instructions. Also be aware that

you will have to sidestep smelly evidence of mule trains gone by as you head down the trail, particularly on the Bright Angel.

From the rim, you cannot anticipate how hot it will become as you descend into the canyon. The National Park Service recommends that you hike during the cooler times of day, eat salty foods, drink one-half to one liter of water or sports drinks for every hour you are hiking, go slowly, rest often, and plan your hike before you go. They suggest that while hiking the canyon you consume twice the number of calories as you usually would, starting with a large breakfast, followed by a full lunch and a snack every time you take a drink. The best times for hiking into the canyon are spring and fall.

BRIGHT ANGEL TRAIL

The Bright Angel Trail is the most heavily traveled inner canyon trail in Grand Canyon National Park. The trail is regularly patrolled by park service rangers and is relatively wide and not as steep as other canyon trails. However, compared to trails in other national parks and wilderness areas, the trail is very steep, and you can expect a joint-jarring, muscle-fatiguing hike into and out of the canyon on the trail.

The trail begins just west of Bright Angel Lodge, the westernmost motel on the rim. This steep trail is 9.4 miles to Bright Angel Campground and descends 4,435 feet into the canyon. The trailhead is near Kolb Studio in Grand Canyon Village. One-and-a-half miles down you'll find the One-and-a-Half-Mile Resthouse, which provides water from May through September, and rest rooms and an emergency phone year-round. If this is your destination, the round-trip will take between two-and-a-half and four hours. A mile-and-a-half farther on is Three-Mile Resthouse, where you will find water during the summer and an emergency phone year-round. At this point, you have descended about 2,000 feet into the canyon; if you turn back now, the round-trip should take you four to six hours. Below Three-Mile Resthouse, you will

Make sure you know where the water sources are before venturing into the canyon and plan accordingly. Although Page Springs is close to Horseshoe Mesa in the inner canyon, the springs are far below the mesa on a treacherous trail. You would be wise to bring enough water down from the rim to last for your entire stay at the campground on the mesa.
TODD R. BERGER

descend Jacobs Ladder, a steep series of switchbacks that underwent extensive trail repair over the winter of 2003–04. The section is a welcome change from the rutted trail hikers experience on the upper portion of the Bright Angel Trail. At Indian Garden, about 4.6 miles from the rim, you will have descended more than 3,000 feet. You will find rest rooms, water, a ranger station, and an emergency phone here. The round-trip from the rim to Indian Garden and back takes six to nine hours. You may camp overnight at Indian Garden (a backcountry permit is required).

The trail splits here. Going to the left, you can continue on to Plateau Point, 6.1 miles from the rim. The round-trip takes 8 to 12 hours. Inexperienced hikers should note that the trail to Plateau Point is not a maintained or patrolled trail. Plateau Point is not recommended as a day-hike desti-

nation from the rim.

If you go to the right, you will reach the River Resthouse 3 miles farther on, which has an emergency phone. The Silver Bridge across the Colorado River is another 1.2 miles. One-half mile farther, you'll find the entrance to Bright Angel Campground. The campground has water, rest rooms, a ranger station, and picnic tables. A few hundred miles further takes you to Phantom Ranch.

During the hottest part of the summer, park rangers recommend that you end your day hike no later than at Three-Mile Resthouse and begin your return to the rim, which, again, will take you twice as long as your descent.

To camp overnight in the canyon, you will need a permit from the Backcountry Information Center (see the Backcountry Camping section earlier in this chapter).

Overnight hikers may also lodge and eat at Phantom Ranch; reservations are required well in advance. Call (888) 297–2757.

GRANDVIEW TRAIL

Grandview Trail begins at Grandview Point east of Grand Canyon Village along Desert View Drive. This is a very steep, unmaintained trail recommended for experienced desert hikers only. The round-trip to Coconino Saddle is 1.5 miles with a 1,600-foot drop in elevation; allow two hours. It is 6 miles round-trip, with a 2,600-foot drop in elevation, to Horseshoe Mesa; the trip takes from 4 to 11 hours. There is a toilet and a designated campsite (backcountry permit required) at Horseshoe Mesa, but there are no other facilities or services (including no water) on this trail.

HERMIT TRAIL

Hermit Trail begins 500 feet west of Hermits Rest, a historic landmark at the westernmost point on Hermit Road. You can get to Hermits Rest by walking along the Rim Trail or by taking the free shuttle bus, which runs March 1 to November 30. Hermit Trail is an unmaintained, steep trail recommended only for experienced desert hikers. The hike to Santa Maria Spring is 5 miles round-trip and descends 1,760 feet into the canyon. The water here must be treated before you drink it. The round-trip to Dripping Springs on the Dripping Springs Trail, which branches off the Hermit Trail 2 miles from the rim, is 7 miles, and the trail descends to 1,700 feet below the rim. Here, too, you must treat the water before drinking it. Narrow sections of this trail require extreme caution. The round-trip to Santa Maria Spring will take five to eight hours. Allow another hour to get to Dripping Springs.

SOUTH KAIBAB TRAIL

The very steep South Kaibab Trail begins near Yaki Point on Desert View Drive. The only access to the trailhead is via shuttle

When hiking at Grand Canyon, whether on the rim or in the inner canyon, it is imperative that you bring along sufficient water (or a sports drink such as Gatorade) and salty snacks, such as saltine crackers. When hiking below the rim, bring along one-half to one liter of water or sports drink for every hour you will be hiking (more in hot weather, less in cooler weather). Eat salty foods every time you stop for a drink. Seek shade, hike slowly (especially uphill), and rest often.

bus March 1 to November 30. The first 1.5 miles of this trail to Cedar Ridge is one of the most popular day hike from the South Rim, offering spectacular views of the main river gorge. The first stopping point on this trail, however, is Ooh Aah Point (we're not kidding!), about three quarters of a mile from the rim. There is no water here or anywhere else along the trail.

At Cedar Ridge you will have descended more than 1,100 feet into the canyon. There is a toilet, but no water. The round-trip from the rim to Cedar Ridge and back takes two-and-a-half to four hours.

Skeleton Point is 3 miles from the rim and 2,040 feet down. The round-trip will take six hours. There is no water here either. Tonto Trail Junction, also known as the Tip Off, is another 1.4 miles; toilets are available here. From the junction you can take the Tonto Trail 4.1 miles to Indian Garden, where there is a campground. The Tonto Trail is not maintained or patrolled; it is recommended for experienced desert hikers only.

The Black Bridge, which allows hikers to cross the Colorado, is 6.7 miles from the rim. Bright Angel Campground is another 0.4-mile hike (follow the signs), and Phantom Ranch is 0.9 mile from the bridge.

Park rangers strongly recommend that you do not attempt to hike to the river and back up to the rim in one day. They recom-

[Facing page] *Hikers on a Grand Canyon Field Institute rim-to-rim backpacking trip make their way into the canyon.* TODD R. BERGER

mend spending at least one night near the river. To camp overnight in the canyon at Bright Angel Campground, you will need a permit from the Backcountry Information Center (see the Backcountry Camping section). Overnight hikers may lodge and eat at Phantom Ranch; reservations are required well in advance. Call (888) 297-2757.

Emergency phones on the South Kaibab Trail are available at Tonto Trail Junction, Bright Angel Campground, and Phantom Ranch.

Hiking in Backcountry Primitive Zones

Backcountry trails in Primitive Zones are not maintained or patrolled. Trails include the Boucher, New Hance, South Bass, Tanner, and Waldron Trails, as well as the inner-canyon Beamer, Clear Creek, Monument, and Tonto Trails. The inner canyon also has the very remote Escalante, Esplanade, and Royal Arch Routes. Almost all of these trails are extremely steep and rocky, and many have no water along their routes. Only experienced Grand Canyon hikers should attempt these trails.

You will need a backcountry permit for all overnight hiking, off-river overnight hikes, and overnight camping in the backcountry, including camping at Indian Garden and Bright Angel Campgrounds. Permits are not required to stay at Phantom Ranch (but you do need reservations). Nor are permits required for day hikes. You should request your backcountry permit on the first of the month four months prior to your trip. For more information on camping below the rim, see the Backcountry Camping section earlier in this chapter.

Backcountry Guides and Tours

Discovery Treks
6890 East Sunrise, Suite 120, Tucson
(520) 760-2249, (888) 256-8731
www.discoverytreks.com
Join Discovery Treks for a guided hike into Grand Canyon. The company provides pickup from Flagstaff or Grand Canyon, transportation to and from the trailheads, tents, backpacks, sleeping bags, sleeping mats, food, and backcountry park permits. Discovery Treks offers a wide range of trips, including hikes into Havasu Canyon, hikes down the Grandview and up the New Hance Trails, day hikes on and below the rim, and hikes from the North Rim. Except for the Bright Angel Trail hike, which is available year-round, hiking treks are scheduled for spring through fall.

Grand Canyon Field Institute
Grand Canyon Village
(928) 638-2485
www.grandcanyon.org/fieldinstitute
Founded in 1993, Grand Canyon Field Institute (GCFI) is the get-dirty-out-in-the-elements arm of the nonprofit Grand Canyon Association, an organization that supports education, research, and other programs for the benefit of Grand Canyon National Park and its visitors. The Field Institute offers dozens of courses and trips, ranging from introductory backpacking trips, photography classes from the rim, and backcountry medicine training, to desert survival and ecology, expert hikes into remote parts of the park, and a white-water rafting trip down the Colorado River. GCFI also runs Learning & Lodging programs,

[Facing page] *The Silver Bridge is one of only two bridges across the Colorado River for more than 270 miles in Grand Canyon National Park. The bridge is 9 miles down the Bright Angel Trail from (and almost a mile lower than) the South Rim.* TODD R. BERGER

which include classes on the South Rim along with a room at one of the park lodges. All trips are led by GCFI instructors, who range from PhDs to well-known authors to expedition hikers with thousands of miles and several decades of Grand Canyon hiking experience. Some trips require instructor approval for participation, and all participants must complete a thorough health questionnaire. If you're a teacher and want to bring the canyon to your classroom, contact GCFI about their Travelin' Trunk program. The trunks contain information about Grand Canyon geology, ecology, and human history, as well as the Colorado River and John Wesley Powell.

Grand Country Trail Guides
Grand Canyon Village
(928) 638-3194, (888) 283-3194
www.grandcanyontrailguides.com
Grand Canyon Trail Guides offers guided hikes into the backcountry of Grand Canyon National Park, including hikes of the Grandview, Tanner, Hance, Bright Angel, South Kaibab, and Hermit Trails. They also offer National Park Service permits, impact fees, food, trail munchies, electrolyte supplements, first-aid supplies, water treatment systems, toiletries, day packs, water bottles, and a backcountry kitchen. Children are welcome. For overnight hikes, plan to make your reservations four to six months in advance. For trips that include river rafting, plan to schedule two years ahead of time.

OUTDOOR ACTIVITIES

Air Tours

Most of the air tour companies at Grand Canyon follow routes specified by the National Park Service and the FAA. The exception is Papillon Air Tours, which is authorized by the Havasupai Tribe to fly helicopters into Supai Village, in addition to flying the two routes that the other companies offer.

All of the helicopter companies flying over the national park follow the same routes. The 45- to 50-minute air tour begins at the airport, flies over the East Rim of the canyon to the confluence of the Little Colorado and Colorado Rivers, turns north and flies over Nankoweap Mesa and Point Imperial, and then turns west to fly over the eastern portion of the North Rim as far as Dragon Head. The flight then turns south and flies back over the canyon to return to the airport.

The 25- to 30-minute tour leaves the airport and flies west to Hermits Rest on the South Rim. The tour then turns north, flying over the canyon to Dragon Head where it makes a U-turn and flies back over the canyon to return to the airport.

All of the companies listed below are at the Grand Canyon Airport on Arizona Highway 64, just south of Tusayan (928-638-2446). Reservations may be made through your hotel or at the air tour company's building. During the winter, it is better to schedule your air tour in advance, as each company requires a minimum number of passengers for each flight. During the summer, you can just walk in and probably find that a tour will be ready to leave fairly soon.

The National Park Service, the FAA, and the air tour operators at Grand Canyon are currently in negotiations to revise these air routes to reduce noise pollution over the canyon. The argument pits environmentalists and hikers, who want to restore "natural quiet" to the canyon, against the air tour companies who maintain that noise pollution is not a problem and that for many people—especially the elderly, young children, and people unaccustomed to the 7,000-foot altitude at the South Rim—this is the only way to see the canyon from anywhere but the rim. When these negotiations will be complete, and when the court challenges by the operators will be exhausted, is not known, so check with the air tour company about routes and prices prior to booking your flight over the canyon.

Flights operate between 8:00 A.M. and 6:00 P.M. in the summer and 9:00 A.M. and 5:00 P.M. in the winter. Flights may be canceled or routes changed without notice due to weather or other safety concerns.

Air Grand Canyon
Grand Canyon Airport, Tusayan
(928) 638-2686, (800) 247-4726
www.airgrandcanyon.com
Air Grand Canyon flies high-wing Cessna T207s and 182s, which hold six or seven passengers who all sit facing forward; the pilot provides live narration. This company's 30- to 40-minute flight takes you along the east side of the South Rim, past the confluence of the Little Colorado and Colorado Rivers, and back to the airport along the same route. The cost is $74 for adults and $44 for children. The 50- to 60-minute tour is the same as other airlines' longer flight; the price is $89 for adults and $49 for children. A longer flight, 90 to 100 minutes, includes the same route as the 50- to 60-minute tour, but extends your flight northward along Marble Canyon all the way to Lake Powell. The cost is $174 for adults and $94 for children. You might also be interested in a combination air tour and river-rafting experience. You'll fly to Lake Powell, land in Page, and take a river-rafting trip down the Colorado to Lees Ferry. From there, ground transport will take you to the Cameron Trading Post and back to the airport. This tour leaves the airport at 8:30 A.M. and returns at 4:30 P.M. The cost is $260 for adults and $240 for children under 13; lunch is included.

AirStar Helicopters
Grand Canyon Airport, Tusayan
(928) 638-2622, (800) 962-3869
www.airstar.com
Flying the Aerospatiale 350B Astar, AirStar Helicopters offers a smooth, quiet, air-conditioned ride, with all passengers in

Visitors from around the world flock to northern Arizona to see one of the wonders of the world. Be sure you make reservations with tour companies well in advance to ensure a spot with the tour of your choice.

forward-facing seats. This is the smallest of the air tour companies at the canyon, and it is owner-operated. Narration is offered in seven languages, and customers receive a free souvenir photograph of their party boarding the aircraft. The 25- to 30-minute tour is $93; the 50- to 55-minute flight is $159; and the 40- to 45-minute tour is $139. A minimum of six passengers per flight is required.

Grand Canyon Airlines
Grand Canyon Airport, Tusayan
(928) 638-2463, (866) 235-9422
www.grandcanyonairlines.com
This company flies 19-passenger twin-engine Vistaliners, with quiet, climate-controlled cabins and all forward-facing seats. The minimum number of passengers per flight is six. They charge $75 for the longer tour. Children ages 2 to 12 are charged $45. French, Dutch, Italian, Spanish, and Japanese narration are available. Reservations are recommended but not required.

Kenai Helicopters
Grand Canyon Airport, Tusayan
(928) 638-2764, (800) 541-4537;
www.flykenai.com
Kenai Helicopters is smaller than some of the other air tour companies and therefore their operators have more time to talk to people. They charge $105 for the shorter flight ($99 for children), and $164 for the longer, with $10 off for children. A minimum of three passengers is needed for each tour. Credit cards and traveler's checks are accepted. In-flight multilingual narration is available.

Don't Let Heat Ruin Your Trip!

Hiking Grand Canyon during the summer months can be a wonderful adventure that you and the kids will always remember. But to prevent it from being an experience you don't want to recall, you need to be aware of some cautions. One of the most important of these is to remember that temperatures in Grand Canyon can exceed 100 degrees, and fatigue, insufficient water and food, and excessively strenuous hiking can lead to life-threatening illnesses.

Heat exhaustion is caused by dehydration. Hikers can sweat out as much as two liters of water per hour. Symptoms of heat exhaustion are pale face, nausea, cool and moist skin, headache, and cramps. Treat heat exhaustion by drinking water, eating high-energy foods (grains, crackers, fruit, nonfat energy bars), resting, and cooling the body. Remember that there is little water and no food available along the canyon's hiking trails. You must carry enough of both for everyone in your party.

Hyponatremia is caused by drinking too much water and losing too much sodium from the body through sweating. The symptoms of water intoxication include nausea, vomiting, altered mental states, and frequent urination. Treat this condition by eating salty foods. If the person seems drowsy, you need to find medical help immediately.

Heatstroke can be fatal—the body can no longer regulate its temperature. Symptoms of heatstroke are flushed face, dry skin, weak and rapid pulse, high body temperature, poor judgment or inability to cope, and unconsciousness. Cool the victim immediately by pouring water on his or her head and trunk, moving him or her into a shady area, fanning, and removing excess clothing. Send someone for help—the victim needs immediate hospitalization and will be airlifted out of the canyon.

Hypothermia is not limited to just cold weather. It can occur as a result of exhaustion and exposure to cold, wet weather (as during a summer rainstorm). The symptoms of hypothermia are uncontrolled shivering, poor muscle control, and a careless mood. To treat this condition, put dry, warm clothes on the victim, provide warm liquids to drink, warm the person by body contact with another person, and find shelter. To help prevent this condition, carry layers of clothing, eat frequently, drink before you feel thirsty, and avoid wet weather if you can. You can get weather information at the visitor center or Backcountry Information Center or by calling (928) 638-7888.

Papillon Grand Canyon Helicopters
Grand Canyon Airport, Tusayan
(928) 638-2419, (800) 528-2418
www.papillon.com

Papillon operates a fleet of Bell jet-powered helicopters from its own heliport at the Grand Canyon Airport. The largest air tour company, Papillon serves hundreds of thousands of passengers annually; reservations are recommended. The 25- to 30-minute North Canyon Tour is $109 for adults and $89 for children. The 40- to 50-minute Imperial Tour is $169 for adults and $149 for children.

Papillon is the only commercial air tour company authorized to fly into Supai

Village on the Havasupai Reservation. They offer a Havasupai Daytime Excursion, with round-trip airfare with tour, landing and entrance fees at Supai Village, and a guided horseback tour to Havasu Falls. The cost is $436 for adults and $416 for children. Papillon also offers air tours over the canyon from Las Vegas.

Land Tours

American Dream Tours
Flagstaff
(928) 527-3369, (888) 203-1212
www.americandreamtours.com
American Dream tours offers a full-day tour of the South Rim of Grand Canyon. Buses depart Flagstaff at 9:15 A.M., Williams at 10:00 A.M., and Tusayan at 11:00 A.M., returning to each of those towns at 6:45, 6:00, and 5:00 P.M. respectively. Pickup service from your hotel or RV park is available. Small, friendly groups and knowledgeable guides travel in 15-passenger club vans. The fare ($67.50 for adults, $42 for children under 10) includes round-trip transportation, a picnic at the canyon under the pines (in good weather), drinks, snacks, and a champagne toast. IMAX tickets are available at a discount. Tours are given in English and German.

Canyon Dave's Geology Tours at Grand Canyon
Grand Canyon Village
(800) 813-5809
www.canyondave.com
Dave Thayer, a.k.a. Canyon Dave, is a Grand Canyon legend. A former teacher of geology and curator of geology at the Arizona-Sonora Desert Museum in Tucson, Canyon Dave now lives on the South Rim, writing books and taking people on the most informative tours about the Grand Canyon available. Canyon Dave runs both Morning Mist tours (starting at 9:00 A.M. and ending at 1:00 P.M.) and Sunset Tours (starting between 1:30 and 4:15 P.M., depending on the time of year, and ending at sunset). He can pick you up at any

of the Grand Canyon area hotels. The tours include stops at multiple canyon viewpoints with discussions of the rock layers, fossils, trees, shrubs, animals, and wildflowers of the canyon. With every topic, Canyon Dave's enthusiasm shines. The tours cost $69 for adults and $39 for children 12 and under.

Grand Canyon Jeep Tours & Safaris
Grand Canyon Village
(928) 638-5337, (800) 320-5337
www.grandcanyonjeeptours.com
Experience the back roads of Grand Canyon National Park and the Kaibab National Forest in an open-air, four-wheel-drive safari vehicle with a guide who knows the geology, history, wildlife, and Native American tribes of the region. The Grand Sunset Tour, about three hours, departs two hours before sunset and takes you through the Kaibab National Forest to overlooks of the Painted Desert, the San Francisco Peaks, and finally, Grand Canyon. Adults pay $53 and children under 12 pay $40. The Canyon Pines Tour follows an 1880s stagecoach trail through the forest to the edge of Grand Canyon. The two-hour tour, which departs at noon, is $48 for adults and $35 for children. The hour-and-a-half Indian Cave Paintings Tour takes you to a petroglyph site in the forest. The trip departs in the morning and in the afternoon and is $35 for adults and $25 for children. The Deluxe Combo Tour includes the Grand Sunset Tour or the Canyon Pines Tour with the Indian Cave Paintings Tour. The Sunset Combo departs three-and-a-half hours before sunset; the price is $83 for adults and $65 for children. There is a two-adult minimum for these tours. Last-minute reservations are honored, depending on availability.

Grand Canyon Motorcoach Tours
Xanterra Parks & Resorts
(928) 638-2631, (888) 297-2757
www.grandcanyonlodges.com
Xanterra, which operates all of the lodges

inside the park, also offers several park tours by motor coach. Options include the Hermits Rest Tour, following Hermit Road along the West Rim with stops at several overlooks ($15.75 per adult; children 16 and under free); the Desert View Tour, with stops at Yavapai Point, Lipan Point, and the Desert View area ($28 per adult; children 16 and under free); and Sunrise and Sunset Tours, with rides to prominent viewpoints for watching the sun's shenanigans (each tour $12.25 per adult; children 16 and under free).

Mule and Horse Trips

Apache Stables
Arizona Highway 64, Tusayan
(928) 638-2891
www.apachestables.com
Guided horse and muleback tours along the South Rim depart from the stables behind the no-longer-in-operation Moqui Lodge during the summer months. One- and two-hour trail rides stroll through the pines of the Kaibab National Forest. Prices run $30.50 and $55.50 respectively. The East Rim Ride goes through Long Jim Canyon to a Grand Canyon viewpoint on the East Rim. This $95.50, four-hour ride is physically demanding and not recommended for everyone. A one-hour evening campfire ride ($40.50) joins a horse-drawn wagon ride at a campfire in the forest where you can roast the hot dogs and marshmallows you have brought along. The wagon ride is $12.50, with a special rate for children under five. Open daily year-round, but the stables often close in wintertime due to cold and/or snow.

Xanterra Parks & Resorts
Grand Canyon
(888) 297-2757
www.grandcanyonlodges.com
A mule trip into Grand Canyon is something you will remember for the rest of your life. All mule trips are operated by Xanterra, which also operates the in-park lodges and restaurants. Mule wranglers select the mules used for rider trips with great care, judging each "candidate" for strength, endurance, and temperament; the mules are then painstakingly trained for their careers. Mules that do not pass the wranglers' muster or do not complete training successfully either never make it to the canyon or are used as pack mules to haul supplies and gear to Phantom Ranch. Mule riders cannot weigh more than 200 pounds and must be at least 4 feet 7 inches tall. Riders cannot be afraid of heights, because the drop-offs in many places along the Bright Angel and South Kaibab Trails include some staggering distances, and mules tend to walk on the outside of the trail. Riders must be able to understand spoken English. Xanterra offers one-day mule trips from the South Rim, down the Bright Angel Trail, to Plateau Point and back. The trip includes a box lunch and runs $129.12 per person. Xanterra also offers overnight mule trips to Phantom Ranch. The trips are offered with either one- or two-night stays in cabins at Phantom Ranch, and include meals. The one-night trip is offered year-round, but the two-night trip is offered November 1 through March 31 only. The one-night trip is $350.39 for the first person, or $623.30 for two people on the same trip. The two-night trip runs $493.76 for the first person, or $832.56 for a pair. Mule rides into the canyon are very popular and are booked many months in advance. Rides are offered daily year-round, weather permitting. Call about reservations as soon as you have finalized your travel plans.

River Rafting

Arizona Raft Adventures
4050 East Huntington Road, Flagstaff
(928) 526-8200, (800) 786-7238
www.azraft.com
Explore the Colorado on a motorized, oar and paddle (hybrid), or all-paddle river trip. Trips range from 6 to 15 days. The company supplies meals, two waterproof

bags, a life vest, a sleeping unit (sleeping bag, pad, and ground cloth), and eating utensils. You bring your clothes, camera, and extra beverages. On motor trips, the minimum age is 10 and the maximum number of guests is 15; on hybrid trips, guests must be at least 12 years old and the maximum number is 15; and on all-paddle rafts, the minimum age is 16 and the maximum group size is 18. Arizona Raft Adventures will make every effort to accommodate people with disabilities and those who require special diets; contact the company with your specifics. A 6-day hybrid river trip runs $1,440 and a 14-day all-paddle trip is $2,740.

Arizona River Runners
Phoenix
(602) 867–4866, (800) 477–7238
www.raftarizona.com
Arizona River Runners offers adventures on the Colorado, from three-day excursions to two-week odysseys. Everything is included in the cost of the trip—river equipment, meals, sodas, transportation, sleeping gear, tent, portable toilet facilities, eating utensils, waterproof bags and containers, life vests, and expert guides; you just bring your personal items, a camera, and a yen for adventure. Six- and seven-day motor trips cover 190 miles in the heart of Grand Canyon from Lees Ferry to Whitmore Wash. From Marble Canyon, the fare for the six-day raft trip is $1,650; add $190 if you want to leave from and return to Las Vegas by air. The eight-day Grand Canyon Adventure travels the full 280-mile length of the canyon, starting at Lees Ferry and ending at Lake Mead. The fare is $1,850; add $60 for round-trip bus transportation to and from Las Vegas. The three-day escape starts in Las Vegas and includes a scenic airplane flight, a day at the Bar Ten Ranch (including horseback riding), a helicopter ride to the canyon floor, 100 miles of adventure on the river, a jet-boat ride to Pearce Ferry, and your optional return by motor coach to Las Vegas. The cost is $825 with an additional $20 for transportation back

to Las Vegas. If you're ready for an oar-powered adventure, try the 13-day journey 225 miles from Lees Ferry to Diamond Creek with ground transportation to Peach Springs. You'll have plenty of time for exploring side canyons on this trip. The fare is $2,595, with an additional $90 for optional bus transportation to and from Las Vegas. A nine-day oar-powered trip starts with a hike from the South Rim to Phantom Ranch where you'll board your craft and travel 135 miles to Diamond Creek. You can opt for ground transportation back to Las Vegas or end your trip at Peach Springs. The fare is $1,675 plus an additional $50 to get back to Las Vegas. The six-day oar trip begins at Lees Ferry and ends at Phantom Ranch, where you will hike out of the canyon. The fare is $1,250; add $50 for ground transportation from Las Vegas the first day. The hike into and out of the canyon is a strenuous 9.5 miles, so you need to be in good shape if you choose either of the last two trips. People with sensory or mobility impairments are encouraged to contact the office to make arrangements for their trip.

Canyoneers, Inc.
Flagstaff
(928) 526–0924, (800) 525–0924
www.canyoneers.com
From a 13-day full river run in a row boat to a 3-day introduction to the wonders of the Colorado River, Canyoneers offers trips to meet anyone's needs and schedule. While the recommended minimum age is 10, Canyoneers has taken passengers from ages 6 to 84 on their trips. The company provides the meals, rain shelters, inflatable sleeping pads, and life vests; you may bring your own or rent a bedroll (on 7- and 13-day trips), which includes a sleeping bag and ground cover. On three- and five-day trips, the boat will carry your bedroll so you do not have to hike into the canyon with it. The All the Grand motorized trip is seven days and 280 miles from Lees Ferry to Pearce Ferry. The $1,800 (peak season) fare covers pre- and post-trip transportation to Flagstaff. Best of the Grand is a

five-day, 193-mile trip from Bright Angel Beach to Pearce Ferry aboard a powered pontoon boat. The fare is $1,375, which includes one night's lodging at Grand Canyon and a guided 9-mile hike to Bright Angel Beach to begin your trip. Best of the Grand with Phantom Ranch, at $1,495, is the same as the Best of the Grand, except that you hike on your own down to Phantom Ranch (9.5 miles with a 5,000-foot change in elevation) and stay at Phantom Ranch the night before you begin your river trip. Travelers who want to spend less time on the river may opt for the Upper Grand—two days and two nights on the river from Lees Ferry to Bright Angel Beach (87 miles) on a powered pontoon boat and a one-day hike out of the canyon. The fare for this trip is $695. Finally, the Upper Grand with Phantom Ranch trip ($895) is two days and two nights on the river on a powered pontoon boat from Lees Ferry to Bright Angel Beach (87 miles), and one day and night at Phantom Ranch at the end of your trip before you hike out of the canyon.

Canyoneers also offers several oar-powered trips. Over 12 days, the CanyonOars Extended Grand covers the entire Grand Canyon, from Lees Ferry to South Cove. Passengers ride in four-person, inflatable boats. Supplies are carried by a motorized pontoon boat. The trip costs $2,700. The CanyonOars Upper meanders over 87 river miles from Lees Ferry to Bright Angel Beach. Participants in this five-day trip must be willing and able to hike the 9 miles from Bright Angel Beach to the South Rim along the Bright Angel Trail. This trip costs $1,450. CanyonOars Best snakes through the lower Grand Canyon, from Bright Angel Beach to Pearce Ferry, over eight days. Participants must hike 9 miles from the South Rim down to Bright Angel Beach. The trip costs $1,895.

Canyon Explorations/Expeditions
Flagstaff
(928) 774-4559, (800) 654-0723
www.canyonexplorations.com

Specializing in oar and paddle trips in Grand Canyon, Canyon Explorations/Expeditions is a family-run business committed to practicing zero impact wilderness ethics on all of their river trips. The outfitter offers all-paddle and hybrid (oar and paddle) trips in a variety of lengths. With the all-paddle trips, participants provide the power, as everyone participates in propelling the raft forward. With the hybrid trips, participants make a daily choice on whether to ride in the oar-powered boat (with guides doing the rowing) or in the paddle-powered boat (with participants doing the paddling). Full Canyon trips travel 226 river miles from Lees Ferry to Diamond Creek. The trips include daily side canyon hikes, allowing multiple chances to explore the canyon. Some of the Full Canyon trips are specialized, including the Hiker's Special (extra time is included in the trip for participants to explore such Grand Canyon sites as Silver Grotto, the Nankoweap ruins, and Elves Chasm) and the String Quartet, which, amazingly, includes an accompanying musical foursome. The Full Canyon trips vary widely in price, depending on the time needed to complete the trip and any special features (like the string quartet). Fees range from $2,670 to $3,695. Canyon Explorations/Expeditions also offers Upper Canyon and Lower Canyon trips. The Upper Canyon trips travel 89 river miles from Lees Ferry to Pipe Creek (Bright Angel Beach) and requires a hike out on the Bright Angel Trail. The Lower Canyon trips require a hike in on the Bright Angel Trail and cover 136 river miles from Pipe Creek to Diamond Creek. The Upper Canyon and Lower Canyon trips also range in price depending on length of time needed to complete the trip, from $1,440 to $2,385.

Colorado River & Trail Expeditions
Salt Lake City, Utah
(801) 261-1789, (800) 253-7238;
www.crateinc.com
Dutch-oven dinners, salad-bar lunches, and hearty breakfasts will keep you going on these exciting river trips through Grand Canyon on a motorized 22-, 33-, or 37-

foot pontoon raft propelled by a 30-horsepower outboard motor or on an 18-foot, oar-powered rowing rig. The company provides you with a sleeping bag, foam pad, ground cloth, waterproof bags, waterproof camera bag, meals, plates, cups and utensils, life preserver, and round-trip transportation from the designated meeting place. The minimum age for Grand Canyon trips is 12. The company is happy to accommodate special needs. The full-canyon, eight- or nine-day motorized trip travels 280 miles from Lees Ferry to Lake Mead and costs $1,900. A nine-day natural history trip 280 miles from Lees Ferry to Pearce Ferry is also $1,900 and focuses on the geology, biology, prehistory, and ecology of the Colorado River in Grand Canyon. You can row and paddle 11 days and 190 miles from Lees Ferry to Whitmore Wash in an 18-foot rowing rig supplemented by an eight-person paddle raft for $2,650. The upper canyon four-day motor trip from Lees Ferry to Phantom Ranch is $900. A five-day rowing and paddling trip following the same route is $1,200. The lower canyon six-day motor trip from Phantom Ranch to Lake Mead is $1,400 and the seven-day rowing and paddle trip 100 miles from Phantom Ranch to Whitmore Wash is $2,100. These trip prices do not include a $25 to $100 fee for optional pre- or post-trip transportation. A 10 percent youth discount is offered on all but the lower Grand Canyon trips.

Diamond River Adventures
916 Vista, Page
(928) 645–8866, (800) 343–3121
www.diamondriver.com
A women-owned and -operated nonprofit enterprise, Diamond River Adventures offers 4- to 13-day motorized and oar trips with guides who have more than 5,000 river miles before they graduate from the company's training program. The company provides life vests, a waterproof tarp, tent, sanitized sleeping bag, mattress pad, eating utensils, and a watertight

metal box for cameras and other personal items. Three meals, snacks, and non-alcoholic drinks are included in the price. Physically challenged adventurers are welcome; call for details. On oar-powered trips, the minimum age is 12; on motorized tours, the minimum age is 8. Full-length trips leave Lees Ferry and travel 226 river miles to Diamond Creek. The 8-day motorized trip runs $1,580, while the 12-day oar trip is $2,480 and the 13-day oar trip $2,570. Rafting on the Upper Colorado takes you from Lees Ferry to Phantom Ranch (87.5 miles), where you will begin your 9.5-mile hike or mule ride out of the canyon. The four-day motorized trip is $800 and the five-day oar trip is $1,175; the six-day oar trip is $1,280. The Lower Colorado River trip is 138.5 miles from Phantom Ranch to Diamond Creek. You hike or ride a mule into the canyon to Phantom Ranch (9.5 miles) in time for lunch, then board your boat to begin your trip. The five-day motorized trip is $1,185 and the eight-day oar trip is $1,915. Mules for packing gear in or out must be arranged separately. Call Xanterra Parks & Resorts at (888) 297–2757. A deposit is required to schedule your trip and the company will book by phone with your credit card number.

Grand Canyon Expeditions Company
Kanab, Utah
(435) 644–2691, (800) 544–2691
www.gcec.com
Eight-day motorized trips from Lees Ferry to Lake Mead on a self-bailing, 37-foot specially designed raft cover 280 miles of rapids and exploration. The company provides transportation to and from Las Vegas, professional guides, all camping equipment, waterproof river bags, deluxe meals, nonalcoholic beverages, and portable toilet facilities. The price is $2,015. Eight-day special interest expeditions cover the same territory but focus on ecology, history, photography, archaeology, or geology. Private charter trips for 1 to 28 people may also be arranged. Dory trips offer a leisurely paced journey

aboard a five-passenger, 18-foot hard-hulled wooden boat with lots of time for exploring. The 14-day trip takes you from Lees Ferry to Lake Mead, and the price is $2,935. This company suggests a minimum age of eight, and they will try to accommodate special diets.

Moki Mac River Expeditions, Inc.
Salt Lake City, Utah
(800) 284-7280
www.mokimac.com
"You have to experience it," says the Quist family, owners of Moki Mac, about rafting the Grand Canyon. Moki Mac offers the opportunity to float the entire length of the canyon. The company provides food, eating utensils, waterproof bags, meals, and sanitation facilities; you bring a sleeping bag, tent, toiletries, and clothes. Special dietary needs can be accommodated, and "differently abled" folks are encouraged to contact the office for pretrip planning. Grand Canyon trips are suggested for people over 12. Moki Mac offers a 280-mile, 8-day motorized trip for $1,663 and a 14-day rowing trip for $2,680. The 6-day rowing trip is $1,180, and the 9-day rowing trip is $1,926. The 6-day trip travels the upper canyon from Lees Ferry to Phantom Ranch. The 9-day trip covers the river from Phantom Ranch to Pearce Ferry. Motorized 33- and 37-foot rafts carry up to 12 guests, and 18-foot rafts (rowed by your guides) carry up to 5 passengers. Optional pre- and post-trip transportation and accommodation packages are available for an extra fee. A deposit is required to make your reservation.

Wilderness River Adventures
Page
(928) 645-3296, (800) 992-8022
www.riveradventures.com
This outfitter offers oar trips and motorized trips in the canyon. From Lees Ferry to Bar Ten Ranch (Whitmore Wash), the eight-day motorized trip on a 15-foot by 37-foot boat powered by a 25-horsepower motor is $2,310; the seven-day trip is $2,040. The minimum age for these trips

is eight. The 12-day oar trip in an 18-foot, traditionally designed rowing rig is $2,905, and the 14-day trip is $3,135. The minimum age for oar trips is 12. A five-and-a-half-day oar trip from Lees Ferry to Phantom Ranch (86 miles) is $1,530 and the Hiker Special, a six-and-a-half-day oar trip from Phantom Ranch to Bar Ten Ranch, is $2,400. The trips to and from Phantom Ranch require a 9.5-mile hike into or out of the canyon. All the other trips include a charter flight at the end of the trip to Las Vegas or Page. The three-and-a-half-day Upper Canyon motorized trip from Lees Ferry to Phantom Ranch (86 miles) requires a hike out of the canyon at the end of the trip. The cost is $940. A four-and-a-half-day motorized trip from Phantom Ranch to Bar Ten Ranch (102 miles) requires a hike 9.5 miles into the canyon. The price of $1,825 includes a charter flight to Las Vegas or Page at the end of your trip. Wilderness trip prices include meals, a waterproof bag, sleeping bag, foam pad and ground tarp, waterproof container for camera, a Colorado River guidebook, and life jacket. People with special needs are encouraged to contact the company so that appropriate arrangements can be made.

SHOPPING

Canyon Village Marketplace and the Inner Canyon Backpacker's Shop, Market Plaza Road, Grand Canyon Village
(928) 638-2262
It will surprise some that Grand Canyon National Park has a full-service grocery store. (It actually has two, as there is a similar though smaller outlet at Desert View.) The prices at Canyon Village Marketplace aren't as outrageous as you might expect (except, perhaps, for ice cream), and this is a good place to stock up on everything from Gatorade to granola for your Grand Canyon adventure. The store also has fresh fruit and vegetables; beer, wine, and hard liquor; some

household items like garden hoses and lightbulbs; and fresh meat. In the same space next to the grocery store, the Inner Canyon Backpacker's store has a surprising variety of high-quality camping items, from GoLite jackets and tents to Merrell hiking boots. The store also has a variety of dehydrated meals, electrolyte powder, smaller necessities like tent stakes and backpack cord stays, a good selection of Grand Canyon and northern Arizona guidebooks, and a huge selection of T-shirts and touristy knickknacks. A one-hour photo lab does business from the front counter in the store. Open daily.

El Tovar Gift Shop
El Tovar Hotel
On the South Rim in Grand Canyon Village
(928) 638-2631, ext. 6356

Located in the El Tovar lobby and open daily, the El Tovar Gift Shop sells fine Navajo, Hopi, and Zuni jewelry; Acoma and Santa Clara pottery; and classy souvenir T-shirts, sweatshirts, and other clothing, including reversible blanket vests. Here you can also buy salsa, jalapeño jelly, and desert hot chocolate offered under the Fred Harvey Desert Trading Company label and items designed by Robert Shields. This is the only shop where you can order reproductions of Mimbreno dinnerware, the service designed by Mary Colter for the El Tovar based on ancient Indian pottery decoration.

Grand Canyon Association Bookstores
Various locations in the park
(928) 638-2481 (GCA Headquarters)
www.grandcanyon.org

With bookstores spread throughout the park, the nonprofit Grand Canyon Association (GCA) serves canyon visitors by providing information, publications, art and photography exhibits, interpretive displays, T-shirts, and maps through their bookstores, on-line, and through mail order, and by offering trips into the canyon through the Grand Canyon Field Institute (GCFI). GCA's profits are donated to the National Park Service at Grand Canyon, and since GCA's founding in 1932, the organization has given the NPS just under $20 million. GCA has five bookstores on the South Rim: the Books & More store at Canyon View Information Plaza, Kolb Studio on the rim just west of Bright Angel Lodge, Yavapai Observation Station, Tusayan Ruin and Museum, and Desert View.

All South Rim GCA stores are open daily year-round.

Hopi House
On the South Rim in Grand Canyon Village
(928) 638-2631, ext. 6383

Located just east of El Tovar, Hopi House was Mary Colter's first building at Grand Canyon, and is a spectacular distinctly southwestern structure perched just back from the rim. It opened a little before the hotel and served not only as a salesroom but also as living quarters for the Hopis who worked there as artists and dancers. Downstairs you'll find Hopi overlay, Navajo silver and turquoise, and Zuni inlay jewelry, including some gorgeous modern pieces. Also have a look at the alabaster stone carvings, the kachina carvings, the Acoma and Navajo pottery, and the genuine Navajo weavings. One room is set aside for media—books, videos, CDs, and calendars—and another small room offers T-shirts and western hats and belts. The really good stuff is in the upstairs art gallery. Stunning Hopi and Acoma pots, large alabaster carvings, excellent kachina carvings, and sumptuous Navajo weavings will take your breath away, but don't get so involved looking at the beautiful art for sale that you forget to look at the building's design and construction. It was built by Hopi stonemasons using rock and timber indigenous to the area. The current salespeople disavow any knowledge of the Hopi ceremonial altar that is recorded to have been placed in the original building, but they do admit that there is a kiva, though it is not open to the public. Hopi House is open daily.

Verkamp's, just east of Hopi House and El Tovar along the Rim Trail, has been peddling tourist items and Native American artwork since 1906. TODD R. BERGER

Verkamp's
On the South Rim in Grand Canyon Village
(928) 638-2242
www.verkamps.com

Located east of Hopi House, this historic building was designed by John Verkamp and opened in 1906. A glowing fire greets you as you walk into this store, much of which is devoted to souvenir items. You will, however, find some good Hopi, Zia, Acoma, Navajo, and San Juan pottery as well as Zuni inlay and Navajo jewelry, and Hopi, Paiute, and Santa Domingo basketry. This is the only shop where we've seen jewelry by Colorado Congressman Ben Nighthorse Campbell, who creates lovely bracelets, both inlay and sandcast silver and gold. Don't miss the excellent silverwork by Bryon, Lynol, and Alvin Yellowhorse in the same case. The store is open daily.

KIDSTUFF

Grand Canyon National Park has a Junior Ranger Program for kids ages 4 to 14. You can pick up a *Junior Ranger* workbook at Canyon View Information Plaza, Yavapai Observation Station, or at the Tusayan Ruin and Museum, and find out which activities are suitable for your kids. Flintsones Bedrock City and the Grand Canyon Experience are also hits with the kids.

GRAND CANYON — NORTH RIM

The North Rim of Grand Canyon National Park is a different world, almost another national park, from the South Rim. One thousand feet higher; considerably wetter and with the varied, thick vegetation to prove it; and much less developed, the land north of the Colorado River offers solitude and wilderness for those looking to get away from crowds and traffic. Inside this section of the park, there is one lodge, one campground, one store selling limited groceries and supplies, one gift shop, one Grand Canyon Association bookstore, one visitor center, one maintained trail leading into the inner canyon, one pub, no shuttle buses, no airport, no train service, and no bank. And the North Rim is closed from late fall to late spring. But if you come prepared and aren't overly picky, you will be able to find everything you need.

What brings people to the North Rim is the wilderness. It's a quiet place, a place filled with the sounds of wind, the call of ravens, and hiking boots clomping on the trail. The North Rim has far more rim-level trails than the South Rim, and visitors can explore many areas without having to endure the bone-jarring descent into the canyon and the lung-expanding climb back out.

The best thing about all of this: You don't give up a thing in terms of scenic beauty. Overlooks are everywhere, and the canyon looks just as remarkable, just as grand, as it does from Mather, Yavapai, and Hopi Points on the South Rim. For those who want to get down into that scenic beauty, the North Kaibab Trail winds down from the 8,000-foot trailhead on the North Rim to the Colorado River, carrying hikers through some of the most dramatic rock formations in Grand Canyon National Park.

GETTING TO THE NORTH RIM

Separated from the rest of Arizona by Grand Canyon itself and from Las Vegas by Lake Mead National Recreation Area, the North Rim of Grand Canyon is remote and takes some planning to reach. This remoteness, and the fact that the North Rim is much less developed for visitors than the South Rim, goes a long way toward explaining why the North Rim has only about 10 percent the number of visitors the South Rim gets every year. In addition, in comparison to traveling to the South Rim, you will need to put more miles on your rental car or the family minivan to reach this out-of-the-way corner of the West. However, the reward is a quieter experience, a much greater feeling of wilderness, and equal if not more spectacular views of Grand Canyon.

By Air

It is not possible to fly directly to the North Rim of Grand Canyon or other parts of the Arizona Strip. The closest major commercial airport is at Las Vegas, 266 miles (six hours) to the west of the North Rim. See the Getting Here, Getting Around chapter for more information on the Las Vegas airport and see the By Car section below for more information on driving to the North Rim from the Las Vegas airport.

U.S. Highway 89A en route to the North Rim of Grand Canyon crosses the Colorado River over the Navajo Bridge. There are two bridges at the site: The original bridge for pedestrians and the current bridge, pictured here, for cars. TODD R. BERGER

By Car

No trains and no bus lines offer regularly scheduled service to the North Rim of Grand Canyon or the Arizona Strip. You will need to get behind the wheel to reach this remote corner of Arizona, and your starting point makes a big difference in how you achieve your destination.

FROM FLAGSTAFF

From Flagstaff, follow U.S. Highway 89 north toward Page. The small town of Cameron lies 46 miles to the north at the intersection with Arizona Highway 64, which leads west to the South Rim of Grand Canyon.

Continue north past Cameron on U.S. 89. As you drive north through the west-ern portion of the Navajo Indian Reservation, notice the westernmost portion of the Painted Desert, a layered landscape of pastel stripes on either side of the highway north of Cameron. U.S. Highway 89 leads 60 miles from Cameron to Bitter Springs. Turn onto U.S. Highway 89A at Bitter Springs toward Marble Canyon and Jacob Lake. Jacob Lake, at the intersection of U.S. 89A and Arizona Highway 67, is 50 miles west. Turn south at AZ 67 to reach the North Rim of Grand Canyon National Park, 45 miles down the road.

FROM THE SOUTH RIM

The North Rim of Grand Canyon is five hours and 215 miles by car or Transcanyon Shuttle from the South Rim. From the South Rim, take Arizona Highway 64 east of

North Rim Weather Conditions

The North Rim is open roughly mid-May until mid-October, depending on weather. The first heavy snowfall in the fall closes Arizona Highway 67, the only access road to the North Rim; with the road's 25 feet of annual snowfall, the state of Arizona doesn't reopen the highway until late spring when that snowpack has melted down. On average, the North Rim is 1,200 feet higher in elevation than the South Rim, and temperatures are generally 10 degrees lower than on the south side of Grand Canyon. Primarily due to the heavy snowfall experienced on the North Rim, you will notice considerably lusher forests in this section of the park and in the Kaibab National Forest on the way to the park. You will also notice deciduous trees in this region, such as quaking aspen, made possible by the North Rim's higher elevation. Similar forests line U.S. Highway 180 from Flagstaff to Valle, a principal route to the South Rim of Grand Canyon and one that rises above 8,000 feet.

Grand Canyon Village toward Desert View. Continue on AZ 64 to Cameron and the intersection with U.S. 89, turn north, and follow the directions to the North Rim given in the previous From Flagstaff section.

Transportation between the South and North Rims of Grand Canyon is available seasonally through Transcanyon Shuttle. The shuttle runs when the North Rim is open, generally mid-May through mid-October, leaving once daily from the North Rim and once daily from the South Rim. Call (928) 638-2820 for more information.

FROM LAS VEGAS

Las Vegas lies 266 miles west of the North Rim of Grand Canyon. To get to the North Rim from Las Vegas, follow Interstate 15 north out of the city toward St. George, Utah. St. George is 116 miles from Las Vegas on I-15. Ten miles north of St. George, turn east onto Utah Highway 9. At Hurricane, 12 miles east of I-15, you have two options to reach the North Rim. Turning south onto Utah Highway 59 (which turns into Arizona Highway 389 at the border) will take you to Pipe Spring National Monument and up to Fredonia. Jacob Lake is 30 miles east on U.S. 89A, and the North Rim is then 45 miles south on AZ 67. The other option is to continue on UT 9 at Hurricane. This is the more scenic choice, as the beautiful road winds through the southeastern corner of Zion National Park, a magnificent destination in itself as well as a bonus scenic encounter if you're continuing on to northwestern Arizona. Utah Highway 9 ends at Mt. Carmel Junction after 55 zigzaggy miles. Turn south here onto U.S. 89 toward Kanab, Utah, 17 miles distant. At Kanab, continue south on U.S. 89A to Fredonia, Arizona, just across the border. Jacob Lake and the intersection with Arizona Highway 67 lie 30 miles east, with the North Rim another 45 miles south on AZ 67.

STARTING YOUR VISIT

The **National Park Service North Rim Visitor Center** (928-638-7864) sits at the end of AZ 67 right next to Grand Canyon Lodge. The visitor center can provide you with additional copies of the *Guide* (the free park newspaper), directions, advice

Accessibility

Wheelchair-accessible rest rooms can be found at the visitor center, general store, and North Rim Ranger Station. The Grand Canyon Lodge can be reached by a lift. The Cape Royal Nature Trail is a 0.6-mile path with canyon views from several overlooks. You can request a wheelchair at the visitor center for use while in the park (there is no fee for this service). Parking permits for disabled drivers may also be obtained at the visitor center. The *Accessibility Guide,* a helpful publication with a lot of information for visitors with disabilities, is available at the visitor center.

on trails and other matters, and anything else you can think of related to Grand Canyon.

The National Park Service offers ranger-led activities on the North Rim, including geology and fossil walks, condor talks, discussions on living with wildfire, and evening programs on a variety of topics. Consult the *Guide* or ask at the visitor center for current topics, times, and meeting places.

Inside the visitor center, the nonprofit Grand Canyon Association's **North Rim Bookstore** offers hundreds of publications about the canyon and the surrounding region. All profits from sales at Grand Canyon Association bookstores directly benefit Grand Canyon National Park.

GETTING AROUND THE NORTH RIM

Upon entering Grand Canyon National Park, AZ 67 leads visitors 13 miles to Grand Canyon Lodge, the North Rim Visitor Center, and Bright Angel Point.

About 11.5 miles from the park entrance, turn right (west) for the **North Rim Backcountry Office.** This is the place to pick up permits and to get your name on the waiting list for backcountry camping. Full details about obtaining permits can be found in the Backcountry Camping section of the Grand Canyon—South Rim and Backcountry chapter.

About 12 miles from the park entrance, turn right (west) on the access road for the North Rim Campground, gas station, laundry and showers, and the general store.

The lodge, visitor center, and Grand Canyon Association North Rim Bookstore are another mile on AZ 67 beyond the intersection with the campground access road.

ACCOMMODATIONS

There is one lodge on the North Rim in the park, Grand Canyon Lodge, operated by Xanterra. There are also lodges 18 miles north of Grand Canyon Lodge, and at Jacob Lake 45 miles north of Grand Canyon Lodge.

PRICE CODE

The following price code is for two adults during the high season, generally between Memorial Day and Labor Day. The codes do not include taxes and other fees.

$	Less than $75
$$	$76 to $125
$$$	$126 to $175
$$$$	$176 to $225
$$$$$	More than $225

The lobby of the Grand Canyon Lodge harkens back to another era. TODD R. BERGER

In-Park Accommodations

Grand Canyon Lodge **$$**
On the North Rim at Bright Angel Point
(888) 297–2757 (Xanterra reservations)
www.xanterra.com
Dating from 1937, the rustic Grand Canyon Lodge is one of the nicest places to rest your body on either rim. A National Historic Landmark, the main lodge building boasts timbered ceilings and floor-to-ceiling limestone walls. Walk straight ahead through the lobby and descend a short flight of stairs to the Sun Room, with windows overlooking the canyon. An outdoor veranda lies to the right, with comfortable chairs facing the canyon and access to a couple of prominent overlooks. This is a great spot to soak up the sun and watch the clouds move across the buttes and spires. The lodge has 161 cabins and 40 motel rooms, ranging in size and price. The Grand Canyon Lodge Dining Room offers fine dining (see the following Restaurants

section), and the lodge also harbors Cafe on the Rim, with snacks, and the Rough Rider Saloon, with libations. You will also find a gift shop, camper store, and post office at the lodge, and the North Rim Visitor Center and Grand Canyon Association North Rim Bookstore are adjacent to the building. Children under 16 stay free.

Out-of-Park Accommodations

Kaibab Lodge **$$–$$$**
On Arizona Highway 67, 27 miles south of Jacob Lake
(928) 638–2389
www.canyoneers.com/pages/lodging.html
Five miles north of the entrance to Grand Canyon National Park on AZ 67, Kaibab Lodge is a convenient, very rustic lodging option for visitors to the North Rim. Opened in the mid-1920s, the lodge now has motel rooms and cabins, a dining room,

and a gift shop. With the exception of the more deluxe Sam's Cabin and Deerview Cabin, none of the rooms has a telephone or television. The lodge is open for guests during roughly the same time frame as the North Rim is open to visitors; that is, mid-May through mid-October. (The lodge often stays open a little later than the North Rim areas—call ahead to check.)

Jacob Lake Inn $$
At the intersection of U.S. Highway 89A and Arizona Highway 67, Jacob Lake
(928) 643-7232
www.jacoblake.com/m-lodgings.html
Located 45 miles north of the North Rim, Jacob Lake Inn has 35 comfortable rooms and cabins. Founded by Harold and Nina Bowman in 1923, the knotty pine-enhanced inn is run by the fourth generation of the Bowman family. The inn has a restaurant and bakery on site (see the following Restaurants section), as well as a grocery store and a gift shop featuring Native American art purchased through local dealers and from the artists themselves. Pets are allowed in most rooms, although having Fido along will cost you an extra 10 bucks.

CAMPING
In-Park Campground

North Rim Campground
Off Arizona Highway 67, 1 mile north of Grand Canyon Lodge
(800) 365-2267 (Spherix reservations)
www.reservations.nps.gov
With 84 sites for tents and RVs (no hookups), some with canyon views, the North Rim Campground is a lovely spot to pitch a tent or park a Winnebago. Sites are $15 per night; $20 for a site with a canyon view. The campground also has some walk-in sites available to backpackers and bicyclists (travelers without a vehicle to park) for the bargain-basement price of $4.00. Showers, Laundromat, a grocery store, and a gas station are nearby.

Out-of-Park Campgrounds

DeMotte Campground
On Arizona Highway 67, 20 miles north of the North Rim
(928) 643-7395 (North Kaibab Ranger District office)
This USDA Forest Service campground within the Kaibab National Forest has 23 sites for tents, trailers, and small RVs (no hookups). The cost is $12.00 per vehicle per night ($6.00 additional for a second vehicle). The campground is generally open the same dates as the North Rim. DeMotte is near Kaibab Lodge, with its restaurant, as well as the North Rim Country Store, with gas, groceries, supplies, camping equipment, and touristy knickknacks. All sites are first-come, first-served.

Jacob Lake Campground
At the intersection of U.S. Highway 89A and Arizona Highway 67, Jacob Lake
(928) 643-7395 (North Kaibab Ranger District Office)
Next door to the Jacob Lake Inn and 45 miles north of the North Rim, this USDA Forest Service campground within the Kaibab National Forest has 53 sites for tents, trailers, and small RVs (no hookups). Jacob Lake Campground also has group sites that can accommodate up to 100 people. Fees for individual sites are $12.00 per vehicle per night ($6.00 additional for a second vehicle), and group rates vary depending on the number of people in the group. The campground is open mid-May to November 1, depending on snowfall. All sites are first-come, first-served.

Kaibab Camper Village
Off Arizona Highway 67 on Forest Road 461, 1 mile south of Jacob Lake
(928) 643-7804
Kaibab Camper Village, 44 miles north of the North Rim, offers RV sites with hookups as well as tent sites. Setting up a

The North Rim receives only 10 percent of the visitors to Grand Canyon National Park, but some argue the views from the north side of the canyon are more spectacular than those from South Rim overlooks. TODD R. BERGER

tent or parking your RV here will set you back $22 for RVs, $12 for tents. The campground is open May 15 to October 15, weather permitting.

Kaibab National Forest

In addition to the DeMotte and Jacob Lake Campgrounds, the Kaibab National Forest allows free, dispersed camping within the forest north of the park. If you choose this option, there are rules that *must* be followed, including not camping closer than a quarter mile from a water source, carrying all trash out of the forest and disposing of it properly, and obeying campfire restrictions in place during your

stay (call 928-643-7395 to check on fire restrictions). The rules are meant not to be annoying or constricting of your lifestyle but to preserve wilderness areas for future generations and to keep wilderness areas wild for the animals that live in the forest. If you are messy and don't believe in zero impact wilderness ethics, do not choose this option. For more information on dispersed camping or the Kaibab National Forest in general, contact the **North Kaibab Ranger District Office** at (928) 643-7395, or stop in the Kaibab Plateau Visitor Center in Jacob Lake. The Web site address for the entire Kaibab National Forest (which has three sections north and south of Grand Canyon National Park) is www.fs.fed.us/r3/kai.

Backcountry Camping in Grand Canyon National Park

See the Grand Canyon—South Rim and Backcountry chapter for more information on inner-canyon hiking and camping. The **North Rim Backcountry Office** is located about 1.5 miles north of Grand Canyon Lodge on Arizona Highway 67. A very limited number of backcountry permits may be available upon your arrival at the park. Show up one day before the first night you want to overnight in the canyon (for example, be there on Thursday if you want to camp in the canyon on Friday), and inquire. This should be a last-resort option only, and be prepared with alternate plans should you fail to secure a permit.

RESTAURANTS

PRICE CODE

The price codes below represent average prices for dinner for two, excluding tax, gratuity, and drinks.

$	Less than $20
$$	$21 to $35
$$$	$36 to $60
$$$$	More than $60

In-Park Restaurants

Grand Canyon Lodge Dining Room $$$
On the North Rim in Grand Canyon Lodge
(928) 638–2612, ext. 160
With the best view from a restaurant on either rim, the Grand Canyon Lodge Dining Room is the sophisticated choice for dining on the North Rim. Serving breakfast, lunch, and dinner in a gorgeous room off the main lobby of Grand Canyon Lodge, the elegant-yet-rustic dining room

seems miles away from roasting wienies over a campfire. The breakfast buffet, with staples such as scrambled eggs and bacon, toast, and coffee, is a popular choice, but many diners choose to pick breakfast dishes off the menu, including the Canyon Breakfast Burrito, with scrambled eggs, diced sausage, beef, onions, green chiles, cheddar cheese, and Lodge Potatoes. For lunch, the dining room offers salivary-gland-pleasing dishes such as the Chicken and Gorgonzola Salad (grilled chicken with dried cranberries, gorgonzola cheese, and toasted walnuts over greens) and the open-face Arizona Cheese Steak Sandwich (rib roast with Monterey Jack cheese and straw onions, served au jus). You do not need a reservation for breakfast or lunch, but for dinner, reservations are required. Like the lodge's counterpart on the South Rim, El Tovar, the Grand Canyon Lodge Dining Room is almost always packed during the prime eating hours, but once you are served your dinner, you will see this isn't because it's the only table-service restaurant on the North Rim. The food is simply magnificent, with such dishes as Prawns with Smoked Cheese Ravioli, Braised Burgundy Lamb Shank, and Alaskan Salmon Salad—although if you are lucky enough to get a reservation at sunset, you may be temporarily distracted from your meal, no matter how tasty. A decent wine list complements meals nicely,

Cafe on the Rim $
On the North Rim in Grand Canyon Lodge
Cafe on the Rim is the fast-eating, cafeteria-style dining choice for those preferring a quick meal without the hubbub of the Grand Canyon Lodge Dining Room. The entrance to the cafe is outside of the front entrance to the lodge, to the right as you approach the lobby doors. Serving breakfast, lunch, and dinner, Cafe on the Rim serves such things as a sausage, egg, and cheese biscuit; Club North Rim Sandwich (bacon, cheddar

cheese, and turkey on sourdough); antipasto salad; and Teriyaki Pork Rice Bowl. The atmosphere recalls fast-food restaurants back home, and the cafe has no canyon view, but the food is good and is served up fast. No phone, so pop in to see what's cookin'.

Out-of-Park Restaurant

**Jacob Lake Inn Restaurant $–$$
and Bakery
At the intersection of U.S. Highway 89A
and Arizona Highway 67, Jacob Lake
(928) 643-7232**
Located at Jacob Lake Inn 45 miles north of the North Rim, this knotty-pine-and-Navajo-rug-decorated establishment serves breakfast, lunch, and dinner, including pancakes, sandwiches, soups, and much more. Specialties include Southwest Baked Chicken and Jägerschnitzel; the homemade pies are to die for. The neighboring bakery specializes in Chocolate Parfait Cookies, carrot cake, and honey whole wheat bread, all great additions to an ad-hoc picnic put together when passing through Jacob Lake.

EXPLORING THE NORTH RIM BY CAR

Outside of the lodge and campground areas, there are few paved roads on the North Rim. Unless you have a high-clearance vehicle, it is best to stay on the paved roads or strike out on foot. About 3 miles north of the visitor center on AZ 67 and about 10 miles from the park entrance, Fuller Canyon Road winds east about 5 miles to the intersection with Point Imperial Road (on the left), which leads another 3 miles to the **Point Imperial** overlook, the highest viewpoint on either rim of Grand Canyon at 8,803 feet. From here you will have unparalleled views of Mount Hayden, the Little Colorado River gorge, Saddle Mountain, Marble Canyon, and the Painted Desert. The overlook has

picnic tables and rest rooms, but make sure you bring your own water and food.

Turning right at the intersection of Fuller Canyon and Point Imperial Roads leads you onto Cape Royal Road, a 15-mile scenic drive across the Walhalla Plateau all the way to Cape Royal. About 3 miles down Cape Royal Road, **Vista Encantada** offers wide views of Mount Hayden and Marble Canyon. The overlook is a nice place to stop for lunch, with picnic tables but no water or rest rooms.

Another 2 miles along Cape Royal Road brings you to the **Roosevelt Point Trailhead.** This loop trail is a mere 0.2 mile long and leads past several stunning overlooks. Roosevelt Point, near the trailhead, towers 8,429 feet above sea level with commanding views of Marble Canyon and the Painted Desert.

The trailhead of the **Cape Final Trail** is 8 miles farther south. The hike to the cape is 2 miles one-way, but the effort will be rewarded with views of Marble Canyon and the first views along Cape Royal Road of the South Rim.

Walhalla Overlook and **Walhalla Glade Ruin** are another mile down Cape Royal Road. The ruin, up a short trail on the western side of the road, is a summertime agricultural site of the ancestral Puebloan people, dating from A.D. 1050 to 1150. The overlook, on the eastern side of the road, offers views of where these same people wintered along the Colorado River in a region known as the Unkar Delta.

Just before reaching Cape Royal on Cape Royal Road, the **Cliff Spring Trail** leads 0.5 mile down a ravine to Cliff Spring (*do not* drink from the spring, as the water may be contaminated). The trail offers nice views of the canyon and passes an ancestral Puebloan granary along the way. The trailhead is at **Angels Window Overlook,** with a nice view of Angels Window, a natural arch in the canyon.

And, finally, at the end of Cape Royal Road, the **Cape Royal Trail** leads 0.25 mile to Cape Royal. The paved trail has views of the canyon along the way, and from the cape you can see the Colorado River,

Angels Window, Wotans Throne, and expansive views of both the eastern and western Grand Canyon. There are rest rooms near the parking area.

If you are driving a high-clearance vehicle, it is worth considering a trip to **Point Sublime,** an accurately named overlook 17 miles west of the North Rim Visitor Center on a rugged dirt road. Note that the road is sometimes impassable in wet weather; check at the North Rim Visitor Center for road conditions. The dirt road branches from AZ 67 about 2 miles north of the visitor center. About a half mile from the turnoff, the road branches left and right. Going left will take you a short distance to Harvey Meadow with access to the Widforss Trail, a 5-mile (one-way) trail through a ponderosa pine forest to an overlook, where you will be blessed with a panoramic view of Buddha Temple, numerous lesser buttes, and the South Rim. Going right continues on toward Point Sublime. Another half mile up the road, veer left onto the dirt Point Sublime Trail Road, which stretches another 15 or so miles west to Point Sublime, a narrow peninsula at an elevation of 7,458 feet sticking far out into the canyon. The point offers views of the Colorado River, the South Rim, and several North Rim overlooks, including a spectacular view of Cape Royal. Picnic tables are available at the point, but there is no water or rest rooms. Despite being on the North Rim, the Point Sublime area is considered part of the backcountry. A limited number of camping permits are available through the Backcountry Office, although you will likely need to secure one well in advance of your arrival at Grand Canyon National Park. See the Grand Canyon—South Rim and Backcountry chapter for more information on backcountry camping permits.

HIKING

As noted, the North Rim area has far more rim trails than the South Rim area. Many are short with a minimal gain or decrease

Hiking in the canyon takes careful planning, including carrying adequate food and water and choosing an appropriate route based on your capabilities and weather conditions. Do not plan an extensive hike in the inner canyon during the summer months, and do not hike to the Colorado River and back in one day at any time of year—even if you are an experienced hiker.

in elevation. Some are paved, although most are not. Many viewpoints not accessible by car can be reached via trails on the rim, and often you will have the viewpoint all to yourself.

The **Bright Angel Point Trail** begins at the corner of the veranda behind Grand Canyon Lodge. The trail leads 0.25 mile (one-way) to Bright Angel Point, a peninsula-like promontory sticking out into the canyon with nice views of Transept Canyon, Roaring Springs Canyon, Bright Angel Creek, the Walhalla Plateau, and the South Rim.

The **Transept Trail** also begins in back of Grand Canyon Lodge and heads northwest 1.5 miles to North Rim Campground. This is a wonderful trail for traveling between your campsite and the creature comforts of the lodge area, although it can be confusing at night. The trail wiggles along the rim of Transept Canyon, with spectacular views of Oza Butte, Widforss Point, and the South Rim.

The **Widforss Trail** is a more serious hike, running 5 miles (one-way) to the canyon edge near Widforss Point. You do not have to hike the entire distance of the trail to get an enjoyable hike, as many nice views of Transept Canyon are to be had in the first couple of miles of the trail. The trail can be accessed from Point Sublime Trail Road, a dirt road that branches west from AZ 67 about 2 miles north of Grand Canyon Lodge. The Widforss Trailhead is about 1 mile up the road to the left.

Spectacular trails through cool aspen and ponderosa pine forests crisscross the North Rim of Grand Canyon. TODD R. BERGER

The **North Kaibab Trail** is the most famous North Rim trail and the only maintained trail leading into the canyon from the North Rim. The trailhead is about 3 miles north of Grand Canyon Lodge. A **hiker's shuttle** carries backpackers to the trailhead from Grand Canyon Lodge twice in the early morning; ask at the lodge front desk for information or to buy tickets ($5.00 for the first person, $2.00 per additional person). Day hikes are possible on the trail, although the trail is extremely steep and the climb back out is guaranteed to get your heart beating rapidly. It is crucial that you bring sufficient water (one quart per hour of hiking time) and food, particularly salty snacks. The Coconino Overlook is a good day-hike destination, about .75 mile (one-way) down the trail, and more hearty day hikers set their sites on Supai Tunnel, 2 miles (one-way) down the trail, where there are water and rest rooms. The North Kaibab Trail runs all the way to the Colorado River, some 14 miles away from and 5,500 feet below the North Rim. *Do not under any circumstances attempt to hike to the river and back in one day.* If you want a more in-depth tour of the inner canyon, obtain a backcountry permit and camp below the rim (see the Grand Canyon—South Rim and Backcountry chapter for more information on backpacking in the canyon).

The **Uncle Jim Trail** is a shorter, rim-level option that begins at the parking area for the North Kaibab Trailhead. The trail runs 2.5 miles (one-way) to Uncle Jim Point, a nice overlook with views of Roaring Springs Canyon, Bright Angel Canyon, Walhalla Plateau, and the South Rim far in the distance.

The **Ken Patrick Trail,** named for the first park service ranger killed in the line of duty, stretches 10 miles (one-way) to Point Imperial, the highest viewpoint on either rim of Grand Canyon. The trail begins at the North Kaibab Trailhead parking area, and features several overlooks and a cool stroll in an aspen–ponderosa pine forest.

The **Point Imperial Trail** leads from Point Imperial, 11 miles northeast of Grand Canyon Lodge, 4 miles (one-way) to the Nankoweap Trailhead. The trail is relatively level and hugs the rim with nice views of the eastern Grand Canyon. The **Nankoweap Trail** is an extremely strenuous, unmaintained, and unpatrolled trail leading into the inner canyon. This trail is for experienced desert hikers only and does not offer any day-hiking opportunities.

There are several trailheads that can be reached by car on the Walhalla Plateau. See the previous Exploring the North Rim by Car section for details.

TOURS

There are no motor-coach tours on the North Rim, but you can see a lot of the rim area and even venture into the canyon if you are willing to mount a four-legged animal.

Canyon Trail Rides
Tropic, Utah
(435) 679–8665
www.canyonrides.com/pkgrandcanyon. html
Canyon Trail Rides offers mule and horseback rides at Grand Canyon National Park as well as at Bryce Canyon and Zion National Parks in Utah. Although the company is headquartered in Utah, you can make reservations or inquire about availability at the desk inside the lobby of Grand Canyon Lodge. The horseback rides stick to the rim, following the Ken Patrick Trail and the Uncle Jim Trail to some nice overlooks. There are one-hour and half-

day options for these trips. The mule trips take you down the North Kaibab Trail into the canyon, to Supai Tunnel for the half-day trip and to Roaring Springs for the full-day trip. Equine trips will set you back $20 for the one-hour ride on the rim to $95 for the full-day mule descent and return to Roaring Springs.

SHOPPING

Hardly a Vegas-style shopper's paradise, the North Rim has a few options if you seek basic groceries or camping supplies, gifts, or books.

Grand Canyon Association North Rim Bookstore
In the North Rim Visitor Center next to Grand Canyon Lodge
www.grandcanyon.org
With bookstores spread throughout the park, the nonprofit Grand Canyon Association (GCA) serves canyon visitors by providing information, publications, art and photography exhibits, interpretive displays, T-shirts, and maps through their bookstores, on-line, and through mail order, and by offering trips into the canyon through the Grand Canyon Field Institute (GCFI). GCA's profits are donated to the National Park Service at Grand Canyon, and since GCA's founding in 1932, the organization has given the NPS just under $20 million. GCA's North Rim Bookstore has a wide body of information, including books, videos, maps, and posters, about Grand Canyon and the surrounding wilderness areas, and is open daily when the North Rim is open to visitors. GCA is also a membership organization, and GCA members enjoy a 15 percent discount at GCA stores at Grand Canyon, discounts at other cooperating association stores in national parks nationwide, invitations to members-only events, discounts on GCFI courses, and more. By shopping at GCA's North Rim store during your visit to Grand Canyon, you will not only find the information and gifts you need, but will also help preserve the future of Grand Canyon National Park.

North Rim General Store
Next to the North Rim Campground
(928) 638-2611
The general store is the only place to buy groceries and camping supplies on the North Rim. The selection is limited, although they can help you out if you're short a tent stake or need more Wonder Bread. They also sell beer and wine, and offer several T-shirts and other touristy items. Open daily when the North Rim is open to visitors.

Grand Canyon Lodge Gift Shop
In Grand Canyon Lodge
The Grand Canyon Lodge Gift Shop, to the left as you approach the front doors of the lodge, offers T-shirts, key chains, coffee mugs, and dozens of other items with "Grand Canyon" prominently featured. Open daily when the North Rim is open to visitors.

LEES FERRY

Although more than 85 miles from the North Rim developed area, Lees Ferry lies on the "north" side of the Colorado River. It is the official starting point for most river trips through Grand Canyon, and marks the boundary of the national park itself. North of Lees Ferry, Glen Canyon National Recreation Area sprawls; south of the spot, Grand Canyon National Park begins. When measuring distance traveled on the river in Grand Canyon, Lees Ferry is considered Mile 0.

You can reach Lees Ferry by turning right on the road shooting north from U.S. Highway 89A just across the Navajo Bridge west of Page. The historic site and boat launch ramp, which includes several historic buildings, is 5 miles north.

Lees Ferry is the only place along 700 miles of the Colorado River where you can drive to the water's edge. This fluke of geography is the reason Lees Ferry exists:

The Navajo Bridge Interpretive Center, just off U.S. Highway 89A after it crosses the Colorado River, offers information on both Grand Canyon National Park and Glen Canyon National Recreation Area. TODD R. BERGER

Until 1928, the ferry that crossed the river here, established in 1872 by Mormon settler John D. Lee, was the only way to cross the river for hundreds of miles. The ferry was deactivated the year before the original Navajo Bridge over the Colorado opened to vehicles.

The National Park Service has established interpretive trails through the historic town as well as the nearby Lonely Dell Ranch. The park service publishes a *Walking Tour Guide* for Lees Ferry, which is available for purchase at the Navajo Bridge Interpretive Center on the western side of the Navajo Bridge or at the ranger station at Lees Ferry.

The Lonely Dell Ranch, so named by one of John D. Lee's 17 wives, is about 700 feet up a dirt road that extends from the Lees Ferry parking area. The site includes an orchard, stone ranch house, log cabins, and a pioneer cemetery.

The Navajo Bridge Interpretive Center is a wonderful resource in a beautiful stone building just across the original Navajo Bridge when approaching from the east. The original bridge, which spans the Colorado River next to the new bridge that supports U.S. Highway 89A, remains open to pedestrian traffic. A parking area is to the right as you approach the new bridge on the highway (park and walk across the old bridge to the interpretive center). The bridges are 467 feet above the river, and the spans stretch 834 feet. The interpretive center has rangers on duty to provide information about both Glen Canyon National Recreation Area and Grand Canyon National Park. You can also buy books and other items in the bookstore inside the interpretive center. There are rest rooms here, but the only water comes from a vending machine.

To take a river trip originating at Lees Ferry, you must make reservations in advance with a commercial rafting company or obtain a private permit; it is not possible to get on river trips by simply going to Lees Ferry. For a list of commercial rafting companies, see the Grand Canyon—South Rim and Backcountry chapter. To get on the very, very, very long waiting list for private river permits, contact the Grand Canyon River Permits Office, Grand Canyon National Park, P.O. Box 129, Grand Canyon, AZ 86023; (800) 959–9164. Applications can be downloaded from the NPS Grand Canyon river Web site, www.nps.gov/grca/river/non_commercial_general_info.htm. There is a $100 application fee and a $100 fee when you actually launch your boat. Those on the waiting list who wish to remain there must submit a Continued Interest Form every year by January 31. Be prepared for a wait of *many* years before a permit is issued. To get a permit is truly a once-in-a-lifetime event, and when applying, it is worth your while to pray for a long and healthy life.

FLAGSTAFF

Surrounded by ponderosa pine trees and delicate aspens, the city of Flagstaff rests at the foot of the San Francisco Peaks. Flagstaff has evolved from a Wild West town to a city with small-town appeal. Its colorful history is a blend of western legends, courageous settlers, and dedicated citizens who have worked to make this mountain town a family community.

The largest city in northern Arizona, Flagstaff is the county seat for Coconino County. The population as of 2003 climbed to nearly 61,000 residents. By the year 2015, the city estimates the population will grow to 80,000.

A high desert town with alpine weather conditions, Flagstaff is just 146 miles north of Phoenix, and at 7,000 feet in elevation, the climates of the two Arizona cities differ dramatically. Flagstaff's pleasurable climate with four distinct seasons has an average January temperature of 42 degrees, and in July the daytime highs hover around 80 degrees. Warm summer days, snowy winters, spring wildflowers, and the glowing gold aspens in fall entice visitors to the north country year-round to explore the endless recreation possibilities.

A transportation hub since the arrival of the railroad in 1881, Flagstaff was once located along the old wagon road to California. Today the city links Interstate 40 to Interstate 17, U.S. Highway 89 to Page and Utah, and U.S. Highway 180 to Grand Canyon. Historic Route 66 passes through Flagstaff.

Tourism is a major source of employment and income for Flagstaff. Government institutions, educational facilities, trucking, and the railroad play important roles in the city's economy. Approximately 19,000 students attend Northern Arizona University. Surrounding communities rely on the historic downtown area and shopping centers for their retail and service needs.

Grand Canyon is just one of the many attractions that bring more than five million visitors to the northland every year. Other sites within a short drive of the city limits include the dormant volcanoes of Sunset Crater National Monument, the ancestral Puebloan ruins of Wupatki and Walnut Canyon, Meteor Crater, and the red rocks of Oak Creek Canyon and Sedona.

But Flagstaff holds its own as a destination in and of itself. Intimate shops, art galleries, unique restaurants, and downtown cafes line the streets. Stop by Heritage Square to people watch or hear local musicians year-round (depending on the weather).

Local museums and scientific research centers work to preserve the history and culture of the Colorado Plateau and to educate and entertain people of all ages. Flagstaff offers social and recreational activities and hosts many annual events and festivals. Community and professional theaters present live performances year-round. The Flagstaff Symphony provides a full concert season from September through May. The San Francisco Peaks, the city's backdrop, offer endless hiking, mountain biking, and cross-country or downhill skiing opportunities.

Flagstaff's motto is: They don't make towns like this any more. Come and experience the spirit and lifestyle that Flagstaff has to offer.

GETTING TO FLAGSTAFF

Since the arrival of the railroad and the earliest pioneers, Flagstaff has been the hub of northern Arizona. Flagstaff sits at the intersection of I-17 (north-south) and I-40 (east-west). U.S. Highways 89 and 180 bring travelers from Grand Canyon to and from Flagstaff.

Flagstaff Vital Statistics

Mayor: Joe Donaldson **Arizona governor:** Janet Napolitano

Population: Flagstaff: 60,880
Arizona: 5,629,870

Area (sq. miles): 64.1

Nickname/motto: Flagstaff, they don't make towns like this anymore.

Average temperatures: July high/low: 82/51
January high/low: 42/15

Average rain/snowfall/days of sunshine: 22.9 inches / 108.8 inches / 300 days

City/state founded: 1881 / 1912

Major university: Northern Arizona University

Important dates in history:

1876   On July 4, travelers raised a flag on a ponderosa pine in Antelope Park, and the area was christened "Flag Staff."

1881   Post office for town of "Flagstaff" established.

1883   On October 21 the Atlantic & Pacific began passenger service from Albuquerque to San Francisco, stopping in Flagstaff en route.

1884   Fire destroyed Old Town. "New Town" was relocated to present-day site near the railroad depot.

1886   Another fire ravaged "New Town," but within six months the town was rebuilt and added 40 more buildings.

1912   Arizona became a state.

1930   The planet Pluto was discovered by Clyde W. Tombaugh at the Lowell Observatory.

1966   Arizona State College became Northern Arizona University.

1990s   Historic restoration of the downtown area.

Major area employers: Coconino County; W.L. Gore Associates; Flagstaff Medical Center; Walgreens Distribution Center; Northern Arizona University; Flagstaff Unified School District

Famous sons and daughters: Eva Marshall—first teacher in Flagstaff; A. E. Douglas—founder of Lowell Observatory and developer of the science of dendrochronology; Anastasia Frohmiller—first woman to run for governor in Arizona; Percival Lowell—famous astronomer; Laura Runke—first female member of Flagstaff's City Council; George Hochderffer—author of *Flagstaff Whoa!*, a historical account of the town; Dr. Harold Colton—founder of the Museum of Northern Arizona; Thomas McMillan—one of the area's first settlers and ranchers; the Babbit Family—economic contributors to Flagstaff's economy.

State/city holidays: New Year's Day; Martin Luther King Day; Presidents' Day; Memorial Day; Independence Day; Labor Day; Veterans' Day; Thanksgiving Day; Christmas Day

Chamber of commerce:
Flagstaff Chamber of Commerce
101 West Route 66
Flagstaff, AZ 86001
(928) 774-4505
www.flagstaff.az.us

Major airports/interstates: Flagstaff Pulliam Municipal Airport; Interstate 40; Interstate 17

Public transportation: Mountain Line Transit (bus system)

Military bases: Camp Navajo

Driving laws: Seatbelts must be worn by front-seat passengers; right turn on red; speed limit is 55 except where marked; speed limit on interstates is 75 except in designated areas.

Alcohol laws: Legal drinking age is 21 years; blood/alcohol level of .08% or higher is DUI in Arizona.

Daily newspaper: *Arizona Daily Sun*

Sales tax: 8.125 percent city/state taxes on all retail sales; 9.89 percent city/state accommodations; 9.31 percent city/state restaurant and bar

Due to weather, northern Arizona is not the easiest place to travel to at times. Mountain weather can strike at any time, so be prepared. If you're looking to escape the heat in the Valley of the Sun, you just need to get "up the hill."

By Air

Flagstaff Pulliam Municipal Airport
6200 South Pulliam Drive, Flagstaff
(928) 556-1234
America West Express (800-235-9292, www.americawest.com) is the only airline flying into Flagstaff Pulliam Municipal Airport, with service to/from Phoenix's Sky Harbor International Airport. The airport is 4 miles south of the city next to I-17. For detailed information about the airport and its amenities, see the Getting Here, Getting Around chapter.

By Bus or Train

Greyhound Bus
399 South Malpais Lane
(928) 774-4573, (800) 231-2222
www.greyhound.com
Flagstaff's Greyhound station is located one-half mile southwest of downtown on Malpais Lane, just north of West Route 66. Greyhound stops in some four dozen locations across Arizona, including Phoenix, Phoenix Sky Harbor Airport, Tucson, Williams, and Winslow, as well as thousands of destinations farther afield.

Amtrak
1 East Santa Fe Avenue (East Route 66)
(928) 774-8679, (800) 872-7245
www.amtrak.com
The Southwest Chief rolls through Flagstaff twice a day (once in each direction) en route between Chicago and Los Angeles.

Flagstaff's train station is just across Route 66 from the historic downtown district. In addition to hosting Amtrak trains, the station houses the Flagstaff Visitor Center. TODD R. BERGER

The Amtrak station is just across East Santa Fe Avenue (East Route 66) from downtown at the San Francisco Street intersection. **Hertz Car Rental** (928-226-0120, 800-704-4473) has an office in the station, and the **Flagstaff Visitor Center** (928-774-9541, 800-842-7293) is also located here. Grand Canyon Railway trains bound for the national park leave from the Amtrak station in Williams (see the Williams chapter for more information).

By Car

Flagstaff is easy to find. If you are traveling east on I-40 from California, or via U.S. 93 from Las Vegas, or west on I-40 from Albuquerque, you'll run right into the city at the intersection with I-17 in north-central Arizona. From Phoenix, Flagstaff is an easy two hours due north on I-17. From the South Rim of Grand Canyon National Park, follow AZ 64 south 28 miles to Valle, and then follow U.S. 180 52 miles to Flagstaff. In winter, U.S. 180 sometimes closes due to inclement weather, and it can be very slippery when there is snow on the ground even when the road remains open. If the weather is iffy, continue past Valle on AZ 64 to Williams, and then follow I-40 east to Flagstaff. To get to Flagstaff from the North Rim of Grand Canyon and the Arizona Strip, follow Arizona 67 north to Jacob Lake, then U.S. 89A east to Bitter Springs and U.S. 89. Flagstaff is about 110 miles south on U.S. 89. U.S. Highway 89 can also be accessed from the Navajo Reservation via U.S. 160.

GETTING AROUND FLAGSTAFF

If you have booked a hotel or bed-and-breakfast in the downtown area, the best mode of transportation is your feet. The two-hour parking restriction makes parking on the north side of the tracks a hassle. Visitors can park a few blocks north of downtown with no restrictions. However, there are no parking restrictions on the south side of town and there are even a few parking lots located behind the chamber of commerce on South Beaver Street, two lots on Phoenix Avenue, and lots on both sides of the Flagstaff Visitor Center/Amtrak train station.

Flagstaff has a city bus system, **Mountain Line Transit** (928-779-6624), with four routes serving most of the city, including Northern Arizona University, downtown, Flagstaff Medical Center, the shopping areas on the south side of the city, Coconino Community College, and the Flagstaff Mall. Buses run roughly every hour between 6:00 A.M. and 10:00 P.M. weekdays and 7:00 A.M. to 5:00 P.M. Saturday; buses do not run on Sunday or major holidays. Adult fares are 75 cents, with one transfer between lines allowed.

Walking and biking are also popular ways to get around town. The Flagstaff Urban Trail System is a peaceful way to traverse the city either by foot or on wheels. (For bike rentals, refer to the Flagstaff Recreation section.) A map of the Flagstaff Urban Trail System can be purchased at the Flagstaff City Hall for $2.00. The Flagstaff Visitor Center has a photocopy of this map for free, but an original copy of the map is suggested.

Car Rentals

Alamo Rent-A-Car
2320 East Lucky Lane (Holiday Inn)
(928) 774-3322

Budget Rent-A-Car
175 West Aspen Avenue
(928) 213-0156, (800) 527-0700
Pulliam Municipal Airport
(928) 779-5235

Enterprise Rent-A-Car
100 North Humphreys Street
(928) 526-1377
3470 East Route 66
(928) 774-9407

ℹ️

Arizona, which is in the mountain time zone, does not observe daylight savings time (except on the Navajo Reservation). When most of the states on mountain standard time move forward one hour in the spring, Arizona does not change its clocks, effectively making the state part of the pacific time zone for six months of the year.

National Car Rental
2320 East Lucky Lane (Holiday Inn)
(928) 779-1975, (888) 868-6204
Pulliam Municipal Airport
(928) 774-3321

Taxi and Limousine Companies

Some local companies offer special rates to various sites and attractions within the region. Contact the individual company for rates and more information.

A-1 Quick Cab and Tours
(928) 214-8294

A Friendly Cab
(928) 774-4444, (800) 853-4445

Mountain Cab Company
(928) 774-7772

Sun Taxi & Tours
(928) 774-7400

ACCOMMODATIONS

Major motel and hotel chains provide the basics, but if you enjoy getting to know the town and its people and are looking for gourmet food and service with a personal touch, Flagstaff is full of charming and unique accommodations that suit any budget. Bed-and-breakfast inns have warm and comfortable atmospheres that make guests feel like family.

Be sure to fully investigate the inns you are considering before making a reservation. Innkeepers are proud of their establishments and willingly answer the questions of potential guests to ensure a quality experience. The best part of staying at inns is that they are centrally located and usually within walking distance of shopping and restaurants. Most inns accept children; however, pets don't seem to be as popular as children, so call ahead to check on this policy. The majority of inns are homes that have been renovated with rooms and suites on the second floor that are not wheelchair accessible, but some may have first-floor, wheelchair-accessible rooms. Nonsmoking inns with outside alternative smoking areas do exist, as do nonsmoking properties. Transportation is provided to and from the local airport, bus and train stations. Summer and winter are Flagstaff's busiest seasons. Rates fluctuate from season to season. Note that the local university hosts various weekend events that attract alumni, students' families, and sports and cultural enthusiasts. Make your reservations early.

PRICE CODE

The following price code is for two adults during high season, which begins in May and ends Labor Day weekend. Snow attracts many visitors and the season picks up again in December and runs through March. Rates are subject to change and do not include tax, gratuities, or other guest services.

$	Less than $60
$$	$61 to $75
$$$	$76 to $100
$$$$	$101 to $125
$$$$$	More than $125

Bed-and-Breakfasts

Aspen Inn   **$$$**
218 North Elden Street
(928) 773-0295, (888) 999-4110
www.flagstaffbedandbreakfast.com
The congenial host of this quaint bed-
and-breakfast, located two blocks east of
Flagstaff's historic downtown, hopes his
guests will pick his brain to find out what
to do and where to go in town. All three
rooms include a private bath, cable TV,
private phone lines, queen-size beds, and
a minifridge stocked with complimentary
beverages and light snacks. The Wilson
Room is perfect for long visits and comes
with a washer and dryer. This house has a
common area for guests. Read a book,
listen to music, or make yourself at home
by the fireplace. A healthy breakfast is
served on Spanish china in the dining
room from 8:00 to 9:00 A.M. The inn's
signature dish is a Spanish "tortilla":
potato pie served with a light mushroom
sauce and a side of turkey sausage. The
innkeeper's wife is from Madrid and her
madre taught her how to make this tradi-
tional recipe.

Birch Tree Inn   **$$$-$$$$**
824 West Birch Street
(928) 774-1042, (888) 774-1042
www.birchtreeinn.com
If a break from the city is what you need,
come to this country-style inn, which
offers plenty of room for lounging on the
wraparound front porch, back deck, and
patio. Take a dip in the Jacuzzi while you
gaze at the star-filled sky. The five rooms
range in price and two come with a
shared bath. Comfortable and spacious,
the inn was built in 1917. You will be
treated like family as you curl up by the
fire or play a round of billiards in the
game room. All rooms are located on the
second floor and each room is decorated
with a theme that pays tribute to the
innkeeper's family, the Southwest, or just
subtle elegance. Afternoon refreshments

are served at 4:00 P.M. daily. A healthy
breakfast is served family style with fresh
fruit. The inn caters to dietary restrictions;
please inform the innkeepers in advance.

Hilltop Bed & Breakfast   **$$-$$$**
701 North Curling Smoke Road
(928) 779-9633, (888) 508-4434
If a secluded cottage off the beaten track
is calling to you, look no further. Awake
each morning in a king-size bed with
trees, birds chirping, and deer grazing
outside your window. Decorated with
antiques, leather furniture, and lace cur-
tains, the cottage has a charming appeal
and plenty of elbow room. The cozy
accommodations include a sitting area,
and a small kitchen with a minifridge,
dishes, coffeemaker, and sink. A Scandina-
vian sauna was installed to ensure that
guests receive the proper amount of
relaxation. Designated a backyard wildlife
retreat by the National Wildlife Federation,
the cottage is located on the top of a 10-
mile-long mesa with trails for hiking, bik-
ing, and cross-country skiing right outside
your cottage door.

Serving only organic ingredients and the
highest quality food, the innkeeper believes
what you eat is as important as where you
stay. A complete breakfast menu is avail-
able. Choose from a hearty southwestern
omelet, pancakes, or a fruit parfait
smoothie. Can't decide? Mix and match
menu items to create the perfect meal.

Hilltop Bed & Breakfast permits guests ℹ️
to bring their small- to medium-size
pets.

The Inn at 410 Bed & Breakfast   **$$$$**
410 North Leroux Street
(928) 774-0088, (800) 774-2008
www.inn410.com
Built in 1894, this elegant inn offers spa-
cious accommodations guaranteed to

soothe the soul. Located 2 blocks north-east of the historic downtown, the inn has four rooms and five suites with private baths, some with Jacuzzi tubs, fireplaces, and private entrances. The names of the rooms are as distinctive as the rooms themselves. "Sunflower Room," "The Southwest," and "Monet's Garden" give you an idea of what the innkeepers are striving for: an intimate setting for an unforgettable getaway. Two suites are available for families. Complimentary beverages and fresh-baked goodies await guests after a day of exploring. Relax by the fireplace in the common area or step outside to the perennial garden. Breathe in the crisp mountain air while rejuvenating in the gazebo. Vegetarian breakfasts are served in the common dining area between 8:00 and 9:00 A.M. The menu changes daily, but guests can count on exotic juices, fresh-baked muffins or breads, and a healthy entree to start their day. The Inn at 410 accepts Visa and MasterCard.

Jeanette's Bed and Breakfast $$$$
3380 East Lockett Road
(928) 527-1912, (800) 752-1912
www.jeanettesbb.com
Resting in the pines with Mount Elden as its backdrop, this Victorian-style home exudes romance. If you decide to take in the scenery or get a breath of fresh air, take a stroll through pine-covered paths or enjoy the porch swing on a warm summer night. All four rooms have private baths, each with a claw-foot bathtub. And what good is a bathtub without homemade soaps and complimentary bubble bath? All rooms have unique features that set them apart, including a private balcony, fireplace, and king-size bed. Enjoy full gourmet breakfasts in the dining room. Guests rave about the Chili Soufflé. Jeanette's accepts Discover, Visa, and MasterCard. No children please.

Hostel

Grand Canyon International Hostel $
19 South San Francisco Street
(928) 779-9421, (888) 442-2696
www.grandcanyonhostel.com
For travelers rolling into Flagstaff with limited funds and an open attitude about communal sleeping, the Grand Canyon International Hostel is an extremely inexpensive alternative just south of Flagstaff's historic downtown. The hostel, located in the former Downtowner Motel, offers both private rooms and bunks in dorm-style rooms, and the rate for either a private room or a bunk includes breakfast and fresh linens (sleeping bags are not allowed on the beds). The Grand Canyon International Hostel is independent and does not offer discounts to hosteling association members. Along with free breakfast, the hostel offers free pick-up service at the Greyhound station, a refrigerator in every room, tours to Grand Canyon and Sedona, high-speed Internet access, a cable TV room with a video library, and two kitchens. The entire facility is nonsmoking, and for those travelers intent on getting a high from something other than the elevation, they best look elsewhere, because the hostel strictly enforces a no-illegal-drugs policy. During the summer, reservations are recommended at least two weeks ahead of time, longer for private rooms.

Motels and Hotels

Flagstaff, a major tourist destination in itself as well as a gateway to some of the most spectacular scenery in the West (and, in the case of Grand Canyon, the world), has wall-to-wall hotels and motels in many parts of town, particularly along Route 66. There are many lovely motels along *East* Route 66, but be aware that almost all of the establishments along the

refrigerator, microwave, coffeemaker, and a table for dining or for use as a work desk. The cost of the room includes a cooked-to-order breakfast. The hotel also has dry-cleaning services, self-service laundry facilities, a gift shop, a business center, a fitness room, an outdoor pool (open seasonally), and a whirlpool. Popular with business travelers and those who prefer a little more elbow room when on vacation, the Embassy Suites Hotel Flagstaff is close to many shops, restaurants, Northern Arizona University, and both interstate highways leading to and from Flagstaff.

Holiday Inn Flagstaff $$$$-$$$$$
2320 East Lucky Lane
(928) 714-1000, (800) 533-2754
www.holidayinnarizona.com/hotels/flgll.html
The Holiday Inn Flagstaff is a convenient and comfortable choice. Located just off I-40 on the east side of Flagstaff, the hotel is about 2 miles from downtown and 7 miles from Pulliam Municipal Airport. The hotel offers a heated, year-round outdoor pool; an indoor pool; fitness room; whirlpool; complimentary shuttles to Pulliam Airport and the Amtrak station; and a National/Alamo rental car desk. Rooms are comfortable and functional, with dataports, in-room movies and video checkout, desks, and a coffeemaker. The hotel allows pets for an additional $25. The hotel also includes a restaurant and lounge.

Hotel Monte Vista $$-$$$$
100 North San Francisco Street
(928) 779-6971, (800) 545-3068
www.hotelmontevista.com
When you arrive in Flagstaff, it's hard to miss the Hotel Monte Vista; its towering sign over the historic downtown announces its presence. The hotel itself is historic, dating from 1926, with four floors of rooms and suites comfortably decorated with furniture and trim hinting at the hotel's historic past. Many of the rooms are named after celebrity guests who once stayed here, including the Bob Hope,

the Spencer Tracy, and the Clark Gable. In the 1950s, the actor John Wayne stayed in a room at the Monte Vista, where he claimed to be visited by a friendly ghost. Ever since, reports of spirit sightings, or at the very least secondhand (and beyond) stories of sightings, have regularly surfaced, although the Monte Vista's alleged spirits are said to be unfailingly friendly. Think Casper. For those seeking a different kind of spirits, the Monte Vista has a lounge featuring live entertainment on Thursday, Friday, and Saturday; a martini menu; and happy hour from 4:00 to 7:00 P.M. daily.

Hotel Weatherford $$
23 North Leroux Street
(928) 779-1919
www.weatherfordhotel.com
The historic Hotel Weatherford was built in 1900 by John Weatherford, who envisioned Flagstaff as the cultural mecca of the West. Since the opening of the grand hotel, the guest list has been impressive. From President Teddy Roosevelt to novelist Zane Grey to painter Thomas Moran, these early-20th-century legends contributed a piece of history to the establishment. The hotel was saved from demolition by the previous owner in the early 1970s and has survived several fires and harsh weather. The eight fully restored rooms on the third floor are decorated in the turn-of-the-20th-century style, without modern amenities (no telephones or TVs in the rooms). The refurbished wood floors, light and airy rooms, and in-house bars and restaurant offer pure relaxation and rejuvenation. Four of the eight rooms come with private baths. Located in the heart of downtown, just 1 block from the Amtrak station, the hotel is within walking distance of restaurants, art galleries, and shopping.

Mormon Lake Lodge $$-$$$$
1 Main Street, Mormon Lake
(928) 774-0462
www.mormonlakelodge.com
Surrounded by oak and pine trees, Mormon

Holiday Inn Flagstaff has a spectacular backdrop of the San Francisco Peaks. TODD R. BERGER

famous highway on the east side of town are right across the street from the Burlington Northern–Santa Fe Railroad tracks, one of the nation's busiest freight arteries. Be warned: The trains rumble through every 15 minutes to half hour.

Most of the following motels and hotels are located a little farther from the tracks in locations that raise the chances of getting a restful night of sleep in comfort. Please note that the hotels and motels on *West* Route 66 border Northern Arizona University rather than the train tracks.

Days Inn Route 66 $
1000 West Route 66
(928) 774-5221
www.daysinnflagstaff.com
If your neighbors back home are impressed by pool size, the Days Inn Route 66, with the largest outdoor pool (open April through October) in northern Ari-

zona, deserves a stay and a couple of backstroke laps during your tour of Flagstaff and environs. The inexpensive hotel offers guests a complimentary deluxe breakfast; lounge; gift shop; complimentary copy of *USA Today;* laundry facilities; cable TV, free HBO, pay-per-view movies, and Nintendo; and dataports. Pets are allowed for a small additional fee. Located about 1 mile south of downtown Flagstaff on West Route 66, the motel is convenient to numerous restaurants and shops.

Embassy Suites Hotel
Flagstaff $$$$-$$$$$
706 South Milton Road
(928) 774-4333
Remodeled in 2003, the Embassy Suites Hotel Flagstaff is an all-suite hotel about 2 miles south of downtown. All rooms have a bedroom, living room, two televisions,

Flagstaff's historic Hotel Weatherford will charm you, with its eight rooms and elegantly restored interior. TODD R. BERGER

Lake Lodge is 25 miles southeast of Flagstaff at the base of Mormon Mountain. Immerse yourself in the seclusion of the Coconino National Forest, which has plenty of hiking trails, lakes for fishing, and horseback riding trails. The rustic, self-sufficient cabins include stove, fridge, wood-burning fireplaces, linens, bedding, and cooking utensils. Choose from one of 16 cabins set on 16 acres of land that range from a cozy cabin for two, stone cabin, split-level for four, or hogan-style cabin that accommodates eight people. Pets are welcome. The nearest store and restaurant is seven minutes away. The store has a limited selection, so stock up on supplies before you leave town. This is cushy camping at its best!

Radisson Woodlands Hotel $$$–$$$$
1175 West Route 66
(928) 773-8888
www.radisson.com/flagstaffaz

The Radisson Woodlands Hotel features 183 comfortable rooms with either a king bed or two queens, as well as several suites. The hotel operates two restaurants: the elegant Sakura Restaurant (see the Restaurants section) serving Japanese cuisine and the casual Woodlands Café and Lounge featuring continental cuisine. The hotel has an outdoor pool, indoor whirlpool, sauna, fitness center, and steam room. The Radisson Woodlands is near the shopping areas on the west side of town and is convenient to I-40 and I-17. Flagstaff's historic downtown is a short drive northeast.

Ramada Limited West $$–$$$
2755 Woodlands Village Boulevard
(928) 773-1111
www.the.ramada.com/flagstaff02431

The Ramada Limited West offers 89 spacious "minisuites," all including a refrigerator, a microwave, an iron and ironing board, and a coffeemaker. The hotel provides a pool, whirlpool, sauna, fitness room, laundry facilities, and a deluxe continental breakfast. The Ramada Limited West does not have a restaurant, but several eating establishments, a grocery store, and a Wal-Mart are just across the street. The hotel, located 4 miles from downtown near I-40, I-17, and Pulliam Municipal Airport, is a scaled-back but wholly acceptable choice among Flagstaff's plethora of hotels.

Residence Inn by Marriott $$$$–$$$$$
3440 North Country Club Drive
(928) 526-5555
www.residenceinn.com/flgri

Located in a quiet residential area on the east side of Flagstaff about 6 miles from downtown, the Residence Inn has 102 comfortable, roomy studio and two-bedroom suites, all with kitchens. Amenities include an outdoor heated pool and whirlpool, exercise room, laundry facilities, fireplaces in some rooms, airport shuttle, and a complimentary buffet breakfast. Pets are allowed for an additional $10. During the summer, the Residence Inn offers an elaborate barbecue dinner every Thursday. There is no restaurant on-site, but dinner delivery is available from some local restaurants, several of which are near the hotel.

Ski Lift Lodge $$
Snowbowl Road
(928) 774-0729, (800) 472-3599
www.arizonasnowbowl.com

Located 14 miles north of Flagstaff at the base of the San Francisco Peaks, this is the perfect spot for a family vacation or a getaway for two. Whether you like to hike, mountain bike, or ski, the "Peaks," as locals refer to it, is the ideal place for outdoor activities.

The lodge has 25 single-room cabins with front porches and fireplaces. The cabins sleep four with two full beds. Some have queen-size beds. The maximum occupancy per room is four. Ask for a roll-away bed if needed. Make reservations early, the lodge—just minutes from the ski lifts—is a popular choice with skiers. A full-service restaurant providing breakfast, lunch, and dinner is open seven days a week. The restaurant will prepare snacks for those on the go.

RESTAURANTS

As you drive into Flagstaff, you will be assaulted by neon lights and fast-food restaurants. Although popular American chain restaurants have invaded Flagstaff, do not despair. Whether you are searching for a fine-dining establishment, a casual cafe, or a haven for vegetarians, Flagstaff is home to eating establishments that will make your taste buds stand at attention. You will find restaurants serving traditional dishes complimented by fresh southwestern ingredients. If you taste something a little out of the ordinary in your marinara sauce, it's probably some fresh-cut cilantro or chipotle chiles.

During the 1800s the number of saloons in Flagstaff outnumbered the number of restaurants seven to one. As American tourism increased during the 20th century, Flagstaff answered the call of supply and demand and built restaurants to accommodate travelers. However, the in-town dining options were still limited prior to the renovation of the historic downtown area in the early 1990s and the subsequent increase in population and tourism. Within the past 10 years, dining options have doubled. Today, Flagstaff is made up of health-conscious people. Perhaps it's the clean air and abundance of outdoor activities that contribute to this healthy attitude. With the current health awareness and popularity of organic foods, locals expect quality ingredients and healthful alternatives. Restaurants have listened to the requests and needs of their customers by providing vegetarian and ethnic dishes. Cafes and restaurants serve coffee drinks made with soy milk and yummy vegan pastries and desserts. Don't worry, carnivores—there are plenty of free-range and hormone-free meat options.

Flagstaff is a town known for its relaxed style and comfortable atmosphere. The dress for restaurants is casual, yet you should feel free to put on a jacket or slip into that little black dress. Don't be surprised if you are sitting next to a table of hikers who have just climbed the San Francisco Peaks, while a well-dressed couple lingering over after-dinner drinks sits at the next table. Self-expression is a way of life in this mountain town. All Flagstaff restaurants are nonsmoking. While breakfast, lunch, and dinner places are scattered throughout town, most of the restaurants featured in this section are in the downtown area or within a 4-mile radius.

PRICE CODE

The costs below represent dinner for two excluding tax, gratuity, and drinks. Menus, times, and prices are subject to change. Most establishments accept cash, major credit cards, and traveler's checks. If a restaurant does not accept credit cards, it is noted in the restaurant listing information.

$	Less than $20
$$	$21 to $35
$$$	$36 to $60
$$$$	More than $60

Beaver Street Brewery & Whistle Stop Cafe $$
11 South Beaver Street
(928) 779-0079
www.beaverstreetbrewery.com
Decorated in dark polished wood, this popular eatery is bound to please the pickiest of eaters. Burgers, wood-fire pizzas, and tasty sandwiches are the specialties of the house. Look for the daily soup and chili specials. The lunch and dinner entrees are always a treat. Start off your meal with a savory fondue made with Beaver Street's own batch of microbrewed beer. Always busy and consistently good, the lively restaurant caters to families and the 30-something crowd. Be ready to wait

on a Friday or Saturday night in the summer or in the dead of winter. Reservations are not taken, thus making patience a virtue. Relax in one of their comfy chairs by the host station or belly up to the bar and try one of the fresh home brews that has made Beaver Street Brewery a household name. The restaurant is wheelchair accessible and is open daily for lunch and dinner.

Black Barts $$$
2760 East Butler Avenue
(928) 779-3142

Black Barts' "Steakhouse, Saloon, and Musical Revue" keeps things hopping with steaks galore and a talented (for the most part) singing waitstaff, all students from Northern Arizona University. Your waitpersons will occasionally apologize that they can't take your order immediately back to the kitchen because they have to "do a number," but on the whole, the bellowing tablehops are attentive, friendly, and right on the money with your order. The food's not bad, either. Naturally, steaks are Barts' strong suit, including the T-bone, porterhouse, New York strip, and filet mignon (for a real spicy treat, top your fillet with the optional peppercorn sauce, a version with a little southwestern heat to it). Barts can also set you up with prime rib (in the smaller Mizus' Cut or larger Barts' Cut), baby-back ribs, broiled salmon, and even a Shrimp 'n' Caesar Salad. Meals come with the Leaves 'n' Weeds Salad; a choice of baked potato, Frenchy Fries, or the quite tasty Rootin' Tootin' Cowboy Beans with Salsa; and sourdough biscuits with honey butter. Desserts include His Mama's Best Cobbler and Snickers Pie. Barts has a full bar, and refills of "sodee water" are always free. Black Barts is open daily for dinner only.

Burritos Fiesta Fresh Mexican Grill $
1530 South Riordan Ranch Road, #4
(928) 774-3600

Burritos Fiesta's Mexican food is indeed fresh—and absolutely delicious. The restaurant is a bit of a hole in the wall tucked away in a nondescript strip mall, but don't let that deter you. Decor is kept to a minimum: Red-check tablecloths complement red vinyl chairs and a red ceiling fan. Piped-in salsa music sets the mood and prepares you to eat the restaurant's yummy specialties; the fish tacos, in particular, are to die for. In addition to individual dishes, Burritos Fiesta offers Family Fiesta platters for 4 to 10 people. Take-out and catering is also available. No matter the size of your party you are bound to savor and enjoy this food. Burritos Fiesta Fresh Mexican Grill is open daily for lunch and dinner.

Buster's Restaurant and Bar $$
1800 South Milton Road
(928) 774-5155

Known as the "local eatery," Buster's is an oasis in the desert. Featuring an oyster bar, fresh fish, and certified Angus steak, its contemporary yet comfortable atmosphere assures a top-notch dining experience. Salads, burgers, steak, and chicken fajitas are lunchtime favorites. Dinner entrees come with a choice of homemade soup or crisp salad. Looking for something a little out of the ordinary? Try the halibut poached in pistachio parchment. The Chicken Sonoma smothered with artichoke hearts, tomatoes, and mushrooms simmered in a Chardonnay will make you a regular customer. Reservations are accepted and diners can choose to eat in the bar or restaurant. The beer list is extensive, sporting numerous imported and domestic beers. The wine list is traditional and features California whites and reds. If a frozen or umbrella-style drink calls, consult the nearest drink list for an original tasty concoction. Buster's is open daily for lunch and dinner and is wheelchair accessible. (See the Nightlife section for more about Buster's.)

Charly's Pub & Grille in the Historic Hotel Weatherford $$
23 North Leroux Street
(928) 779-1919
www.weatherfordhotel.com

Built in 1900, this casual lunch or dinner institution takes the customer on a historic sojourn back to the early 20th century. The proprietors of Charly's saved the building from destruction 25 years ago. Since the purchase, the building has been under a constant restoration and renovating process. Seasonal outdoor dining is available for lunch and dinner. The lunch menu includes sandwiches, southwestern dishes, and fresh salads. Dinner at Charly's features traditional pub food and innovative entrees including steak, fish, and chicken. The Salmon Escondido is wrapped in a cornhusk with peppers and onions, and simmered in a teriyaki and prickly pear marinade. All dinner entrees come with homemade soup or salad. The wine list is well-rounded and the beer list is extensive, including locally brewed and imported beers. Reservations are accepted for parties of six or more.

If late-afternoon drinks and appetizers are called for, take the stairs up three flights (there is no elevator) to the Zane Grey Ballroom. Decorated in turn-of-the-20th-century style, with a fully restored bar from Tombstone, Arizona, the room is elegant but casual. Stroll along the restored balcony that wraps around the building for some of the best views of the city and the peaks. Open from 5:00 P.M. until closing, the Zane Grey serves drinks and yummy appetizers. Try one of its imported beers on tap and piping-hot, baked spinach artichoke dip. (See the Nightlife section for more about Charly's Zane Grey Ballroom.)

Cottage Place Restaurant   **$$$**
126 West Cottage Avenue
(928) 774-8431
www.cottageplace.com
This is one of Flagstaff's true fine-dining experiences. Set inside a Craftsman-style home built in 1909, the restaurant's intimate yet comfortable atmosphere is a favorite among locals and tourists. The service is attentive and friendly without being obtrusive. Cottage Place serves a traditional continental/American menu, with table-side specialties. The Caesar Salad for Two combines crisp romaine lettuce with a classic Caesar dressing and is prepared table side. Chateaubriand for Two includes a tenderloin roast carved table side and served with garlic duchess potatoes and tomato Provençal. The menu also includes beef, veal, fresh seafood, and vegetarian dishes. To complete your succulent meal, dessert is a must. Choose one of the many homemade options from the dessert tray. The Chocolate Decadence, a flourless chocolate cake topped with chantilly crème and served with raspberry puree, is to die for. Cottage Place also serves a prix fixe menu with optional wine pairings Thursday through Saturday evenings, with six courses including a flambé dessert. The restaurant serves beer and wine; the extensive wine list includes more than 250 varieties, and the list has routinely won the Award of Excellence from *Wine Spectator* magazine. Reservations are required. Cottage Place is open for dinner Tuesday through Saturday.

Crown Railroad Café   **$**
3300 East Route 66
(928) 522-9237
2700 South Woodlands Village Boulevard
(928) 774-6775
With an electric toy train circling the dining rooms of both locations of the Crown Railroad Café and decidedly 1950s diner atmospheres, kids tend to love stopping in at both locations for eats. The Crown serves breakfast, lunch, and dinner seven days a week, and diners show up all day long for solid food like the meat loaf; a variety of burgers with fresh fries; big, floppy pancakes; and omelets not meant for small appetites. Both restaurants serve beer and wine, and you can pay with your Visa or MasterCard (cash is also accepted).

Dara Thai   **$$**
14 South San Francisco Street
(928) 774-0047
As you walk into this lively restaurant, you will notice the brightly painted walls with

palm trees, exotic flowers, and the line of people. The decorated walls will promptly put you in the right frame of mind. Relax and enjoy the experience. Try a Singha, a Thai beer, or a refreshing mai tai while you wait for a table. The restaurant specializes in coconut curry sauces, and all dishes can be made vegetarian and as spicy as you like. They use the star system to rate the spiciness. Two to two-and-a-half stars is medium; five stars is hot. Then comes Thai hot or extra Thai hot. Pad Thai is a house favorite, rice noodles in a sweet sauce topped with ground peanuts, chicken, and shrimp. Another favorite is the Gaeng Kari, a yellow coconut curry sauce with potatoes, carrots, peppers, and your choice of chicken, beef, pork, or deep-fried tofu. Dara Thai is open for lunch and dinner every day. Reservations are accepted for parties of four or more.

Jitters Gourmet Coffee and Cafe $
3504 East Route 66
(928) 526-6964

This bright atmosphere is sure to make a morning person out of anyone. Unique gift items (including homemade fudge), local and regional newspapers, and colorful tabletops ensure a morning, afternoon, or evening well spent. The breakfast menu is limited. Choose from pastries, cereal, or a breakfast bagel sandwich with your choice of bagel, scrambled egg, and cheese (ham is optional). The lunch menu is delightful. Jitters is known for homemade soup, gourmet sandwiches, and a personal touch. Have a special request or in a funky mood? Just ask the friendly staff and they will personalize your order. All menu items from the six varieties of quiche, to the

Whether it's a cold blustery day, or you are just looking for an afternoon treat, head to Macy's European Coffee House, Bakery, and Restaurant for a delicious Macy's hot chocolate with homemade whipped cream.

sticky buns, to the chocolate walnut fudge are homemade. In addition to the great food and casual atmosphere, Jitters has specialty coffee drinks and a variety of teas. Outdoor seating is available. Jitters is open seven days a week. The cafe does not accept credit cards.

La Bellavia $
18 South Beaver Street
(928) 774-8301
Brandy's Restaurant and Bakery $
1500 East Cedar Avenue, #40
(928) 779-2187
www.brandysrestaurant.com

La Bellavia has been a Flagstaff institution since 1976. The encore to the popular La Bellavia restaurant was the opening of Brandy's in 1993. Whether you decide to dine at the downtown location or the eastside restaurant you will not be disappointed. La Bellavia serves wonderful, fresh breakfast and lunch items in their small, casual space downtown. The restaurant often features the work of local artists on the walls, and the ceiling is intriguingly painted with clouds. An outdoor patio area surrounded by a white picket fence makes for lovely summertime eating. The restaurant serves a variety of pancakes, muffins, quiches, soups, and sandwiches, including the Beaver Street Club and Eggs Neptune. La Bellavia is open daily for breakfast and lunch.

Brandy's menu is a mix of traditional breakfast and lunch items and unique dishes that are made from scratch. All of the recipes are Brandy's own concoctions. Everything from the hollandaise sauce to the peaches-and-cream danish is homemade. Breakfasts are, to put it simply, huge. Just try and finish a stack of Swedish oat pancakes with hot cinnamon apple topping. Phoenicians (people from Phoenix) drive for two-and-a-half hours just for the award-winning trout and eggs. All breakfasts come with a choice of potatoes or buttermilk pancakes, and toast or English muffin. Both breakfast and lunch menus offer vegetarian options galore.

Brandy's Art Gallery

As you enter Brandy's Restaurant or La Bellavia you will notice the aroma of fresh-roasted coffee, the case of homemade pastries, and the colorful artwork hanging on the walls. Why does the owner of these popular restaurants choose to decorate the walls with artwork? Because amidst the talented and diverse community of Flagstaff, Brandy realized she had the perfect venue to support local artists. By combining food and art, Brandy's and La Bellavia offer a place for people to come together as a community. The regular clientele comes to enjoy good food and to discuss and critique the displayed artwork, which stimulates conversations between staff and customers. Most diners would not expect to walk in and find the work of Navajo artist Shonto Begay hanging above them as they eat their breakfast.

Flagstaff and its surrounding areas have a tremendous number of talented artists who are looking for exposure, and this venue features local and professional artists who clamor to get on the two-year waiting list.

As a mother of two, Brandy realizes the importance of introducing art to children. Local high schools are invited each year to display the work of their students. The kids enjoy bringing their parents, knowing that their work is displayed. Brandy also dedicates a month to the Plein-Air Artists of Northern Arizona and to the Hozhoni Foundation, a foundation for developmentally disabled adults, who produce artwork in pencil, acrylics, and woodwork. Each show lasts for a month and the artist is welcomed with a reception, which is open to the public. Check for reception dates and times in *Flagstaff Live!* While you're checking out the art, be sure to peruse, mingle, and sample some of Brandy's famous goodies.

The Reuben with avocado and tomato is a hit. Brandy's is open daily for breakfast and lunch and serves dinner Tuesday through Saturday.

**Macy's European Coffee House,
Bakery, and Restaurant $
14 South Beaver Street
(928) 774-2243
www.macyscoffee.com**
This in-house bakery and restaurant caters to vegetarians, vegans, and anyone who loves good food. All menu items are made on the premises and, in the Macy's tradition, "baked with love." Breakfast, lunch,

and dinner are served daily. Check out the bakery case to see the fresh, homemade specialties of the day. The chalkboard menus include vegetarian sandwiches served on whole wheat molasses bread, salads, and breakfast specials from steamed eggs with the veggies of your choice to oatmeal to breakfast couscous. Don't walk by the daily special board. Try the ever-changing lasagna special prepared with fresh pasta. All items on the specials chalkboard come with salad greens and whole wheat molasses bread. The coffee is roasted in Macy's own roaster every morning. An eclectic blend of people

meet here to play chess, chat, and eat delicious home-baked goodies. The walls are covered with paintings by local artists. The staff is always friendly and ready to help. People from all walks of life are welcomed here; this place has a true community spirit. Macy's does not accept credit cards.

Main Street Grill and Catering $
16 East Route 66, Suite 103
(928) 774-1519

If you hear the sound of singing voices coming from a restaurant kitchen, go no farther. That's just the staff of Main Street Grill, and you know you are in the right place. Gourmet sandwiches, quality ingredients, and lunch items with a twist are the house specialties. Try the Main Street Philly, a half loaf of shepherd's bread stuffed with steak, chicken, or veggies, with cheese, onions, chiles, and a side of marinara; the smoked turkey sandwich piled high with avocado, sprouts, and Havarti cheese; or the Caesar salad with fresh turkey or portobello mushroom and roasted garlic. All salads are made with organic greens with your choice of a homemade dressing. The specials board has two daily homemade soups. Don't miss Mulligatawny Wednesday. This creamy curry soup is combined with apple and chicken to delight the senses. Save room for dessert. The cappuccino brownie is pure decadence and you won't mind skipping dessert for a week. Place your order at the counter, slide into one of the retro-style booths, and get ready for a mouth-watering experience! Main Street is open Monday through Saturday for lunch only and does not accept credit cards.

Mamma Luisa Italian Restaurant $$
2710 North Steves Boulevard
(928) 526-6809

Italian food like your mother (if she were Italian) would make. Walking through the door of this establishment is like walking into Little Italy in New York City. The restaurant is warm and cozy with red-check tablecloths. The recipes come from the original owner's mama who was from Italy. As the restaurant changed hands, the present chef kept the recipes intact, but added vegetarian options. The cuisine is a combination of northern and southern Italian with thick red sauces, tangy pesto, or rich marsala. Dedicated to serving the finest wine and food, Mamma Luisa promises all entrees are made to order, including the lasagna. Chicken, veal, and shrimp dishes are the specialties. Ask for the daily special, and if you're lucky *zuppa pesce* will be featured. Mamma Luisa's is open daily for dinner. Reservations are accepted and recommended on the weekend.

Martans Burrito Palace $
10 North San Francisco Street
(928) 773-4701

Right in the heart of downtown Flagstaff you'll find a little bit of Mexico. Postcards from locals and tourists alike hang on the walls. These are testimonies of trips taken, hometown greetings, or just a simple "thank you" from customers around the world. The atmosphere is as homemade as the food. Seat yourself if you can find a table. What better way to start the day off than with an order of homemade chorizo con huevos or the ever popular *chilaquiles,* scrambled eggs mixed with onions, corn tortillas, enchilada sauce, and topped with cheddar and Jack cheese? All breakfasts are served with rice, beans, and hash browns. Lunches are more than generous. Look for the daily special, and posole with corn or flour tortilla is always on hand. This is a great place to go before a big hike or if you're on your way to Grand Canyon. Open daily for breakfast and lunch. Martans does not accept credit cards.

Pasto $$
19 East Aspen Avenue
(928) 779-1937

As you turn onto Aspen Avenue, the smell of garlic will lead you in the right direction. A local favorite, this restaurant's intimate setting, with its crisp white linen tablecloths, is perfect for a first date or a large party. Dark stone walls complement

The intimate Pasto restaurant, on East Aspen Avenue in downtown Flagstaff, serves fine Italian food in an elegant yet comfortable atmosphere. TODD R. BERGER

this affordable yet elegant Italian eatery. Tantalizing dishes await you as your dining experience begins with a plate of drizzled olive oil for dipping chunks of fresh, crusty bread. For a more than auspicious beginning, the Prince Edward Sound mussels appetizer with chunks of garlic and ripe tomatoes is a must. The entrees include various types of homemade pasta with nine tempting sauces that range in spiciness and flavors. The atomic marinara with crushed red pepper and cayenne is for adventurous eaters only. Entrees include chicken, veal, and seafood dishes. The Balsamic Salmon is poached and simmered with artichoke hearts, mushrooms, and fresh basil, and served over orecchiette (an ear-shaped pasta). The attentive and friendly servers are well educated in wine. The wine selection is sure to please the toughest of palettes. Or you can choose from a selection of imported and local microbrewed beers. All desserts are homemade. The tiramisu, made especially by the owner, is a must. Reservations are recommended. Ask for a table for two by the window. A great view of the downtown area gives you a feel for the local scene. Pasto is open daily for dinner.

Pesto Brothers Deli Market Ristorante $$
34 South San Francisco Street
(928) 913–0775
www.pestobrothers.com
Pesto Brothers has been catering (no pun intended) to the culinary needs of Flagstaff for several years now and has consistently delighted all who dine here. Their motto, "For the love of food," can be tasted in their robust sandwiches stuffed with imported cheeses and meats and dripping with tasty oils and sauces. Pesto Brothers offers a nice selection of imported cheeses (raclette, blue Stilton, taleggio, and belletoile among others), Greek and Italian olive oil, Belgian chocolates, Italian meats (prosciutto di Parma, cappacola, and Genoa salami, etc.) and, of course, homemade pesto. You can

order a sandwich (don't forget a canolli) and eat in the cozy, relaxed dining room. You are bound to overhear the conversations of NAU students and faculty discussing the likes of Hemingway, the pros and cons of prescribed forest burns, or just how fabulous their sandwiches are. Pesto Brothers also offers take-out and catering and is open for lunch Monday through Saturday and for dinner Tuesday through Saturday.

The Place: Mike and Rhonda's
Restaurant   **$**
3518 East Route 66, Suite 107
(928) 526–8138
21 South Milton
(928) 774–7008
Known for their breakfasts, Mike and Rhonda's two locations are prime destinations for locals, students, and families. With cheap prices and specialties like biscuits and gravy, most patrons go away well satiated. Both restaurants are open daily for breakfast and lunch, and Tuesday through Saturday for dinner. The restaurants accept Visa and MasterCard, and neither serves alcohol.

Sakura Restaurant   **$$–$$$**
Radisson Woodlands Hotel
1175 West Route 66
(928) 773–9118
If an entertaining and exotic evening is planned, try the Japanese menu at Sakura, which was nominated by *Food & Wine* magazine as one of the top 100 restaurants in the Southwest. Customers may either dine at a table or sit at a Teppanyaki grill. (Pick the grill!) A trained Teppan chef prepares teriyaki or hibachi-style chicken, beef, and seafood dishes in traditional Japanese fashion. The New York steak and lobster combination is a favorite among regulars. All dinner entrees come with soup, steamed rice, and fresh vegetables. Any sushi lover will devour the made-to-order specialties. Ask for the daily sushi specials and current market prices. A wine list, Japanese

beers, and sake are available. Sakura is open daily for dinner. Reservations are highly recommended.

ATTRACTIONS

Mingling Native American influences and western tradition, Flagstaff is a city that is surrounded by natural wonders and a diverse cultural history.

While you visit local museums, ancient ruins, and historic homes, you will glimpse the lives of the pioneers and Native Americans who have cultivated this land and made this area their home. Visitors will learn about native plant life, hike to ancient pueblos, and admire turn-of-the-20th-century architecture. As you take time to understand past generations, you will discover a rich heritage that is continuing into the future. Flagstaff is proud to hold onto its identity by preserving natural and popular attractions for locals and visitors to share. It is not one strand that defines this city, but rather a multitude of fibers that have been woven together to produce a thriving community.

The Arboretum at Flagstaff
4001 South Woody Mountain Road
(928) 774-1442
www.thearb.org
The arboretum is dedicated to helping visitors understand the native plants of the Colorado Plateau. At 7,150 feet in elevation, the arboretum is an educational adventure. Study one of the 250 types of herbs in the herb garden, or view the San Francisco Peaks from the 1.2-mile nature trail. Visit the constructed wetlands or the solar greenhouse. Bring your binoculars; there are guided bird walks. Educational outings and programs are offered for children and adults. The arboretum is open daily April 1 to December 15 and is located 3.8 miles south of West Route 66 on Woody Mountain Road. Admission is $4.00 for adults, $3.00 for seniors, $1.00 for children 6 to 12, and kids under 6 are admitted free. (See

the Flagstaff Kidstuff section for more on educational programs.)

Arizona Historical Society Pioneer Museum
2340 North Fort Valley Road
(928) 774-6272
www.infomagic.net/~ahsnad
The Pioneer Museum was first a hospital, then a boarding home, before it was bought by the Historical Society in 1960 and turned into a museum. The museum specializes in exhibits that are representative of the history of Flagstaff and northern Arizona. In addition to displaying an extensive collection of artifacts, photographs, and memorabilia, the museum sponsors annual exhibits such as *Playthings of the Past,* and annual events, such as the Wool Festival. (Refer to the Flagstaff Annual Events section for more information.) Admission is free to the Pioneer Museum, but donations are greatly appreciated. The museum is open Monday through Saturday.

Elden Pueblo Indian Ruins
U.S. Highway 89 North
(928) 526-0866
Elden Pueblo, which is still being excavated, offers a unique opportunity to understand the archaeology of the ancestral Puebloan people of northern Arizona. The ruins are located just past the Mount Elden Lookout trailhead on the left side of U.S. 89. Visitors have a choice between the self-guided tour, which allows you to observe the ruins without disturbing them, or participation in a group dig coordinated by the Elden Pueblo Archaeology Program. This educational program teaches archaeological skills, concepts, and laws. Open daily.

Lowell Observatory
1400 West Mars Hill Road
(928) 774-3358
www.lowell.edu
Learn about the wonders of the sky at Lowell Observatory. The public can view the daytime sky through specially

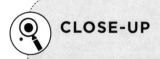
Elden Pueblo

Introduce yourself and your children to the wonders of archaeology, and to the indigenous peoples who once lived in the area around Flagstaff, with a quick tour of Elden Pueblo, just a few minutes north of downtown on U.S. Highway 89.

This partially excavated archaeological site was inhabited by the Sinagua (see-na-wa) who lived in the Flagstaff area from about A.D. 700 to 1400. The word *Sinagua* means "without water" and refers to the semiarid high desert conditions of this area.

The Sinagua at Elden Pueblo built aboveground stone houses like those some of the Pueblo tribes occupy today. They made brownware and redware pottery and traded their pots for items such as shells, jewelry, macaws, minerals, and copper bells. Some of the trade items came from as far away as Mexico. You can learn more about the *Sinagua* by visiting the Museum of Northern Arizona, Wupatki National Monument, and Walnut Canyon National Monument.

The 70 rooms that make up Elden Pueblo, which is named for the mountain behind the site, were inhabited from about A.D. 1070 to 1275. A large "dormitory" room suggests that Elden Pueblo may have been a center of trade, as was Wupatki.

In 1926, Dr. Jesse Walter Fewkes, an archaeologist for the Smithsonian Institution, excavated some of the rooms at Elden Pueblo. While the site was not made into a national monument as he had hoped, it is nonetheless open to the public year-round. Modern-day Hopi, a Pueblo people who now live on three mesas northeast of Flagstaff, consider Elden Pueblo to be a place important in their ancestral history. They call it "Pasiovi" or "Pavasioki."

To get to the pueblo, drive north on U.S. 89 past the Flagstaff Mall on your right. The sign for the pueblo is on your left, just before the traffic light at Townsend-Winona Road. Parking is plentiful, and there is no entrance fee.

Self-guided tours are available at this site, which is used to train archaeologists. The forest service holds several Public Dig Days, usually on weekends, in the summer and the fall, during which adults and children can help professional archaeologists excavate the site and look for treasures—pottery shards, feathers, bones of animals used for food, and the remains of tools.

As at all archaeological sites you visit, do not remove anything, however insignificant it may seem. Vegetation, pot shards, stones, pebbles—everything here is part of the archaeological record.

For more information and a schedule of educational activities held at Elden Pueblo, write Coconino National Forest, Archaeology Section, 2323 East Greenlaw Lane, Flagstaff, AZ 86004 or visit the Coconino National Forest office on U.S. 89 just about a mile south of the pueblo.

filtered telescopes. Tours include a presentation explaining the beginnings and history of Lowell Observatory. Preceding the presentation, the public is invited to tour the telescopes. There is also a hands-on exhibit for children and adults of all ages. The observatory is located 1 mile west of downtown Flagstaff. Open daily; call the observatory for special events and hours. Remember that the observatory tours and events are weather permitting. (For more information about viewing the night sky, see the Flagstaff Nightlife section.)

Museum of Northern Arizona
3101 North Fort Valley Road
(928) 774-5213
www.musnaz.org
Founded in 1928, the Museum of Northern Arizona has more than five million pieces in its permanent collections and is home to a life-size skeletal model of Dilophosaurus, a carnivorous dinosaur of the Colorado Plateau. Dedicated to preserving the natural and cultural history of the Colorado Plateau, the museum sponsors year-round events, exhibits, and seminars for children and adults, including the Heritage Program, a summerlong celebration of Native American art. The museum is open daily and is located on U.S. Highway 180 on the way to Grand Canyon. Admission is $5.00 adults, $4.00 seniors, $3.00 college students, and $2.00 children ages 7 to 17. Members get in free.

Northern Arizona University
North Campus
South San Francisco Street
(928) 523-5511
www.nau.edu
With its sandstone buildings and white pillars, the 100-year-old North Campus of NAU is a testimonial to Flagstaff at the turn of the 20th century. Old Main was built in 1894 and was originally proposed to be a home for juvenile delin-

quents. The town objected and the building eventually became the Northern Arizona Normal School in 1899. Other buildings of interest on North Campus include the Blome Building and North Morton Hall, which is believed to be haunted. (Old Main is now home to the Old Main Gallery; see the Flagstaff Arts section.)

Riordan Mansion State Historic Park
409 Riordan Road
(928) 779-4395
www.pr.state.az.us/parkhtml/riordan.html
This historic building was built in 1904 and has 40 rooms with more than 13,000 square feet of living area. Interesting features of the Riordan home are the rustic log-slab siding exterior, volcanic stone arches, and hand-split wooden shingles. The park's visitor center offers a slide program, exhibit area, and a children's "touch table." A guided tour of the interior of the mansion is the only way to see it. Don't miss the holidays tours at the mansion during the month of December (See the Flagstaff Annual Events section for more information.) The park is surrounded by six acres of pine and has picnic tables for visitors. The park is open daily and is located next to Northern Arizona University. Reservations are recommended for tours. Call Riordan Mansion for current hours and entrance fees.

RECREATION

Flagstaff boasts almost 300 days of sunshine a year throughout its four distinct seasons. The diverse terrain of the Colorado Plateau ensures plentiful outdoor recreational activities any time of the year. Whether you are a hardcore outdoor enthusiast or a first-time skier, people of all fitness levels will agree that the scenery is beautiful and the outdoor recreational activities are endless.

The Museum of Northern Arizona, on North Fort Valley Road (U.S. Highway 180) north of downtown Flagstaff, houses everything from prehistoric sandals worn by the ancestral Puebloan people to a life-size model of a Dilophosaurus. TODD R. BERGER

Bike Rentals

Pedal your way through the streets of downtown, coast along the Flagstaff Urban Trail System, or plan a mountain bike excursion for the whole family with the help of the following bike shops. Suggested mountain bike rides can be found in the Coconino National Forest chapter. (Refer to the Flagstaff Shopping section for more information on bike shops.)

Absolute Bikes
18 North San Francisco Street
(928) 779-5969
www.absolutebikes.com
This shop located in historic downtown Flagstaff rents front- or full-suspension mountain bikes. Rentals start at $25 for front-suspension and $35 for full-suspension mountain bikes. Absolute also sells many of the major brands of mountain bikes, road bikes, and hybrids, as well as all of the equipment you need for the saddle, from Yakima car racks to Oakley sunglasses. Open daily.

Cosmic Cycles
901 North Beaver Street
(928) 779-1092
This shop can get you up and riding with their selection of rigid-, front-, or full-suspension mountain bikes ($25 for front-suspension and $45 for full-suspension mountain bikes). Look for it near the Flagstaff Medical Center. Cosmic Cycles is open Monday through Saturday.

Single Track Mountain Bikes
575 West Riordan Road
(928) 773-1862
Single Track can outfit the entire family with state-of-the-art mountain bike rentals. Front-suspension rentals (only) are $25.00 for the first day, after which the price decreases $5.00 each day. So the second day would be $20.00, and so on. Single Track is open daily from late March to early November, and Monday through Saturday from November to late March.

Don't forget to wear your helmet! If you are renting bikes to cruise around downtown or try a new mountain bike trail, rent helmets for the whole family.

Bowling

Starlite Lanes
3406 East Route 66
(928) 526-1138
Starlite Lanes has 16 lanes with automatic scoring. Open bowling is available to the public every Saturday. They even have Bumper Bowling for kids. Starlite Lanes has a cocktail lounge, a satellite dish, and a full-service Pro Shop. The cost per game to bowl ranges from $2.00 to $3.00, depending upon the day of the week. Shoe rental is $1.75. Prices are the same for kids and adults. Open daily. Call ahead for open-bowling times.

Camping and RV Parks

These accommodations make camping and roughing it in the outdoors a little bit easier.

Black Barts RV Park
2760 East Butler Avenue
(928) 774-1912
Black Barts offers all the necessary amenities for camping, including an antiques store, full hookups, general store, shower, laundry, and steakhouse with saloon. RV spaces with full hookups are $20 per night.

Flagstaff KOA
5803 North U.S. Highway 89
(928) 526-9926, (800) KOA-FLAG
www.koakampgrounds.com
Flagstaff KOA is conveniently located on U.S. Highway 89 as you enter Flagstaff from Page or Utah. The KOA is close to the Flagstaff Mall and other shopping conveniences. Flagstaff KOA offers showers,

If you are visiting northern Arizona from July through September, be prepared for monsoon season. The sometimes-wicked afternoon storms will roll in with dark clouds and heavy winds. During monsoon season, try to plan your outdoor recreational activities for early morning, and don't forget to bring your rain jacket.

laundry, general store, and camp kitchen for breakfast. The campground is open all night with night drop or morning payment options. Tent sites are $22 per night and RV spaces with full hookups are $28 per night.

Fort Tuthill Campground
Arizona Highway 89A
(928) 774-3464
co.coconino.az.us/tmp/
This campground is close to town, the Flagstaff Urban Trail System, shopping, and restaurants. It also offers the seclusion of ponderosa pines for those who want to commune with nature without giving up store and shower amenities. The campground is 3 miles south of Flagstaff at exit 337 off Interstate 17. Tent and RV sites with partial hookups are available. Sites without hookups are $9.00 per night, and sites with partial hookups are $13.00 per night.

Woody Mountain Campground and RV Park
2727 West Route 66
(928) 774-7727, (800) 732-7986
This is luxury camping at its best! Woody Mountain Campground has a heated outdoor swimming pool, store, laundry, playground, propane, and tent and RV camping spaces with full hookups. Tent sites are $16 per night; RV sites are $21 per night.

 Buffalo Park has exercise stations that will encourage fun and fitness any day of the week.

City Parks and Recreation

For general information on Flagstaff's city parks and recreation departments, call (928) 779-7690, or visit the Web site www.flagstaff.az.gov.

Bark Park
600 North Thorpe Road
Dog lovers and their dogs can roam freely inside this enclosed park, which is divided into areas for large and small dogs. From May through October, dogs can refresh themselves at a hose bib. Humans have their own sitting area.

Buffalo Park
West of Gemini Drive off Cedar Hill
Buffalo Park has 163 acres of natural plateau and hills. Known for its breathtaking views of the San Francisco Peaks and Mount Elden, the park has a 2-mile walking/jogging course with exercise stations. Runners, walkers, and cross-country skiers enjoy this expansive acreage. Buffalo Park is adjacent to McPherson Park.

Bushmaster Park
3150 North Alta Vista Road
Bushmaster Park is Flagstaff's most popular park because it offers outdoor amenities for the whole family, including picnic facilities, footpaths, playgrounds, tennis and basketball courts, and a BMX skate park.

McPherson Park
1650 North Turquoise Drive
McPherson Park is made up of 43 acres and connects with Buffalo Park by various hiking trails. The park has outdoor tennis courts and playground equipment, and is home to the Jay Lively Activity Center, the seasonal ice and roller skating rink. (Check out the Jay Lively listing later in this chapter.)

Thorpe Park
245 North Thorpe Road
The recreational opportunities are endless

at this community park. Playgrounds, hiking and running trails, tennis and basketball courts, and lighted ball fields offer year-round family entertainment. Thorpe Park is home to Northern Arizona's premier disc golf course.

Urban Trail System
Flagstaff Visitor Center, 1 East Route 66
(928) 774-9541, (800) 842-7293
This citywide network of trails is closed to motorized transportation. Twenty miles of trails connect neighborhoods, schools, and community activity centers, while providing alternative methods of transportation and exercise. Open year-round, this trail system offers bicycling, running, cross-country skiing and walking opportunities for both visitors and residents. A map of the Flagstaff Urban Trail System can be purchased for $1.00 at the Flagstaff City Hall in the Parks and Recreation office, 211 West Aspen Avenue, (928) 774-5281.

Cross-country Skiing and Snowshoeing

Flagstaff Nordic Center
U.S. Highway 180, past Arizona Snowbowl
(928) 779-1951 ext. 195
www.arizonasnowbowl.com
The Flagstaff Nordic Center is 13 miles north of Flagstaff on U.S. 180. The center has more than 40 kilometers of groomed ski trails and 15 kilometers of snowshoe trails. Equipment rentals and private and group lessons are available. An all-day pass (9:00 A.M. to 4:00 P.M.) is $10.00. Kids seven and under are admitted free. The day snowshoe pass is $5.00. Open daily from mid-December through April as long as snowpack permits skiing. Call ahead for current conditions.

Ski, snowboard, or ride the skyride at the Arizona Snowbowl for free on your birthday. Valid identification is needed for your complimentary ticket. Kids 7 and under and seniors 70 and older ski or sky ride for free year-round.

Discovery Programs

Museum of Northern Arizona Discovery Programs
3101 North Fort Valley Road
(928) 774-5211
www.musnaz.org
For students of all ages, the Discovery Programs offer field studies, workshops, and intergenerational excursions designed to promote the arts, sciences, history, and cultures of the Colorado Plateau. Call to make reservations. The program runs June through September. (For more information about the Museum of Northern Arizona, see the Flagstaff Attractions section.)

Golf

Continental Country Club Golf Course
2380 North Oakmont Drive
(928) 527-7997 (information)
(928) 527-7999 (tee times)
Although Flagstaff does not have as many golf courses as the Phoenix area, it makes up for the lack of quantity with Continental Country Club Golf Course, home to the Northern Arizona University women's golf team. The 6,029-yard course is considered one of the state's finest. The course is open daily March or April through November, weather permitting, and offers tee times up to 14 days in advance. Summer rates are $22 to walk and $34 to ride during the week. Call for weekend rates.

The Northern Arizona University Lumberjacks sports teams play many of their home matches at the J. Lawrence Walkup Skydome, including the football, basketball, track and field, men's soccer, and lacrosse teams. TODD R. BERGER

Hayrides and Cookouts

Arizona Snowbowl
Snowbowl Road
(928) 774-4481
www.arizonasnowbowl.com
Get a true taste for the West with a hayride and an outdoor meal. Day or evening cookouts are available. Reservations are required; make your reservations in advance. A hayride runs $10, with additional charges for the "cowboy cookout" option. Open every day except Wednesday.

Horseback Riding

Arizona Snowbowl
Snowbowl Road
(928) 774-4481
www.arizonasnowbowl.com
Take a one-hour ride through the Coconino National Forest with experienced wranglers. Enjoy the quiet and solitude of northern Arizona on horseback. All rides begin and end at the Fort Valley Barn on U.S. Highway 180 and Snowbowl Road. Guided horseback rides start at 8:00 A.M. and the last ride leaves at 5:00 P.M. Open every day except Wednesday. Call for reservations and rates.

Flying Heart Barn
8400 North U.S. Highway 89
(928) 526-2788
Let experienced wranglers show you the ropes and the scenery as you ride along the trails of the Coconino National Forest. Daylong sightseeing trips along well-maintained trails are available, as are one- and two-hour trail rides. Open for rides Monday through Saturday year-round. Rides may not be available when the weather is bad. Contact Flying Heart for current rates and times.

Hitchin' Post Stables
4848 Lake Mary Road
(928) 774-1719, (928) 774-7131
Hitchin' Post Stables offers rides for all levels of riders. Explore Native American ruins and caves in Walnut Canyon or take the sunset ride to an authentic western campsite with cowboys cooking over an open fire and live entertainment. Hayrides and pack trips are available. Open daily. Rides may not be available when the weather is bad. Call for current rates.

Ice/Roller Skating

Jay Lively Activity Center
1650 North Turquoise Drive #B
(928) 774-1051
Skating is fun exercise for kids of all ages (and adults too!). Roller skating begins in June and ends in the beginning of August. Ice-skating season runs mid-September through the end of April. Lessons, public skating, and hockey are offered. Open daily. Contact the activity center for admission prices and open skating hours.

River Trips

Several river outfitters operate out of Flagstaff, organizing trips on the Colorado River through Grand Canyon and elsewhere throughout the Southwest. For more information, see the Grand Canyon—South Rim and Backcountry chapter.

Rock Climbing

Vertical Relief
205 South San Francisco Street
(928) 556-9909
www.verticalrelief.com
With more than 6,000 square feet of climbing space and 40-foot walls, Vertical Relief offers quality rock-climbing lessons and equipment for locals and travelers. Indoor climbing allows people of all ages and abilities to experience rock climbing in a safe and managed atmosphere. Day passes are $14 ($12 for students). Vertical Relief is open seven days a week.

Skiing/Snowboarding

Arizona Snowbowl
Snowbowl Road
(928) 779-1951
www.arizonasnowbowl.com
The Arizona Snowbowl has a vertical drop of 2,300 feet and 32 trails for beginners through experts. Arizona gets most of its snowfall during the spring, and the mountain may be open as late as April or early May. Snowbowl offers ski and snowboard packages and daily private, group, and children's lessons. The packages include a ski lift ticket, rentals, and a two-hour lesson. You can purchase half- and full-day passes for children and adults. Full-day passes are $40 for adults, $22 for children ages 8 to 12, and $20 for seniors.

Snowbowl also has a full-service equipment rental and repair shop and two restaurants (each with its own bar). The Agassiz Lodge features live music on weekends.

Skyrides

The Scenic Skyride at Arizona Snowbowl
Snowbowl Road
P.O. Box 40, Flagstaff 86002
(928) 779-1951
www.arizonasnowbowl.com
This is truly a wonderful way to experience the breathtaking views of northern Arizona. The skyride will take you to an elevation of 11,500 feet with more than 70 miles of amazing scenery. The trip is 25 minutes one-way in an open chairlift. The lift is open daily 10:00 A.M. to 4:00 P.M. from Memorial Day through Labor Day. After Labor Day the lift operates on

The Snowbowl skyride offers scenic views of northern Arizona and Grand Canyon, but be prepared for the change in elevation and in weather. Bring a jacket and wear sneakers or hiking boots to ensure a safe and enjoyable trip.

Friday, Saturday, and Sunday only through mid-October. The cost for adults 13 and up is $10.00; seniors pay $8.00; and the cost for kids ages 8 to 12 is $6.00; kids 7 and under and seniors 70 and older are admitted free. Group rates are available.

SHOPPING

Flagstaff is the retail center for northern Arizona with numerous strip malls and shopping centers. The Flagstaff Mall features national stores and is located on the east side of town. However, in this section we direct you to the quaint boutiques, shops, and trading posts that reflect the true feel of the city.

The downtown area has a concentration of shops, restaurants, and unique gift stores where you will find the perfect souvenir for yourself and anyone on your list. From hand-crafted jewelry to quality outdoor gear to gourmet chocolate, you will find it here. Park your car, stroll through the streets, window-shop, and enjoy the crowd-free streets and the sunshine on your face.

Antiques

Carriage House Antique and Gift Mall
413 North San Francisco Street
(928) 774-1337
Voted best antiques shop in the "Best of Flagstaff" for the past 11 years, Carriage House Antique and Gift Mall is an antiques lover's dream. From furniture, to vintage clothing, to china and silver, you will find a little bit of everything here. This antiques haven is open daily.

The Dragon's Plunder
217 South San Francisco Street
(928) 774-1708
The Dragon's Plunder houses antiques reminiscent of treasures you would find in your grandmother's attic, including collectibles, furniture, and used books. The Dragon's Plunder can be found on the northwest corner of South San Francisco Street and Butler Avenue. Open daily.

The Scenic Skyride at Arizona Snowbowl offers a spectacular view of the Coconino National Forest and surrounding lands. TODD R. BERGER

Books

Aradia Bookstore
116 West Cottage Avenue
(928) 779-3817

Intriguing independent bookstores are becoming a rare breed in Flagstaff and elsewhere, but downtown's Aradia Bookstore is bucking the mass-taste trend with a diverse collection of books on the Southwest, children's books, books and music for women, books on holistic health, Native American literature, and a good selection of greeting cards, magazines, and calendars. Aradia also has a wide selection of new age books, cassettes, and music. Aradia is 2 blocks south of the railroad tracks. Open Monday through Saturday.

Starrlight Books
15 North Leroux Street
(928) 774-6813

Find high-quality new, used, and rare books at Starrlight Books. This quiet bookstore encourages people to browse through their small but particular selection of titles, which includes a children's book area. Starrlight Books focuses on science, Native American, and southwestern titles. Starrlight is open daily.

Clothing

Animas Trading Co.
1 East Aspen Avenue
(928) 773-0004

Shop at Animas and bring out your inner free spirit, hippie, and flower child. This store offers clothing for men, women, and children who wish to wage peace and look great doing it. The women's clothing is made of light cotton and hemp fabrics. It brings out the feminine, gypsy, earth goddess in all who wear it. Be sure to accessorize your clothes with the proper beaded bag, oversize straw hat, retro sunglasses, and platform flip-flops. Once you are properly attired, purchase some incense, candles, and a bumper sticker

that says "My karma ran over your dogma" (or something equally amusing), and you will be well on your way to nirvana. Open daily.

Gene's Western Wear & Shoe Hospital
111 North Leroux Street
(928) 774-3543
www.geneswesternwear.com

Do the clear blue skies and open range make you want to wear a Stetson hat? Do you hear the call of the wide-open spaces and suddenly need a pair of Tony Lama boots? Gene's can outfit the entire family from head to toe in full western apparel. They have a full line of felt and straw hats, shoelaces, boots, and more. This is your cowboy and Native American jewelry headquarters. Gene's is open daily.

Favorites to Wear
10 North Leroux Street
(928) 774-7516

Favorites offers one of the finest selections of women's fashions in northern Arizona. Whether you are looking for that special outfit or a comfortable sweater, Favorites has it. They also have accessories to complete any outfit, including jewelry, hair clips, and lingerie. Favorites is open Monday through Saturday.

Incahoots Vintage Clothing and Costumes
9 East Aspen Avenue
(928) 773-9447

This vintage clothing and costume rental shop is busting at the seams with retro wear from the disco dancing days of the '70s, the groovy '60s, the rocking '50s, and the swinging '40s. You will find classic Levis, albums, and rare turn-of-the-century clothes. Incahoots is open daily.

Sage Brush Trading Co.
Old Town Shops, 120 North Leroux Street
(928) 773-1625

Specializing in stylish and comfortable clothes for men, women, and kids, Sage Brush knows that quality counts. That's why there is a lifetime warranty on every

Gene's Western Wear & Shoe Hospital on North Leroux Street will gladly dude you up or resole your snakeskin boots. TODD R. BERGER

item sold in the store. Sage Brush has a complete line of leather accessories, including shoes, hats, and briefcases. Sage Brush is open daily.

Convenience Stores/ Markets

New Frontiers Natural Marketplace
1000 South Milton Road
(928) 774-5747
This "healthier kind of supermarket" has all-natural and preservative-free food. From hemp products to hormone-free meat to bulk selections, New Frontiers is a healthy alternative for the conscientious eater. Check out the deli's great salads, fresh baked goods, and homemade soups. New Frontiers is open daily.

Pay-N-Take Downtown Market
12 West Aspen Avenue
(928) 226-8595
If you forgot film for your camera or need Advil or snacks for the road, Pay-N-Take will have it. A full espresso bar and tasty homemade pastries are also available. The espresso bar can serve a draft beer or a glass of wine if the mood strikes you. Open daily, this place is a favorite local haunt from happy hour to closing Thursday through Saturday. (See the Flagstaff Nightlife section for more information.)

Gifts

All That Jazz
8 North Leroux Street
(928) 774-6234
Whatever you are looking for, you will find it here. This small shop is packed with sterling silver jewelry and bath and body products that will make you smile and smell good too. They have T-shirts, journals, candles, toys, frames. . . . Must we go on? The owners have done a fine job of stocking their store with eclectic and contemporary gifts for everyone on your souvenir list (even yourself!). All That Jazz is open daily.

Black Hound Gallerie
Old Town Shops, 120 North Leroux Street
(928) 774-2323
One of the most intriguing things about this store is the window display. There is always something hanging in the window that will make a passerby do a double take or help initiate a conversation between strangers. Black Hound has eclectic and mostly off-the-wall gifts, posters, and prints from the masters of art to the legends of jazz. You will enjoy the journals, cards, refrigerator magnets, and pasta that resembles human body parts. Hmm . . . Black Hound Gallerie is open daily.

Candles by Night
113 West Phoenix Avenue
(928) 774-1461
Out on West Phoenix Avenue, even before you enter Candles by Night, your senses will begin to stir. Delicious aromas of vanilla, musk, verbena, lavender, and more flow out to greet you from the open, half door of artist Kelly O'Hair's sensually intoxicating store and studio. Glass candleholders in vibrant colors shine in the windows, casting rays of light across the sumptuously decorated store. The rich oranges, browns, reds, yellows, and purples of her stunning candles massage your eyes. Kelly's cat Niko—part Siamese, part tabby—reclines on a red velvet sofa. On the other side of the store, water falls on glistening stones in a small fountain. It is impossible to keep your hands off of the beautiful, texturally pleasing, aromatic treasures in Candles by Night. Open Monday through Saturday.

Mountain Christmas of Flagstaff
14 North San Francisco Street
(928) 774-5101

It is Christmas every day on San Francisco Street. How could you be a Scrooge with the delightful smell of seasonal spices and selection of hot chocolates warming even the meanest Scrooge's heart? Mountain Christmas sells ornaments, decorations, and seasonal collectibles, including Matchbox and Department 56 items. Open daily (year-round).

P.J. Chilcottage
Old Town Shops, 120 North Leroux Street
(928) 774-0009

At P.J. Chilcottage, you will learn the art of pampering yourself with bath salts, lotions, and massage oils. Rejuvenation is a must as you choose among quality bedding, robes, and P.J.s. Try the "soap bar." Spoil yourself with a piece of Mango Madness or Cinnabun. The whole family can be clean, relaxed, and happy with the help of this store. P.J. Chilcottage is open daily.

Sacred Rites and McCabes' Music
8 North San Francisco Street
(928) 556-0018
www.sacredrites.com

Need a narrow-necked ceramic *doumbek*? What about a standard sitar, bowed psaltry, or a Native American flute (E minor)? Maybe you have been searching for just the right Brasileiro CD for your upcoming samba party or just want to chill to the mesmerizing tunes of Sheila Chandra. Or perhaps your garden shrine just won't be complete until you have found the perfect brass Shiva Nataraja, Celtic cross, menorah, or St. Cecelia plaque. Then Sacred Rites is the store for you. The musical knowledge and expertise combined with a deep understanding of the sacred nature of music of owners Kelly and Tessie McCabe make this a must stop for the musically and spiritually inclined—and they always have tea and cookies on hand, too. Just be forewarned: Even if you can't carry a tune or believe

the entire spiritual world can be understood through a spreadsheet, if you bang on a bodhran at Sacred Rites, you will buy it. Open daily.

Zani Futons & Frames
9 North Leroux Street
(928) 774-9409, (800) 294-9409

As you walk into this store you will feel as if you walked into someone's house. That's because the owners have used the entire space to display their wonderful selection of jewelry, bedding, furniture, cards, journals, and unique gifts. The word is that Zani may be haunted, so don't be surprised if you notice something move out of the corner of your eye. Zani can ship your purchases anywhere, and is open Monday through Saturday.

Jewelry

Jeff Karl Jewelers
204 East Route 66, Suite 204-B
(928) 773-8914

With more than 20 years of experience, Jeff Karl Jewelers is a full-service (repairs are done on the premises) fine jewelry store that specializes in wedding sets and has an extensive selection of Bulova and Seiko watches for men and women. Jeff Karl is known for his uniquely designed custom jewelry. The store is open Tuesday through Saturday.

Native American Trading Companies

Puchteca Indian Goods
20 North San Francisco Street
(928) 774-2414

This store features Native American paintings, pottery, jewelry, and Hopi kachinas. From the Navajo pottery of Alice Cling, to the Hopi pottery of James Nampeyo, to the paintings of the famous artist Harrison Begaye, Puchteca Indian Goods is the only

store in town that hosts an exclusive list of artists. Puchteca is open daily.

Thunder Mountain Traders
20 East Route 66
(928) 779-5291
www.thundermountaintraders.com

This trading company features an extensive collection of cowboy and Native American art, Navajo, Hopi, and Zuni jewelry, books, pottery, and paintings. Be sure to say hello to "Scooter," the owner's dog and Thunder Mountain's official greeter. The store is open daily.

Winter Sun Trading Company
107 North San Francisco Street
(928) 774-2884
www.wintersun.com

A Flagstaff institution since 1976, Winter Sun Trading Company is part gallery and part herb shop. The art gallery features local and Native American artists and has an extensive collection of authentic Hopi kachina carvings. Winter Sun has a large selection of herbs, natural beauty products, teas, and tinctures for optimum health. Winter Sun is open Monday through Saturday. Open Sunday in December only.

---

i

Winter Sun Trading Company sells all-natural beauty products. These face and skin products do not contain alcohol, glycerin, or synthetic chemicals.

Outdoor Clothing/ Gear/Equipment

Absolute Bikes
18 North San Francisco Street
(928) 779-5969
www.absolutebikes.com

Absolute Bikes is your downtown full-service bike store with quality mountain,

road, and recreational bikes and cycling apparel. Absolute rents mountain bikes and can accommodate all sizes. Group rentals are available. Professionally trained mechanics are on duty. Absolute Bikes is open daily.

Aspen Sports
15 North San Francisco Street
(928) 779-1935

Specializing in quality outdoor gear, clothes, and equipment that will help you breeze from one season to the next, Aspen Sports also rents everything for the outdoor enthusiast from cross-country skis, to snowboards, to telemark skis. It is the only shop in town where you can rent white-water rafts and sea kayaks. Aspen Sports is open daily.

Babbitt's Backcountry Outfitters
12 East Aspen Avenue
(928) 774-4775

Babbitt's is stocked with outdoor equipment, apparel, and clothing for all your outdoor needs. With a full-service rental shop, books, maps, and technical gear, Babbitt's is located on the corner of Aspen Avenue and North San Francisco Street. Open daily.

Babbitt's Fly Fishing Specialist
15 East Aspen Avenue
(928) 779-3253

Specializing in everything that makes the ideal fly-fishing experience, Babbitt's is an angler's haven for equipment, clothing, books, maps, and that hard-to-find gift for your favorite angler. Call for the latest fly-fishing classes. Babbitt's also sells Arizona State Fishing Licenses. Open daily.

Cosmic Cycles
901 North Beaver Street
(928) 779-1092

"If you don't like it, bring it back." This motto has been echoed by this full-service bike shop since 1971. Cosmic Cycles guarantees their products and ensures all customers will receive prompt, friendly service. A mechanic is on duty at all times.

Babbitt's Backcountry Outfitters on East Aspen Avenue in downtown Flagstaff offers everything from fleece to Gookinade to fit the needs of anyone wishing to venture into the wilderness. TODD R. BERGER

Check out their cycling apparel, equipment, and hydration systems. Cosmic Cycles is open Monday through Saturday.

Peace Surplus
14 West Route 66
(928) 779-4521
www.peacesurplus.com
Providing northern Arizona with quality outdoor gear since 1976, Peace Surplus has something for everyone. They carry low, medium, and high-end products that are affordable by anyone's standards. They stand by their ever-popular slogan: "If it's outdoors—it's us." Peace Surplus is open daily.

Single Track Mountain Bikes
575 West Riordan Road
(928) 773-1862
For nearly 15 years, Single Track has provided more than bikes to the Flagstaff community. A full-service bike shop known for its efficient and friendly service, Single Track features a complete line of bike accessories, apparel, and equipment, including hydration systems. Professional mechanics are on duty at all times. Single Track has mountain bike rentals for the whole family. Open daily from late March to early November, and Monday through Saturday from November until late March.

Skip the lines at the ski resort, Peace Surplus rents cross-country and downhill skis and snowboards for children and adults.

NIGHTLIFE

When the sun goes down on this small mountain town, put on your dancing shoes! Live entertainment is found on almost every downtown street corner, from funky jazz to hip-hop to toe-tapping bluegrass. Strolling the streets on a starry evening promises to be just as entertaining as the clubs themselves. Street performers provide outdoor entertainment even on the coldest Flagstaff nights. Donations are accepted and always appreciated. Flagstaff is home to Northern Arizona University's 19,000 students, which means there are quite a few college bars with long waiting lines.

Don't worry, barhopping isn't the only thing to do in town. Many of the downtown restaurants serve dinner until 10:00 P.M., but there are a few late-night options mentioned in this section. Special art gallery shows and functions are scheduled throughout the year; check the local arts and entertainment newspaper *Flagstaff Live!* for a complete listing of events and times. Flagstaff has community theater, a symphony, and a university offering top-notch entertainment. Contact individual organizations for a schedule of events and ticket prices.

Bars and Nightclubs

Flagstaff police enforce the state's drinking and driving laws. If you are pulled over with a blood level of .08 percent or more you will spend the night in jail. The best advice is don't drink and drive, and ask a bartender to call a taxi for you. The legal drinking age in the state of Arizona is 21. Supermarkets, liquor stores, and bars sell alcohol until 1:00 A.M. Most bars turn into nightclubs at 9:00 P.M. and charge a small cover to enter. All bars are smoking establishments unless otherwise noted. If you look 35 years of age or younger be prepared to show your ID. If you aren't carrying a U.S. driver's license, passport, or military ID, you will be turned away at the door. Dancing alone or in a group is encouraged—whether you are young or old. The thing about Flagstaff is that the locals like and know how to have fun.

The Alley
22 East Route 66
(928) 774-7929

The Alley is preserving the tradition of its previous owners by continuing to supply "the best music in northern Arizona." Within the Alley's walls, you will find the hottest local, regional, and national bands any day of the week. The stage is in the back of the club and the rustic wooden floor is great for dancing. The down-home atmosphere welcomes both locals and visitors. Pictures of locals and employees hang from the stone walls. Look for the daily drink specials to wet your whistle. On a quiet night, the Alley has a foosball table and two pool tables for entertainment. This building was once home to one of the original bars in town. There is a cover charge for the music, ranging from $1.00 and up.

Beaver Street Brewery & Whistle Stop Cafe
11 South Beaver Street
(928) 779-0079

This upbeat and energetic meeting place for the 30-something-and-over crowd invites great conversation and good times with friends. Serving wine, specialty drinks, and handcrafted ales and lagers brewed on the premises, Beaver Street is a great place for Sunday Bloody Marys, after-the-movie munchies, and just plain socializing. Open seven days a week, Beaver Street serves food in the bar (from a limited menu) until 11:00 P.M. (For more information about Beaver Street Brewery, refer to the Flagstaff Restaurants section.)

Buster's Restaurant & Bar
1800 South Milton Road
(928) 774-5155

A big-screen TV, plenty of tall round tables, and a fireplace are welcoming features on a cold Flagstaff night or for a Sunday-afternoon football game. The beer list is extensive, sporting 66 imported and domestic beers. Happy hour begins at 4:00 P.M. and continues until closing with great drink and appetizer specials. If you are not in the mood to watch the game, slide into a comfortable booth, sip on a margarita, and nosh on some of the tasty appetizers from the only oyster bar in town. If you're in the mood for something different and decadent, consult the nearest drink menu for either a fruity frozen or creamy concoction. Open seven days a week, Buster's serves appetizers in the bar until 11:00 P.M. (Also see the Flagstaff Restaurants section.)

Charly's Pub & Grille in the Historic Hotel Weatherford/Zane Grey Ballroom
23 North Leroux Street
(928) 779-1919
www.weatherfordhotel.com

The band starts at 9:00 P.M. and so do your feet. Dance the night away in Charly's Bar with the local and regional bands who have made this place a local institution. If the dance floor gets too crowded, climb the stairs to the third floor and relax in the turn-of-the-20th-century-style Zane Grey Ballroom. Completely renovated with a restored wraparound balcony and an antique bar from Tombstone, Arizona, this dark and intimate room boasts a fireplace and quaint tables for two. If you have a larger party, feel free to pull a few tables together. The balcony has outside seating and is an interesting way to view the nightlife scene down below. (Also see the Flagstaff Restaurants section.)

Flagstaff Brewing Company
16 East Route 66
(928) 773-1442

The crowd that congregates at the Flagstaff Brewing Company is a mixture of young and old people who just want to have a good time. Brewing beer since 1994, the brewery features seasonal home-brewed ales and lagers on tap. Happy hour is Monday through Friday from 4:30 to 6:30 P.M., and all FBC pints are $2.00. The full bar is stocked with premium liquors and offers one of the finest scotch and bourbon selections in town, with more than 52 single malts to choose from. Just ask your bartender or server for a suggestion. Live entertainment fills the place Thursday through Saturday, and Wednesday night is "Dead Night," when you can hear the best live tapes and recordings from fellow Grateful Dead aficionados. The outside patio is open year-round, so you can soak up the sun, watch the clouds roll in, or watch the snow fall from the sky while you enjoy your beer. Every Saturday night from Memorial Day until late September, FBC hosts their "Party on the Patio" with live music, drink specials, and lots of dancing under the stars.

The drinking age in Arizona is 21. If you look 35 years old or younger be prepared to show proper ID to enter a bar or club. Proper ID consists of a valid U.S. driver's license, passport, or military ID card. If you do not have your ID you will not get in.

Mogollon Brewing Company
15 North Agassiz Street
(928) 773-8950
Old-town rustic and comfortable, this bar and nightclub makes you feel right at home—probably because over 95 percent of the bar was rebuilt using recycled materials mostly from torn-down Flagstaff buildings. Even the wooden bar is made from an old chicken coop. Mogollon makes its own handcrafted beer on the premises. Amber, stout, pale, wheat, and seasonal ales are available on tap. The Sampler Platter is a taste for those who can't decide. Growlers and Mogollon bottled beer are for those who can't stay but are happy to take a brew home. There is live entertainment six nights a week. Happy Hour is from 4:00 to 7:00 P.M. Monday through Friday. Mogollon serves food until midnight. The menu includes pizza, subs, calzones, and apps!

Museum Club
3404 East Route 66
(928) 526-9434
Built in 1931, the Museum Club is the largest log cabin in Arizona. Put your cowboy boots on and get your country fix here. Every Thursday, Friday, and Saturday live music starts at 9:00 P.M. Learn how to two-step on Thursday; dance lessons are free and start at 6:00 P.M. A DJ spins your favorite dance tunes Tuesday and Wednesday nights. Ask the bartender for the weekend drink specials. Expect to pay a $4.00 cover charge on nights with music (live or DJ). The Museum Club opens daily at 11:00 A.M.

Pay-N-Take Downtown Market
12 West Aspen Avenue
(928) 226-8595
This small market also doubles as a happy haunt for locals. The bar area is intimate and the crowd is large on Thursday, Friday, and Saturday when it's open until 1 A.M. Pay-N-Take features local brews on tap and wine by the glass. (For more information about the market see the Flagstaff Shopping section.)

Uptown Billiards
114 North Leroux Street
(928) 773-0551
There are many places to play pool in Flagstaff, but Uptown Billiards is the classiest pool hall in northern Arizona, and it's nonsmoking. A haven for pool sharks, novices, and anyone who wants to have a good time, Uptown is home to 10 full-size tournament tables, as well as fine house cues and pool balls. If the tables are full, get on the waiting list and enjoy one of the 35 imported and specialty beers on tap. The martini menu features more than 106 tempting mixes for your drinking pleasure. Slip some money into the CD jukebox and listen to a few of the local musicians crooning over coffee and the beloved Colorado River. Uptown Billiards opens daily at 1:00 P.M.

The Wine Loft
17 North San Francisco Street (2nd Floor)
(928) 773-9463
www.thewineloft.com
Tucked away on the second floor, high above the main drag, this is one of Flagstaff's best-kept secrets. Don't be intimidated if you don't know the difference between a White Zin and a Red Zin, this place is warm and inviting. Slide into one of the large comfortable bar chairs and ask your wine expert or bartender for his or her suggestion. The well-educated and attentive staff is passionate and knowledgeable about their wines and will assist you in choosing a wine. The Wine Loft has more than 300 wines to select from. Grab a table by the window to view the passersby or chat at the long spacious bar. A baby grand sits next to the polished dance floor. Check *Flagstaff Live!* for nightly entertainment, wine tastings, and special events.

Offbeat Things to Do at Night

Macy's European Coffee House & Bakery
14 South Beaver Street
(928) 774-2243
If the smoky bar scene doesn't appeal to you, maybe a late-night game of chess at Macy's will. People come here to converse, meet friends, or just read. Open until midnight Thursday through Saturday, Macy's serves homemade pastries and sandwiches until 9:00 P.M. Specialty coffee drinks and a large assortment of teas are served until midnight. Thursday is Open Mic Night. Bring your guitar or recite your favorite poetry. Friday is Jazz Night and Saturday's entertainment is usually a surprise. (See the Flagstaff Restaurant section for more about Macy's.)

Lowell Observatory
1400 West Mars Hill Road
(928) 774-3358
www.lowell.edu
View the constellations and learn about the wonders of the night sky at Lowell Observatory. Weather permitting, Lowell offers nighttime tours Wednesday, Friday, and Saturday. The tour includes a presentation describing the history and campus of the observatory, followed by telescope viewing. Call for the current tour times and special events.

KIDSTUFF

Flagstaff's cultural and recreational activities welcome people of all ages, including kids and adults who still think they are kids. Most Flagstaff residents bring their children to the symphony, art gallery openings, or outdoor concerts. There aren't many enforced age restrictions, except of course in bars and nightclubs. Children are allowed in establishments that serve food and alcohol until 9:00 P.M. If you're traveling through Flagstaff with your kids, they will surely be interested in the following Kidstuff options.

Bowling

Starlite Lanes
3406 East Route 66
(928) 526-1138
Bowling can provide hours of family fun on a rainy day. Starlite has Bumper Bowling for kids. The cost per game for children and adults ranges from $2.00 to $3.00, depending upon the day of the week. Shoe rental is $1.75. (For more information about Starlite Lanes, refer to the Flagstaff Recreation section.)

Horseback Riding

Flying Heart Barn
8400 North U.S. Highway 89
(928) 526-2788
Let an experienced wrangler guide you through the Coconino National Forest. One- and two-hour or daylong trips are

The Slipher Building is one of several structures on the Lowell Observatory campus. Founded in 1894 on a hill just west of downtown Flagstaff, the observatory offers spectacular views of not only the heavens but of Flagstaff and the San Francisco Peaks as well. TODD R. BERGER

available. Call for seasonal rates. (See the Flagstaff Recreation section for more information.)

Hitchin' Post Stables
4848 Lake Mary Road
(928) 774-1719, (928) 774-7131
Discover Walnut Canyon's Native American ruins and caves on horse with guided tours. Hitchin' Post Stables also offers pack trips, hayrides, and a sunset ride to an 1880s wagon train campsite. Call for rates. (For more information, refer to the Flagstaff Recreation section.)

Arizona Snowbowl
6355 U.S. Highway 180
(928) 774-4481
www.arizonasnowbowl.com
Horseback ride through the pristine Coconino National Forest. The ranch offers one- and two-hour rides. Group hayrides and cowboy cookouts also are available. (See the Flagstaff Recreation section for more information.)

Ice/Roller Skating

Jay Lively Activity Center, McPherson Park
1650 North Turquoise Drive, #B
(928) 774-1051
Kids and adults will enjoy indoor ice skating from September through April and indoor roller skating during June, July, and August. Call the rink for public session times and prices.

Museums

Arizona Historical Society Pioneer Museum
2340 North Fort Valley Road
(928) 774-6272
www.infomagic.net/~ahsnad
The popular exhibit *Playthings of the Past* will appeal to children of all ages. The exhibit showcases toys, dolls, games, and children's books from the past, and gives children an interesting way to learn about the pioneer history of the West and particularly of Flagstaff. The museum is open Monday through Saturday 9:00 A.M. to 5:00 P.M. and is closed on Sunday. There is no admission fee, but donations are appreciated. (For more information about the Pioneer Museum, refer to the Flagstaff Attractions and Annual Events sections.)

Museum of Northern Arizona
3101 North Fort Valley Road
(928) 774-5213
www.musnaz.org
The museum welcomes children with activities scheduled throughout the summer. During the summerlong Heritage Program, kids will learn about Native American culture. Call for a more detailed schedule. The museum sponsors Discovery Programs, designed for the whole family, which emphasize the science, art, and culture of the plateau region. River trips, campouts, and bike excursions are only a few examples of the family trips offered. The Discovery Programs include day and weekend trips. The museum is open seven days a week from 9:00 A.M. to 5:00 P.M. (For more about the Museum of Northern Arizona, see the Flagstaff Attractions section.)

Parks, Plants, and Recreation

For more information on the area's parks, call the Flagstaff City Parks and Recreation Department at (928) 779-7690, or visit www.flagstaff.az.gov.

The Arboretum at Flagstaff
4001 South Woody Mountain Road
(928) 744-1442
www.thearb.org
Introduce your child to the native plants of the Colorado Plateau. Fun-filled educational programs for kids are scheduled

throughout the season; call for an updated events listing. The arboretum offers guided tours, beginning at 11:00 A.M. and 1:00 P.M. daily. Admission is $4.00 for adults, $3.00 for seniors, $1.00 for children 6 to 12, and free for children under 6. The arboretum is closed from December 16 until March 31.

Bark Park
600 North Thorpe Road

Families traveling with kids and dogs will enjoy this park. Dog lovers of all ages and their dogs can roam freely inside this fenced area. The park is divided into a small area for small dogs and a larger area for large dogs. Water is available from a hose bib May through October and humans have their own sitting area.

Buffalo Park
West of Gemini Drive off Cedar Hill

Buffalo Park has 163 acres of natural plateau and hills. The 2-mile walking/jogging course gives kids plenty of room to roam. A good place for strollers, big kids, and toddlers. (See the Flagstaff Recreation section for more information.)

Bushmaster Park
3150 North Alta Vista Road

This park has its own BMX skate park, plenty of playground facilities, and a spacious picnic area. (For more information, see the Flagstaff Recreation section.)

McPherson Park
1650 North Turquoise Drive

McPherson Park connects with Buffalo Park by various hiking trails. Children will enjoy the outdoor tennis courts and playground equipment. (For more information, see the Flagstaff Recreation section.)

Thorpe Park
245 North Thorpe Road

This community park offers endless recreational opportunities, including playgrounds, trails, tennis and basketball courts, and lighted ball fields. (Refer to the Flagstaff Recreation section for more information on Thorpe Park.)

Rock Climbing

Vertical Relief
205 South San Francisco Street
(928) 556-9909
www.verticalrelief.com

Let your kids' minds reach new heights at Vertical Relief. Climbing builds muscles, increases flexibility, and improves coordination at all ages. Vertical Relief offers a variety of programs for kids 5 to 18 and guided outdoor trips as well. Purchase a day pass for $12.00 for students K through grad school. A belay lesson for $6.00 is required before using the facility. Vertical Relief is open daily. Call for details. (For more information about Vertical Relief, see the Flagstaff Recreation section.)

Theater

Magic Curtain Productions Youth Cultural Center
2575 East Seventh Avenue
(928) 526-3787
www.magiccurtain.org

The only children's theater in Flagstaff, Magic Curtain Productions is a unique organization where children are the stars of the show. Plays, activities, and workshops are scheduled throughout the year. Previous performances include *Annie,* *Winnie the Pooh,* and *Cinderella.* Call for dates and times of productions.

THE ARTS

Flagstaff's art community has undergone many changes within the past decade; the dedicated artists' community and concerned citizens have banded together to enhance the quality of art in Flagstaff. Art galleries are packed with creations by local artists. Music has experienced a resurgence with the help of the Spectrum Series sponsored by Northern Arizona University in conjunction with its 100th anniversary. This series has brought national acts to town and put Flagstaff on the map. The Flagstaff Symphony entertains audiences with eight concerts and special guest performances throughout the year. The symphony has also joined forces with NAU to implement the Summer Arts Program. The program includes concerts and live theater performed on the NAU campus. Local community and children's theater have survived changes and challenges as well. Flagstaff Cultural Partners, an arts and science agency, plays a major role within the arts, culture, and science communities.

During the Wild West days, the community of Flagstaff encouraged and appreciated different forms of art. Flagstaff was once a major stop along the transcontinental route to California, which brought with it filmmakers, writers, and famous painters, such as Thomas Moran, who brought to the world the wonders of the West on canvas. His paintings immortalized Grand Canyon and Native American cliff dwellings of the region. The popularity of southwestern art declined between the 1930s and the 1960s, but the art world of the 1960s witnessed a western revitalization, which was found in the popularization of cowboy art.

Women artists have played an important, but sometimes silent, role within the art world, as earlier historians did not recognize or record many of their contributions. Mary Colton, who founded the Museum of Northern Arizona with her husband, Harold, instituted programs designed to rejuvenate the interest and quality of Native American art. An artist originally from Philadelphia, Colton was intrigued by the enigmatic Colorado Plateau, and many of her paintings are of southwestern landscapes.

Whether you are looking for tickets to the Flagstaff Symphony, a show in Phoenix, or a production on the university campus, NAU Downtown (right off of Heritage Square), 6 East Aspen Avenue, (928) 523-1628 is your local ticket connection.

A longtime painter of Arizona landscapes, Lillian Wilhelm Smith gained further recognition as the first and only woman to illustrate the western novels of Zane Grey.

In this section, we explore the artistic happenings that bring forth the area's newest stars and shape Flagstaff's art scene. Visitors and locals alike can count on seeing memorable performances, meeting members of the passionate artistic community, and viewing quality craftsmanship in intimate venues.

Galleries

Downtown Flagstaff boasts a gallery on almost every street corner. With intimate settings and diverse media selections, you'll welcome the chance to browse around Flagstaff's galleries and acquaint yourself with local artists and their work any day of the week.

Mark your calendar for the first Friday of each month and head downtown for the Artwalk. This "gallery hop" offers lively conversation, complimentary hors d'oeuvres, and the best artwork that northern Arizona has to offer.

Participating galleries and shops include Arizona Handmade Gallery, Aspen Fine Arts, High Desert Gallery, Old Main Gallery, Starrlight Books, and West of the Moon. Stroll through the downtown area, browse in the participating galleries, and meet local artists. Participating galleries are open from 6:00 to 8:00 P.M. Pick up a map at any of the participating galleries.

Arizona Handmade Gallery
13 North San Francisco Street
(928) 779-3790

The name of this gallery fits. Everything in the gallery is handcrafted by Arizona artists. Enjoy the vast array of jewelry, ornaments, clothing, and ceramics by local artisans. The gallery is open daily.

Don't forget the First Friday Artwalk, which takes place—you guessed it—the first Friday of every month from 6:00 to 8:00 P.M. Call (928) 774-0465 for more information.

The Artists Gallery
17 North San Francisco Street
(928) 773-0958
www.theartistsgallery.net

Since 1992, the Artists Gallery has showcased the finest arts and crafts from more than 40 northern Arizona artists. With blown glass, woodworking, and sculpture, this contemporary cooperative features quality craftsmanship and is a favorite among locals and visitors. The Artists Gallery is open daily and is located in the historic downtown.

Aspen Fine Arts
123 North San Francisco Street
(928) 226-1483

Aspen director Dorothy M. Simousek and her partner, Bryan Bru, have created an airy, light-filled, inviting gallery in downtown Flagstaff. Simousek says that diversity is her goal, and she hopes to appeal to various tastes with the art she offers for sale. The artwork includes modern Southwest Native American art, watercolors by an artist from Moscow, art by early-20th-century residents of Flagstaff, pottery, jewelry by Zygmurt Klechowicz, photography by Philip Johnson (one of the Navajo Code Talkers), ancient Chinese pieces from estate sales, and the popular folded, painted-fabric artwork of Carolyn

Batchelor. The breadth and variety of work in Aspen Fine Arts makes it a lovely place to visit. Simousek says that owning Aspen Fine Arts might not make her rich, but it makes her happy.

Old Main Gallery
NAU, North Campus, Old Main Building
(928) 523-3471

Displaying nationally acclaimed contemporary art, Old Main Gallery offers workshops and scheduled lectures throughout the year. The gallery is open Tuesday through Saturday. Old Main Gallery is located on North Campus in the Old Main building on the corner of Knoles and McMullen Circle. Admission is free.

Richard E. Beasley Gallery
NAU, Central Campus, Performing and Fine Arts Building
(928) 523-3549

One of the university's two galleries, the Beasley Gallery's exhibits reflect the School of Fine Arts' current academic year. The gallery's highlights include a Faculty Art Show, juried exhibits for students, and a Bachelor of Fine Arts exhibit from graduating seniors. Admission is free.

West of the Moon
111 East Aspen Avenue
(928) 774-0465

Named for a Norwegian folktale, West of the Moon's primary focus is to support local artists. The smallest gallery in northern Arizona (the room is 11 by 15), West of the Moon has instituted the philosophy that quality, not quantity, is what defines them. You will find an eclectic mixture of photography, beadwork, jewelry, and sculpture.

Music and Theater

Whether you enjoy community theater, the symphony, or a night of jazz, you will be delighted by the variety of performances around town.

Canyon Movement Company
2812 North Isabel Street
(928) 774-3937
http://members.aol.com/_ht_a/canyon
movement/company/

Canyon Movement Company was established in April 1993 and has been performing dance, educating dancers, and educating the public about dance ever since. Through an annual spring concert, numerous other concerts, workshops, educational residencies, and its dance school, Canyon Dance Academy, directed by Gina Darlington (a professor of dance at Coconino Community College), Canyon Movement Company continues to inspire and reach a wide audience.

Flagstaff Symphony Orchestra
113 East Aspen Avenue
(928) 774-5107
www.flagstaffsymphony.com

The Flagstaff Symphony is composed of 75 professional and community members. From Chabier's *Espana* to Moussorgsky/ Ravel's *Pictures at an Exhibition,* each season's program is a blend of international influences and talented performers that will dazzle audiences. Recently the Flagstaff Symphony and Northern Arizona University joined forces to provide a Summer Music and Theater program. Call the symphony office for a calendar of events and ticket information, or stop by the box office.

Magic Curtain Productions Youth Cultural Center
2575 East Seventh Avenue
(928) 526-3787
www.magiccurtain.org

Enjoy a night of theater performed by an all-children cast. Come out and support the budding performers of the Flagstaff community. Previous performances include *Annie, Winnie the Pooh,* and *Cinderella.* (For more about Magic Curtain, see the Flagstaff Kidstuff section.)

Northern Arizona University Theater
(928) 523-5661, (800) 520-7214
www.nau.edu/cofa

Enjoy a night at the theater with the talented NAU College of Fine Arts. Performances are held in the Clifford White Theater and Ardrey Auditorium on Central Campus.

Theatrikos Theater Company
11 West Cherry Avenue
(928) 774-1662

In May 1972, a small group gathered in the basement of the Historic Hotel Weatherford to discuss the possibility of forming a community theater group. Today, Theatrikos thrives as Flagstaff's premier community theater group and produces six shows a season. Previous performances include Neil Simon's *Jakes' Women, Diary of Anne Frank,* and *True West* by Sam Shepard. Look for performance schedules, previews, and reviews in *Flagstaff Live!* or call the Theatrikos box office for more information.

Theatrikos has discounted tickets for Sunday matinees. Call for current performance listings and times.

ANNUAL EVENTS

Ideal weather, friendly atmosphere, and beautiful scenery make Flagstaff a prime destination for year-round events. Residents are proud of their roots and enjoy reminiscing about the past. Stop any old-timer on the street and you will see how sentimental the locals are. Many of Flagstaff's annual events blend together the history, traditions, and industries that have contributed to the making of the town. This section provides the month-to-month coverage for the happenings in northern Arizona. Most of the events are sponsored by local organizations and the Flagstaff Chamber of Commerce, 101 West Route 66, (928) 774-4505; the Flagstaff Visitor Center, 1 East Route 66, (800) 842-7293; and the Flagstaff Convention and Visitors Bureau, 323 West Aspen Avenue, (928) 779-7611.

January is a quiet month in northern Arizona, but if the town is blessed with snowy weather, outdoor activities abound. (Refer to the Flagstaff Recreation section.) Also consult the calendar events listing in the *Arizona Daily Sun* and the weekly arts and entertainment newspaper, *Flagstaff Live!*, for an up-to-the-minute schedule of musical, cultural, and family-oriented events. Keep in mind that times and dates are subject to change.

Northern Arizona University hosts a variety of concerts, sporting events, exhibits, and theatrical performances. For additional information, contact NAU's Central Ticket Office (928) 523-5661 or www.nau.edu.

February

Flagstaff Winterfest
Flagstaff Chamber of Commerce
101 West Route 66
Entire month of February
(928) 774-4505
www.flagstaffchamber.org
Winterfest is a celebration of snow. Restaurants, local accommodations, and businesses partake in the fun. Weekend highlights include sled dog races, nordic and alpine skiing competitions, snowboard and snowshoe events, stargazing, children's activities, cultural events, and other fun-filled entertainment.

Ski Events
Arizona Snowbowl
Throughout February and March
(928) 779-1951
www.arizonasnowbowl.com
The Arizona Snowbowl and the Flagstaff Nordic Center offer winter events for all levels of skiers, including the Mountain Sports Cup, Arizona Citizens' Cup, Arizona Special Olympics Winter Games, and the Grand Canyon State Winter Games competitions. Contact the Arizona Snowbowl for times and dates.

March

Arizona Ski and Golf Classic
Arizona Snowbowl
Fourth weekend in March
(928) 779-1951
www.arizonasnowbowl.com
The weekend event begins in sunny and warm Phoenix with four-person teams competing in a golf tournament on Saturday. Sunday, the teams travel north to the high country of Flagstaff for a modified slalom ski race at the Arizona Snowbowl. Spectators are welcome. This event is for those who like extremes.

Archaeology Day
Museum of Northern Arizona
3101 North Fort Valley Road
End of March
(928) 774-5213
www.musnaz.org.
The museum focuses on the indigenous peoples that inhabit the Colorado Plateau. This fun-filled day for children and adults includes special activities and events about southwestern archaeology.

May

Movies on the Square
Heritage Square
Friday nights in May and June
(928) 779-6929

At around 7:00 P.M., or a tad later or earlier depending on darkness' arrival, family movies are shown outside in downtown Flagstaff.

The Scenic Skyride at Arizona Snowbowl
Memorial Day to Labor Day
(928) 779-1951
www.arizonasnowbowl.com

This is truly a wonderful way to experience the breathtaking views of northern Arizona. The skyride takes you to an elevation of 11,500 feet, with more than 70 miles of amazing scenery. The trip is 25 minutes one-way in an open chairlift. At the top, a forest ranger will be on hand to answer questions about the biology and geology of the region. After the scenic skyride, enjoy an afternoon hike and lunch on the deck. The lift is open daily 10:00 A.M. to 4:00 P.M. from Memorial Day through Labor Day. After Labor Day the lift operates on Friday, Saturday, and Sunday only through mid-October.

Heritage Program
Museum of Northern Arizona
3101 North Fort Valley Road
Memorial Day to Labor Day
(928) 774-5213
www.musnaz.org

During the annual Heritage Program, the Museum of Northern Arizona honors the creativity of Native American and Hispanic artists of the Colorado Plateau. The weekend-long family-oriented events include exhibits featuring the arts and crafts of the Hopi, Navajo, Zuni, and Pai. Children's activities are scheduled throughout the weekend. Representatives from Native American and Hispanic groups perform traditional dances. Contact the museum for a schedule of events.

June

Flagstaff's Historic Walks
June through September
(928) 774-8800

Each semester Northern Arizona University offers the REEL Women Film Series sponsored by the Women's Studies program. Films are free, open to the public, and are shown at Cline Library on NAU's Central Campus. For more information call (928) 523-3300.

Join Flagstaff historians Richard and Sherry Magnum, dressed in turn-of-the-20th-century costumes, as they lead educational and entertaining tours through Flagstaff's historic downtown area. The guides offer unique information and anecdotes about downtown's buildings and inhabitants. The tours begin at the Flagstaff Visitor Center and are scheduled every other Sunday at 10:00 A.M. A special tour is available on July 4. All tours are free, but call for reservations.

Concerts in the Park
Wheeler Park
Every Wednesday in June
(928) 779-7690

Flagstaff Parks and Recreation host this concert series every Wednesday during June, between 6:00 and 8:00 P.M. in Wheeler Park, located across from the City Hall, 211 West Aspen Avenue. The series features local and regional musicians. Bring a blanket or chair to this toe-tapping event.

Wool Festival
Arizona Historical Society Pioneer Museum
2340 North Fort Valley Road
First weekend in June
(928) 774-6272

The earliest European settlers introduced sheep to the Flagstaff area and began an industry that played an important economic role in Flagstaff until the mid-1900s. Paying tribute to these settlers and their flocks, this festival features a sheep wagon from the museum's collection; sheep, goat, and llama shearing; and livestock and

Looking for a place to picnic? Grab a blanket and go to Wheeler Park, between Aspen Avenue and Birch Street on Humphreys. The park has sturdy trees for climbing.

fleece judging. Food is prepared in Dutch ovens and on griddles, just as it was in the sheepherding days. Felting, spinning, dyeing, and weaving demonstrations are held throughout the weekend.

Flagstaff Heritage Days
Flagstaff Visitor Center
1 East Route 66
Multiple days between Memorial Day and Independence Day
(928) 774-9541
Heritage Days is a celebration of the heart and soul of the American West. Many events take place during 12 action-packed days. During the Pine Country Rodeo, top rodeo contenders compete in roping and riding events. The Great Fiesta Del Barrio pays homage to the culture and customs of the Hispanic community. The popular Route 66 Festival and car show drives into Flagstaff. Other events include the Arizona Dream Cruise and Route 66 Car Rally, dances, mixers, and kids' carnival rides.

The Annual Fajita Cook-off
Second Saturday in June
(928) 773-9269
The culture of Hispanic Flagstaff is on display at this sizzling event. Call for location and times.

July

Coconino County Horse Races
Fort Tuthill Coconino County Park
South Arizona Highway 89A
Fourth of July
(928) 774-5139

Featuring thoroughbred and quarter horse races, the Coconino County Horse Races are held annually over the Fourth of July weekend at Fort Tuthill Downs. Distances range from 350-yard sprints to 1-mile endurance races. This event draws a large crowd, so be sure to arrive early.

Festival of Arts and Crafts Extraordinaire
Northland Hospice
First weekend of July
(928) 779-1227
This fund-raiser benefits the Northland Hospice and features entertainment, food, children's activities, and arts and crafts from artisans around the country.

Flagstaff's Fabulous 4th Festivities
Flagstaff Visitor Center
1 East Route 66
Fourth of July
(928) 774-9541
Celebrate Flagstaff's favorite holiday—the Fourth of July—with an old-fashioned community parade. Citizens go all out as they dress in turn-of-the-20th-century costumes. The parade takes place in the historic downtown area. Get there early to see decorated floats, live music, and locals doing their thing.

August

Flagstaff Summerfest
Fort Tuthill Coconino County Fairgrounds
South Arizona Highway 89A
First week of August
(928) 774-5139
Flagstaff Summerfest is the coolest place to be in the summer. This three-day celebration of fine arts and crafts features 200 juried artists from across the country. More than 40 musicians from throughout the West perform on three stages, while an array of fine foods tempts your senses. A hands-on activity area for children provides entertainment for the whole family.

September

Coconino County Fair
Fort Tuthill Coconino County Fairgrounds
South Arizona Highway 89A
Labor Day weekend
(928) 774-5139
For the past 50 years, the Coconino County Fair has been the largest county fair in northern Arizona. Enjoy live music performed on outdoor stages, a demolition derby, livestock auction, and an arts-and-crafts festival. The kids will love the petting zoo, carnival rides, and all the hot dogs, popcorn, and cotton candy. For ticket prices and information on this event, contact the Fort Tuthill Coconino County Fairgrounds.

Labor Day Arts and Crafts Festival
Labor Day
(928) 779-6176
Looking for something to do over the Labor Day weekend? Take the family to this arts-and-crafts festival and enjoy the food, entertainment, and regional artists' displays. Local musicians perform throughout the festival. Admission is free. This is an alcohol-free event.

Annual Bed Race
Down Aspen Avenue
Last Saturday in September
(928) 523-1642
The bed race includes a parade, banquet, silent auction, and hilarious racing competition. Come join the fun as teams from businesses and community groups push "beds" down Aspen Avenue.

Flagstaff Festival of Science
Flagstaff Visitor Center
1 East Route 66
End of September into beginning of October
(800) 842-7293
www.scifest.org
A great educational experience for the whole family, this 10-day event is filled with fun and family-oriented learning activities, including field trips and interactive exhibits. Local museums, observatories, and other scientific facilities offer open houses. Events take place at locations throughout the Flagstaff area. For more information, contact the Flagstaff Visitor Center.

October

Flagstaff Symphony Guild's "Elegant Affair"
Last Saturday in October
(928) 522-0549
To benefit the Flagstaff Symphony Guild, this grand event includes a luncheon, silent auction, and champagne served butler style. Support for the silent auction comes from donations made by Arizona sports teams and local businesses. Auctioned items include great vacation giveaways, antique jewelry, and gift certificates. Dillard's Department store presents their famous Elegant Affair fashion show, which features fall and holiday fashions perfect for a night on the town, cruises, or any social function. Reservations are required.

November

Voices from the Past
Lowell Observatory
1400 West Mars Hill Road
Entire month of November
(928) 774-2096
www.lowell.edu
Combining astronomy, history, and theater, Voices from the Past introduces visitors to famous astronomers and scientists from the past. This program, performed by the observatory staff, re-creates the lives of such astronomers as Galileo, Copernicus, Caroline Herschel, Maria Mitchell, and Percival Lowell himself. A tour of the night sky follows. The series usually runs Friday and Saturday nights with at least two performances each night. Call ahead for times and nighttime visibility.

The preparation for Little America's Lights Festival begins in October. The entire staff of Little America Hotel is responsible for decorating the hotel grounds. Temporary help is hired to facilitate the effort. Two million lights, 500 luminarias, and 400 floating candles greet locals and visitors to the northland as they kick off their holiday season. If you are coming from out of town and would like to stay at the hotel, make your reservations early.

Handel's *The Messiah*
Northern Arizona University
Late November
(928) 523-5661
A Flagstaff holiday gem, this performance showcases the talents of NAU's student soloists, chamber orchestra, and chorus. The concert is normally held in late November; however, the date varies, so contact the university for further information.

Playthings of the Past
Arizona Historical Society Pioneer Museum
2340 North Fort Valley Road
November through January
(928) 774-6272
Children and adults will enjoy learning about toys that came before computers and handheld games. The toy exhibit features dolls, trains, cars, and other playthings from the 1880s through the 1960s.

December

Annual Holiday Lights Festival
Little America Hotel
2515 East Butler Avenue
Nightly from the Saturday after Thanksgiving to mid-January
(928) 779-7979, (800) 435-2493

Forget the hustle and bustle of the holidays! The Little America Hotel kicks off the holiday season with more than two million decorative lights. This sight, and the celebration that surrounds it, are sure to start your holiday season right. The ceremony takes place on the Saturday after Thanksgiving with a visit from Santa, live entertainment, caroling, and complimentary cookies and warm beverages. Local high school choirs sing Christmas favorites.

Holiday Tours at Riordan Mansion
Riordan Mansion State Historic Park
409 Riordan Road
Throughout December
(928) 779-4393
Experience the joys of Christmas past with a guided tour of the historic Riordan Family Mansion. Well-informed guides lead tours of this living piece of Flagstaff history and share Christmas folklore and traditions both past and present. The mansion is decorated in turn-of-the-20th-century style with wreaths, garland, and a tree trimmed with old-fashioned ornaments. The staff recommends making reservations.

Pinecone Drop
Hotel Weatherford
23 North Leroux Street
New Year's Eve
(928) 779-1919
You haven't celebrated the arrival of the New Year until you have done so in historic downtown Flagstaff watching a giant pinecone plummet at the stroke of midnight.

WILLIAMS 🚂

I n 1880 the rough-and-ready railroad construction town of Williams boasted a population of 500 people. Today more than a million visitors a year stop in this small town (population 3,000) on their way to Grand Canyon, only 55 miles to the north. Williams is a town that seems never to have left the era when Route 66 was the road to adventure. You'll find quaint, restored shop fronts, a 1950s soda fountain, and a B&B that was once a bordello, to name just a few of the attractions here. A short drive from town takes you to high-country lakes, oak and aspen forests, and designated wilderness areas.

The Williams town site was established in 1874 and named for "Bill" Williams, an early-19th-century beaver trapper who worked the Rocky Mountains and the canyons of the Mogollon Rim of northern Arizona. He was one of the few who survived the harsh life of the trapper. Some believe he was killed in 1849 in southern Colorado by Ute Indians at the ripe old age of 62.

The transcontinental Atlantic and Pacific Railroad began construction in the Flagstaff-Williams area in about 1880. The railhead reached Williams on September 1, 1882, and like all the other towns that had at one time been at the end of the railroad as it moved from east to west, Williams was now a town of gambling halls, dance-hall girls, and scoundrels. The local newspaper's pages were filled with stories of shootings, lynchings, vendettas, and other crimes. One story in 1882 reported that George Rich, deputy sheriff of Williams, resigned—he was suspected of being one of the men who had robbed a Williams liquor store.

In the 1890s copper was discovered north of Williams and a rail line to the mines, financed by eastern capitalists, was built to transport the ore 45 miles from the Anita mines. The mining boom lasted less than a decade before it went bust in

1899. The Atchison Topeka & Santa Fe Railroad took over the railway built for the mines and extended it to Grand Canyon. Prior to this, the only way for tourists to visit the canyon was by taking a back-breaking eight-hour stagecoach ride. Now they could ride the train for $3.95. The first trainload of tourists reached the canyon in the fall of 1901. Williams took that opportunity to declare itself "The Gateway to the Grand Canyon."

Tourism increased when Route 66 went through Williams beginning in 1926. This was a lifesaver for the town, because by the mid-20th century the forests were logged out and the livestock industry was becoming less profitable. Williams would need to rely more and more on tourism for its economy.

In 1968 the railroad to Grand Canyon stopped operating. More people were now visiting Grand Canyon by car and it was no longer profitable to run the train back and forth from Williams. In 1984, the new Interstate 40 bypassed Williams. The section of Route 66 that went right through the middle of town no longer existed, and Williams began to decline as tourists simply drove on by.

The Grand Canyon Railway reopened in 1989 due to the courageous (and costly) efforts of Max and Thelma Biegert. Thanks to the refurbished Grand Canyon Railway and the efforts of the town's restauranteurs and shop owners, Williams is once again a main entry point for visitors to all of northern Arizona—and to Grand Canyon in particular.

The mountain near the town is also named after Bill Williams. The mountain itself is a cluster of volcanic spires surrounded by 12 volcanic domes and some lava flows. The mountain is about 4 million years old. Since the volcanoes in this area erupted first in the west, Sitgreaves Mountain is about 2.5 million years old, and Kendrick Peak about 2 million. The eruptions of San Francisco Mountain occurred from about 2.8 million years to 200,000 years ago. San Francisco Mountain and the surrounding peaks are often referred to as the San Francisco Peaks. Native American tribes in the area have their own names for these mountains, which are sacred to them. Sunset Crater, the most recent active volcano of the San Francisco Volcanic Field, began erupting in A.D. 1064 and continued to be active for about 200 years.

ACCOMMODATIONS

Williams offers visitors a choice of motels, hotels, or bed-and-breakfasts.

PRICE CODE

The following price code is for two adults during the high season, generally between Memorial Day and Labor Day. The codes do not include taxes and other fees.

$	Less than $60
$$	$61 to $75
$$$	$76 to $100
$$$$	$101 to $125
$$$$$	More than $125

Fray Marcos Hotel and Resort $$$$
235 North Grand Canyon Boulevard
(928) 635–4010, (800) THE–TRAIN,
www.thetrain.com
Adjacent to the Grand Canyon Railway depot, the plush Fray Marcos Hotel offers a turn-of-the-20th-century atmosphere and modern amenities, including air-conditioning, hair dryers, and TVs. The 196 rooms (some nonsmoking) are decorated in the Southwest style, and the lobby is graced by genuine Remington sculptures and original oil paintings by Kenny McKenna. A flagstone fireplace in the lobby and an authentic 19th-century hand-crafted bar in Spenser's Lounge, which serves drinks, pizza, and appetizers, add to the atmosphere of old-time luxury. You can also enjoy the heated indoor swimming pool, a hot tub, and the fitness room. Max and Thelma's Restaurant is next door, and historic downtown Williams is just a few blocks away.

The original hotel, like the depot, was completed in 1908; it was one of the Harvey Houses built by the Santa Fe Railroad to make rail travel more civilized. The current building, similar in style to the original, was finished in 1995. Staying here entitles you to a discount on Grand Canyon Railway trips and packages. The hotel has eight wheelchair-accessible rooms. An extra $10 per person is charged for more than two adults in a room, with a maximum of four adults per room. Children under 18 stay free.

Legacies Bed and Breakfast $$$$$
450 South Eleventh Street
(928) 635–4880, (928) 370–2288
www.legaciesbb.com
The elegant and upscale, stucco-and-stone Legacies is a romantic choice for visitors to Williams. The foyer and large main room of the inn boast 17-foot ceilings, and the dining area has a large stone fireplace with 12-foot-tall arched windows to either side. A curved oak stairway winds from the foyer to the three guest rooms. The 600-square-foot Legacies Suite, the best room in the inn, features a canopied king-size bed, as well as a spectacular bathroom with a double-head shower, an onyx Jacuzzi tub that can be illuminated from below, and onyx countertops. The suite includes a separate sitting room with satellite TV, desk, and free-standing gas fireplace. Other rooms include the themed Hawaiian Room and Route 66 Room. All rooms are nonsmoking, and pets are not allowed. If you are looking for a place near

Grand Canyon to rekindle the flames of romance far from unromantic tourist buses and crowded overlooks, Legacies will definitely put a grin on your face.

Quality Inn Mountain Ranch $$$
6701 East Mountain Ranch Road
(928) 635-2693, (866) MTRANCH
www.mountainranchresort.com

If you want a quiet haven as your starting point for exploring Williams and the Grand Canyon area, this 73-room motel is perfect. Set back in the cool pines and away from the railroad tracks, it is just 7 miles east of Williams. Rooms have air-conditioning, TVs, hair dryers, and coffeemakers. In good weather, you can enjoy the swimming pool and whirlpool, tennis, basketball, and a putting green. For the children, an inviting lawn is a wonderful place to play after long hours in the car. Nonsmoking rooms are available, and the motel is wheelchair accessible. There is a $10 charge for each extra person over age 12 in the room. Pets are allowed with a $20 nonrefundable fee; major credit cards are accepted. The restaurant has a view of the San Francisco Peaks and serves breakfast (included in the room rate) and dinner. This motel is also the headquarters for Mountain Ranch Stables (see Recreation).

The Red Garter Bed and Bakery $$$
137 West Railway Avenue
(928) 635-1484, (800) 328-1484
www.redgarter.com

Originally an 1897 saloon and bordello, this bed-and-breakfast in the middle of the downtown historic district has four nonsmoking rooms, three of which accommodate two adults each and one of which accommodates four. The rooms, which are kept quite simple, have queen beds, private baths, and color TVs, but no phones. Children over the age of eight are welcome. The continental-plus breakfast comprises items from the on-site bakery, including bagels, cinnamon buns, and strudels. Fresh fruit, juice, and coffee are also served. None of the rooms is wheelchair accessible. Ask owner John Holst to

tell you about the building's colorful history—from bordello to flophouse to barbecue joint to warehouse. He has a scrapbook that he'll be happy to share, and be sure to ask about the two-story outhouse. He may also be willing to tell you about the ghosts that guests and employees have reported seeing on the premises. Major credit cards are accepted, and reservations are recommended.

Route 66 Inn $
128 East Route 66
(928) 635-4791, (888) 786-6956

Within walking distance of everything in town, this 20-unit inn is housed in a historic 1930s three-story building. Some rooms are family units with three beds, a refrigerator, and a microwave. All rooms have color TV with HBO, air-conditioning, and phones (local calls are free). You can hook up your laptop to the Internet using a phone line in the office. From April through September, the room rate includes a continental breakfast. Staying here entitles you to a 15 percent discount at Pancho's and discounts on package train, helicopter, and other tours arranged through the inn. The hosts will be happy to make your travel arrangements for you or to help you plan your trip. You can also take advantage of FedEx and UPS service at the inn, and there is a small gift shop. Nonsmoking rooms are available, but wheelchair-accessible rooms are not. A $5.00 charge applies to extra people in the room, and pets require a $5.00 nonrefundable fee.

RESTAURANTS

PRICE CODE

The price codes below represent average prices for dinner for two, excluding tax, gratuity, and drinks.

$	Less than $20
$$	$21 to $35
$$$	$36 to $60
$$$$	More than $60

CLOSE-UP

Route 66

Perhaps nothing has so captured the postwar American imagination as Route 66—fast cars, open spaces, and unlimited freedom and adventure.

Designated Route 66 in 1926, the 2,448-mile Mother Road linking Chicago and Los Angeles was completely paved in 1938. During the Depression, the road took desperate families from the Midwest's Dust Bowl to the golden opportunities of Southern California. This is the trip described in John Steinbeck's *The Grapes of Wrath.*

After World War II, America started making cars again, which had been impossible during the war because the necessary raw materials were needed for building military vehicles. Americans wanted big cars, and gasoline was so cheap that gas stations offered incentives for people to buy it. Route 66 was made more popular by the 1946 Bobby Troup song, "Get Your Kicks on Route 66," which has been recorded by artists as different as Perry Como and the Rolling Stones.

By the early 1950s, America's lust for adventure on the open road had outstripped the capacity of the two-lane byways through the small towns of the West and Southwest—Gallup and Holbrook, Winslow, Flagstaff, and Williams. Partly to make life easier for travelers, and partly to make sure that the country's road system was adequate for moving military personnel and equipment, America began a massive highway construction project, building interstates linking all major cities. The 1960s TV series *Route 66* depicted an era that was fast disappearing.

Most of the section of Route 66 that came through New Mexico and northern Arizona was replaced by Interstate 40, a limited-access road that bypassed the towns and cities that had relied on Route 66 to bring tourists—and tourist dollars. Williams, in 1984, became the last town on Route 66 to be bypassed by I-40.

Some sections of the old road, however, still exist. The main street through Williams, Bill Williams Avenue, and the main street through downtown Flagstaff, Santa Fe Avenue, have been redesignated as Historic Route 66. Some other stretches of the road are still accessible.

Max and Thelma's Restaurant $$
123 North Grand Canyon Boulevard
(928) 773-1976
www.thetrain.com
Have breakfast, lunch, or dinner at Max and Thelma's, adjacent to the Williams Depot and Fray Marcos Hotel. Children will enjoy the model electric train of the Grand Canyon Railway that circles this railroad-theme steakhouse/buffet. Tourists can begin the day with an all-you-can-eat breakfast buffet, including eggs, pancakes, omelets, and more. Lunchtime also features an all-you-can-eat buffet. For dinner, a barbecue buffet will fill you up, or try an entree from the menu. Favorites are steak, salmon, and ribs. A full-service bar may help you relax after a day of sightseeing. Open every day year-round except Christmas, Max and Thelma's is wheelchair

Put some '50s tunes on the CD player and begin in downtown Williams. Go east on I-40 to the Pittman Valley exit. Turn left after the exit, go over the highway, and turn right onto Route 66. Follow the road to the forest boundary where the historic portion of 66 ends. From Flagstaff, access this portion of the road from the Bellemont exit off I-40. This paved and gravel-surfaced stretch of road is about 22 miles one-way and is accessible by passenger cars year-round. Round-trip driving time is one to one-and-a-half hours.

Route 66 is no longer one continuous road across northern Arizona, but sections of the highway still lead through the towns and forests of the high desert. Here, Route 66 motors on through downtown Williams.
TODD R. BERGER

accessible and there is plenty of parking. When you've finished your meal, visit the large gift shop for your souvenir purchases. Major credit cards are accepted.

Pancho McGillicuddy's Mexican Cantina $
141 Railroad Avenue
(928) 635-4150
It's worth having a meal here just to

experience the elegance of eating in this historic building with 15-foot-high arched windows and a painted tin ceiling. The walls of the restaurant area are decorated with charming hand-painted murals in Mexican designs. Everything here is good and the menu includes fajitas, enchiladas, chili relenos, and fish tacos. A city parking lot across the street and wheelchair accessibility make this an

The City of Williams Visitor Center is at 200 West Railroad Avenue. The phone numbers are (928) 635-4061 or (800) 863-0546. The center is open seven days a week year-round.

easy and convenient stop whether you're just driving through or staying for a few days in Williams. The restaurant is open daily for lunch and dinner. It's within walking distance of many of Williams's motels, a good thing because Pancho's serves 30 types of tequila and is famous for its margaritas. Credit cards are welcome.

Pine Country Restaurant $
107 North Grand Canyon Boulevard
(928) 635-9718

This is where the locals eat, mostly because of the gorgeous pies and home-style cooking. A family-style restaurant with checked tablecloths and bentwood chairs, as well as a few booths, the restaurant serves basic home cooking—burgers, sandwiches, and full chicken and steak dinners, some of which you might feel obliged to taste before moving on to the 7-inch-high pies with beautiful flaky crusts. You won't have trouble parking—a city parking lot is just across the street. Reservations are a good idea here because the place can fill to overflowing very quickly as people enjoy this comfortable, fun setting. Open daily for breakfast, lunch, and dinner, the eatery accepts credit cards and personal checks and is wheelchair accessible.

Twister's 50's Soda Fountain and
Route 66 Café $
417 East Route 66
(928) 635-0266
www.route66place.com

Were you a teenager in the 1950s? Then this is an opportunity to revisit those days of poodle skirts and sock hops. The soda fountain features '50s treats—old-fashioned cream sodas, shakes and malts, root beer floats, and cherry cokes. Ice cream delectables are made with Dreyer's ice cream. You can also try the burgers, hot dogs, generous sandwiches, fries, and chili dogs while listening to hits from the days when Route 66 was the main road across the country. Open seven days a week, with a continental breakfast and light lunch and dinner menus, Twisters accepts credit cards but no out-of-town checks.

ATTRACTIONS

Grand Canyon Deer Farm Petting Zoo
6752 East Deer Farm Road
(928) 635-4073, (800) 926-3337
www.deerfarm.com

Located 8 miles east of Williams (exit I-40 at Deer Farm Road), the Grand Canyon Deer Farm Petting Zoo is a wonderful place to pull off the highway to placate antsy kids and to put a warm spot in the hearts of their parents. Fawns are in abundance during the summer, and the adult deer here will eat right out of your hands—the petting zoo has mule deer, sika deer, axis deer, and reindeer. However, the farm doesn't limit itself to members of the deer family. You can also cozy up to, among others, pygmy goats, pronghorn, turkeys, wallabies, potbellied pigs, a bison, donkeys, and llamas. The farm is open year-round (weather permitting). Children under two are admitted free.

Grand Canyon Railway
Williams Depot
(928) 773-1976, (800) THE-TRAIN
www.thetrain.com

For the adventure of a lifetime, board the Grand Canyon Railway at the historic 1908 Williams Depot (take exit 163 off Interstate 40 and drive a half mile south) and ride the train to Grand Canyon. A vintage steam or diesel engine pulls the old iron horse through valleys, pine forests, high desert plains, and small canyons. As the piercing whistle blows and you leave the depot at 10:00 A.M., you'll have a view of

The Red Garter Bed and Bakery offers guests the chance to overnight in a turn-of-the-20th-century bordello. TODD R. BERGER

Amtrak has partnered with Grand Canyon Railway to make rail travel to the canyon an easy option now that the Southwest Chief stops in Williams. Call (800) USA-RAIL for information on Amtrak service.

the majestic San Francisco Peaks. Be sure to get to the depot early—you won't want to miss the Wild West shootout at the depot before the train departs. On the two-and-a-quarter-hour ride, uniformed conductors show you old-fashioned courtesy, and costumed strolling musicians will entertain you with country tunes.

The train takes you right to the 1910 Grand Canyon Depot on the South Rim, just steps away from El Tovar Hotel. You'll have more than three hours to explore the South Rim of Grand Canyon on your own. Be sure not to miss El Tovar, Hopi House, and Bright Angel Lodge's restaurant at Grand Canyon Village.

The railway also offers escorted motor-coach rim tours to some of the most popular scenic overlooks to give you a more encompassing look at one of the most visited natural wonders of the world. See Mohave Point, Pima Point, the Abyss, and Hermits Rest. Fred Harvey Company offers three different motor-coach tours, all of which include lunch.

At 3:30, the train whistle will blow and you'll begin your return journey. An Old West train robbery, complete with bad-men armed with blazing pistols, will make you think you're riding the train through the territory a century ago when the first train from Williams pulled out of the station in 1901.

You'll arrive at 5:45 in time to visit the gift shop and free railway museum back at the Williams Depot. Passengers may also stay overnight at the canyon and return to Williams the next day, and one-way tickets for the train are available.

The railway offers several classes of service for your trip. Coach Class puts you in an authentic 1923 Harriman railroad car with reversible seats so you and your friends can sit facing each other. Coach Class cars seat 88 passengers; each car has its own rest room. Club Class gives you the additional benefit of being able to order drinks at an old-fashioned, fully stocked mahogany bar in your railroad car, which seats 58. Coffee and pastries are served in the morning. First Class service will find you in a comfortable recliner. Fruit, pastries, coffee, and juice are served in the morning, and on the return journey you will be offered appetizers and champagne. Other alcoholic beverages are also available. The Deluxe Observation Class passengers enjoy all the amenities of First Class in an upper-level enclosed glass dome from which to view the scenery. Children over 11 years old are welcome. Finally, the Luxury Parlor Car gives you all the advantages of Observation Class, but in an elegant coach with an open-air rear platform, perfect for taking pictures. Some cars can be reserved in advance for groups and special events. Wheelchair access to the train and rim tours is limited, so be sure to inquire in advance. The Grand Canyon Railway operates every day except Christmas Eve and Christmas Day.

One- to four-night package tours are also available, including one designed specially for guests 55 and older. A one-day tour from Las Vegas includes round-trip airfare, the train ride, a motor-coach tour of the rim, and lunch. Call or write for details and prices. Amtrak has partnered with Grand Canyon Railway to make rail travel to the canyon an easy option now that the Southwest Chief stops in Williams. Call (800) USA-RAIL for information on Amtrak service.

RECREATION

**Elephant Rocks Golf Course
(928) 635-4936 (pro shop and clubhouse)
www.thegrandcanyon.com/golf**
This 18-hole, par 72 municipal golf course is a mile west of town near exit 161 off Inter-

The Grand Canyon Railway employs an old-fashioned steam locomotive to pull the train from Williams to the South Rim of Grand Canyon in summertime. TODD R. BERGER

state 40. After exiting the highway, take a right and drive 1.5 miles; the golf course will be on your right. In addition to driving your ball down the fairways, you will be able to practice on the driving range and the putting and chipping greens. The pro shop offers club rentals, balls, clothing, bags, and other accessories. Golf carts are available. Tee times may be reserved up to a week in advance. Visa and MasterCard are accepted. The golf course is open from early April to November, but these dates may vary depending on the weather.

Williams Ski Area
Bill Williams Mountain
(928) 635-9330

A poma lift that reaches 8,150 feet takes you to five main runs for beginner, intermediate, and advanced skiers. Adventuresome skiers are also allowed to make their own trails through the trees. Beginners may want to use the rope lift. A day lodge serves snacks, and the ski school offers complete equipment rentals for downhill and cross-country skiing and snowboarding. Kids will enjoy the indoor child play area. Four miles south of town, the ski area is open Thursday through Sunday during the ski season. Usually Williams can count on enough snow for skiing from mid-December through mid-April. Be sure to call ahead to find out if the ski area is open.

Mountain Ranch Stables
Quality Inn Mountain Ranch
6701 East Mountain Ranch Road
(928) 635-0706

One of the best ways to get a sense of the West is to take a horseback trail ride through the beautiful Kaibab National Forest. This stable maintains about 25 horses, so it has suitable mounts for almost anyone. Most rides are one or two hours, but

The Williams Health Care Center at 301 South Seventh Street, (928) 635-4441, is open daily 8:00 A.M. to 8:00 P.M.

longer rides can be arranged, or enjoy a hayride and cookout with cowboy singing. Take exit 171 off Interstate 40, 7 miles east of Williams. The same proprietors also operate Stable in the Pines, 100 Circle Pine Road, (928) 635-2626 or (800) 732-0537. Both stables are open April through September or longer, depending on weather.

Kaibab National Forest

In 1934, the Tusayan National Forest and forest service land north of Grand Canyon were combined to form the Kaibab National Forest, one of six national forests in Arizona.

This forest borders both the North and South Rims of Grand Canyon and covers 1.5 million acres at elevations from 5,500 to 10,418 feet (at the top of Kendrick Peak). At higher elevations, the forest is mostly ponderosa pine with alpine meadows and mixed conifers. At lower elevations, expect to see mostly juniper and pinyon.

Travel is restricted to foot and horseback only in the 115,000 acres of designated wilderness, including Saddle Mountain Wilderness and Kanab Creek Wilderness on the North Rim of Grand Canyon and Kendrick Peak Wilderness and parts of Sycamore Canyon Wilderness near Williams.

Photographers and nature lovers will enjoy seeing the wildlife of the forest, which includes mule deer, elk, pronghorn, and black bear, as well as smaller animals, reptiles, and birds, such as bald eagles, other raptors, and marsh birds. One animal, the Kaibab squirrel, is found only on the Kaibab Plateau. You can distinguish it from the Abert squirrel by its dark body and white tail. The best time to see wildlife is from the beginning of May through the beginning of November when the roads are open.

The natural and cultural resources of the forest are protected and regulated by the stewardship of USDA Forest Service rangers who administer rules on ranching, lumbering, and homesteading, build lookouts to fight fires, and build and maintain trails and roads into the forest.

For more information about the forest, stop by the City of Williams/Kaibab

National Forest Visitor Center at 200 West Railroad Avenue in Williams, call (928) 635-4061 or (800) 863-0546, or visit the forest's Web site at www.fs.fed.us/r3/kai.

Beale Wagon Road

The Beale Road crosses the Williams Ranger District of the Kaibab National Forest from east to west north of Interstate 40. The road's hiking and horseback riding trails are accessible at Laws Spring, about 20 miles northeast of Williams.

Laws Spring is a water hole where you will see rock carvings inscribed by members of the 1858 Beale Expedition as well as petroglyphs left by Native American travelers, and you can walk to a small section of the original Beale Road. Travel on Beale Road by motorized vehicle is prohibited. To get to Laws Spring from Williams, take Arizona Highway 64 about 5 miles to Spring Valley Road (Forest Road 141). Turn right and drive 7 miles to FR 730. Turn left and go 3 miles to FR 115. Turn left and continue 1.5 miles to FR 2030. Follow the sign to the parking area. Laws Spring is a short walk. FR 115 and FR 2030 are not suitable for passenger cars, only for high-clearance vehicles, such as 4x4s or pickup trucks. You can get information on other access points to the Beale Wagon Road and maps at the City of Williams/Kaibab National Forest Visitor Center in Williams.

HIKING AND CAMPING

Dozens of trails around Williams will keep the intrepid hiker busy. They will take you through forests, canyons, meadows, parks, and historic sites. Difficulty varies from quite easy to quite strenuous, especially at these altitudes (6,800 to more than 10,000 feet). For a detailed description of more than 30 hikes in and around Williams, pick up a copy of *Williams Guidebook* by Richard and Sherry Magnum (Flagstaff, Arizona: Hexagon Press, 1998).

Seven developed campgrounds on the Kaibab National Forest offer tables, drink-ing water, pit toilets, and fire grates. Reservations are not needed, and campsites are allocated on a first-come, first-served basis. Most are open only during the summer. Backcountry camping is allowed throughout most of the forest.

For more hiking and camping information, contact the Kaibab National Forest at (928) 635-4061 or (800) 863-0546, 200 West Railroad Avenue, Williams, or visit their Web site: www.fs.fed.us/r3/kai.

Circle Pines KOA
1000 Circle Pines Road
(928) 635-4545, (800) 732-0537
www.koa.com

Nestled in the tall pines, this well-equipped campground has 45 tent sites and 120 pull-through RV sites (97 with hookups), as well as cabins. Take a minivacation right here and enjoy horseback riding, hayrides, an indoor heated swimming pool, and two spas. For the basics, Circle Pines KOA offers flush toilets, a laundry, hot showers in a tiled bathroom, a grocery store, and a gift shop. Kids will stay entertained with the playground and miniature golf course. The campground offers a van tour of Grand Canyon and a free shuttle to the Grand Canyon Railway. Don't forget to ask for your discount coupon for the railroad. Take exit 167 off Interstate 40 to 1000 Circle Pines Road. Major credit cards are accepted, and the campground is open year-round.

Red Lake Arizona Campground
8850 North Arizona Highway 64
(928) 635-9122, (800) 581-4753

Red Lake, 10 miles north of Williams on AZ 64, was settled in 1896 and served as a camp for Chinese laborers working on the railroad to Grand Canyon. This four-acre site is much more than a campground, offering an independent hostel, 14 tent sites, 14 RV sites with hookups, a deli, and a gift shop. The hostel has European-style dormitories that hold up to four people in each room as well as private rooms. Everyone shares the common room with a TV, refrigerator, microwave, and free coffee. Guests make and strip their own beds.

Tenters and hostel guests share the bath-house, which has separate toilet and shower facilities for men and women. Groups should call for special rates. The campground is open year-round, and reservations are strongly recommended. Pets are not allowed in rooms but are welcome at the tent sites. The proprietors will be happy to make reservations for you for air tours, helicopter rides, and river running. Major credit cards are accepted. To reach the campground, take Arizona Highway 64 north off Interstate 40. Go 8.2 miles and the facility will be on your right.

SHOPPING

Dusty Bunch Gallery
517 East Route 66
(928) 635-5332
The whimsical life-size carvings of Old West cowboys and Indians make this a place your kids won't let you drive by. The painted wood carvings are done by Kowalski and Sons, who also create wood bears in all sizes. Owner Linda Odijk carries a full complement of souvenirs for your gift shopping. Her Navajo jewelry and Zuni fetishes are purchased directly from Native American artists. The shop is open daily. Summer hours run into the late evenings so that people on day tours out of Williams will have a chance to shop here. You can pay for your purchases with a major credit card, traveler's checks, or personal checks up to $100.

The Route 66 Place
417 East Route 66
(928) 635-0266
www.route66place.com
Since this large souvenir gift shop is attached to Twister's 50's Soda Fountain, this is a one-stop mecca for the Route 66 enthusiast. The large gift shop has everything you can imagine (and some you probably can't) related to Route 66, from T-shirts to key chains to mugs. You should also check out the selection of western wear and Minnetonka moccasins. Open daily.

ANNUAL EVENTS

May

Mountain Men Rendezvous Days
Buckskinner Park
Memorial Day weekend
(928) 635-4061
Join trappers right out of the 19th century at this festival of black powder shoots, trading, and 1800s crafts at Buckskinner Park in south Williams. Trappers show off their expertise with flintlock and caplock rifles and pistols, and traders sell small leather pouches, old-style clothing, beads, guns, knives, tomahawks, blankets, and fur hats.

Today's Buckskinners re-create the legendary fur-trading time by dressing in period clothing, living in tepees or primitive shelters, shooting muzzleloading black powder rifles and pistols, and throwing tomahawks and knives in friendly competition. Some who attend rendezvous days are still trappers, but most are hunters and outdoorsmen. In the early 1990s, about 150 trappers were licensed by the Arizona Game and Fish Department to trap beaver, fox, coyote, bobcat, raccoon, ringtail, and badger.

This family weekend is too good to miss. It is full of unusual and fun events. In addition to the activities in the park staged by the mountain men, all ages can enjoy downtown events—a parade, arts and crafts, food vendors, street entertainment, and a dance.

July

Small Town Fourth of July
Downtown Williams
July Fourth
(928) 635-4061
This Fourth of July celebration includes an old-fashioned parade, outdoor entertainment, an ice cream social, barbecue, and a craft fair in downtown historic Williams. After dark, you'll be treated to a spectacu-

lar show of fireworks with Bill Williams Mountain as the backdrop.

August

Cowpunchers Reunion Rodeo
First weekend in August
(928) 635-9526
Real working cowboys get together for this big rodeo held at the Rodeo Grounds.

September

Labor Day PRCA Rodeo
Labor Day weekend
(928) 635-4061
Spend Labor Day weekend in Williams at this rodeo featuring top professional

rodeo cowboys. This big-time rodeo includes bull riding, barrel racing, bucking broncos, and all the other traditional rodeo events. Watch the rodeo parade on Saturday, and join in the barn dancing later in the day.

November

Mountain Village Holiday
Thanksgiving to New Year's Day
(928) 635-4061
A million Christmas lights adorn this small mountain town during Mountain Village Holiday, with a Parade of Lights on the second Saturday in December. Hayrides, craft sales, arts shows, and shopping make this a good time to visit Williams.

SEDONA

Although its population hovers around 17,000, Sedona welcomes an estimated 3.5 million visitors a year, making it the second most popular visitor destination in the state of Arizona, next to Grand Canyon. A tourist, recreation, resort, and art mecca, Sedona rests at the center of Red Rock Country, an area that affords panoramic views, monolith rock formations, and a mild climate that appeals to visitors of all ages.

Located 120 miles north of Phoenix and 30 miles south of Flagstaff, Sedona was established in 1902 but not incorporated until 1988. Sedona sits at an elevation of 4,500 feet and spreads across two bordering counties: Coconino and Yavapai.

Visitors often ask, "When is the best time of year to visit Sedona?" By far, the best answer to this question is any time of year. Each season offers its own special nuances. Come in the fall and camp among Oak Creek Canyon's explosion of autumn color. Take refuge from snow and ice in Sedona's mild winter. Watch wildflowers bloom during the spring. And every month is ideal to participate in the area's endless outdoor activities. The forest service stocks Oak Creek with trout from Memorial Day through Labor Day. Arizona Highway 89A, which runs through Oak Creek Canyon, was named one of the most beautiful drives in America by Rand McNally. In 2003, *USA Weekend* magazine chose Sedona and the surrounding Red Rock Country as the most beautiful place in the United States.

Tourism is Sedona's main economic force, and the city prides itself on its locally owned businesses that strive to preserve Sedona's small-town character. Though you can find a four-star hotel, Sedona is also home to quaint bed-and-breakfasts, accommodations for the whole family, and a variety of camping possibilities.

A major cultural center for the arts in the West, Sedona is home to more than 40 galleries and a multitude of artists and writers. Spend a few days here to shop, dine, and explore other attractions in northern Arizona—visit Jerome's old mining town, dance the night away on Prescott's Whiskey Row, or take a day trip to Grand Canyon.

Ancient ruins and geological evidence dating from A.D. 700 surround the area and add to its cultural mystique. This land is sacred to Native Americans. People of all walks of life come to Sedona every year to explore the power of the world-renowned vortexes. Pioneers, surveyors, and trappers came to the area in the early 1800s. In the early 1920s author Zane Grey wrote *Call of the Canyon* and later convinced producers to film the silent movie in Sedona. Since then hundreds of movies, TV commercials, and music videos have been filmed in Sedona.

Still a well-kept secret among visitors to northern Arizona, Sedona is an unforgettable experience, and we hope you enjoy every minute of it.

GETTING TO SEDONA

The Sedona region is divided into three major sections: Oak Creek Canyon, Red Rock Country, and the three communities of Sedona (Uptown Sedona, West Sedona, and the Village of Oak Creek). Tourist activity centers mainly within Uptown and West Sedona. The quintessential Y intersection connects Arizona Highway 89A and Arizona Highway 179. Arizona 89A, the "Main Street" for both Uptown and West Sedona, connects the Sedona region with the city of Prescott (63 miles southwest of Sedona) and Flagstaff (28 miles north). Travelers looking to access the intersection of Interstate 17 and Interstate

40 will take AZ 89A north to Flagstaff. Visitors are encouraged to take the 14-mile scenic AZ 89A from Flagstaff. The trip down the switchbacks of Oak Creek Canyon is considered the most beautiful scenic road in the country.

By Air

Sedona Airport only deals with charter and private planes. For more information about the facilities at the airport call (928) 282-4485. Travelers can fly into Phoenix Sky Harbor International Airport and rent a car or take a shuttle to Sedona. It takes about two hours to drive from Phoenix (except during rush hour) and seems to be the least complicated of the options.

Phoenix is the hub for America West Airlines (800-235-9292 reservations). Many of the major airlines have daily flights to Phoenix including Continental Airlines (800-525-0280 reservations), United Airlines (800-241-6522), and American Airlines (800-433-7300 reservations). For information about Sky Harbor Airport call (602) 273-3300.

Ten rental car companies serve Phoenix Sky Harbor International Airport. See the section on the airport in the Getting Here, Getting Around chapter for contact information.

By Car

SEDONA VIA GRAND CANYON

If you are driving from the south entrance of Grand Canyon, take U.S. Highway 180 to Flagstaff. Grand Canyon Village (south entrance) is 80 miles northwest of Flagstaff. Once you are in Flagstaff follow U.S. 180 until you reach Humphreys Street. Make a right on Humphreys and follow it until you meet Santa Fe Avenue. Turn right onto Santa Fe Avenue, which rounds a bend under the railroad bridge and soon becomes Milton Road. Milton Road takes

you directly out of town to Interstate 17 South. From I-17 South, take the exit marked Pulliam Airport and take scenic AZ 89A to Sedona or take I-17 South to the Sedona exit. Travel time is approximately two hours.

From the North Rim of Grand Canyon, take Arizona Highway 67 to Jacob Lake. At Jacob Lake head east on U.S. 89A, which will tie into U.S. 89 and bring you directly into the east side of Flagstaff. Instead of driving through town, travelers can bypass the traffic and take the exit marked I-40 and I-17 South (Phoenix). Once you have exited, you will be on I-40. Take the exit marked I-17 South (Phoenix). Now you will have two choices: to take scenic AZ 89A (look for the exit off of I-17 South marked Pulliam Airport, AZ 89A) or take I-17 South to the Sedona exit. It takes approximately five hours to get to Sedona from the North Rim.

Road conditions change rapidly at higher elevations, especially in winter. Call the automated road conditions number, (888) 411-7623, for up-to-the-minute traveling information.

SEDONA VIA PHOENIX

Take Interstate 10 East and look for the exit marked Interstate 17 North. Take I-17 North to Arizona Highway 179 (exit 298) and continue 15 miles to Sedona. This exit allows visitors access to the Village of Oak Creek. Driv-ing time is approximately two hours.

By Shuttle

Ace Xpress
(928) 639-3357, (800) 336-2239
Ace Xpress provides door-to-door service to and from the airport by reservation only. Ace Xpress does not provide service on Thanksgiving and Christmas Day.

Sedona Vital Statistics

Mayor: Dick Ellis   **Arizona governor:** Janet Napolitano

Population: Sedona: 17,000
                     Arizona: 5,629,870

Area (sq. miles): 15

Nickname/motto: Arizona's Scenic Sensation

Average temperatures: July high/low: 95 F/65 F
                                       January high/low: 55 F/30 F

Average rain/snowfall: combined: 8.8 inches

Average days of sunshine: 300

City founded: 1902; incorporated in 1988

Important dates in history:

1863   President Abraham Lincoln signed the congressional bill that established the Territory of Arizona. Resting at the center of the new territory was the area that would become the Sedona region.

1872–73 General Crook began his offensive against the Yavapai and Tonto Apache Tribes.

1875   Native Americans were moved from the Camp Verde Reservation to the San Carlos Reservation in eastern Arizona. More than 200 Native Americans died on this walk. The Yavapai call this forced relocation the "March of Tears."

1879   The Abraham James family became the first residents of what is today known as Sedona.

1895   A school was established in Oak Creek Canyon.

1900   Yavapai and Tonto Apache Indians were granted permission by the federal government to return to the Verde Valley area and Sedona region.

1902   Sedona was named by Ellsworth Schnebly for his sister-in-law, Sedona.

1910   The first school was established in Sedona.

1914   The first road through Oak Creek Canyon was completed.

1923   Western author Zane Grey published *Call of the Canyon*. Oak Creek Canyon is one of the settings for the novel.

1939   W. W. Midgley Bridge was dedicated in Oak Creek Canyon.

1956   Chapel of the Holy Cross was completed.

1970   Population of Sedona reached 2,000.

1975   Honanki Cliff Dwellings, built by the Southern Sinagua 800 years ago, was listed on the National Register of Historic Places.

1987   Sedona's population reached 9,000.

1988   Sedona incorporated as a city.

1995 The Sedona International Film Festival and Workshop was founded.

2001 Sedona's population reached 17,000.

2003 *USA Weekend* magazine chose Sedona and the surrounding Red Rock Country as the most beautiful place in the United States.

Major area employers: Double Tree Sedona; Enchantment Resort & Spa; Los Abrigados Resort & Spa; Sedona/Oak Creek Unified School District

Famous sons and daughters:

John James "Jim" Thompson: He became the first settler at Indian Gardens in Oak Creek Canyon.

Sedona Schnebly: The town was named after her in 1902.

The Abraham Jones Family: This family became the first residents of what is today known as Sedona.

Jesse Jefferson "Bear" Howard: An escaped convict from California, he used the alias "Charles Smith Howard" and hunted bear in the Sedona region. He sold the meat in Flagstaff. His great size and imposing demeanor earned him the nickname "Bear."

Ellsworth Schnebly: Brother of Theodore Schnebly, he was the person who suggested that the town be named after his sister-in-law, Sedona.

Theodore Schnebly: Husband of Sedona Schnebly, Theodore was made Sedona's first postmaster in 1902.

William W. Midgley: A grocer, state senator, and county supervisor, Midgley actively promoted road development in the Oak Creek/Sedona area.

State/city holidays: New Year's Day; Martin Luther King Day; Presidents' Day; Memorial Day; Independence Day; Labor Day; Veterans' Day; Thanksgiving Day; Christmas Day

Chamber of commerce:
Sedona–Oak Creek Chamber of Commerce and Visitors Center
331 Forest Road
(928) 282-7722 or (800) 288-7336

Major airport: Sky Harbor International Airport (Phoenix)

Driving laws: Seatbelts must be worn by front-seat passengers; right turn on red; speed limit is 55 except where marked; speed limit on interstates is 75 except in designated areas.

Alcohol laws: Legal drinking age is 21 years; blood/alcohol level of 0.8% or higher is DUI in Arizona.

Newspaper: *Sedona Red Rock News,* a biweekly.

Sales tax: 7.5 percent city/county/state taxes on all retail sales; 10.5 percent city/county/state accommodations; 7.5 percent city/county/state restaurant and bar

The road through Oak Creek Canyon to Sedona has been widely described as the most beautiful drive in the United States. TODD R. BERGER

Sedona Phoenix Shuttle
Sedona
(928) 282-2066, (800) 448-7988
This service provides six daily shuttles to and from the Phoenix airport (except for Thanksgiving and Christmas). The 10-passenger van is comfortable and air-conditioned. Shuttles pick up at the Super 8 Motel in West Sedona and at the Bell Rock Inn in the Village of Oak Creek. Advance reservations are required. Fares fluctuate; call for current rates.

GETTING AROUND SEDONA

Walking along Oak Creek Canyon can be precarious, as cars tend to drive fast along the narrow road. Uptown Sedona is pedestrian friendly. Shops, galleries, and restaurants line both sides of the street. However, while on narrow Arizona Highway 179 and busy West AZ 89A, stick to driving. Remember: Visitors are looking at the outrageous rock formations and are not always watching the road. The trick is to use defensive tactics; we suggest keeping bikes to the designated mountain bike trails surrounding the area.

Taxis and Limousines

Bob's Sedona Taxi
(928) 282-1234

Sedona Limousines
(928) 204-1383, (800) 775-6739

ACCOMMODATIONS

Surrounded by rugged red rocks, acres of national forest land, and ancient Native American ruins, Sedona visitors can spend the day hiking along famous rock formations or riding in a jeep on dirt roads and then return to their top-notch accommodations with first-class amenities. This paradoxical community appeals to many vacationers who want the best of both worlds: to play hard all day and relax in luxury at night.

Wherever you decide to stay, hosts or resort staff will point you in the right direction to find a particular piece of art, gourmet coffee, or an ideal spot to watch the sunset. Each of the accommodations listed has a reputation for providing excellent customer service and the "extras" that make the difference. Plush robes, afternoon goodies, and gourmet breakfasts are just a few of the perks you can expect when staying in Sedona.

Sedona's peak season is from February through June and from September through the end of December. It is common for accommodations to offer special winter rates from the end of December to the beginning of February. Most guests are return guests and make their reservations a year in advance, so plan your trip early. However, if you find yourself driving into Sedona during the high season without reservations, do not hesitate to check with establishments, especially during the week. Midweek cancellations are more common than weekend ones; plus weekday rates are cheaper.

Most of the accommodations are non-smoking. Call and check if the accommodation accepts pets. If they don't, many establishments will happily put guests in touch with a kennel service or take care of the arrangements themselves.

This section is divided geographically: Arizona Highway 179, Oak Creek Canyon, Uptown Sedona, and West Sedona. Resorts, inns, and bed-and-breakfasts are combined in each section.

PRICE CODE

Prices are based on two-person occupancy and are subject to change. Prices do not include gratuity, room service, or an extra person in the room. (The average

fee for an extra person is $5.00, but some accommodations charge up to $45.00.)

$	Less than $65
$$	$66 to $95
$$$	$96 to $150
$$$$	$151 to $200
$$$$$	More than $200

Arizona Highway 179

Canyon Villa
Bed-and-Breakfast Inn $$$-$$$$
125 Canyon Circle Drive
(928) 284-1226, (800) 453-1166
www.canyonvilla.com

Majestic views of Red Rock Country are as close as your own balcony or patio. This 11-room inn with private baths is elegantly furnished, intimate, and quiet. Guest rooms include individual climate control, whirlpool tubs, remote color TV, telephone, and ceiling fans. Breakfast is served in the dining room between 8:00 and 9:00 A.M. and includes fresh fruit, breakfast entree, and homemade cinnamon rolls. A continental breakfast is available for early and late risers.

The Inn on Oak Creek $$$$-$$$$$
556 Arizona Highway 179
(928) 282-7896, (800) 499-7896
www.sedona-inn.com

The elegant rooms have spa tubs, gas fireplaces, private baths, and plush robes, and make for a romantic getaway any day of the week. A gourmet breakfast is served from 8:00 to 9:30 A.M. Guests are treated to complimentary hors d'oeuvres each day at 5:00 P.M. The inn is within walking distance of shops, galleries, and restaurants.

Within the Los Abrigados Resort & Spa is the Red Rock Spring Farmer's Market. The market has fresh seasonal fruits and vegetables and the hottest to the mildest salsas.

Los Abrigados Resort & Spa $$$$$
160 Portal Lane
(928) 282-1777, (800) 521-3131
www.ilxresorts.com

Adjacent to Tlaquepaque Arts and Crafts Village, Los Abrigados Resort & Spa's 180 luxurious suites rest in the heart of Sedona. Guests enjoy strolling through the 22 acres of lush landscaping and Spanish-style plazas and walkways. Suites have a separate living area, bedroom, and balcony, and many come with a fireplace and patio spa. Los Abrigados is home to the Sedona Spa, where guests experience luxurious pleasures like facials, manicures, and the eucalyptus steam room. The resort has three restaurants on the grounds. On the Rocks Bar & Grill offers casual dining, Steaks & Sticks has prime beef at its best, and for fine Italian dining try Joey Bistro. For more information on these restaurants, see the Sedona Restaurants section.

The Penrose Bed-and-Breakfast $$$$
250 Red Butte Drive
(928) 284-3030, (888) 678-3030
www.thepenrose.com

The Penrose features five guest rooms and is tucked away in a residential neighborhood one-half mile from AZ 179. Each room has a private bath with either a two-person shower or a double Jacuzzi with separate shower. All rooms have east-facing windows offering majestic views of red rock formations and private balconies or patios. A complete breakfast is served from 8:00 to 9:00 A.M. in the breakfast room or outside on the deck. Vegetarian and low-fat meals are available upon request. The Penrose offers complimentary afternoon hors d'oeuvres, nighttime snacks, and refreshments any time of the day.

Radisson Poco Diablo
Resort $$$-$$$$$
1752 South Arizona Highway 179
(928) 282-7255, (800) 528-4275
www.radisson.com/sedonaaz

The Radisson Poco Diablo Resort is great for a weekend getaway or family vacation. The resort has a 9-hole par 3 golf course,

Los Abrigados offers convenient, elegant accommodations in Sedona. The resort's champagne brunch is widely praised. TODD R. BERGER

heated pool and spa, and tennis and rac-quetball courts. The rooms are spacious and include wet bar, refrigerator, and Nintendo. You won't have to leave the resort if you don't want to. Enjoy your meals indoors or outdoors at the resort's two restaurants, T. Carl's (see the Sedona Restaurants section for more information) and 10th Hole Lounge.

Oak Creek Canyon

Briar Patch Inn $$$-$$$$$
3190 North Arizona Highway 89A
(928) 282-2342, (888) 809-3030
www.briarpatchinn.com
These romantic cottages, furnished with Native American art, have wood-burning fireplaces and private patios. Designed for comfort and relaxation, Briar Patch Inn is a secluded getaway on more than eight acres along Oak Creek. Guests start the day with a homemade breakfast in the privacy of their cottage, fireside in the lounge, or creekside.

The Canyon Wren $$$-$$$$
6425 North Arizona Highway 89A
(928) 282-6900, (800) 437-9736
www.canyonwrencabins.com
Looking for that special place to celebrate a birthday or anniversary, or just looking for an intimate escape? The Canyon Wren exudes romance with its private accommodations. The three chalet-style cedar cabins have an open loft bedroom with queen bed and outside deck, complete kitchen with dining area, private bath with whirlpool bathtub, wood-burning fireplace, and patio or deck with gas grill. Continental breakfast is served daily.

Garland's Oak Creek Lodge is surrounded by organic fruit orchards. A greenhouse is located in the orchard where Garland's grows organic vegetables and herbs.

Don Hoel's Cabins, north of Sedona in Oak Creek Canyon, offers a woodsy, quiet atmosphere.
TODD R. BERGER

Don Hoel's Cabins $$$
9440 North Arizona Highway 89A
(928) 282-3560, (800) 292-4635
www.hoels.com
In the heart of Oak Creek Canyon's pines, you will find 19 charming cabins that can accommodate a family or are cozy enough for two. Family cabins come with full kitchens and some cabins have gas-log fireplaces. A continental breakfast is served each morning in the "Parlor," a community cabin with TV and telephone for guests to utilize.

Garland's Oak Creek
Lodge $$$$-$$$$$
8067 North Arizona Highway 89A
(928) 282-3343
www.garlandslodge.com
Guests have to ford Oak Creek (with the help of a paved road) to enjoy the secluded and intimate Garland's Oak Creek Lodge. The lodge's 16 cabins are hidden on nine acres, with four cozy cab-

ins that overlook the creek. The larger cabins have a spacious sitting area and wood-burning fireplace. Full breakfasts and dinners are included with lodging. A light snack is served with afternoon tea daily. The lodge is open April 1 through November 15. For more about Garland's restaurant, see the Sedona Restaurants section.

Oak Creek Terrace Resort $$$$
4548 North Arizona Highway 89A
(928) 282-3562, (800) 224-2229
www.oakcreekterrace.com
Casual and comfortable, Oak Creek Terrace Resort is an oasis along the banks of Oak Creek. The resort has suites, bungalows, and family units. Bungalow and family units include fireplace, minikitchen, and private deck with outdoor barbecue. Relax by the creek in a hammock or in a swing built for two. Small pets are allowed. There is a $25 nonrefundable fee for pets.

Sedona Reál Inn $$$-$$$$$
Arizona Highway 89A at 95 Arroyo
Piñon Drive
(928) 282-1414, (877) 299-6013
www.sedonareal.com
Don't let the hotel amenities fool you.
Behind the luxurious accommodations,
you'll find an all-suites inn with a friendly
atmosphere and an attentive staff. Suites
come with private decks, fireplaces,
Jacuzzis, refrigerators, and microwaves.
Continental breakfast is served daily.

Uptown Sedona

Apple Orchard Inn $$$-$$$$$
656 Jordan Road
(928) 282-5328, (800) 663-6968
www.appleorchardbb.com
Just minutes away from Uptown Sedona,
Apple Orchard Inn is secluded among the
pines. Each of the six rooms is custom
designed with Jacuzzi tubs. Spend the
day by the pool or have an invigorating
massage in the massage room. Start your
day with a gourmet breakfast on the red
rock patio or in the dining room. Afternoon snacks and evening hors d'oeuvres
are served daily.

**L'Auberge de Sedona
Resort** $$$$-$$$$$
301 L'Auberge Lane
(928) 282-1661, (800) 272-6777
www.lauberge.com
Choose from an intimate cottage with fireplace that sits along the banks of Oak
Creek, the European lodge with canopied
king-size beds, or the charming rooms at
the Orchards at L'Auberge, which offers
spectacular views from private balconies or
patios. After a morning walk by the creek,
spend the afternoon soaking in the Jacuzzi
or sipping a drink poolside. Enjoy the gourmet cuisine of L'Auberge, an elegant
French restaurant, or the relaxed atmosphere of the Orchards. For more information about L'Auberge and the Orchards, see
the Sedona Restaurant section.

Matterhorn Lodge $$-$$$
230 Apple Avenue
(928) 282-7176
www.arizonaguide.com/matterhorn/
The Matterhorn Lodge sits perched high
above Uptown Sedona. Each room has a
picture window looking out on the beauty
of the surrounding red rocks, plus a balcony or patio near the room. The lodge
has an outdoor whirlpool spa and heated
pool, in-room refrigerators and complimentary coffee, and cable TV. If you're
bringing your pet, ask about designated
pet rooms.

West Sedona

Boots & Saddles $$$-$$$$$
2900 Hopi Drive
(928) 282-1944, (800) 201-1944
www.oldwestbb.com
For a true western experience with spec-
tacular views of the red rocks, Boots &
Saddles has four custom-designed rooms
that will bring out the cowboy or cowgirl
in any guest. This casual yet romantic B&B
offers in-room spa tubs, homemade and
hearty breakfasts, and afternoon appetiz-
ers. Some rooms come with fireplaces; all
rooms have a TV/VCR, telephone, and
refrigerator.

**Casa Sedona Bed &
Breakfast Inn** $$$$-$$$$$
55 Hozoni Drive
(928) 282-2938, (800) 525-3756
www.casasedona.com
Nestled in a tranquil setting surrounded
by stunning red rocks, this secluded inn's
private guest rooms come with fireplaces,
spa tubs, and refrigerators. A healthy,
gourmet breakfast is served outside
(weather permitting) each morning
between 8:00 and 9:30 A.M. Breakfast
includes entree, fresh fruit, and baked
goods. A "side bar" is always available
with homemade granola, cereal, and
yogurt. Afternoon appetizers are served
from 5:00 to 6:00 P.M.

Enchantment Resort   **$$$$$**
525 Boynton Canyon Road
(928) 282-2900, (800) 826-4180
www.enchantment.com

Tucked away among Boynton Canyon's red rocks and cedar forests, Enchantment Resort's spacious suites can be joined together to create one- or two-bedroom casitas or haciendas. All guest accommodations have private decks. The resort offers a wide variety of activities, including nature walks, yoga, tai chi, swimming, and tennis. Enchantment has two 18-hole championship golf courses for guests. World-renowned spa services are also available.

The Yavapai Room is open for breakfast, lunch, and dinner. For more about the resort's restaurant, see the Sedona Restaurants section.

Enchantment Resort has facilities just for kids ages 8 to 12. Camp Coyote is dedicated to arts, crafts, and outdoor activities. Trained counselors will introduce campers to the wonders of Boynton Canyon. Call the resort for registration.

Sky Ranch Lodge   **$$-$$$$**
Airport Road
(928) 282-6400, (888) 708-6400
www.skyranchlodge.com

These cozy, secluded rooms and cottages have fireplaces and kitchenettes. The lodge offers 75-mile panoramic views in every direction. You will feel close to heaven here. Guests enjoy six acres of lush gardens, year-round pool and spa facilities, and relaxing streams and ponds.

A Territorial House Bed & Breakfast   **$$$-$$$$**
65 Piki Drive
(928) 204-2737, (800) 801-2737
www.oldwestbb.com

Experience western hospitality at this friendly bed-and-breakfast. The spacious rooms include stone fireplaces, whirlpool tubs, and private decks. All rooms come with private baths. The hearty, homemade breakfasts provide plenty of energy for tourists looking to tackle the highlights of Sedona. Families are welcome.

RESTAURANTS

Casual eateries, four-star restaurants, and steak houses await you in Sedona. The relaxed atmosphere of the town permeates the restaurants. The dress code is casual, but if you want to dress up, feel free. Only a few of the upscale eating establishments require dinner jackets for men, but be sure to ask when you call to make your reservations. As for reservations, make them. This is a busy resort town; if you don't want to wait more than an hour for dinner, you will heed this recommendation.

Since this is a resort town, restaurants accept all major credit cards with the exception of Diner's Club. But ask as you make your reservation, not as you are paying your bill. There is no law in Sedona that prohibits smoking in restaurants; however, most establishments only allow smoking in the bar area and don't have a smoking section in the restaurant. Outside dining is available at most restaurants. The mild climate and beautiful scenery entice visitors to dine outdoors during the summer, fall, and spring months. Once the sun goes down, even during the summer, the nights cool off, so be prepared and bring a sweater or jacket.

In this section, the restaurants are divided geographically: Arizona Highway 179, Hillside Sedona, Tlaquepaque Arts and Crafts Village, Oak Creek Canyon, Uptown Sedona, and West Sedona.

PRICE CODE

The price codes below represent average prices for dinner for two, excluding tax, gratuity, and drinks.

$	Less than $20
$$	$21 to $35
$$$	$36 to $60
$$$$	More than $60

Arizona Highway 179

Joey Bistro $$
Los Abrigados Resort & Spa,
160 Portal Lane
(928) 204–JOEY
www.ilxresorts.com
This fun, classic-Italian eatery's menu features homemade pasta, seafood, and chicken dishes. The desserts are "ta die for." The decadent Italian specialties include tiramisu, cannoli, and cheesecake. The crisp, white linen tablecloths add to the casual elegance of the bistro-style restaurant.

On the Rocks Bar and Grill $$
Los Abrigados Resort & Spa,
160 Portal Lane
(928) 282-1777
www.ilxresorts.com
Sports enthusiasts, locals, and visitors agree that this bar and grill's relaxed atmosphere and tasty menu items are a winning combination. The ribs, rotisserie chicken, and wood-fire pizzas are local favorites. On the Rocks has the only 10-foot TV screen in Sedona, and is open daily for lunch and dinner. See the Sedona Nightlife section for more information.

Steaks & Sticks $$
Los Abrigados Resort & Spa,
160 Portal Lane
(928) 204-7849
www.ilxresorts.com
Featuring steak, chops, seafood, and grilled specialties, Steaks & Sticks wows guests with their open kitchen and custom-made brass accouterments. Dining guests are invited to sit at the tiled counter facing the cooking area to watch the chef create. Choose from a full bar with imported beer, spirits, and Los Abri-

gados Resort & Spa's private-label wine. Steaks & Sticks is open every day except Tuesday for dinner. Reservations are recommended. A billiards room is adjacent to the restaurant. For more information about the Billiards Club see the Sedona Nightlife section.

Hillside Sedona

Javelina Cantina $$
671 Arizona Highway 179
(928) 282-1313
This popular eating establishment serves Sonoran-style Mexican cuisine with southwestern flair. The menu has traditional south-of-the-border favorites, fresh salads, and seafood dishes. The margarita menu is extensive. Javelina Cantina is open daily for lunch and dinner.

Shugrue's Hillside Grill $$
671 Arizona Highway 179
(928) 282-5300
Shugrue's Hillside Grill has spectacular views of the red rocks and a continental menu that will knock your socks off. The seafood is so fresh it makes you wonder how close Sedona really is to the ocean. The chef uses fresh ingredients and Cajun spices to create dishes featuring chicken, seafood, and veal. Shugrue's Hillside Grill is open daily for lunch and for dinner.

T. Carl's at Radisson $-$$
1752 South Arizona Highway 179
(928) 282-7333
www.pocodiablo.com
T. Carl's is open daily for breakfast, lunch, and dinner. The breakfast menu includes traditional dishes from French toast to waffles to southwestern favorites like the Breakfast Burrito with fresh chiles. On Sunday, T. Carl's serves a champagne brunch. Lunch features grilled sandwiches, southwestern dishes, and salads. The dinner menu is continental with seafood, steak, and chicken dishes. T. Carl's has a full bar.

Tlaquepaque Arts and Crafts Village

El Rincon Restaurante Mexicano $$
336 South Arizona Highway 179,
Suite A112
(928) 282-4648
www.elrinconrestaurant.com

Guests will enjoy the "Arizona-style" Mexican cuisine. Locals come back for the Green Chile and Shrimp Rellenos and the Spinach Cream Cheese Enchiladas. Sit inside by the fireplace or outside under the sycamore trees. El Rincon has the No. 1-rated Margaritas in Sedona. The restaurant is open daily for lunch and open Tuesday through Sunday for dinner.

René at Tlaquepaque $$-$$$
336 South Arizona Highway 179, Suite 118
(928) 282-9225
www.rene-sedona.com

Nestled in the Mexican courtyard of Tlaquepaque is René at Tlaquepaque, an exquisite and elegant dining experience. The continental menu has traditional and intriguing seafood, vegetarian, pasta, and game dishes. The country French ambience—with delicate lace curtains and superb service—is one reason why you will want to make reservations. Outdoor seating in the courtyard is available, weather permitting. Don't forget to ask for the dessert tray. It changes daily, and if you're fortunate, flourless chocolate cake will be a dessert option. René is open daily for lunch and dinner.

Secret Garden Café $$
336 South Arizona Highway 179,
Suite 66
(928) 203-9564

Bright yellow walls and lush plants invite customers to bring a book and stay for a while. The outdoor seating provides a private getaway for one or two. The quiche bar and selection of homemade pastries offer a light reprieve from the traditional American breakfast. The lunch menu features grilled veggie and meat sandwiches, fresh salads, and soups. All menu items are homemade. The Secret Garden is open daily for breakfast and lunch.

Oak Creek Canyon

Garland's Oak Creek Lodge $$-$$
8067 North Arizona Highway 89A
(928) 282-3343

Dinner at Garland's is a treat. Cocktails start at six, the dinner bell rings at seven. The one-entree special menu begins with homemade bread, soup, and garden salad. Entrees range from beef filet and rack of lamb to fresh fish and breast of duckling. Specify beforehand if you are vegetarian or have other dietary restrictions. Choose from a fine selection of wines to complement your dinner. Exquisite desserts and coffee or teas top off the meal. Limited dinner reservations are available for those not staying at the lodge. Garland's is open daily for breakfast, afternoon tea, and dinner. See the Sedona Accommodations section for more about Garland's Oak Creek Lodge.

Uptown Sedona

Black Cow Cafe $
229 North Arizona Highway 89A
(928) 203-9868

Kids and adults will enjoy the homemade ice cream, home-baked goodies (including breakfast items and pastries), and gourmet sandwiches. There is also a full espresso bar for the much-needed afternoon pick-me-up. Black Cow Cafe is open daily for breakfast and lunch, with baked goods and coffee drinks only available through the dinner hours.

The Cowboy Club/
Silver Saddle Room $$$
241 North Arizona Highway 89A
(928) 282-4200
www.cowboyclub.com

The Cowboy Club is open for lunch and dinner, serving southwestern delicacies.

The menu has unique and tasty options including buffalo, rattlesnake, certified Angus beef, and fresh seafood dishes. Decorated in dark wood with western detail, the Cowboy Club offers casual dining, perfect for families and large parties. The Silver Saddle Room is open for dinner and serves the same menu as the Cowboy Club, but offers a romantic atmosphere. The menu in the Silver Saddle Room also includes sorbet intermezzo, appetizers, and dessert amusé. All menu items are made from scratch. Breads, pastries, and desserts are made in the restaurant's own bakery. The Cowboy Club is open daily for lunch and dinner. Reservations are recommended.

L'Auberge de Sedona Restaurant $$$$
301 L'Auberge Lane
(928) 282-1667
www.lauberge.com
Featuring gourmet French cuisine, L'Auberge serves an award-winning a la carte or prix fixe menu by European-trained master chefs. Step inside and enjoy the ambience of this country French inn with imported fabrics, fine china, and excellent service. The wine list is extensive and will please the most discriminating of palettes. L'Auberge serves breakfast, lunch, and dinner, as well as a gourmet Sunday brunch. The brunch buffet includes omelets, international cheeses and pâtés, fresh-baked breads, and more. Outdoor dining is available along the banks of Oak Creek. Reservations are recommended.

Orchards Bar and Grill $$
254 North Arizona Highway 89A
(928) 282-7200
www.lauberge.com
Influenced by its French cousin, L'Auberge, this American grill offers a casual setting and can accommodate large parties or an intimate party of two. The menu features chicken, beef, and seafood dishes, traditional and southwestern breakfast items, and fresh salads and homemade soup for lunch. Look for the nightly dinner specials. Orchards serves breakfast, lunch, and dinner daily. Reservations are suggested. For more

about Orchards, see the Sedona Nightlife section.

Orchards has live entertainment Thursday, Friday, and Saturday during Sedona's high season. Kick back, have an after-dinner cordial, and listen to the acoustic music of some of the region's most talented musicians.

Takashi Japanese Restaurant $
465 Jordan Road
(928) 282-2334
www.takashisedona.com
The extensive menu features teriyaki, tempura, sukiyaki, teppan yaki, and sushi. Dinner entrees include vegetarian, chicken, beef, and seafood options, and include salad, miso soup, rice, and tea. Takashi is open Tuesday through Friday for lunch, and Tuesday through Sunday for dinner. In good weather, enjoy your meal in the restaurant's outdoor seating. Reservations are suggested.

West Sedona

Casa Rincon & Tapas Cantina $$
2620 West Arizona Highway 89A
(928) 282-4849
www.rinconrestaurants.com
Casa Rincon offers a variety of tapas (appetizers), soups, salads, and traditional Southwest dishes including tamales, tacos, enchiladas, and burritos. A kids' menu is also available. Casa Rincon is open daily for lunch and dinner. For more about Casa Rincon & Tapas Cantina see the Sedona Nightlife section.

Dahl & DiLuca Ristorante
Italiano $$$-$$$$
2321 West Arizona Highway 89A
(928) 282-5219
Guests will feel like they stepped into an authentic Italian restaurant in Italy. Dark-tile

The Heartline Cafe offers fresh ingredients and delicious meals. TODD R. BERGER

floor, cherub fountains, and Italian paintings decorate the long, intimate room. The menu is filled with northern and southern Italian dishes. All ingredients are fresh and the pasta is homemade. The chef specializes in seafood and veal dishes. The desserts are as delightful as the dinner menu. Open daily for dinner. Reservations are required.

The Heartline Cafe $$-$$$
1610 West Arizona Highway 89A
(928) 282-0785
For a casual evening or an elegant affair, experience the original creations at Heartline Cafe. All menu items are made from scratch with only the freshest ingredients. The menu features seasonal dishes, but you can always count on quality and healthy seafood and vegetarian entrees. Heartline Cafe has a full bar and an extensive wine list. Reservations are suggested. Open daily for lunch and dinner.

Judi's Restaurant and Lounge $$
40 Soldiers Pass Road
(928) 282-4449
Tucked away in La Posada Shopping Plaza, this local eatery continues to deliver great food in an intimate setting. Known as "Sedona's best kept secret," Judi's Restaurant serves a continental menu. Guests will have a hard time deciding between the baby back ribs, fresh seafood, and hearty pasta dishes. Judi herself makes all the desserts from scratch, including the ice cream. The restaurant is open daily for lunch and dinner. Dinner reservations are suggested.

Keiser's West $
2920 West Arizona Highway 89A
(928) 204-2088
This is food like your mother would make—the breakfasts are big, and your coffee cup is bottomless. Locals agree that Keiser's serves the tastiest French toast in town.

Lunch is a delight with hickory-smoked sandwiches. Dinner is a tradition, with chicken, ribs, and pork basted in Keiser's secret sauce. Early-bird dinner specials are from 4:30 to 6:30 P.M. The atmosphere is casual, so roll up your sleeves and dig in. Keiser's West is open Monday through Saturday for breakfast, lunch, and dinner, and Sunday for breakfast and lunch.

Rainbows End Steakhouse and Saloon $-$$
3235 West Arizona Highway 89A
(928) 282-1593
If you are searching for good steaks, ribs, and chicken, look no further. Rainbows End serves large portions of homemade "grub" that will fill your stomach and warm your heart. The service is friendly and attentive. You'll feel like a local after spending an evening here. After dinner, the band starts, so put on your cowboy boots. For more information about the Rainbows End weekend entertainment, see the Sedona Nightlife section. The restaurant is open Monday through Friday for lunch and dinner, and Saturday and Sunday for dinner only.

Yavapai Room at Enchantment Resort $$-$$$
525 Boynton Canyon Road
(928) 282-2900
www.enchantment.com
Plan an intimate evening dinner, a relaxing lunch, or start your day with the breakfast buffet at the Yavapai Room. The menus incorporate local, regional, and traditional ingredients and the outcome is memorable. Guests will love the food and enjoy the breathtaking views of Boynton Canyon. The Yavapai Room is open daily for breakfast, lunch, and dinner. Reservations are required for all menus.

ATTRACTIONS

While exploring Red Rock Country, be sure to break away from the souvenir shops

Rainbows End Steakhouse and Saloon has free dance lessons every Tuesday and Wednesday. Lessons begin between 8:00 and 8:30 P.M.

that line the streets of Uptown Sedona and immerse yourself in the history of the area. Besides the picturesque landscape, Sedona and the surrounding region have a story to tell. Ancient ruins and historic monuments provide insight to the past.

Visitors will be introduced to the ancient Sinagua Indians who lived in the region from A.D. 650 to about A.D. 1400, when the culture mysteriously vanished. While some Sedona residents believe extraterrestrials abducted the ancient culture, there is no evidence to support this theory, and scientists remain perplexed as to why the people left as they were tending to tasks such as preparing a meal. Tuzigoot and Montezuma National Monuments and Palatki and Honanki sites are silent testaments to this lost culture and other Native American tribes.

Fort Verde State Historic Park is the site of several major battles between the U.S. Cavalry and Yavapai and Apache Indians. Jordan Historical Park is a tribute to the earliest settlers of Sedona.

This section includes historic and ancient monuments, museums, Native American sites, an arts-and-crafts village, area parks, a chapel, a theater, and one of the best places to watch the sunset.

Museums and Parks

Fort Verde State Historic Park
125 East Holloman Street, Camp Verde
(928) 567-3275
During the late 1880s, this site was the base for General Crook's U.S. Army scouts and soldiers as they fought against the Apache and Yavapai Indians. Visitors will be intrigued by the military history of the park.

Located southwest of Sedona, 3 miles east of Interstate 17 in Camp Verde, Fort Verde is open every day except Christmas. The entrance fee is $3.00 for adults and $1.00 for children ages 7 through 13. (For more about Fort Verde State Historic Park, see the Sedona Kidstuff section.)

Jordan Historical Park/
Sedona Heritage Museum
735 Jordan Road
(928) 282-7038
www.sedonamuseum.org
This museum is a tribute to Sedona's earliest settlers. The four acres were once home to Jordan Orchards. The grounds include exhibits on antique farm equipment, an apple-processing shed, and the Jordan house, now home to the Sedona Heritage Society. Admission is $3.00 for adults and children over 12. Children under 12 years of age are admitted free. Open daily.

National Monuments and Native American Ruins

Honanki Ruins
Sedona Ranger District
(928) 282-4119
These 700-year-old ruins are a sacred place, once home to three different cultures: the Sinagua Indians and the Yavapai and Apache Nations. Many of the pictographs have been destroyed by weather and by vandals, but much of the rock art covering the walls is still well preserved. As you approach the site, the main room is to the left, and it has a circular clan symbol painted on the ceiling. As visitors proceed to the right of the site, they will find smaller rooms with preserved rock art.

Honanki Ruins are 6 miles as the crow flies northwest of Sedona, acessible through a series of forest service routes stretching out from Dry Creek Road on the western edge of town. Stop at one of the visitor centers in town for specific directions, as the route is confusing if you lack a map and can be impassable in bad

weather. The site is open daily. Entrance fee is $5.00 for adults. Children 16 and under are admitted free.

Montezuma Castle National Monument
2800 Montezuma Castle Road,
Camp Verde
(928) 567-3322
www.nps.gov/moca
An ancient, five-story cliff dwelling, Montezuma Castle has 20 well-preserved rooms. Early settlers were awestruck by the dwelling, which was built by Sinagua Indians in the 12th and 13th centuries, and named it after the Aztec king, Montezuma. The monument is open every day except Christmas. Children under 16 are admitted free. There is a $3.00 entrance fee for adults.

Palatki Ruins
Sedona Ranger District
(928) 282-4119
These ruins are the cliff dwellings constructed by the Southern Sinagua, who inhabited the area from approximately A.D. 650 to about A.D. 1300. This site is known for its 3,000- to 6,000-year-old pictographs. The symbols painted in red are believed to be the work of mainly the Archaic cultures. The animal and human pictographs painted in yellow are believed to be the work of the Sinagua. The charcoal drawings of men on horseback were done in more recent times by the Yavapai or Apache, around the time the Spanish introduced the horse to the New World.

Palatki Ruins are 9 miles northwest of Sedona and 3 miles northwest of Honanki Ruins. As with Honanki Ruins, stop at one of the visitor centers in town for specific directions, as the route is confusing if you lack a map and can be impassable in bad weather. Both ruins can be visited in a single trip. There is a $5.00 entrance fee per car. The ruins are open daily.

Tuzigoot National Monument
Tuzigoot Road, Clarkdale
(928) 634-5564
www.nps.gov/tuzi

Tlaquepaque Arts and Crafts Village offers upscale shops and restaurants in a beautiful complex reminiscent of an Italian village. TODD R. BERGER

Tuzigoot National Monument, which encompasses 43 acres, was built by the Sinagua Indians in the 13th century. The original pueblo had 110 rooms and second and third stories. Talks and guided tours are offered daily (depending upon the availability of the staff). The monument is open daily except Christmas. There is a $3.00 entrance fee for adults.

Other Attractions

Chapel of the Holy Cross
780 Chapel Road
(928) 282-4069
In 1956, a local architect, inspired by the completion of New York City's Empire State Building, built this shrine 250 feet high in Sedona's red rock landscape. The chapel is open daily. Although it does not still function as a working chapel, a Catholic prayer service is held on Monday evenings.

SuperVue Theatre
Oak Creek Factory Outlets
6615 Arizona Highway 179
(928) 284-3214
This motion-picture venue offers a "virtual tour" of Sedona, shown on a four-story-high screen with digital surround sound. Viewers will take a historical journey and see how this unique region was created. There is a show every hour on the hour except for 3:00 P.M. Admission is $7.50 for adults and $5.00 for children 3 to 11. The theater is located on Arizona Highway 179 at Jacks Canyon Road. Open daily.

Tlaquepaque Arts and Crafts Village
336 South Arizona Highway 179
(928) 282-4838
www.tlaq.com
When visitors come to the arts-and-crafts village Tlaquepaque, they encounter more than quaint galleries and shops: They experience a cultural treat as they stroll along cobblestone courtyards where sycamore

The Chapel of the Holy Cross is built right into a red rock bluff just east of Sedona.
TODD R. BERGER

trees provide shade from the warm Sedona sun. A landmark since the 1970s, Tlaquepaque has exceptional restaurants, entertaining events, and enchanting galleries and shops. It's open daily.

For more about the restaurants in Tlaquepaque, see the Sedona Restaurants section. Tlaquepaque's annual events are referenced in the Sedona Annual Events section. Shops at Tlaquepaque are listed in the Sedona Shopping section. For more information about the galleries, see the Sedona Arts section.

Sunset Views

Sedona offers many spectacular places to watch the sunset. Airport Mesa offers unobstructed views and visibility up to 70 miles. Take Arizona Highway 89A past the Y toward West Sedona. As you reach the top of the hill, a sign for Sedona Airport will be on your left. Follow the road and find a romantic spot to share the sunset.

RECREATION

Sedona is a favorite spot for visitors and locals alike to enjoy outdoor activities. Situated in the heart of Red Rock Country, Sedona has recreational activities for people of all ages. Surrounded by monolithic rock formations, rugged countryside, and vast open land, outdoor enthusiasts can explore the mysterious area by foot, jeep, horse, mountain bike, or hot air balloon. The mild temperatures and constant sunshine will have you outdoors enjoying the fresh air in no time.

Air Service and Charters

Arizona Helicopter Adventures
235 Air Terminal Drive
(928) 282-0904, (800) 282-5141
www.arizonahelicopteradventures.com

View Sedona's famous red rocks, explore canyons, and visit ancient Native American ruins with Arizona Helicopter Adventures. You will hear an in-flight narrative by a skilled pilot, while enjoying a comfortable ride in a Bell Jet Ranger Helicopter. For information about trips and rates, contact Arizona Helicopter Adventures.

Red Rock Biplane Tours
1225 Airport Road
(928) 204-5939, (888) TOO-RIDE
www.redrockbiplanetours.com
Journey through the Red Rock Country of Sedona in a Waco open cockpit biplane. The pilot flies from the rear cockpit while passengers sit in the front cockpit. Contact Red Rock Biplane Tours for more information.

Sky Safari
1225 Airport Road
(928) 204-5939, (888) TOO-RIDE
www.sedonaairtours.com
Sky Safari offers fully narrated local tours, charter services, and destination flights to Grand Canyon, Lake Powell, Monument Valley, and Laughlin, Nevada. The aircrafts can hold three to five passengers plus the pilot. Call Sky Safari for times, different destinations, and current rates.

Balloon Rides

Northern Light Balloon Expeditions
(928) 282-2274, (800) 230-6222
www.sedona.net/fun/balloon
This early-morning adventure starts at sunrise and ends with a gourmet picnic. The cost is $135 per person. Children must be 42 inches tall to ride in the balloon. Northern Light Balloon Expeditions will pick you up from your hotel. Call ahead for reservations.

For up-to-the-minute weather conditions call (928) 774-3301.

Sedona temperatures average 10 degrees cooler than Phoenix and 10 degrees warmer than Flagstaff.

Red Rock Balloon Adventures
175 Palo Verde Circle
(928) 284–0040, (800) 258–3754
www.redrockballoons.com

Explore the Red Rock Country by balloon at sunrise. This company flies deeper into Red Rock Country than any other. After the flight, a champagne breakfast is served. Passengers will receive a previously filmed flight video as a souvenir. The cost is $165 per person.

Sky High Balloon Adventures
175 Palo Verde Circle
(928) 204–1395, (800) 551–7597
www.skyhighballoons.com

If you are looking for something a little out of the ordinary, try "Splash and Dash!" Beginning at sunrise, pilots have passengers floating through the air before they make a dramatic landing on the water. Hold on! Then you ascend into the air again and land on a solid surface. A champagne picnic in the forest after the ride is included. Sky High will pick passengers up at their hotel. The cost is $150 per person. Children must be at least 4 feet tall. Call Sky High Balloon Adventures for more information.

Camping

All designated national forest service campgrounds in the Sedona area have toilets, picnic tables, and fire rings and are wheelchair accessible. The cost per night for one vehicle is $16.00. A $5.00 fee is charged for the second vehicle. There is a $3.00 fee for visitors who want to picnic

Remember: If you pack it in, pack it out. Keep Sedona clean. Don't litter.

in the campgrounds between 10:00 A.M. and 4:00 P.M. A $15.00 fee will be charged to picnickers after 4:00 P.M.

All campgrounds have spigots for drinking water except for Bootlegger. If you have questions, contact the Sedona Ranger District, (928) 282–4119; for reservations call (877) 444–6777.

Bootlegger
This small yet beautiful campground is a good fishing spot nestled among ponderosa pines in Oak Creek. Bootlegger has 10 camping sites, and RVs and trailers are not allowed. Only one vehicle is allowed per unit. The campground is open April 15 through October 31. If you are coming from Sedona, Bootlegger Campground is 9.1 miles north of Sedona on Arizona Highway 89A past the Junipine Resort on your left.

Cave Springs
Cave Springs is a secluded campground, ideal for both couples and families. It has 80 sites and is one of the largest campgrounds in the area. Cave Springs allows two cars per unit and RVs and trailers up to 36 feet. This campground fills up quickly. Call ahead for reservations. Cave Springs is 11.9 miles north of the Y intersection in Sedona on Arizona Highway 89A.

Chavez Crossing Group Camp
Chavez has three sites that can accommodate group campers. Two of the sites can hold 10 to 30 people, while the third site holds up to 50 campers. Walk along the nature trail by the creek and enjoy privacy and seclusion at this campground. Camping fees are $45 at the sites for 10 to 30 campers; a $65.00 fee is charged for the third site. The campground is 2.1 miles south of the Y intersection on Arizona Highway 179.

Manzanita
This campground is open all year and has 19 camping sites. One vehicle per site is allowed. RVs up to 24 feet are allowed; trailers are not allowed in this campground. Campers should arrive early; this

is a popular place to camp. Visitors will enjoy walking or relaxing by the creek. Campers: Beware of poison ivy.

Pineflat East and West

These campgrounds are across the highway from one another and are 12.9 miles north of the Y intersection in Sedona on Arizona Highway 89A. Pineflat East visitors can enjoy access to the Cookstove Trail. This shaded campground is open from April 1 to November 15. There are 21 sites available and RVs and trailers up to 36 feet are allowed. Reservations are not necessary. Pineflat West has 37 sites and is open from March 1 through November 15. This campground can accommodate RVs and trailers up to 36 feet; two vehicles per site are allowed. Pineflat West has trail access on either side of the creek.

Dispersed Camping

Here a few suggestions for campers looking to escape the crowded campgrounds and find seclusion in Coconino National Forest. This is real camping; there are no amenities available in the national forest. Camping in dispersed areas of the national forest is only allowed for 14 days. If you park a car anywhere in the Red Rock Country of the Coconino National Forest (with the exception of developed campgrounds), you must display a daily, weekly, or annual Red Rock Pass. These passes cost $5.00, $15.00, and $20.00 respectively. You can buy a pass at any of the Gateway Visitor Centers (along Arizona Highway 89A just south of Flagstaff, in Sedona, in West Sedona, and in Oak Creek), by calling the Red Rock Ranger District office in Sedona (928–282–4119), or by going on-line to www.redrock country.org/redrockpass. Note that if you don't park a car, you don't need a pass (bikers and hikers can leave their cars in Sedona, head out of town under human power, and explore the area for free).

Beaverhead Flat Road

Take Arizona Highway 179 past the Village of Oak Creek for 3 miles. Beaverhead Flat Road or Forest Road 120 is on the right-hand side of the road.

House Mountain

Take Arizona Highway 179 south of the Village of Oak Creek to Beaverhead Flat Road (Forest Road 120). Drive 2 miles on FR 120, which leads directly to House Mountain.

Sycamore Street/Deer Pass Drive

Drive 6 miles west of Sedona on Arizona Highway 89A until you reach Forest Road 525. Take FR 525 north for 2.5 miles to Forest Road 525C. Get out and camp!

Visitors with a fishing license can stop almost anywhere along Oak Creek and throw in a fishing line. Watch for signs that warn against trespassing. Be aware of areas that are restricted to swimmers and are private property.

Fishing

If you want to fish in Oak Creek Canyon, you must first purchase a fishing license. Fishing licenses can be purchased at Safeway, Bashas, or participating sporting good stores.

Gon' Fishen
30 Kashmir Road
(928) 282-0788

Your fishing guide Jim McInnis will take you to secluded fishing holes, provide transportation, lunch, and basic fly-fishing instruction. Equipment can be rented and private fishing lessons are available. Contact Jim for more information and an unforgettable fishing experience.

Oak Creek Canyon is an idyllic spot, great for fishing or contemplating. TODD R. BERGER

Rainbow Trout Farm
North Arizona Highway 89A, Oak Creek Canyon
(928) 282-5799
Pay $1.00 and you will be armed with bucket, pole, and net. Be ready to catch some trout. You cannot throw back what you have caught. The fee per fish ranges from $3.99 to $6.95 depending on the size and weight. Rainbow Trout Farm is open seven days a week year-round. A fishing license is not required at the trout farm. Barbecue grills and picnic facilities are available.

Golf

Canyon Mesa Country Club
500 Jacks Canyon Road, Oak Creek
(928) 284-0036
A private course that is also open to the public, this 9-hole executive course is well maintained and offers putting and chipping facilities. Greens fees are $15 to walk plus an additional $10 for a cart.

Oak Creek Country Club
690 Bell Rock Road, Oak Creek
(928) 284-1660, (888) 703-9489
Three decades ago, Robert Trent Jones Sr. designed this traditional-style 18-hole golf course. Today it is one of the most played courses in the Sedona area. The $75 greens fee includes a cart. Call for tee times.

Sedona Golf Resort
35 Ridge Trail Drive
(928) 284-9355, (877) 733-9882
www.sedonagolfresort.com
This championship 18-hole course has received more than one four-star rating from *Golf Digest*. The views of the surrounding red rocks makes this an unforgettable golfing experience. Contact the Sedona Golf Resort for tee times and fees.

Hiking

Whether you are looking for wildlife, archaeological sites, or an afternoon walk, Sedona's hiking trails are bound to please everyone. Don't forget to bring plenty of water and to wear sunscreen.

Allen's Bend Trail
Easy
This tranquil 0.5-mile walk takes you along Oak Creek through an old orchard. The trail provides access to the creek for fishing, swimming, and picnicking. To find the trailhead, go north on Arizona Highway 89A to milepost 376.7. Make a right and park in the lot for Grasshopper Point. There is a $3.00 fee. This trail is not recommended for horses.

Bell Rock Pathway
Easy
This 3.5-mile trail is the widest in the state. Members of the local organization Red Rock Pathways helped to build the trail that offers stunning views of Bell Rock and Courthouse Butte. To reach the Bell Rock Pathway, take Arizona Highway 179 south. Just beyond the Sedona Methodist Church you will see the trailhead is on the east side of the road.

Brins Mesa Trail
Moderate
This trail begins at the edge of town and exposes the hiker to unobstructed views of the red rocks. Bring a map along this 3-mile trail so you can identify Coffee Pot Rock, Wilson Mountain, Chimney Rock, and other rock formations. Take Arizona Highway 89A for 3.1 miles to Dry Creek Road. Turn right onto Dry Creek Road and drive for 1.9 miles to unpaved Forest Service Road 152 and turn right. Go 2.4 miles on FR 152 and turn right for Brins Mesa Trail Forest Service Road 119.

Secret Canyon Trail
Moderate
This 4.2-mile trail climbs from 4,640 feet

to 5,300 feet, and the first 2 miles follow an old, flat roadbed. The rest of the trail traverses in and out of the bottom of the canyon and is used by both hikers and equestrians. To access the trailhead, drive on Arizona Highway 89A for 3.1 miles to Dry Creek Road. Turn right onto Dry Creek Road and drive 1.9 miles to Forest Service Road 152. Make a right onto FR 152 and drive northeast for 3.4 miles to the parking area for Secret Canyon Forest Service Road 121.

Horseback Riding

A Day in the West & Sedona Photo Tours
252 North Arizona Highway 89A
(928) 282-4320, (800) 973-3662
www.adayinthewest.com
Step back in time and visit an authentic western movie town by horseback. A Day in the West provides guided horseback rides and cowboy cookouts with all the fixins'! Contact A Day in the West for reservations and rates. (See Tours for more about Sedona Photo Tours.)

Sedona Red Rock Tours
270 North Arizona Highway 89A
(928) 282-6826, (800) 848-7728
www.redrockjeep.com
Experience the "Old West" with Sedona Red Rock Tours. Riders will be surrounded by national forest and will view some of Sedona's most stunning red rock formations. Call Sedona Red Rock Tours for reservations and rates. See Tours for more information about Sedona Red Rock Jeep Tours.

Trail Horse Adventures
85 Five J Lane
(928) 282-7252, (800) 723-3538
www.trailhorseadventures.com
For the complete western experience, Trail Horse Adventures offers hayrides, sunset rides, cattle drives, and western entertainment. Call Trail Horse Adventures for corporate and family rates and special events.

Mountain Biking

Pedal your way through the pine forests and the desert landscapes of Sedona on numerous bike trails. Visitors can rent mountain bikes at Mountain Bike Heaven, 1695 Arizona Highway 89A, (928) 282-1312, and at Sedona Bike & Bean, 6020 Arizona Highway 179, (928) 284-0210.

Broken Arrow
Moderate
Broken Arrow provides scenic views, awesome rock formations, and a sink hole. This trail can get a bit tricky (some might say technical) and fluctuates from easy to hard riding terrain. To access the Broken Arrow trail, take Arizona Highway 179 south from the Y intersection 1.4 miles to Morgan Road, which is on the left. The trailhead is at the end of Morgan Road.

Cathedral Rock
Moderate
This 10.9-mile trail ranges from easy to expert. The clincher of this ride is a swimming hole, a welcome relief for tired and sweaty riders. To access the trail, take Arizona Highway 179 south from the Y intersection for 4 miles until you come to an intersection with Back o' Beyond Road on the right. Take Back o' Beyond Road 0.7 mile to the trailhead on the left.

Deadman's Pass
Easy to Moderate
This 6.4-mile singletrack takes you through the backcountry north of Sedona. The trail goes mostly downhill through rough, rocky sections. To access the trailhead, take Arizona Highway 89A through West Sedona to Dry Creek Road. At Dry Creek Road make a right and follow the road until it ends at a Y intersection. Before the intersection, the road turns into Boynton Pass Road. Turn right onto Long Canyon Road at the Y intersection. Drive for 0.6 mile; the trailhead is on the left.

Mountain bike trails abound in the Coconino National Forest around Sedona. Mountain Bike Heaven can get you in the saddle if you come to town without fat-tire transportation.
TODD R. BERGER

Dry Creek Road
Easy
Beginning mountain bike riders will enjoy the smooth forest road and spectacular views, but remember the return trip is uphill. To reach the Dry Creek Road Trailhead, take Arizona Highway 89A through West Sedona and turn right onto Dry Creek Road. Dry Creek Road turns into Boynton Pass Road. Bikers will want to head right at the Y intersection and park their car here as well.

Parks

Red Rock Crossing/Crescent Moon Ranch Day Use Area
Upper Red Rock Loop Road
(928) 282-4119 (Red Rock Ranger District)
Families will enjoy swimming under the towering red cliffs. Picnic tables are available. To access Red Rock Crossing, take

Tune your radio to 1500 AM for more information about Sedona's parks.

West Arizona Highway 89A to Upper Red Rock Loop Road. Overnight camping is prohibited. There is a $7.00 fee per vehicle.

Red Rock State Park
4050 Red Rock Loop Road
(928) 282-6907
www.pr.state.az.us/Parks/parkhtml/ redrock.html
The park was founded to preserve the natural habitat of Oak Creek and to provide educational activities for adults and kids. The park also offers hiking trails, picnic facilities, and special programs. Red Rock State Park is located on Lower Red Rock Loop Road off of West Arizona Highway 89A. There is a $5.00 entrance fee per vehicle.

Slide Rock State Park
6871 North Arizona Highway 89A
(928) 282-3034
www.pr.state.az.us/Parks/parkhtml/
sliderock.html
This natural waterslide is one of the most popular parks in Arizona. The park, besides offering relief from the summer heat, has picnic tables, barbecue grills, fishing, and nature trails. Slide Rock State Park is located 7 miles north of Sedona in Oak Creek Canyon. A $5.00 entrance fee is charged per vehicle.

Tennis

Play a set of outdoor tennis surrounded by the beautiful red rocks of Sedona. These private clubs are also open to the public. Reservations are required and there is a $10 fee to play: Radisson Poco Diablo Resort, 1752 South Arizona Highway 179, (928) 282-7333; and Sedona Racquet and Fitness Club, 100 Racquet Road, (928) 282-4197.

Posse Grounds Park
Posse Grounds Road
(928) 282-7098
Bring the family here to enjoy the playground facilities, have a picnic, or play tennis. This park is located in West Sedona on Posse Grounds Road.

Tours

Blue Feather Tours
(928) 284-3343
www.bluefeathertours.com
Blue Feather Tours will pick you up at your hotel and take you through Oak Creek Canyon and along Historic Route 66. The tour will then introduce you to the beauty of the Painted Desert and stop at a Navajo trading post. The next stop is Grand Canyon. Passengers will stop at lookout points and walk along the rim. Tours can be personalized to accommodate a group

of five or more. Two-day excursions to Monument Valley and Canyon de Chelly, and to the Hopi Reservation, are available. Call Blue Feather Tours for rates, departure times, and reservations.

Pink Jeep Tours and Ancient Expeditions
204 North Arizona Highway 89A
(928) 282-5000, (800) 8-SEDONA
www.pinkjeep.com
Explore the desert country of Sedona in a pink jeep. Take a tour to the ancient Native American ruins with professional and knowledgeable guides. Pink Jeep Tours offers exclusive "world famous" four-wheel-drive adventures, customized tours, and special events. Contact Pink Jeep for more information and reservations.

Sedona Adventures 4X4 Tours
276 North Arizona Highway 89A
(928) 282-3500, (800) 888-9494
Specializing in customized tours of Sedona's canyons and monuments, Sedona Adventures will take you on the off-road experience of your life. Call Sedona Adventures for group rates and reservations.

Sedona Nature Excursions
(928) 282-6735
www.rahelio.com
Embark on a spiritual journey in the Red Rock Country to the world-renowned vortices of Sedona. Your guide will customize your tour to include healing ceremonies, nature walking, or meditation. Contact Rahelio for more information.

Sedona Photo Tours
252 North Arizona Highway 89A
(928) 282-4320, (800) 973-3662
www.adayinthewest.com
Sedona Photo Tours range from "mild to wild" and offer some of the best photographic opportunities. Learn about Native American customs, geology, and history while experienced guides offer great photography tips. Don't forget your camera!

Sedona Red Rock Jeep Tours
270 North Arizona Highway 89A
(928) 204-4320, (800) 848-7728
www.redrockjeep.com
Sedona's renowned cowboy tour company also offers 4x4 jeep and jeep-helicopter tours, and special personalized events. Ride along the same trail traveled by General George Crook during the final Apache campaign in 1871-72. Contact Sedona Red Rock Jeep Tours for more information.

Sedona Vortex Connections
Angel Valley Ranch
13513 Angel Valley Road
(928) 204-9322, (800) 393-6308
www.sedonavortex.com
Sedona Vortex Connections will help make your visit to Sedona a life-changing experience with its nurturing tours to the renowned vortices. Contact Sedona Vortex Connections for details on tours and rates.

SHOPPING

Even the most hesitant of shoppers will agree that Sedona is a shopper's paradise. Visitors enjoy strolling through the stores and along cobblestone courtyards as they eye some of the most unique gifts under the sun.

One of the major retail areas is located in Uptown Sedona, on Arizona Highway 89A. Don't be startled by the abundance of souvenir shops. Seek and you shall find, and you will find a little of everything within a convenient walking distance—arts, crafts, jewelry, western wear, and clothing stores with a "southwestern" flair.

South of AZ 89A, below the Y, on both sides of Arizona Highway 179 you will find bookstores, mineral shops, and clothing boutiques. Hillside Sedona is on AZ 179 and has scenic views, sculpture gardens, boutiques, and southwestern furnishings. Tlaquepaque Arts and Crafts Village is located at the Y. Shoppers will

The Book Loft specializes in out-of-print book searches. Visit the bookstore, or call (928) 282-5173 to find your title.

enjoy the Spanish colonial architecture, bending sycamores, and flower-filled courtyards. The major draws in the Village of Oak Creek are the factory outlet stores and a few specialty shops.

Numerous shopping centers, professional plazas, and specialty shops line West AZ 89A.

This section is divided geographically: Arizona Highway 179, Hillside Sedona, Oak Creek, and Tlaquepaque. Then we head to Uptown Sedona and West Sedona.

Arizona Highway 179

The Book Loft
175 Arizona Highway 179
(928) 282-5173
Specializing in regional guidebooks, the Book Loft has 10,000 new, used, and rare books. Try their organic coffee by the cup or take a pound of it home with you. The Book Loft is open every day except Tuesday.

Crystal Castle
313 Arizona Highway 179
(928) 282-5910, (800) 688-2665
www.crystalcastle.com
Crystal Castle has products to soothe your mind and soul, including aromatherapy products, new age music, books, bells, chimes, jewelry, rocks, and crystals. Crystal Castle is open daily.

Ramsey's Rocks and Minerals
152 Arizona Highway 179
(928) 204-2075
Since 1949 Ramsey's has offered a large selection of Arizona gems, crystals from around the world, and quality minerals. Jewelry is custom made by artist Jeffrey Goebel. Ramsey's is open daily.

Victorian Cowgirl
204 Arizona Highway 179
(928) 203-9809, (888) 804-9040
www.easy-finder.com/brochures/vcgirl
For a classic look, Victorian Cowgirl combines the elegance of the Victorian age and the freedom of the West. Victorian Cowgirl, featuring women's clothing, unique bridal wear, and accessories, is open daily.

Hillside Sedona

Favorite Clothing Co.
671 Arizona Highway 179
(928) 282-0995
Featuring contemporary natural fiber clothing, Favorite Clothing also has its own line of handmade batik clothing for women and children. This natural shop also has accessories, jewelry, and gift items. The store is open daily.

Hillside Prints & Framing
671 Arizona Highway 179
(928) 282-6567
Hillside Prints & Framing has a great selection of prints, posters, and original art of Sedona and the Southwest. After you have picked out your piece, they will happily frame it for you too.

The shop also carries note cards, postcards, and gift items. Hillside Prints & Framing is open daily.

Santa Fe Savvy
671 Arizona Highway 179
(928) 204-9848
Decorate your home with the spirit of the West. Santa Fe Savvy has leather furniture, end tables, bookcases, dressers, and so much more. Santa Fe Savvy is open daily.

Steppes
671 Arizona Highway 179
(928) 204-0606
Get lost in this quaint boutique for hours and discover Brighton leather goods and gifts, women's clothing, and accessories. Steppes is open daily.

The Wine Basket at Hillside
671 Arizona Highway 179
(928) 203-9411
Immerse yourself in the decadence of the Wine Basket. They have gourmet everything, from chocolates to pastries to imported coffee. The Wine Basket has California, New Zealand, French, Chilean, and Italian wines. Specialty baskets can be designed and shipped from the store. The Wine Basket is open daily.

Village of Oak Creek

Oak Creek Factory Stores
6600 Arizona Highway 179
(928) 284-2150, (888) 545-7227
Oak Creek Factory Stores feature more than 30 national store chains. From Bass to Anne Klein to Geoffrey Beene, the stores have a large selection of clothing and home furnishings at discounted prices. The factory stores are open daily.

Sedona Bike & Bean
6020 Arizona Highway 179
(928) 284-0210
Sedona Bike & Bean can outfit you for all your cycling needs, with bike clothing and accessories for men, women, and children. They also rent mountain bikes for the family (ages eight years and up). Wondering what the Bean part is about? Sedona Bike & Bean has an espresso bar with specialty drinks and snacks. Sedona Bike & Bean is open daily.

Tlaquepaque Arts and Crafts Village

Cocopah
336 South Arizona Highway 179,
Suite C101
(928) 282-4928

Cocopah has beads, shells, ethnic pieces, jewelry kits, and jewelry-stringing materials. Call for their color bead catalog. Cocopah is open daily.

Kitchen Wizard
336 South Arizona Highway 179, Suite D101
(928) 282-3905
The Kitchen Wizard has southwestern spices, condiments, cookbooks, and fun accessories for the home. Kitchen Wizard is open daily.

The Melting Pot Candle Shoppe
336 South Arizona Highway 179,
Suite C106
(928) 204-9881
The Melting Pot has candles, candle holders, and accessories. They feature candles and accessories made by local artists. The Melting Pot is open daily.

The Storyteller Bookstore
336 South Arizona Highway 179,
Suite B105
(928) 282-2144
The Storyteller has southwestern children's books, and hardcover and softcover books about Sedona, the Southwest, and Native American tribes. They also have music, hiking maps, and guides. The Storyteller is open daily.

Torke Weihnachten Christmas
336 South Arizona Highway 179,
Suite A116
(928) 282-2752
Featuring glass pieces and ornaments from Poland and Germany, Torke Weihnachten also has holiday collectibles and Christmas art from the Southwest. Torke Weihnachten is open daily.

Uptown Sedona

Looking West
242 North Arizona Highway 89A
(928) 282-4877
Featuring ladies' fashions with a taste of

Kitchen Wizard at the Tlaquepaque Arts and Crafts Village has a fresh salsa bar where you can sample before you make your purchase.

the Southwest, Looking West has a selection of locally made clothing and accessories. The store is open daily.

Richard David for Men
301 North Arizona Highway 89A
(928) 282-4662
Richard David features men's clothing and accessories. Even the most hesitant of male shoppers will like the selection of sportswear, golf wear, and casual outerwear. Richard David is open daily.

Rollies Camera Shop
297 North Arizona Highway 89A
(928) 282-5721
www.rolliescamera.com
Rollies Camera Shop is a full-service shop that specializes in film, accessories, and of course cameras. Ask about their overnight processing policy. Rollies Camera Shop is open daily.

Sedona Fudge Company
257 North Arizona Highway 89A
(928) 282-1044
Calling all sweet tooths! Sedona Fudge Company has homemade fudge in assorted flavors, truffles, toffee, cookies, and more. This candy heaven is open daily

The Worm Book & Music Store
207 North Arizona Highway 89A
(928) 282-3471
www.sedonaworm.com
The Worm Book & Music Store specializes in western, health, and travel books and hardcover and softcover fiction. Featuring world, classical, and Native American music, the Worm also has a large children's book section. The store is open daily.

Offering general-interest books and a first-class travel section, including lots of titles on Sedona, the Worm feeds the mind from its little shop in Uptown Sedona. TODD R. BERGER

West Sedona

Bob McLean Custom Boot Maker
40 Soldiers Pass Road
(928) 204-1211
Manufacturing quality handmade western boots and belts, Bob McLean will measure and fit you in the shop. Customers choose from only the finest leather. The store will ship anywhere in the United States. The store is open daily.

Canyon Outfitters
2701 West Arizona Highway 89A
(928) 282-5293
Canyon Outfitters will dress and outfit you with quality equipment for your outdoor adventure. They also have a large selection of USGS topo maps, area hiking maps, and books. Canyon Outfitters is open daily.

Gift Baskets of Sedona
Bashas' Shopping Center
160 Coffee Pot Drive
(928) 282-7747
You will find a gift basket for any reason and season here. Baskets are designed especially for you. They will do the shopping or you can shop and they will assemble the basket for you. Or try one of their unique creations, like the Southwest Basket with cactus pot holders and prickly pear jelly. The Get Well Basket comes with crossword puzzles and fresh-squeezed juices. These baskets make great gifts for the person who has everything. Gift Baskets of Sedona is open Monday through Saturday.

Lightin' Up of Sedona
1370 West Arizona Highway 89A
(928) 282-7902
For all your cigar needs, Lightin' Up has

the finest selection of cigars, pipes, and accessories from around the world. Lightin' Up is open Monday through Saturday.

Mexidona
1670 West Arizona Highway 89A
(928) 282-0858

Featuring handcrafted imports, Mexidona has Mexican colonial furniture, home and garden decor, and ethnic and folk art at reasonable prices. Take a piece of the Southwest home with you! Mexidona is open daily.

Sedona Clothing Company and West Fork Men's
1710 West Arizona Highway 89A
(928) 204-9390

Both men and women can find casual or dressy attire for any occasion. Open daily, Sedona Clothing Company and West Fork Men's will even gift wrap your purchases at no extra charge.

Wayne B. Light Custom Jewelry
3000 West Arizona Highway 89A
(928) 282-2131, (800) 894-2131
www.wayneblight.com

Featuring custom designs and traditional jewelry for men and women, this store's extensive selection includes pendants, rings, earrings, and tie tacks, all in your choice of precious metals or diamonds. Wayne B. Light is open daily.

NIGHTLIFE

As a resort town, Sedona hums through the day, but the nights seem quiet under the star-filled sky. Most people like to rest at night so they can tackle the following day's activity-packed itinerary. But there is plenty to do here once the sun goes down.

Live entertainment is everywhere. Solo acts and bands fill the bars. Whether you like to two-step or listen to rock 'n' roll, you can find your choice of music almost any night of the week during the high season (from February to April and from September through the end of December). Free

Tour the Sedona Clothing Company's sewing factory, 1710 West Arizona Highway 89A, Monday through Friday 10:00 A.M. to 6:00 P.M.

dance lessons are given everywhere. Sedona nightclubs hear their Spanish roots and offer salsa lessons and then they listen to their western roots and provide two-step and country line dancing.

If dancing isn't up your alley, Sedona also has quiet and intimate establishments that encourage conversation and provide quality local and regional entertainment.

Most resorts have family activities and bars so visitors don't have to leave the grounds. If you are looking for a night out or for a nightcap after dinner, keep in mind Arizona's strict enforcement of DUI laws. Sedona is a small city. It won't take more than 10 to 15 minutes to reach your destination by cab.

Casa Rincon & Tapas Cantina
2620 West Arizona Highway 89A
(928) 282-4849
www.rinconrestaurants.com

Featuring live entertainment almost every night, Casa Rincon will have you dancing in the aisles or at least in your seat. Local and regional bands perform on Friday and Saturday beginning at 9:00 P.M. The music entertainment on weekend nights changes regularly. Guests can expect to hear Motown, reggae, and rock 'n' roll. Special entertainment is scheduled for Sunday. Call for an updated schedule of events. Wednesday night is Ladies' Night starting at 5:00 P.M., with drink specials all evening. For more about the Casa Rincon & Tapas Cantina, see the Sedona Restaurants section.

The Laughing Coyote
West Arizona Highway 89A
(928) 282-1842

Here the music is as eclectic as the crowd. This is where the locals hang out. Bands play every Wednesday, Friday, Saturday,

and Sunday starting at 9:00 P.M., except for Sunday, when the music starts at 7:00 P.M. Ladies, come out on Wednesday, this is your night. Drink specials, free pool, and jukebox music start at 7:00 P.M.

Oak Creek Brewing Co.
2050 Yavapai Drive
(928) 204-1300
Get a taste for what the locals drink at Oak Creek Brewing Co. Handcrafted stouts, ales, and seasonal beers are made on the premises. Wine and soft drinks are also served. Look for entertainment almost every night of the week. A full band is featured Friday and Saturday nights beginning at 9:00 P.M. Dancing is mandatory. Live solo entertainment is every Sunday, Tuesday, and Thursday. Times fluctuate, so call ahead for exact schedule.

On the Rocks Bar and Grill
Los Abrigados Resort & Spa
160 Portal Lane
(928) 282-1777
www.ilxresorts.com
Come watch the game on the giant 10-foot screen, or relax with a glass of Los Abrigados private label wine. On the Rocks Bar and Grill has appetizers and offers a lighter menu for snacking. The bar is open until 1:00 A.M. For more about On the Rocks Bar and Grill, see the Sedona Restaurants section.

Orchards
254 North Arizona Highway 89A
(928) 282-7200
www.lauberge.com
Visitors will enjoy the quaint bar and casual atmosphere with entertainment every Thursday, Friday, and Saturday. Enjoy live acoustic music from 7 to 9:30 P.M. Local and regional musicians play here. For more about Orchards, see the Sedona Restaurants section.

Rainbows End Steakhouse and Saloon
3235 West Arizona Highway 89A
(928) 282-1593
Rainbows End has something for anyone who wants to dance. Learn the latest country swing dance moves every Tuesday night, and every Wednesday night learn how to country line dance. If country isn't your cup of tea, try Rainbows End on the weekend when they feature live country, Motown, or classic rock bands. The music starts at 9:00 P.M. Call for a listing of bands. For more about Rainbows End, see the Sedona Restaurants section.

Steaks & Sticks
Los Abrigados Resort & Spa
160 Portal Lane
(928) 204-7849
www.ilxresorts.com
This room has pool, backgammon, and small intimate tables for conversation. The room opens at 11:00 A.M. The bar is open from 5:00 P.M. 'til 1:00 A.M. and is stocked with fine wine, premium liquors and cordials, and imported beer. For more on Steaks & Sticks, see the Sedona Restaurants section.

KIDSTUFF

Forget the video games here. Sedona is nature's playground, with endless outdoor recreational activities that will appeal to kids from all walks of life. Whether your kids enjoy hiking, taking nature walks, or swimming in outdoor, pristine pools, Sedona has it.

Your kids can learn from Sedona as well. Introduce your child to ancient Native American cultures and tour historic forts and home sites of Sedona's first settlers.

Fishing

Rainbow Trout Farm
North Arizona Highway 89A
Oak Creek Canyon
(928) 282-5799

Plan to spend the day fishing along Oak Creek with the family. Pay $1.00 and the entire family will be armed with bucket, pole, and net. And after the kids fish to their heart's content, cook the catch of the day right at the farm. Barbecue grills and picnic facilities are available. Rainbow Trout Farm is open seven days a week year-round. For more information about Rainbow Trout Farm, see the Sedona Recreation section.

Hiking

Hiking trails in the Sedona area offer scenic views, a chance to see wildlife, or just a pleasant way to spend the day with your child. The trails are usually dry and exposed to sunlight: Don't forget to bring plenty of water and to wear sunscreen.

Allen's Bend Trail
Easy

This easy 0.5-mile walk takes you along Oak Creek through an old orchard. The trail provides access to the creek for fishing, swimming, and picnicking. For more information about the trail, see the Sedona Recreation section.

Bell Rock Pathway
Easy

This 3.5-mile trail offers stunning views of Bell Rock and Courthouse Butte. To reach the Bell Rock Pathway, take AZ 179 south just beyond the Sedona Methodist Church. The trailhead is on the east side of the road. For more information about this hike, see the Sedona Recreation section.

Brins Mesa Trail
Moderate

Bring a map (you can get one at the Sedona Chamber of Commerce) along this 3-mile trail so you can identify Coffee

Pot Rock, Wilson Mountain, Chimney Rock, and other rock formations. For more information, refer to the Sedona Recreation section.

Horseback Riding

A Day in the West & Sedona Photo Tours
252 North Arizona Highway 89A
(928) 282–4320, (800) 973–3662
www.adayinthewest.com

What child would not want to visit an authentic western movie town by horseback, take a guided horseback ride through Red Rock Country, or have a cowboy cookout with all the fixins' under the star-filled Sedona sky? Contact A Day in the West for reservations and family rates.

Trail Horse Adventures
85 Five J Lane
(928) 282–7252, (800) 723–3538
www.trailhorseadventures.com

For the complete western experience, Trail Horse Adventures offers hayrides, sunset rides, cattle drives, and western entertainment. Call Trail Horse Adventures for family rates and special events.

Movies

SuperVue Theatre
Oak Creek Factory Outlets
6615 Arizona Highway 179
(928) 284-3214

Kids will love the adventurous motion picture shown at the SuperVue that offers a "virtual tour" of Sedona. There is a show every hour on the hour except for 3:00 P.M. Admission is $5.00 for children ages 3 to 11; adults pay $7.50. For more about the SuperVue Theatre, see the Sedona Other Attractions section.

National Monuments and Native American Ruins

Honanki Ruins
Sedona Ranger District
(928) 282-4119

The 700-year-old ruins are regarded as a sacred place to two different cultures: the Yavapai and Apache Nations. The walls are covered with well-preserved rock art. Different colored markings differentiate between inhabitants and time periods. The site is open daily. Entrance fee is $5.00 for adults. Children 16 and under are admitted free. For more about Honanki Ruins, see the Sedona Attractions section.

Montezuma Castle National Monument
2800 Montezuma Castle Road,
Camp Verde
(928) 567-3322
www.nps.gov/moca

Montezuma Castle, a well-preserved cliff dwelling, is five stories tall and has 20 rooms. The structure was built by the Sinagua during the 12th and 13th centuries. Early settlers discovered the ancient cliff dwelling and named it after the Aztec king, Montezuma. Junior Ranger Program activity guides are provided upon request. This program is designed to educate children about the prehistoric environment of the ancient pueblo. The monument is open every day except Christmas Day. Extended summer hours run from Memorial Day through Labor Day. Children under 16 are admitted free; adults pay $3.00.

Visitors are asked to refrain from touching the rock art. Oil from your hand can cause deterioration. Please respect the sites, as they are sacred places to Native Americans.

Palatki Ruins
Sedona Ranger District
(928) 282-4119

The Southern Sinagua constructed these cliff dwellings and lived in the area from approximately A.D. 650 to A.D. 1300. This site is known for the well-preserved pictographs that date back 6,000 years. Palatki Ruins are open daily. There is a $5.00 entrance fee per car. For more information about Palatki Ruins, see the Sedona Attractions section.

Tuzigoot National Monument
Tuzigoot Road, Clarkdale
(928) 634-5564
www.nps.gov/tuzi

Tuzigoot National Monument was built by the Sinagua in the 13th century, and the original pueblo had 110 rooms with second and third stories. Junior Ranger Program activities are designed to educate children and develop awareness of the park's prehistoric environment. Junior Activity Guides are distributed upon request. The monument is open daily except Christmas. There is a $3.00 entrance fee for adults.

Parks

Fort Verde State Historic Park
(928) 567-3275

Fort Verde was the primary base for General Crook's army during the Indian campaigns that were fought in the 1880s. Most of the original buildings stand today, including the officers' quarters and the headquarters building, which is now the fort's museum. The park is in the town of Camp Verde, 3 miles east of Interstate 17, and is open every day except Christmas. The entrance fee is $3.00 for adults and $1.00 for children ages 7 through 13. (For more about Fort Verde State Historic Park, refer to the Sedona Attractions section.)

Posse Grounds Park
Posse Grounds Road
(928) 282-7098

Are your kids tired of shopping and browsing through art gallery after art gallery? If they are, bring the family here to enjoy the playground facilities, have a picnic, or play tennis. The park is located in West Sedona.

Red Rock Crossing/Crescent Moon Ranch Day Use Area
Upper Red Rock Loop Road
(928) 282-4119 (Red Rock Ranger District)
Families will enjoy swimming under the towering red cliffs in the clear waters of Oak Creek. Picnic tables are available. To access Red Rock Crossing, take West Arizona Highway 89A to Upper Red Rock Loop Road. For more information, see the Sedona Recreation section.

Red Rock State Park
4050 Red Rock Loop Road
(928) 282-6907
www.pr.state.az.us/Parks/parkhtml/redrock.html
This nature and wildlife preserve is a family-oriented park with hiking trails, picnic area, and guided tours. The visitor center has daily programs and slide presentations. The entrance fee is $5.00 per vehicle and a $1.00 fee is charged to pedestrians, equestrians, and bicyclists. To preserve and protect the natural environment in the park, dogs, swimming, and camping are prohibited.

For more information about Red Rock State Park, see the Sedona Recreation section.

Slide Rock State Park
6871 North Arizona Highway 89A
(928) 282-3034
www.pr.state.az.us/Parks/parkhtml/sliderock.html
This popular recreational site is known for its natural 30-foot waterslide. Plan on spending the day here! The park also has a picnic area, barbecue grills, a nature trail, and fishing. The entrance fee is $5.00 per vehicle and $1.00 per person (walking in). Refer to the Sedona Recreation section for more information.

Swimming Holes

Swimming in the pristine waters of Oak Creek is a wonderful way to spend the day. The swimming holes and wading options are abundant. Visitors can pull off the side of Arizona Highway 89A (just about anywhere). Don't forget to bring plenty of drinking water and sunscreen, and wearing a hat is always recommended. Most of Sedona's parks have access to the creek. If you would rather have facilities to accommodate the family, refer to the Parks section in this chapter.

Grasshopper Point
Arizona Highway 89A
You'll have too much fun jumping off these cliffs into the cool creek water. Or if you want a little more seclusion, rock hop down the creek and you can sit with your feet in the water and enjoy your own personal pool! Grasshopper Point is located between Oak Creek Canyon and Uptown Sedona. The point is well marked so it's not hard to find.

THE ARTS

Art within the community of Sedona comes in various shapes and sizes. It can be found inside galleries, at decorative outdoor venues, and in the landscape. Nature has played an artistic role as it etched the magnificent red rocks with the help of the sand, seas, and wind. Ancient civilizations left their artistic mark as well in the form of petroglyphs and pictographs. Art is everywhere you look in Sedona. Whether you like to gallery hop, listen to chamber music, or enjoy community theater, the artistic presence is essential to this community's existence.

Sedona was home to western art legends Joe Beeler and John Hampton as well as internationally acclaimed surrealist artist, Max Ernst, who rented his home to Egyptian-born American sculptor Nassan Gobran. Known for his sculpture *Capricorn*, Gobran decided to make Sedona his home

and envisioned making Sedona a center for the arts. In 1961 he saw his dream turn into a reality when land was purchased and proposed as the site for the Sedona Arts Center. This artistic institution was to be a center for national and local art shows. Today the Sedona Arts Center is also dedicated to promoting visual and performing arts for all levels of experience.

Another turning point in the city's history was the birth of one of the most successful and influential art organizations in the United States. Cowboy Artists of America was founded in 1965 in a back booth of what is now the Cowboy Club, a popular eatery in Uptown Sedona.

Today the community enjoys its colorful artistic past while still looking to the future. More than 300 artists call Sedona home. More than 40 art galleries showcase the work of local, regional, and international artists.

The galleries are spread throughout the city, but Sedona is not limited to galleries. The Sedona Arts Center is home to the Sedona Arts Center Community Theatre. The Sedona Chamber Music Society provides year-round concerts at venues around northern Arizona, including Grand Canyon.

A recent addition to the art community is the Sedona Cultural Park. This outside arena and educational facility hosts such Arizona favorites as concerts as well as performances by the Phoenix Symphony and Sedona Jazz on the Rocks.

Galleries

HILLSIDE SEDONA

Blue-Eyed Bear
671 Arizona Highway 179
(928) 282-4761
www.blueeyedbear.com

If you are looking for contemporary Native American jewelry, Navajo folk art, and Zuni fetishes designed by the most prominent artists, Blue-Eyed Bear has one of the most extensive collections in Sedona. Open daily, the shop offers elegant Native American jewelry and crafts, quality, and affordability.

The Clay Pigeon
671 Arizona Highway 179
(928) 282-2845
This gallery is known for setting standards for Southwest contemporary crafts. Specializing in sculpture, ceramics, and jewelry, the Clay Pigeon is also located in Uptown Sedona, 250 North Arizona Highway 89A, (928) 282-2862, and is open daily.

Compass Rose Gallery
671 Arizona Highway 179
(928) 282-7904
www.oldmaps.com
This gallery has an intriguing collection of 16th- to 19th-century maps from the world over. Compass Rose has also one of the largest collections of Native American photography, as well as some of Audubon's original etchings and engravings. The gallery is open daily.

Geoffrey Roth Ltd.
671 Arizona Highway 179
(928) 282-9550, (800) 447-7684
www.geoffreyrothltd.com
Select craftsmen and jewelers have been chosen from across the country and Europe to complement the elegant work of Roth. Geoffrey Roth Ltd. carries a fine selection of jewelry, timepieces, accessories, and exotic hardwood creations. Look for the first Geoffrey Roth Ltd. under the bell tower in Tlaquepaque Arts and Crafts Village, Arizona Highway 179. The second gallery is next to Javelina Cantina at the Hillside Marketplace. Both locations are open daily.

Scherer Gallery
671 Arizona Highway 179
(928) 203-9000
Since 1968, the Scherer Gallery has fea-

How to Buy Art and Jewelry

As you browse through art gallery after art gallery, you finally decide you would like to purchase a piece of authentic art or jewelry. Why not? How many times do you come across true southwestern art?

The actual purchase of art can be intimidating. But it need not be. The most important rule to remember is that you like what you are buying. If you follow this rule, you're sure to appreciate and enjoy your piece of art for years to come, regardless of whether or not its value increases.

The second step is to learn as much as you can about the artist. Don't feel awkward; a smart consumer is an informed consumer. Ask for the artist's biography and bibliography. Ask for a list of collectors, galleries, or museums that display the artist's work.

Know what is out there. Tour as many galleries as you can. Get a feel for the craftsmanship and quality that is available. Many art aficionados will return to a gallery several times to ask more questions and to see the piece one more time.

Practice the same shrewd purchasing skills when buying jewelry. The market has a wide range of styles, quality, and pricing. Be sure to ask if a piece is solid gold, silver, or merely plated. Sometimes nickel is used on less expensive items.

If you are interested in a piece of Native American jewelry, ask for the name of the jeweler and what tribe he or she is from, and ask to see other pieces created by the artist.

Remember to enjoy the experience. Take the time to research and educate yourself about your possible purchase. This is part of the fun.

tured the work of local and internationally acclaimed artists. Some of the more outstanding selections include sculpture, studio art glass, and photography. The gallery is open daily.

HOZHO CENTER

Exposures International Gallery of Fine Art
561 Arizona Highway 179
(877) 278-7483
www.exposuresfineart.com
Art aficionados will get lost among the largest fine art display in Arizona. Encompassing 20,000 feet, the gallery showcases bronze and stone sculptures, fine art photography, ceramics, and glass. Collectors will covet the complete works of the area's most prolific artists. The gallery is open daily.

Garland's Navajo Rugs
411 Arizona Highway 179
(928) 282-4070
www.garlandsrugs.com
Garland's offers quality Native American arts and crafts, including Hopi kachina carvings, Navajo sand paintings, Pueblo pottery, handwoven baskets, and the largest selection of Navajo rugs purchased directly from Navajo weavers. These authentic pieces of art include hard-to-find floor rugs and colorful blankets. Garland's is open daily.

Lanning Gallery
431 Arizona Highway 179
(928) 282-6865
www.lanninggallery.com
This contemporary gallery features jewelry, sculpture, paintings, handmade paper,

and beautifully designed hand-painted furniture. Lanning Gallery is open daily.

Turquoise Tortoise Gallery
431 Arizona Highway 179
(928) 282-2262
www.turqtortsedona.com
Since 1971, Turquoise Tortoise Gallery has assisted both the seasoned collector and the novice buyer in purchasing only exceptional Native American art. The expansive selection will take your breath away. Choose from oil and acrylic paintings, sculpture in bronze and other metals, and custom-made jewelry. The gallery is open daily.

Visions Fine Art Gallery
251 Arizona Highway 179
(928) 203-0022
A unique gallery that focuses on enhancing your quality of life, Visions Fine Art Gallery features spectacular contemporary art that the buyer is bound to fall in love with. Visions Fine Art is open daily.

TLAQUEPAQUE ARTS AND CRAFTS VILLAGE

Bearcloud Gallery
336 South Arizona Highway 179,
Suite C107
(928) 282-4940
Rod Bearcloud Berry's work is reminiscent of the romantic painters of the 1800s. Each piece captures the connection between Earth and the heavens. The gallery is open daily.

El Prado Galleries, Inc.
336 South Arizona Highway 179,
Suite E101
(928) 282-7390, (800) 498-3300
Antiques collectors and art lovers will enjoy browsing among this gallery's antique furniture works by nationally acclaimed artists. This gallery features traditional, western, contemporary, and impressionist paintings, sculpture, and ceramics. El Prado is open daily.

Isadora Handweaving Gallery
336 South Arizona Highway 179,
Suite A120
(928) 282-6232
The gallery is a celebration of handcrafted and handwoven garments, accessories, and jewelry. This wearable art has the spirit of the Southwest woven into it. Isadora is open daily.

Kuivato Glass Gallery
336 South Arizona Highway 179
Patio Azul, Suite B122
(928) 282-1212
This gallery sets itself apart from the other galleries in town because it has an exclusive collection of glass art and sculpture by American artists. Kuivato is open daily.

OAK CREEK CANYON

Garland's Indian Jewelry
3953 North Arizona Highway 89A
(928) 282-6632
Tucked beneath the oak trees in the canyon, you'll find Garland's, a gallery featuring southwestern-style and Native American jewelry, kachina carvings, pottery, baskets, and paintings. Garland's is open daily.

Hoel's Indian Shop
9589 North Arizona Highway 89A
(928) 282-3925
For the past 45 years, Hoel's has been dedicated to selling authentic Native American art. Featuring Pueblo pottery, Hopi kachina carvings, jewelry, baskets, and Navajo rugs, Hoel's Indian Shop is open daily.

UPTOWN SEDONA

Joe Wilcox Fine Arts
271 North Arizona Highway 89A
(928) 282-2548
www.sed-biz.com/wilcoxfinearts/
This fine art gallery proudly represents award-winning artists who work in oils, pastels, and bronze. The gallery is open daily.

Jordan Road Gallery
305 Jordan Road
(928) 282-5690
www.jordanroadgallery.com
As you enter the Jordan Road Gallery, prepare to view the most eclectic art in the area. The gallery boasts one of the finest collections of fine art, sculpture, paper, and works on canvas in a variety of mediums and diverse subject matter. Jordan Road Gallery is open daily.

Zonies Galleria
215 North Arizona Highway 89A
(928) 282-5995
www.zoniesgalleria.com
Showcasing the arts and crafts of Arizona artists, this gallery offers pottery, jewelry, home decor, and kaleidoscopes. Zonies Galleria is open daily.

Music and Theater

Canyon Moon Theatre Company
1370 Arizona Highway 89A
(928) 282-6212
www.canyonmoontheatre.org
Artistic director Mary G. Guaraldi founded Sedona's professional theater company in 1997 with a mission of bringing high-quality theatrical presentations to northern Arizona. After five years at the Sedona Arts Center, Canyon Moon moved into a new, custom-built, intimate theater building in West Sedona in March 2002. Past performances include *I Hate Hamlet, Steel Magnolias,* and *Proof.* Tickets can be purchased at the box office, by phone, on-line, at Bonni's Fashions in West Sedona, or at Rycus Corner Stationers in the Village of Oak Creek.

Chamber Music Sedona
(928) 204-2415
www.chambermusicsedona.org
Continuing to gain national and international attention, this is Arizona's only organization that performs chamber music year-round. Enjoy world-class concerts in the beauty of Sedona. Contact Chamber Music Sedona for more information.

Sedona Arts Center
15 Art Barn Road
(928) 282-3809, (888) 954-4442
www.sedonaartscenter.com
The Sedona Arts Center is a nonprofit membership organization dedicated to the performing and visual arts. An affiliate with Children's Classic Caravan, the arts center provides educational programs and activities for all levels of experience. The gallery shop displays and sells the work of 120 local and regional artists. The exhibition gallery rotates exhibits by local and regional artists, and sponsors group and juried shows. Contact Sedona Arts Center for a complete schedule of events.

Sedona Cultural Park
1725 West Arizona Highway 89A
(928) 282-0747
www.sedonaculturalpark.org
Encompassing 50 acres in western Sedona, Sedona Cultural Park is an outdoor venue for live entertainment, an educational center for children and adults, and a park preserve. The park offers hiking trails, musical performances, and nature walks all surrounded by the majestic beauty of Red Rock Country. The park is now home to Sedona Jazz on the Rocks, Sedona Arts Festival, and the Flagstaff Symphony Pops Concerts. Contact the Sedona Cultural Park for a schedule of events and more information.

Shakespeare Sedona
Red Rock Auditorium, Red Rock High School
(928) 203-4TIX, (800) 780-ARTS
www.shakespearesedona.com
Past performances include *A Funny Thing Happened on the Way to the Forum, Twelfth Night,* and *Romeo and Juliet.* Tickets can be purchased through the Sedona Cultural Park. Performances are offered from the beginning of June through the end of July.

ANNUAL EVENTS

Sedona residents are proud of the caliber of events that occur throughout the year, blending their community's diverse culture, strong artistic influence, and taste for fun. Local organizations provide artistic and fund-raising events for the whole family. Many visitors return year after year to partake in the annual festivities.

In this section we list musical events, duck races, and cultural gatherings from March through December. If you visit Sedona during the months of January and February, expect a quiet city.

March

Sedona International Film Festival
First weekend of March
(928) 282-0747, (800) 780-ARTS
Featuring American and international independent films, documentaries, animation, shorts, and features, the Sedona International Film Festival is a weekend-long celebration of cinema. The event is usually scheduled for the first weekend in March, but venues vary from year to year so call ahead. The festival honors film personalities and schedules panel discussions and interactive workshops. Contact the film committee for more information.

St. Patrick's Day Parade
March 17
(928) 204-2390
Put on your green and get ready as locals line the streets of Uptown Sedona to watch floats, merrymakers, and leprechauns pass by. Contact the Sedona Main Street Program office for parade time and more information.

Sedona Chamber Music Festival attracts more than 4,000 annually. Get your tickets early, and be sure to make your hotel reservations in advance.

April

Great Northern Arizona Duck Race
Los Abrigados Resort & Spa
160 Portal Lane
First weekend in April
(928) 204-2390
This charity fund-raiser is a collaboration between the Sedona Main Street Program and Boys & Girls Club of Sedona. The event is held creekside at Los Abrigados and benefits various adult and children's charities. Please call to adopt a duck or to find out more about this fun and popular event.

May

Sedona Chamber Music Festival
Mid-May
(928) 204-2415
This magical and prestigious event attracts more than 4,000 music lovers and features guest artists and quartets. Performances are scheduled for various locations. Call for more information.

June

Sedona Taste
Los Abrigados Resort & Spa
160 Portal Lane
Second weekend in June
(928) 282-0122
Come out and taste fine food and drink at the creekside resort of Los Abrigados. This event benefits the Boys & Girls Club of Sedona. Call for tickets early, as this is a popular event that sells out quickly.

July

Buy the People for the People Auction
L'Auberge de Sedona Resort
301 L'Auberg Lane
(928) 282-2834
This charity auction is organized by the

Adult Community Center and Sedona Main Street Program. It all happens at the elegant L'Auberge Resort. Local galleries and artists donate work to be auctioned. Call for tickets.

Annual Fourth of July Celebration
Sedona Cultural Park
(928) 254-0338
Celebrate the Fourth surrounded by the beautiful red rocks of Sedona. Sponsored by the Sedona–Oak Creek Canyon Lions Club, festivities include food, live music, games, and fireworks.

September

Fiesta del Tlaquepaque
Tlaquepaque Arts and Crafts Village
336 South Arizona Highway 179
Mid-September
(928) 282-4838
www.tlaq.com
For the past three decades, the annual Fiesta del Tlaquepaque has brought the courtyard of the arts-and-crafts village to life with live mariachi bands and flamenco dancers performing throughout the day. Taste the food and appreciate the art of the Hispanic and Native American Southwest. Festivities begin at 10:00 A.M. Admission is free.

Sedona Jazz on the Rocks Festival
Sedona Cultural Park
1725 West Arizona Highway 89A
(928) 282-1985
Called "the event you'll always remember in a place you'll never forget," Jazz on the Rocks features famed musicians and of course breathtaking scenery and views. Call for more information, dates, and concert schedule.

October

Sedona Sculpture Walk
First weekend in October
(928) 204-7119

Sponsored by Sedona Arts Center, this event brings artists from across the country to display their work. Exhibits are placed throughout the city and range from monumental bronze to small marble or wood sculptures.

Sedona Arts Festival
Sedona Red Rock High School
995 Upper Red Rock Loop Road
Mid-October
(928) 204-9456
This celebration combines arts and crafts and cuisine from some of Sedona's finest restaurants. Regional musicians provide live entertainment, and locals and visitors alike agree that this event is one of the nation's top art festivals.

November

Red Rock Fantasy of Lights
Los Abrigados Resort & Spa
160 Portal Lane
Thanksgiving through first week
in January
(928) 282-1777
This holiday extravaganza lights up the town with more than one million lights and 50 displays. Bring your family and get a jump start on the holiday season.

December

Festival of Lights
Tlaquepaque Arts and Crafts Village
Second weekend in December
(928) 282-4838
www.tlaq.com
Thousands of luminaries light up the cobblestone courtyards for the month of December. Kick off your holiday season with live music and dancers.

COCONINO NATIONAL FOREST

F eaturing some of the highest mountains in the state, the Coconino National Forest is a fascinating blend of alpine tundra, coniferous forest, and high desert. Encompassing 1.8 million acres, the Coconino National Forest is the world's largest contiguous ponderosa pine forest.

In this chapter, we explore the forest's Volcanic Highlands area, which includes the San Francisco Peaks, and the Plateau Country area, with its rolling terrain that extends from the foot of the peaks and is home to Arizona's largest natural lake. The Coconino National Forest also encompasses most of the Red Rock Country around Sedona southwest of Flagstaff (see the Sedona chapter for more information) and the Mogollon Rim district well to the south of Flagstaff in central Arizona, which is beyond the scope of this book. Outdoor recreational activities abound, with endless hiking, mountain biking, fishing, boating, and relaxing options. Note that tent and RV camping are available at dozens of sites within Coconino National Forest. These sites offer few amenities and are often primitive, although drinking water is available. The fee to camp is between $8.00 and $12.00. Unless otherwise posted, eight people are allowed to camp at each site. For more information, contact the Coconino National Forest, 2323 East Greenlaw Lane, Flagstaff, (928) 527-3600. Or visit their Web site, www.fs.fed.us/r3/coconino.

 At 12,663 feet, Humphreys Peak is the highest mountain in Arizona. The peaks are sacred to the area's Native people. Please leave the area as you found it.

VOLCANIC HIGHLANDS/ THE SAN FRANCISCO PEAKS

Campgrounds

Bonito Campground
Peaks Ranger Station
5075 North U.S. Highway 89, Flagstaff
(928) 526-0866
Bonito Campground is named for the Bonito Lava Flow that covered the area about 900 years ago. Sunset Crater National Monument is located just beyond the boundaries of the campground. Also nearby is Wupatki National Monument. Both Sunset Crater and Wupatki have visitor centers featuring self-guided tours. The 44 campsites include tables, fire rings and cooking grills, drinking water, and toilets. To access the campground, drive 12 miles northeast of Flagstaff on U.S. Highway 89. Turn east (right) onto Forest Road 545 and drive 2 miles to Bonito Campground. The campground is open from late March/early April to mid-October. There is an $8.00 to $12.00 fee per vehicle per night (single family), and a $5.00 fee per vehicle for day use. (Prices are subject to change.) Tents, motor homes, and trailers under 42 feet are permitted. There are no utility hookups.

Little Elden Springs Horse Camp
Peaks Ranger Station
5075 North U.S. Highway 89, Flagstaff
(928) 526-0866
At the base of Mount Elden, this campground is designed especially for horse lovers. Each of the 14 sites allows easy access for trucks and horse trailers. Riding trails are accessible from the campground. Little Elden has water, picnic tables, rest rooms, and hitching rails. Larger sites can

The Coconino National Forest stretches across a vast area centered on Flagstaff, encompassing radically different topography ranging from the Volcanic Highlands, seen here, to Red Rock Country. TODD R. BERGER

accommodate vehicles up to 35 feet. There is an $8.00 to $10.00 campsite fee per night. To access the campground, drive 5 miles northeast of Flagstaff on U.S. Highway 89. Turn west (left) onto Forest Road 556 and drive 2 miles. Make a right onto FR 556A and follow this road into the campground.

Hikes

The following trails are found within the San Francisco Peaks area. For more information, contact the Peaks Ranger Station, 5075 North U.S. Highway 89, (928) 526–0866.

Elden Lookout Trail
Difficult
The Fat Man's Loop Trail (see following hike) provides access to the Elden Look-

out Trail. When the trail splits, you will stay to the left. The trails are clearly marked for Elden Lookout and Fat Man's Loop. As you reach the top of the loop, follow the sign for Elden Lookout, continue up the mountain for 2 miles, and then climb 2,000 feet to the summit of Mount Elden. This hike provides great views and offers an introduction to the diverse flora and fauna of the area with shrubs and smaller trees usually found at lower altitudes. This hike is 6 miles round-trip and takes approximately four hours.

Fat Man's Loop
Easy
From downtown Flagstaff, head east on Route 66 (which turns into U.S. Highway 89) to the Peaks Ranger Station. As you pass the Flagstaff Mall on your right, you will see the sign MOUNT ELDEN TRAILHEAD. The parking lot for the trail is on the north side

Lava River Cave: A Natural Museum

This museum is like no other museum. There isn't a front door you can walk through; the entrance is a hole in the ground that you must crawl through. The cave appears today as it did shortly after its formation almost 700,000 years ago. Molten rock from a volcanic eruption in Hart Prairie cooled and solidified in only a few brief moments.

Historians believe the Lava River Cave was discovered in 1915 and that Flagstaff residents visited the cave to collect ice to use for refrigeration.

The cave contains a variety of lava flow features. "Flow ripples" can be found farther inside the cave. These ripples give the appearance of a flowing river. "Splash-downs" are hardened rocks that fell into the lava flow and froze. "Long cracks" can be found in the floor, ceiling, and walls. These "cooling cracks" formed as the lava cooled and hardened. Iciclelike formations formed after the floor and ceiling hardened. Experts believe hot gas shot through the cave, remelting the floor and ceiling. "Lavasicles" are drips of remelted lava that form and quickly harden.

The "lava tube" is the longest cave of its kind in Arizona. The temperature in the cave during the summertime is about 42 degrees Fahrenheit.

You will need to dress properly, wear sturdy shoes, and bring two to three flashlights; the only natural light inside the cave comes from the entrance. Unfortunately, the Lava River Cave was defaced by graffiti in the past, but it has recently been cleaned up. Help preserve the Lava River Cave for all to enjoy. Visitors are asked to report any damage to the park service. Please do not build fires inside the cave. If you see litter you can help by packing it out with you.

To get to the Lava Cave take Humphreys Street to U.S. Highway 180. Drive north on U.S. 180 for 9 miles and turn left onto Forest Road 245. Follow the road for 3 miles to Forest Road 171 and turn south 1 mile to where FR 171A turns left. You will only be a short distance from the entrance of the Lava River Cave. The access road is closed in winter.

of the street. As you begin the hike you will pass through a pole fence. Follow the trail until it splits. The trail is clearly marked; choose between Fat Man's Loop and Elden Lookout. You can access this easy 2-mile loop from either trail. Fat Man's Loop has a more gradual ascent. Along the route there are a number of fascinating rock formations, and hikers can view the Flagstaff suburbs and surrounding countryside. Estimated hiking time is one hour.

Humphreys Trail
Difficult

From downtown Flagstaff, take Humphreys Street north to U.S. Highway 180. Follow U.S. 180 for 7 miles until you reach Snowbowl Road. Take Snowbowl Road for 7 miles until you reach the first parking lot on the left. The trail begins at the far end of the lot. The first few miles of the trail are dark, filled with fir, spruce, and aspen trees. As you ascend, the forest opens up to a small meadow. At 3.75 miles the footing is rocky and not very good. At 4 miles you can see into the Inner Basin of the peaks and enjoy the magnificent views. The top of the trail is above timberline and windy and cold. Bring plenty of water and food on this hike. You will climb from 9,500 feet to 12,663 feet, the highest point in Arizona. Be wary of the effects of the change of altitude, bring plenty of water and food, and rest often. This is a 9-mile hike round-trip; plan to hike for at least six hours.

Kachina Trail
Moderate

As you follow Snowbowl Road to its end, turn right into the first parking lot at the ski resort. The trail begins at the end of this lot. This 5-mile trail (one-way) begins in aspen and fir and is a must during the fall when the leaves are changing. This is a gradual hike that descends through meadows, aspen forests, and wildflower fields. But remember what goes down must come up. Allow for plenty of time to climb back to the trailhead.

Oldham Trail
Moderate

This trail is part of a developed trail system around the Mount Elden and Dry Lakes area of Flagstaff. Take San Francisco Street north and turn right onto Forest Avenue (which turns into Cedar Avenue). At the top of Cedar Avenue turn left onto Gemini. The trail begins at the fence in the rear of Buffalo Park. Just follow the main graveled path that cuts straight through the park, not the exercise route. This 5.5-mile route traverses fields, cliffs, and pine forest and takes approximately four hours.

Weatherford Trail
Difficult

This 17-mile round-trip trail climbs through a scenic canyon on the southeast side of the San Francisco Peaks. Along the trail, you will find an ammunition can chained to a log. Inside is a logbook where you can add your own entry and see who has been there before you. At the end of the trail is a pond (during wet seasons). This is a great place to see wildlife. To access the Weatherford Trail, go north on Humphreys Street to U.S. Highway 180. Take U.S. 180 to Snowbowl Road and turn right (7.3 miles). Follow Snowbowl Road to the 9.7-mile point, where you will see an unpaved road, Forest Road 522, that heads to the right. Follow FR 522 to the fork in the road at 9.8 miles. Take the left fork and drive for 13.7 miles. You will see a parking lot at the end of the road. Park in the lot; you will see a trail behind the parking lot. There is a trail sign. Believe it or not, this is the easiest way to hike to the top of the San Francisco Peaks.

Mountain Biking

Novice and advanced riders will enjoy the singletrack trails, grand scenery, and gratification of a hard but fun workout through some of Arizona's prettiest places.

Dry Lake Hills
Difficult

This ride might sound a bit confusing, but what a fun ride! The trail starts at the Schultz Creek parking area. It climbs, rolls, and descends all in 9.3 miles. Dry Lake Hills bypasses and traverses other trails in the Mount Elden/Dry Lake trail system. Begin with a climb up Rocky Ridge Trail and head toward Elden Lookout Road. Follow the Lookout Road until you reach the steep Lower Brookbank Trail up to Dry Lake Hills. Then head over to Little Gnarly Trail and head back down to Schultz Creek Trail and back to the parking area. To get to the Dry Lake Trailhead, take U.S. Highway 180 north. At milepost 218.6 you will see a sign for Schultz Pass; take a right. Follow the road until the pavement ends, go through the gate, and take a short, steep right down into a parking area. A sign marking the trailhead says ROCKY RIDGE TRAIL.

There are hundreds of red rock pinnacles and spires among the Coconino National Forest land surrounding Sedona. The best views can be had from the hiking trails that crisscross the region. TODD R. BERGER

Fisher Point
Easy

This is an easy 7.2-mile singletrack for the novice rider. The trail takes you to a cave at the entrance to the isolated and quiet Walnut Canyon. Bring along a picnic and enjoy the scenery. To start the ride, take Butler Avenue east. At Lone Tree Road there is a stoplight, head south on Lone Tree or make a right. Follow Lone Tree Road under the freeway. When the road makes a sharp right, go straight on the dirt road and follow it until the trail splits after the first mile. (You can go either way because the trails reunite a mile later.) The trail splits again another mile later. Stick with the trail that goes to the right; it takes you directly to Fisher Point. You will return the way you came. This ride could take two hours; the time does not include lounging.

Flagstaff Nordic Ski Center
Easy to Moderate

We know the sign reads NORDIC SKI CENTER, but after the snow has melted and the tracks have dried, the Nordic Ski Center has free, paved trails without any difficult climbs. Bikers will enjoy the views of the San Francisco Peaks and the peacefulness of the surrounding aspen groves. Take U.S. Highway 180 north of Flagstaff past the Arizona Snowbowl about 8 miles. The Nordic Ski Center is on the right-hand side of U.S. 180. You will see the sign. Don't worry, you can't miss it.

Waterline Road
Moderate

This ride has a steep climb but allows access to the same superb views of the peaks. The ideal time for this ride is between May and October. Head north on

U.S. Highway 89 to Lockett Meadow Road at milepost 431.2. Take the 4.5-mile road up to Lockett Meadow, where you will find plenty of places to park. Follow the trail up to the "cabins." At the cabins, turn right. Now it will be a pleasant ride to Abineau Canyon. This excursion totals 14 miles. The hardest part is the 1 mile up to the cabins. Plan on this being an all-day adventure, and bring plenty of water and snacks!

THE PLATEAU COUNTRY/MORMON LAKE

Home to the area's largest natural lake, the Plateau Country is made up of open meadows, rolling hills, and endless prairies. A large population of elk and antelope graze the open land, while bald eagles and osprey also make their homes here. This is a year-round destination, offering hiking, boating, fishing, and cross-country skiing. For more information, contact Mormon Lake Ranger District, 4373 South Lake Mary Road, Flagstaff, (928) 774-1147.

Boating/Fishing

For fishing (and hunting) information, contact Arizona State Game and Fish, 3500 South Lake Mary Road, Flagstaff, (928) 774-5045. Fishing licenses are required.

Lake Mary Fishing Boat Rentals
480 Lake Mary Road
(928) 774-1742
Whether you like to canoe, row, or drive a 14-foot fishing boat, this rental shop has the watercraft for you. All boats can be used at any lake within a 35-mile radius of this rental shop. The shop is open May through September. Buy your bait or rent your fishing poles here.

Campgrounds

Ashurst Lake and Forked Pine Campgrounds
To reach Ashurst Lake and Forked Pine Campgrounds, drive 19 miles south of Flagstaff on Lake Mary Road and turn east onto Forest Road 82E. The campgrounds are 4 miles up the road. Ashurst Lake Campground has 33 sites, as well as drinking water and toilets. Forked Pine Campground, with 25 sites, is next to Ashurst Lake Campground. Both campgrounds allow tents and small RVs; neither has utility hookups.

Dairy Springs and Double Springs Campgrounds
Near Mormon Lake 24 miles southeast of Flagstaff, each of these campgrounds has 27 sites for tents and small RVs (no utility hookups). Both campgrounds are open May 1 through October 15. To reach the campgrounds from Flagstaff, follow Lake Mary Road 20 miles southeast to Forest Road 90. Turn west onto FR 90 and drive 3.5 miles to Dairy Springs Campground or 4.6 miles to Double Springs.

Lakeview/Pine Grove Campgrounds
These campgrounds have easy access to Upper Lake Mary and Lake Mary Road. Lakeview Campground is surrounded by a grassy hillside and offers 30 sites for tents and small RVs. Nearby Pine Grove Campground is bordered by open meadows and has 46 sites for tents and small RVs. Both campgrounds have tables, fire rings, cooking grills, and drinking water. To reach the

If the region has experienced a long dry season, the lakes may not have enough water to accommodate boating or fishing. Contact the Mormon Lake Ranger District (928-774-1147) for up-to-date conditions.

campgrounds, drive 16 miles southeast of Flagstaff on Lake Mary Road. Lakeview Campground will be to your left. Another 3 miles down Lake Mary Road will bring you to Pine Grove Campground, to your right.

Dispersed Camping

It is legal to camp in nondeveloped areas in most of the Coconino National Forest. No permit is needed (except the Red Rock Pass in the Red Rock Country section of the forest—see the Sedona chapter for more information), and there is no cost to pitch your tent at some remote overlook or deep in a ponderosa pine forest. However, there are some regulations for dispersed camping, and following a few simple rules will protect the forest, leave it in good condition for those who follow, and avoid a hefty and deserved fine from a ranger.

- Campers can stay in the Coconino National Forest no more than 14 days during any 30-day period.
- Camping or campfires are not permitted within the city limits of any of the towns in the forest.
- Camping is allowed only on public land.
- Camping is not allowed within a quarter-mile of a water source.
- Camp at least 200 feet from major roadways and at least 20 feet from forest roads.
- Camp at least 1 mile from a developed campground.
- Do not camp in or drive through open meadowlands.
- Choose a camping spot that has been used before whenever possible.
- Firewood can be gathered around your camping area, but it is illegal to collect wood and load it in a vehicle for use outside the forest.
- Pets are allowed but must be kept leashed at all times.
- Pack out everything you brought in, including all garbage.

- Bury all human and pet waste under at least 7 inches of dirt.
- Campfires are allowed provided there are no fire restrictions in effect (call the Mormon Lake Ranger District at 928-774-1147, or any of the other district offices, to check on restrictions). If a pit is not already available at your campsite, clear the brush and needles 10 feet around the pit area and surround the pit with large stones. Do not build a fire if there are high winds. Use water or dirt to thoroughly put out your fire. Coals must be cold to the touch before a fire area can be left unattended.

Hikes

Lake View Trail #132
Moderate

Follow Lake Mary Road 23 miles (milepost 323.6). Turn right onto Mormon Lake Road. At 28 miles, you will see a sign for Lake View Trail. Turn right here and follow the gravel road and signs to the 28.2 mile sign near the rest rooms at the campground. A sign marking the trail will be to your left as you enter the Double Springs Campground. Most of the 2-mile hike weaves through ponderosa pine, oak, and aspen. For a majority of the hike you will not understand why the trail is named Lake View, but as you reach the lava cliff at the top, the views of Mormon Lake are unobstructed and plentiful. Depending on the amount of moisture the area has received, the lake might be full or it might be a grassy pasture with a small body of water at its center. This moderately easy hike will take a little over an hour to complete if you walk fast, but why bother? Enjoy the view!

Ledges Trail #138
Easy

This easy, 1-mile trail connects with the Mormon Mountain Trail and takes you through a pine forest to a basalt cliff with great scenic views of Mormon Lake. Along the way you will encounter ledges for which the trail is named. This is an excellent place to observe wildlife; you may spot elk or mule deer by the lakeside. To access the Ledges Trail, follow Lake Mary Road to the 23-mile mark (milepost 323.6.) Turn right onto Mormon Lake Road; you will see a sign marked DAIRY SPRINGS AMPHITHEATER. Turn right here and follow the gravel road to the 27-mile marker; there is a large sign at the parking lot marking the trailhead. Ledges and Mormon Mountain Trails begin at Dairy Springs Campground.

Mormon Mountain Trail #58
Moderate

A popular trail for cross-country skiers, Mormon Mountain Trail also connects with the Ledges Trail. Follow the white triangles to reach the top of the mountain. The 3-mile trail climbs through aspen, fir, and spruce. Before you reach the top of the mountain, you will pass through an old-growth forest that has been logged. Various places along the trail offer views of Mormon Lake, tree-covered hills, and open meadows below. (See Ledges Trail for directions.)

Lakes

The Plateau Country/Mormon Lake region is studded with lakes, unlike just about everywhere else in Arizona. Given the inherent dryness to the region and the drought in recent years, many of the lakes are low or even temporarily nonexistent. And they are also quite small, particularly if your idea of a lake is Lake Powell or Lake Mead (or Lake Michigan). If you're thinking of tying up the boat behind the RV and hitting the road for a few days of fishing or water-skiing in the region, call the Mormon Lake Ranger District at (928) 774-1147 for information on lake levels.

Many of the lakes have nearby maintained campgrounds, and dispersed camping is also permitted in many areas of the national forest. See the Campgrounds and Dispersed Camping sections for more information.

Ashurst Lake

Twenty miles southeast of Flagstaff, Ashurst Lake is stocked regularly with rainbow and brook trout. The lake is also popular for canoeing, windsurfing, and boating. A boat ramp is available; boat motors are limited to eight horsepower or less. Visitors enjoy the panoramic views, sightseeing, biking, photography, and picnicking in the area.

Lower Lake Mary

The smaller of the twin lakes Lower and Upper Lake Mary, this lake is nonexistent during dry spells. When Lower Lake Mary does have water, anglers are lined up on the banks ready to catch northern pike and catfish. Whether the lake has water or not, the surrounding land is still an ideal location to fly a kite, have a picnic, or just relax. A boat ramp is available; boat motors are restricted to eight horsepower or less. To get to the lake from Flagstaff, drive 8 miles south on Lake Mary Road. A parking lot is on the western side of the road.

Marshall Lake

Marshall Lake is a marshy body of water bursting with wildlife. At sunset an elk might wander through the muddy meadow, or you may spot a bald eagle soaring overhead. This lake is a valuable wildlife habitat managed by the Arizona Game and Fish Department and Ducks Unlimited. The northwestern side of the lake is closed to vehicles. The lake area is open in early May and closes in mid-October. To get to Marshall Lake from Flagstaff, drive 9 miles on Lake Mary Road. Turn left onto Forest Road 128 and drive 3 miles to the lake. The last mile is unpaved and may be impassable due to mud or snow. When the ground is dry, the road is passable in a passenger car.

Mormon Lake

When Mormon Lake is full, it is an excellent place to fish, boat, and windsurf. It is also a good place to watch for hawks, ospreys, cranes, and an occasional bald eagle. The shoreline offers numerous spots for picnicking, hiking, or just kicking back with your feet resting in the cool water. Dairy Springs and Double Springs Campgrounds are nearby. A country store, restaurant, and service station are also just down the road.

Upper Lake Mary

The Arizona Game and Fish Department stocks this long, narrow lake with northern pike, channel catfish, walleye, crappie, and trout. Upper Lake Mary is the twin lake of Lower Lake Mary and is the primary source of drinking water for the city of Flagstaff. The lake is popular with water-skiers and boaters. There are two paved boat ramps at the parking area near the dam and an additional ramp at Lake Mary Narrows Recreation Area. Boat camping is permitted only on the south shore of the lake. Camping is permitted only in Lakeview Campground (see the Campgrounds section). Swimming is allowed, but it is not recommended. To reach the lake from Flagstaff, drive 12 miles on Lake Mary Road.

NAVAJOLAND

The Navajo are the largest Native American tribe in the United States, with a population of about a quarter million people. The Navajo Reservation covers 27,000 square miles in three states—Arizona, New Mexico, and Utah. About 170,000 people live in Diné Bikéyah, or Navajoland. Most of the remaining Navajos live in border towns such as Flagstaff and Gallup and in other urban settings like Phoenix.

HISTORY

According to Navajo tradition, the Diyin Diné planned the universe with holy pollen and all spiritual beings and natural forces existed in a mist in complete harmony. A disagreement between Father Sky and Mother Earth ensued, and 12 sacred Diyin Diné (Darkness, Early Dawn, Evening Twilight, Sun, First Talking God, Second Talking God, Turquoise Carrier Boy, One Corn Carrier Girl, White Corn Boy, Yellow Corn Girl, Corn Pollen Boy, and Ripener Girl) preserved the universe by creating a covenant between male and female, with the sun to rule the day and the moon and stars to rule the night. Harmony was restored.

First Man and First Woman emerged and were given a sign from the universe, a mist, within which First Man and First Woman found First Male Talking God with a newborn child, White Shell Woman. She was named Changing Woman at puberty. Changing Woman gave birth to the Hero Twins, Monster Slayer and Born for Water. The twins, with the help of Spider Woman, found out that their father was Sun. The twins overcame many obstacles as they journeyed to meet their father and through those trials, they developed courage. Their father gave them the tools necessary to fight the Challengers of Life.

When the Twins returned to earth, they began to slay the Challengers of Life. Only Old Age, Hunger, Poverty, and Sickness remained. Thus began the existence of the Diné on earth.

The Holy People placed the four sacred mountains to protect the area in which the Diné were to live. Sisnaajini or Yoolgaii Dziil (White Shell Mountain) is in the east. This mountain, also called Mount Blanca, represents male, spring, dawn, and the beginning of life.

The mountain to the south is Tsoodzil or Dootl'izhii (Turquoise Mountain of Strength). This male mountain represents summer, adolescence, and leadership, as well as power and authority over the sky. Also known as Mount Taylor, this mountain is near Grants, New Mexico.

Dook'o'oosliid or Diichili Dziil, the Abalone Shell Mountain of Strength, is in the west (near Flagstaff) and is also known as Humphreys Peak. It is a female mountain and represents fall, adulthood, and the physical strength of life.

Dibé Ntsaa or Baashzhinii Dzil is Black Jet Onyx Mountain on the north. Also known as Mount Hesperus, it is a female mountain that represents old age and harmony. This mountain, near Durango, Colorado, along with the moon, is the ruler of night.

According to archaeologists, the Diné, whom the Spanish called Navajos, came to the Southwest 500 to 700 years ago from northwestern Canada where they were hunters and gatherers. They are an Athapaskan people, related to the Native American tribes of the Northwest Coast and the Apaches.

By the time the Spanish arrived in the mid-16th century, Dinétah, the first Navajo homeland in the Southwest, occupied much of the area that had been abandoned by the ancient Anasazi, or ancestral Puebloan people. The Diné were seminomadic hunters and gatherers, though they may also have grown some maize. They made pottery, wove baskets, and traded with the Pueblo tribes who lived along the Rio Grande. Within a few hundred years of coming to the Southwest, they were planting corn, beans, and squash.

The earliest recorded contact between the Navajo and the Spanish was with the Antonio de Espejo expedition of 1582–83. According to Spanish accounts, the meeting at the base of Mount Taylor began as a friendly one, but resulted in hostilities. Warfare was the hallmark of relations with the Spanish throughout the 17th century. Petroglyphs in Canyon del Muerto in northeastern Arizona record the arrival of Spanish armies in the area. By the early 1600s, the Navajo had acquired horses and iron tools from the Spanish invaders through trade with colonists in New Mexico.

From the 1500s to the 1800s, the Navajo fought the Spanish and other Native American tribes, including the Utes and the Comanches. They also formed alliances with some tribes, including the Acoma Pueblo and the Hopi, which led to Puebloan influences taking hold among the Navajo, including the herding of sheep and goats.

Narbona was a much-respected headman from the Chuska Mountains. He was able to negotiate a peace treaty with the Spanish in 1819, but when Mexico gained independence from Spain in 1821, hostilities resumed as the New Mexicans raided the Navajo for slaves. Narbona and a Mount Taylor Navajo, Antonio Sandoval, negotiated a peace treaty with the Mexicans. In 1833, they visited all of the Navajo bands, asking them to stop fighting the Mexicans and to return Mexican livestock. The Mexicans, however, did not keep their promise to return Navajo livestock and slaves, so warfare resumed under the leadership of Hastiin Ch'ilhaajinii, whom the Mexicans called Manuelito. In the meantime, Sandoval had joined the Mexicans in attacking other Navajo bands in order to protect his own band who lived near Mount Taylor.

The U.S. Army joined the war in the mid-1840s. In 1846, Navajo leaders, including Narbona, Sandoval, Manuelito, and Zarcillos Largos, and more than 500 other Navajos met to make peace with the Mexicans and Americans. They negotiated the Bear Spring Treaty with Colonel Doniphan, but the Navajo leaders could not speak for all Navajo bands, and so Navajo raids continued. A new and equally unsuccessful treaty was negotiated in 1848.

In 1849, Indian Agent James Calhoun met with Navajos under the leadership of Narbona. Narbona and six other Navajos were killed by the U.S. Army. Narbona had been one of the Navajo leaders who wanted peace, but after his death, Manuelito, who wanted revenge, was the most influential leader, and the bloody conflicts continued. Navajos were routinely taken as slaves by the New Mexicans, a practice that continued even after the Civil War.

Anglo-European settlement put tremendous pressure on the Navajo resources as Mexicans and Anglos usurped Navajo grazing lands for their own sheep. By the late 1850s, hostilities between the Navajos and the U.S. government were ongoing, and war was formally declared by the United States on September 8, 1858. In the meantime, another Navajo warrior and leader, Barboncito, had emerged.

In April 1860, the Navajo, under the leadership of Manuelito and Barboncito, attacked the U.S. Army's Fort Defiance and were barely repulsed. But in September 1861 a group of Navajo women and children, who had gone to Fort Fauntleroy to collect rations promised them under one of the several U.S.-Navajo treaties, were massacred.

The next year, Brigadier General Carleton became the military commander for New Mexico. Having defeated the Mescalero Apaches, he moved against the Navajo, first demanding that they surrender and move to Fort Sumner in New Mexico. His strategy was to force the Navajos to become farmers and live in small towns, where they would, he believed, forget their language and customs. He pursued a scorched-earth policy to force the Navajos to move.

In the winter of 1863–64, Kit Carson invaded Canyon de Chelly, where Barboncito's band was living, and took 200 prisoners. All through the winter, starving Navajos surrendered at Fort Canby and Fort Wingate. In the winter and early spring of 1864, the U.S. government moved more than 4,000 Navajos from Fort Wingate and Fort Defiance to the banks of the Pecos River, known as Bosque Redondo. The terror and hardship of the Long Walk, which covered several hundred miles in sleet, snow, and cold, are still remembered and bitterly recounted. The march was intentionally brutal, since the soldiers' intent was to eradicate the Navajo. By March of the next year, more than 9,000 Navajos were incarcerated at Fort Sumner, although several thousand, some under the leadership of Manuelito and Barboncito, had avoided capture. In August 1864 Barboncito and a few of his band surrendered at Fort Wingate and Manuelito and 23 followers surrendered in 1866.

The rations allotted for the captives were never sufficient, no shelter was provided, and fodder for the animals was inadequate, so the Navajos' livestock starved. Smallpox swept through the camps, killing more than 2,000 Navajos. For four years, the Navajos' crops failed and the prisoners starved and died of disease during an illegal incarceration that began during the administration of President Abraham Lincoln.

By 1868, partly because settlers were disturbed by the presence of Navajos so far east, the U.S. government negotiated the 1868 treaty with the Navajo. Seven Navajo headmen—Delgadito, Barboncito, Manuelito, Largo, Herrero, Armijo, and Torivio—met with U.S. Peace Commissioners. Barboncito, as spokesman for the Navajos, argued successfully for the Navajos that they be allowed to return to their land in the Four Corners area rather than be sent to live with other Indians on reservations in Oklahoma, Mississippi, and Florida.

The Navajos were accorded a 3.5-million-acre reservation, an area equal to about 10 percent of the land they had occupied before the Long Walk. Several million acres were added to the reservation between 1878 and 1934, but some of those acres, which had been part of the Hopi Reservation, have been returned to the Hopis by U.S. government courts as part of the settlement of the Navajo-Hopi land dispute. The Treaty of 1868 remains the binding agreement between the U.S. government and the sovereign Navajo Nation.

The Navajos walked home and began the difficult process of rebuilding their homesteads. The U.S. government provided each family with seeds, farm tools, and two sheep, from which they began to rebuild their flocks. The period after the Navajo returned to their land brought in the era of trading posts and the beginning of the tourist trade, as well as the establishment of government boarding schools that children were forced to attend despite many families' strong objections. Off-reservation boarding schools persisted as the main educational opportunity for Navajo children until the 1930s, when some reservation day schools were built.

In the early 1900s, oil was discovered on the reservation, and in 1922 Midwest Oil Refining Company struck oil near Shiprock. In 1923 the U.S. government set up a tribal council of 12 delegates and 12 alternates to lease the oil and gas resources.

Thirty-six hundred Navajos served in the armed forces during the Second World War, bringing much-needed money to the tribe. The Navajo language was used by some of these servicemen to create a secret code that was never broken by the Japanese. The Navajo Code Talkers have been recognized for their invaluable service in winning the war for the Allies by both the federal government and the Navajo Nation.

Visiting the Navajo Nation

Respect the privacy of the residents of Navajoland by not entering houses or hogans uninvited, not knocking on doors, not yelling or throwing things, especially near sacred sites, observing quiet hours between 11:00 P.M. and 6:00 A.M., and recognizing that tepees are always used for religious purposes, and therefore, you should not intrude.

Obey all tribal laws and regulations. Do not enter areas that are marked off limits or that you have been told not to enter. Stay on designated trails unless your tour guide says otherwise. Rock climbing and off-trail hiking are not allowed without permission from the Navajo Parks & Recreation Department in Window Rock, nor is off-road travel by dune buggies, ATVs, jeeps, or motorcycles.

Do not touch or remove any artifacts, plants, rocks, or animals.

Use trash containers, and do not litter or burn or bury debris.

Alcoholic beverages and firearms are strictly prohibited.

If you want to take photos, ask first, and remember that a gratuity is always appreciated. Photographing for commercial use requires a special permit.

Attend a dance or an event only after you have confirmed that visitors are welcome. If it is a religious event, behave as you would in a church or synagogue. Do not disturb any event by pushing your way to the front or blocking someone's view, and do not ask questions about what is happening.

Do not applaud unless it is clearly acceptable to do so.

If you are asked to leave a private religious event, do so quietly and promptly.

Use permits are required for hiking, camping, and backcountry use. Contact the Navajo Parks & Recreation Department, P.O. Box 9000, Window Rock, AZ 86515; (928) 871-6647. For hunting, fishing, trapping, and boating licenses, contact Navajo Fish & Wildlife, P.O. Box 1480, Window Rock, AZ 86515; (928) 871-6451/6452.

After the war, the Indian Claims Commission was set up to compensate Native American tribes for the land that had been taken from them. Norman Littell was hired as attorney for the Navajo, and he began a campaign to assert Navajo rights. The government's termination policy of the mid-1950s, which sought to end the federal government's treaty responsibilities to Native American tribes, actually worked to strengthen the council as the Bureau of Indian Affairs withdrew from the tribe's affairs.

In the late 1950s, oil and gas reserves were discovered in the Four Corners area, and revenues from those leases and Littell's legal work to affirm the tribe's sovereignty added to the tribal government's ability to act on behalf of the Navajo. By the end of the decade, the tribe had assumed responsibility for water development, emergency welfare, the building of chapter houses, tribal enterprises, and the court system on the reservation. Littell was fired in 1966 when he failed to win more than a compromise in one decision in the Navajo-Hopi land dispute.

The council decided at the end of the decade to allow the strip mining of Black Mesa for coal to power the generators that would support the development of the new cities of the Southwest. The decision was as controversial here as it was on the Hopi Reservation. In the mid-1970s, Exxon signed an agreement with the tribe to mine uranium on reservation lands. The tribal council had signed the agreement though it had inadequate information about the health hazards of mining uranium and the difficulty of restoring the land after the mining. Navajo miners and millers worked without safety gear and took the radioactive dust on their work clothes back to their homes. Despite the passage of the Radiation Exposure Compensation Act, the federal government (which is responsible for overseeing mineral leasing on Native American lands) has still done little to help the miners or their families.

The exploitation of mineral resources is the major revenue-producing enterprise on the Navajo Nation, and while much of the tribe's revenues are derived from mineral leases, most of the profits go to the corporations that hold those leases, and the tribe has never had the capital to extract and process the minerals itself.

Navajos on the reservation live in a largely rural area with pockets of more urban environments. Some are traditional farmers and ranchers living without electricity or running water. Others live in the urban centers of Window Rock (the capital), Shiprock, and Tuba City.

The Navajo Nation Tribal Council meets in Window Rock, and 88 delegates from the 110 chapters, or communities, make the laws and decisions for the people in a representative form of government.

Navajo Nation chapters were established in 1923, along with the tribal council, as units of agricultural administration. They subsequently became community centers for the largely rural, dispersed population. Each chapter elects a president, vice president, and secretary. Chapters hold regular meetings, rather like town halls, to decide on matters of local importance and to meet with their representatives to the Navajo Nation Tribal Council. Tribal programs, such as building or economic development programs, are administered through chapter government.

Most chapters have chapter houses, which provide services and facilities for chapter members. Chapter houses are usually built near recently dug wells or other water sources and therefore can provide facilities for bathing, laundering, and cooking. Chapters also organize community events, such as fairs, rodeos, sports, social dances, clinics, and educational classes.

The Navajo Nation elects a president and a vice president every four years. When the Tribal Council is not in session, 12 standing committees of the Navajo Nation Council carry on the work of the nation. In 1998, the Local Governance Act, giving more authority to the chapters rather than to the central government in Window Rock, was passed. Shonto Chapter became the first to be certified under the act.

The Navajo language is spoken widely, and it is the only language used in Navajo prayers, songs, and religious ceremonies. Traditional medicine men use songs, prayers, and ceremonies to cure illness or protect from harm a person who has been exposed to a dangerous situation or experience. The more than 50 ceremonies that may be used are performed at specified times for particular purposes; they may last from several hours to nine days. The medicine man may also use sandpaintings as part of the ritual.

GETTING AROUND NAVAJOLAND

Navajoland, the local name for the Navajo Reservation, sprawls over much of northeastern Arizona; the reservation boundaries then stretch east into New Mexico and north into Utah. The reservation borders Grand Canyon National Park and Glen Canyon National Recreation Area, and is easily reachable from Flagstaff via either U.S. Highway 89 or Interstate 40.

This chapter presents information in a clockwise manner, starting with Cameron in the western part of the reservation and circling around to Window Rock on the New Mexico border. Visitors choosing to visit Navajoland from the east via U.S. Highway 191 from I-40 or Indian Route 12 from I-40 can find what they are looking for by paging through the chapter in reverse.

The closest commercial airport to Navajoland is Flagstaff Pulliam Airport. Amtrak does not stop within the reservation, but you can take the train to the nearby cities of Gallup, New Mexico; Winslow, Arizona; or Flagstaff. Likewise, Greyhound does not travel through the reservation, but buses stop in Holbrook, Winslow, and Flagstaff. (See the Getting Here, Getting Around chapter for more information on all of these options).

CAMERON

Cameron, a small chapter of the Navajo Nation, is 52 miles east of Grand Canyon Village on Arizona Highway 64 and 54 miles north of Flagstaff on U.S. Highway 89. The visitor center, (928) 679-2303, is at the intersection of the two highways.

The Little Colorado River cuts through solid rock at Cameron. The river is usually dry here, but during spring snowmelt and after summer thunderstorms, the riverbed has water in it, and flash floods may even occur. From Cameron, the Little Colorado descends 2,000 feet to meet with the Colorado River 30 miles to the northwest.

Cameron Trading Post and Motel
U.S. Highway 89, Cameron, AZ 86020
(928) 679-2501, (800) 338-7385,
www.camerontradingpost.com
One mile north of the intersection of Arizona Highway 64 and U.S. Highway 89 is the historic Cameron Trading Post, founded in 1916 by Hubert and C. D. Richardson. Open daily, the trading post combines modern economic practices and traditional trading post customs—Native Americans sell and trade their arts-and-crafts items here for merchandise and groceries, and the trading post also accepts credit cards.

Inside the trading post you will find a wide range of arts and crafts created by artisans from many of Arizona's tribes. The store is full of Navajo rugs; Acoma, Hopi, Santa Clara, Jemez and Navajo pottery; Tohono O'odham basketry; Navajo stone carving and sandpaintings; Naatsilid pottery; and Navajo, Hopi, and Zuni jewelry. Pendleton blankets, western-style hats and belts, regional-interest books, and the usual collection of T-shirts and inexpensive souvenirs complete the collection. In the center of the store is a counter selling many flavors of delicious, locally made fudge. The grocery store/commissary at the back of the building stocks everything from snacks and sodas to nails and 25-pound sacks of Blue Bird flour.

Near the Navajo rugs, look for a small display of rock art. These are small petroglyph-like carvings on sandstone done by local children using nails as their carving implements. All proceeds from the sale of these charming souvenirs goes to benefit the Cameron Youth Project and the Dzil Libei Elementary School. The rock art carving project was started by a teacher at the school to buy the children books to take home and keep.

The trading post is open daily year-round except for Christmas Day and a half-day on Thanksgiving.

Walk through the trading post to the restaurant. A huge sandstone fireplace dominates the back wall of windows overlooking the Little Colorado. A decorated tin ceiling and handmade wooden display cabinets add to the Old West charm. The walls display magnificent basketry, kachina carvings, and Navajo rugs.

The restaurant serves a varied menu of American, Mexican, and Navajo food, including Navajo tacos, green chili stew, and Navajo stew (beef, carrots, celery, and onions in a thick gravy, served with fry bread). A Navajo taco is a plate-size piece of Navajo fry bread topped with a spicy combination of ground beef, mild green chili, beans, cheese, lettuce, and tomato. Both locals and tourists come here for breakfast, lunch, and dinner. Reservations are not required, and the restaurant is wheelchair accessible.

Don't leave without ordering Navajo fry bread—a soft, sweet dough rolled thick and deep-fried to a golden brown, served with honey and butter, though some folks prefer to eat it just with salt. You can order it for breakfast, lunch, or dinner. It is a treat you won't soon forget!

The motel has 66 rooms, each with stunning hand-carved and decorated beds, vanities, bureaus, and valances in southwestern mission style. Smoking and nonsmoking rooms are available and two rooms are wheelchair accessible. All rooms have TVs, and most have balconies overlooking a terraced garden oasis. The gardens here were recently restored and the outdoor area has a large barbecue and fountains. Reservations for motel rooms are strongly recommended. Reservations are held until 7:00 P.M. unless guaranteed with a credit card or full prepayment is received before your arrival date. Cancellation requires a 24-hour notice prior to your arrival date.

For museum-quality artwork, visit the gallery across the parking lot from the trading post. The artwork here is absolutely top quality. Rugs, paintings, basketry, jewelry, Hopi kachina carvings, Apache burden baskets, bronze sculptures, and modern steel and glass furniture share this space with antique Native American beadwork, weaving, and other art. Be sure to ask the salesperson to let you see the second floor of the gallery. If the front door of the gallery is locked, the salesperson is probably showing visitors the second floor. Knock on the door and wait a few minutes, or ask in the trading post for another salesperson to open the first floor for you. Even if you cannot afford to buy the magnificent pieces here, the friendly and helpful staff will provide a unique opportunity to learn more about authentic Native American art.

The trading post complex also features a Texaco gas station, telephones, rest rooms, and a post office, as well as RV sites with full hookups.

Navajo Arts & Crafts Enterprise
P.O. Box 464, Cameron, AZ 86020
(928) 679–2244

Established by the Navajo Nation in 1941 to promote traditional Navajo arts and crafts, the Navajo Arts & Crafts Enterprise at the intersection of U.S. 89 and AZ 64 offers high-quality, genuine Navajo arts—rugs, silver and turquoise jewelry, sandpaintings, and pottery—as well as Pendleton blankets, backpacks, pillows and purses, yarn, moccasins, and T-shirts. For the music lover, an extensive collection of cassettes and CDs by Native American artists makes the stop worthwhile. Among the books offered are some out-of-print scholarly texts and anthropological studies reprinted by the University of Arizona's Arizona Books on Request at (800) 426–3797, www.uapress.arizona.edu.

Navajo Arts & Crafts Enterprise has three other stores—in Window Rock at the intersection of AZ 264 and Indian Route 12, (928) 871–4095; in Kayenta at U.S. 160 and U.S. Highway 163, (928) 697–8611; and in Chinle at U.S. Highway 191 and Indian Route 7, (928) 674–5338. Open daily.

Outside Cameron

Anasazi Inn and Gray Mountain Trading Post
U.S. Highway 89, Gray Mountain
(928) 679–2214, (800) 678–2214

The Anasazi Inn, 10 miles south of Cameron on U.S. Highway 89, features 112 homey rooms. Convenient to Grand Canyon and to Wutpatki and Sunset Crater National Monuments, this motel is open year-round and has satellite TV and an outdoor swimming pool. Pets are welcome at an additional charge; reservations (for both you and your pets) are recommended. The small trading post just across the highway has an abundant selection of souvenirs, maps, T-shirts, and other tourist sundries, as well as a few Navajo rugs and Minnetonka hats and moccasins.

The Navajo Arts & Crafts Enterprise in Cameron is one of several such businesses on the Navajo Reservation selling authentic Native American artwork purchased directly from artists. TODD R. BERGER

A restaurant adjacent to the trading post has a low-key but spacious dining room with a player piano and Native crafts. Since this restaurant is not on the Navajo Reservation, beer and wine are available. Navajo tacos are the favorite entree for both locals and tourists. The restaurant opens early for breakfast and stays open through a late dinner hour.

Here at Gray Mountain you can also buy gasoline and some groceries, find public telephones, and mail home your purchases at the post office branch in the trading post.

Anasazi Inn and Gray Mountain Trading Post Restaurant are open daily for breakfast, lunch, and dinner. The trading post is also open daily. However, both are closed during the off-season, roughly early November through late March. The motel is open year-round.

Little Colorado River Gorge Navajo Tribal Park

Drive 10 miles west of Cameron on AZ 64 to reach the Little Colorado River Gorge Navajo Tribal Park. This overlook, maintained by the Navajo Nation, offers a spectacular view of the narrow Little Colorado Gorge, which is cut through Paleozoic rock. The river has only seasonal flow, so you are most likely to see it running during summer monsoon season (July to September) and during spring snowmelt. The overlook area has Portajohns and a Navajo market.

THE PAINTED DESERT

Stretching in a long curve from the town of The Gap on U.S. Highway 89 about 30 miles north of Cameron across the Navajo and Hopi Reservations to Petrified Forest National Park, the 160-mile-long Painted Desert is a series of mesas, buttes, and South Dakota–style badlands layered in gorgeous pastel colors of pink, orange, red, blue, gray, and purple. The drive on U.S. 89 north of Cameron and then on U.S. Highway 160 toward Tuba City winds directly through this remarkable landscape. The Painted Desert is also prominent in the Petrified Forest area, from the national park west to Winslow.

The colorful layers of the Painted Desert were caused by varied amounts of minerals in the strata and differing rates of deposit when the sediments formed. Layers that formed more slowly have higher concentrations of iron and aluminum, which leaves behind pink, orange, and red sediments. Layers that formed more quickly lack oxygen and tend toward the gray, purple, and blue sides of the color spectrum.

As you drive toward Tuba City on U.S. 160, the highway climbs steeply onto the Coconino Plateau. About 4.5 miles east of the U.S. 160/U.S. 89 junction, a small sign on the north side of the highway directs you to dinosaur tracks embedded forever in the once-muddy flats. The dinosaurs that left these tracks walked on two legs with a stride of about 7 feet. Their short front legs were probably used for clasping food. There is no entrance fee to see the tracks.

Tuba city is another 10 miles east through the Painted Desert.

TUBA CITY

A plaque on a sandstone monument near the Tuba City Boarding School commemorates Chief Tuba (or Tuve). The monument, erected in 1941, says that Chief Tuba was a Hopi of the water and corn clans. He was born in 1810 and died around 1887. In 1865, he acted as a scout for Kit Carson's U.S. expedition.

Natural springs attracted Hopi, Navajo, and Paiute Indians to this area for many generations. Mormon missionaries arrived as early as 1859. In 1875, Chief Tuba, having been converted to Mormonism, gave the spring and the land around it on which Tuba City now stands to Mormon pioneers in return for protection from his enemies. The Mormons laid out the city and built their structures using cut stone from nearby sites.

Navajo Rugs

Weaving is a way of life for many of the 30,000 Navajo women who make rugs today. Navajo weavers believe the art of weaving was taught to the Navajo by Spider Woman, who built a loom according to the instructions of the Holy People.

Traditionally, women raise and herd the sheep that produce the wool for the rugs. They shear the sheep in the spring, a task that must be done with manual, not electric, clippers. Once the fleece is removed from the animal, it is combed, or carded, and stickers and burrs are removed by hand. The tools used for this and all other aspects of creating a rug are often made by the weaver herself. The carded wool ends up in a loose roll, ready for spinning.

To spin the wool, the weaver uses a spindle made of a long, tapered shaft of wood and a flat round whorl. The roll of wool is attached to the spindle and spun as many times as necessary to create the right thickness and tightness for the kind of yarn being made. Yarn for the warp (the vertical yarns in the weaving) is thinner and tighter than yarn for the weft (the horizontal yarns that create the design).

The yarn is removed from the spindle and wound into a skein, which is then washed in warm, soapy water. The yarn must then be dried by hanging it to set the spin so it does not unravel.

Now the yarn, if it is not going to be used in its natural color of white, brownish-black, gray, or brown, is ready for dying, and the precise color that can be achieved depends on the kinds of plants used, the time of year when they are picked, the part of the plant used, the kind of metal container in which the plant is boiled, and the other elements that are added to the dye bath. Among the many dozens of plants useful for creating the colors in Navajo rugs are rabbitbrush, sagebrush, mistletoe, wild carrot, cliff rose, cedar, oak, wild holly, and lichen. Today weavers may also buy yarn that has already been dyed, or they may use aniline (synthetic) dyes that produce colors similar to natural plant dyes. One of the most interesting purchases you can make while visiting Navajoland is a dye chart, which holds some of the plants used for dying wool and shows you strands of colored yarn dyed with those particular plants.

Navajo women construct their looms from logs or two-by-fours, or they may use two trees or two poles of the hogan. The loom must be square, and it must be sturdy enough to hold the tension of the warp. Warping a large loom may take several hours, and it is traditional to do all of the work at once, without interruptions from children or from attending to other tasks.

Then the weaving can begin, although the weaver has been planning the design for this particular rug all along. Navajo rugs are woven in a tapestry weave—the weft yarns are woven over and under the warp yarns, which do not show in the finished piece. In addition to the loom, the weaver uses battens, a weaving fork, and shuttles, all of which she may have made herself or which may have been passed down to her by her mother or grandmother.

The weaver may carry the design in her head, or she may draw it out on paper. The weaving will take many hours of physically demanding and mentally challenging work. The rug is not only an object, but also a process, and everything that happens during the weaving is part of the final piece. Some weavers put in a spirit line, a contrasting piece of yarn from the inner portion of the design through the border. This practice, and the prayers associated with weaving, help ensure that the weaver will be able to weave another rug when the one she is working on is finished.

Navajo women have been perfecting the art of weaving for nearly 400 years. Not so many decades ago, one could purchase a Navajo rug for 50 cents a square foot. Fortunately, that has changed, as the skill and artistry of rug weaving have become recognized and appreciated. Many women support their families with the proceeds from their weaving, and some say that this work, although difficult and demanding, is particularly appealing because it allows them to stay home and care for their families.

From the delicate pastels of Burntwater and Wide Ruins rugs to the vibrant reds and blacks of the Ganado Red and Chief's Blanket, there are dozens of styles of Navajo rugs that you will soon learn to recognize. Some, like Two Grey Hills, are associated with particular geographical areas, and others, such as the Eye Dazzler, with particular time periods. Other styles include pictorials, which show scenes from everyday life, and *ye'ii bicheii* rugs, which depict ceremonial Navajo dancers.

Every Navajo weaving is a work of art, and every rug is different. Today, many weavers sign their works, and a photograph of the weaver may be attached to the rug at the trading post. While the weavings are called "rugs," often they will be hung on walls rather than placed on the floor.

You will soon learn what style appeals most to you, and this (and what you can afford) will determine what you want to buy, whether you are thinking of purchasing just one rug or starting a collection. You can begin to evaluate the quality of a piece by looking for symmetry, square corners, an even texture to the weaving, and consistent colors in the piece as a whole. Eventually you will want to learn to distinguish between natural dyes and synthetic ones and between commercial yarns and the ones made by the weaver herself.

You can find Navajo rugs at galleries, in museum gift shops, and at upscale shops in Sedona and Phoenix, but you can also find some of the most beautiful ones at the trading posts, such as the Cameron Trading Post, the Tuba Trading Post, and the Hubbell Trading Post National Historic Site in Ganado, where you might also be fortunate enough to see weavers demonstrating their craft. Some weavers sell their work directly to the public.

A particularly good map for this area is Guide to Indian Country of Arizona, Colorado, New Mexico, Utah, published by the Automobile Club of Southern California. The map is widely available in this area, or it may be ordered from Grand Canyon Association, P.O. Box 399, Grand Canyon, AZ 86023; (800) 858-2808; www.grandcanyon.org.

The Mormons, however, could not get clear title to the land and the settlement was taken over by the U.S. Indian Agency in 1903.

Tuba City, with a population of 7,300, is now the administrative and trade center for the Western Navajo Agency. It is 1 mile north of the junction of Arizona Highway 264, which leads to the Hopi mesas, and U.S. Highway 160, which travels through Kayenta to Monument Valley. U.S. 160 travels through Mesozoic sedimentary rocks formed in the Triassic and Jurassic periods. Here, as near Cameron, the area was periodically covered with water. The brilliantly colored rock formations all around you are evidence of the ancient floodplains and sand dune deposits.

The town is governed as one of the 110 Navajo chapters, with a chapter president, vice president, treasurer, and secretary. Chapters elect delegates to send to the Navajo Nation Council in Window Rock.

Temperatures during the summer range from the high 90s (degrees Fahrenheit) to lows in the mid 50s. During the winter, expect daytime highs of about 50 degrees and overnight lows in the mid to high 20s. The elevation of Tuba City is approximately 5,000 feet and the average precipitation is less than 10 inches a year.

Motels

PRICE CODE

The following price code is for two adults during the high season, generally between Memorial Day and Labor Day. The codes do not include taxes and other fees.

$	Less than $75
$$	$76 to $125
$$$	$126 to $175
$$$$	$176 to $225
$$$$$	More than $225

Diné Inn Motel $$$
U.S. Highway 160 and Peshlakai Avenue, Tuba City
(928) 283-6107

A nicely designed exterior and very basic rooms describe this 15-room motel. Rooms have full baths, air-conditioning, and cable TV.

One room is wheelchair accessible and all rooms are nonsmoking. Prepare to pay extra for additional people and pets. Reservations are recommended during the holiday season.

Greyhills Inn $
Greyhills Drive, Tuba City
(928) 283-4450

If you're traveling on a budget, this is the place to stay. The Greyhills Inn is a training site for high school students who want to get into the hotel management and hospitality industry. Students take courses at Northern Arizona University and in the business department at the high school, then work in the motel to get real-life experience.

The motel recently redesigned its patio area in the southwestern style, adding tables and chairs, trees, flowers, outside heaters, and other features. The Quaility Inn Navajo Nation donated many of the new furnishings.

The inn offers 32 rooms, all nonsmoking, and all with shared baths. The wheelchair-accessible rooms have central airconditioning, TVs, and telephones for local calls. Pets are not allowed and the inn takes only MasterCard and Visa. The facility is open year-round except for Christmas Day and New Year's Day. Reservations are recommended.

Quality Inn Navajo Nation $$$–$$$$
**Main Street and Moenave Road,
Tuba City**
(928) 283–4545, (800) 644-8383
This 80-room motel has a peaceful, com-
fortable feel. The lobby is decorated with
fascinating old photographs and historic
descriptions of the area and the people
who lived here. Quiet music plays in the
background, and on your way to your
room, you'll see wall murals by Native
American artists in the hallways.

The rooms are spacious and well fur-
nished in the southwestern style. All the
rooms have full baths, cable TV, and
queen-size beds, as well as coffeemakers
and air-conditioning. Smoking and non-
smoking rooms are available and some
rooms are wheelchair accessible.

Pets are accepted only in smoking
rooms, and the additional fee is $20.
There is also a charge for more than two
people in a room. A 24-hour advance
notice is required for cancellation of reser-
vations, which are recommended, espe-
cially around the holidays and during the
Western Navajo Fair usually held the sec-
ond or third weekend of October.

Call the motel to find out about the
RV park with full hookups, cable TV,
shower, and laundry facilities.

Restaurants

PRICE CODE

The price codes below represent average
prices for dinner for two, excluding tax,
gratuity, and drinks.

$	Less than $20
$$	$21 to $35
$$$	$36 to $60
$$$$	More than $60

Hogan Family Restaurant $
**Main Street and Moenave Road,
Tuba City**
(928) 283-5260

The menu runs the gamut from Mexican
to Navajo to American food; an unusual
feature is a full salad bar. The Navajo tacos
are quite good here.

The Hogan is open every day for
breakfast, lunch, and dinner. The atmosphere is casual and nonsmoking. The
restaurant is next door to the Tuba Trading Post in the Quality Inn Navajo Nation,
so there is plenty of parking.

This is a frequent meeting place for
locals and visitors, which can sometimes
lead to utter confusion. Arizona does
not observe daylight savings time. The
Navajo Reservation, however, does. But
the Hogan Restaurant, like the trading
post and the motel, is on a small piece of
private property within the reservation,
so the restaurant, trading post, and
motel are on mountain standard time. If
you're in the restaurant at 3:00 P.M. on a
July afternoon, it will be 2:00 P.M. when
you walk across the street to Kate's
Restaurant.

Kate's Cafe $
**Edgewater Drive and Main Street,
Tuba City**
(928) 283-6773
Kate's Cafe is a local favorite and you will
probably see more Tuba City residents
than tourists here. The restaurant is on
Edgewater Drive; turn east at the Tuba
Trading Post. Since Tuba City recently
renamed all of its streets, people may not
immediately know where Edgewater Drive
is, but everyone knows where the trading
post is located.

This place is so casual that it feels
more like an old-time diner than a
restaurant. You can get mostly plain
American fare here—steaks, chops,
pasta, salads, and sandwiches. Favorites
are the avocado, lettuce and tomato
sandwich; the 12-ounce T-bone; and
huevos rancheros. Kate's is open daily
for breakfast, lunch, and dinner. Parking
is plentiful and reservations are out of
the question, but you probably won't
have to wait for a table.

The Tuba Trading Post in Tuba City has been selling Native American artwork, including high-quality Navajo rugs, since 1870. TODD R. BERGER

This restaurant does not take credit cards, so be sure to have enough cash on hand to pay for your meal.

Shopping

Tuba Trading Post
**Main Street and Moenave Road, Tuba City
(928) 283-5441**
One mile north of the junction of U.S. Highway 160 and Arizona Highway 264, this historic trading post dates back to 1870. The octagonal building was constructed in 1905 and has been remodeled several times. The trading post, like a traditional hogan, faces east to catch the rising sun.

You can find high-quality, authentic artwork here, including spectacular Nava-jo rugs, fine Hopi and Navajo pottery, Zuni, Navajo, and Hopi jewelry, Zuni carvings, superb Hopi kachina carvings, prayer fans, and basketry. The trading post also sells western-style hats and belts, moccasins, books, CDs and cassettes, Pendleton blankets, jackets, pillows, and the usual collection of inexpensive tourist keepsakes. Particularly endearing are some examples of Navajo folk art, including teddy bears made of Blue Bird flour sacks and toddler-size dolls made of fabric and clothed in traditional-style dress.

Check at the trading post to find out about upcoming public events on the Navajo and Hopi Reservations. The staff is friendly and very helpful.

The trading post, like the Quality Inn motel and restaurant beside it, are owned by the Babbitt Brothers on a small piece of private land on the Navajo Reservation. It's open daily.

TUBA CITY TO BLACK MESA

Your drive northeast from Tuba City to Kayenta will take you through some spectacular landscapes culminating in the exotic spires, pinnacles, and buttes of Monument Valley. About 37 miles north of Tuba City, you can't miss the stunning rock formations known as Elephant Feet on the north side of the highway. Not far beyond is a pullout where you can stop to take a photograph.

You will pass Tonalea, and to the east is Black Mesa, which records the existence of vast floodplains and advancing and retreating seas. The lagoon deposits of vegetation and animal life lie atop Black Mesa, which supplies the coal deposits being strip-mined by Peabody Coal Company. To the east and south, Black Mesa rises and divides into the finger-shaped mesas of Hopiland.

At the intersection of U.S. Highway 160 and Arizona Highway 564, look south to see a massive conveyor belt that carries strip-mined coal off Black Mesa. The conveyor belt crosses the highway on an "overpass" and takes the coal to the huge storage towers just north of the highway. From here the coal is loaded onto the train that takes it to Navajo Generating Station in Page, Arizona. About a quarter of the power generated at this power plant is used to pump Central Arizona Project water uphill from the Colorado River in western Arizona to the urban centers of Phoenix and Tucson.

The power plant created an obnoxious haze over Grand Canyon, but it was approved before the environmental protection movement of the 1970s. However, in 1991, the Environmental Protection Agency, responding to a lawsuit brought by environmental groups, issued regulations to reduce emissions from the plant. Later, the EPA, Grand Canyon Trust, the Environmental Defense Fund, and the power plant settled the suit with an agreement that Navajo Generating Station would, among other conditions, reduce its emissions of sulfur dioxide by 90 percent no later than 1999. These conditions have, indeed, been met.

NAVAJO NATIONAL MONUMENT

Navajo National Monument lies 9 miles north of U.S. Highway 160 at the terminus of Arizona Highway 564. This monument was established to protect three cliff dwellings of the ancestral Puebloan people: Betatakin, Keet Seel, and Inscription House.

These places were, for a brief period at the end of the 13th century, home to the descendents of Paleoindians who had probably arrived at least 10,000 years earlier. The Basketmaker Culture emerged around A.D. 700. This culture is named for the superb baskets the people made (some of which were so finely woven they could be used to carry water). Baskets, made of twigs and grasses using a coiling technique, were also used for cooking and storing food. Artisans today employ a similar technique to make finely decorated baskets from sumac twigs, and many of these baskets are sold at gift shops and trading posts around Kayenta.

The Pueblo Culture, which followed, dominated this area until about A.D. 1300 by which time the Colorado Plateau was largely abandoned. Today's Hopi people refer to the members of this culture, their ancestors, as the *Hisatsenom*. The Navajo call the builders of these magnificent cliff dwellings the *Anasazi,* which means "ancient enemies" or "ancient ancestors" and until recently archaeologists also used the Navajo term. Today they usually refer, instead, to the "ancestral Puebloan people."

The ancestral Puebloan people were related to and traded with the peoples of cultures to the south, the Hohokam and the Mogollon. They lived in small villages and began to build aboveground structures. Though they did not know the sophisticated masonry techniques used by the people who built at Chaco Canyon and Mesa Verde, the builders of Betatakin and Keet Seel constructed cliff dwellings ranging in size from 10 to 200 rooms. As at other cliff-dweller sites, the ancestral Puebloan people built their living quarters in alcoves that faced south or southeast to catch the sun's warmth in the winter and to take advantage of the cliff overhangs to provide shade during the summer.

Alluvial flats along the bottom of the canyon, which today are mostly eroded away, provided good farmland watered by a high water table in the canyon bottom and flood irrigation. (Even 100 years ago, Tsegi Canyon was probably much greener than it is today—severe erosion, drought, and overgrazing have taken their toll.) In addition to growing corn, squash and beans (the "Three Sisters" of the ancestral Puebloan diet), the people kept domesticated turkeys and possibly dogs.

While the tradition of basketmaking continued, pottery was better for some uses, such as storing water and cooking. The ancestral Puebloan people used the coil and scrape technique that is still used by Hopi potters. They also made corrugated pottery, leaving some or all of the coils unscraped and incising designs on the outside of the container, which would have made the contents of the pot cook more quickly.

Kayenta-area pottery was particularly well made. In addition to the typical ancestral Puebloan black-on-white pots, Kayenta potters also made a polychrome pottery that was widely traded.

The cliff dwellings you see at Navajo National Monument today were built, occupied, and abandoned within a brief 50-year period from about A.D. 1250 to 1300. Did the inhabitants leave because of drought, erosion, deforestation, or other environmental factors? Were they attacked by outsiders? Did their religious and philosophical beliefs tell them it was time to continue their migrations? No one knows for sure.

Betatakin is a Navajo word that means "ledge house." The Hopi, who still make annual pilgrimages to this and other sites along their ancestral migration routes, call this place Kawestima. This spectacular ruin is located in a sandstone alcove near a spring. It is less than a mile away from bottomlands at the mouth of the canyon that would have been perfect for growing crops.

The Sandal Trail, which originates at the visitor center at Navajo Nation Monument, takes you to an overlook from which you can see Betatakin across the canyon. A telescope is available, but you might want to bring your own binoculars or camera with a telephoto lens to get a good look. The self-guided trail is 1 mile round-trip and quite steep in places. Allow about 45 minutes to go down and come back up. Along the trail, signs identify various plants and explain how the plants were used by ancient dwellers and how the Hopi and Navajo use them today. This trail is not recommended for wheelchairs.

From Memorial Day through Labor Day, park service rangers conduct tours to Betatakin. The 5-mile trip takes about five hours and is a very strenuous hike, descending 700 feet into the canyon. The tour, which is free, departs once a day at 8:15 A.M., although rangers add a second hike to the ruins around midday during busy holiday weekends. The number of hikers for each tour is limited to 25. You must carry your own water, and the trip is not recommended for people who have heart or respiratory ailments.

As at all archaeological sites, you are reminded not to touch or remove anything, however insignificant it may seem to you. Also, at Navajo National Monument, you need to remember at all times that the area has been preserved in as natural a state as possible, so falling rocks, flash floods, and falls are dangers, as are snakes, rodents, and scorpions. Be alert at all times, and hang on to the kids. Pets must be on leashes.

The Hopi call Keet Seel Talastima. Construction at the cliff dwelling that you see

Betatakin Ruins at Navajo National Monument can be viewed from the Sandal Trail, which begins at the visitor center. TODD R. BERGER

today on the west side of Keet Seel Canyon started around A.D. 1250. Between 1272 and 1276, the population grew quickly as more immigrants arrived. Eventually Keet Seel probably housed 125 to 150 people in more than 150 rooms. The population here seems to have been less stable than at Betatakin. Families moved out and others moved in during its brief period of occupation, and archaeologists identify a larger variety of artifacts and building techniques here than at Betatakin. Two features of this ruin indicate a high level of community organization: the construction of a retaining wall running 180 feet across the eastern half of the ruin and the existence of three wide streets that connect different parts of the village. Keet Seel also includes four kivas, each unique, again suggesting that several distinct groups of people built and inhabited this cliff dwelling.

After A.D. 1286, construction at Keet Seel stopped and the village declined as more and more families moved out. Before they left, however, they sealed the doorways of many rooms containing jars of corn, and they embedded a large log in masonry above an access ladder to the village. Did they mean to return one day?

You will need a backcountry permit, obtainable at the visitor center, to visit Keet Seel, which is open from Memorial Day through Labor Day. Only 20 visitors a day are allowed to visit, and the 8.5-mile trail is a strenuous climb. Once you reach the site, rangers will escort you on a tour of the ruin. The trip will take you at least a day to complete; hikers may camp for one night in the canyon. Reservations are required for this free tour.

Inscription House, the third cliff-dweller site at Navajo National Monu-

Navajo National Monument's Aspen Trail begins near the visitor center and winds its way down to a viewpoint overlooking an aspen and fir forest, most unusual at this elevation.
TODD R. BERGER

ment, is too fragile to allow any visitors at all.

Navajo National Monument has a campground with 31 sites for tenting and RV use that is open year-round on a first-come, first-served basis. RVs may not exceed 27 feet in length. Wood and charcoal fires are not allowed at the campground, but camp stoves are okay to use. No hookups are available, though the campground does have rest rooms, a camper service sink, and running water. Expect cold temperatures and deep snow during the winter. Food and gasoline are available at the Black Mesa Trading Post at the intersection of U.S. Highway 160 and Arizona Highway 564.

The visitor center provides exhibits and books, videos, and posters for sale, as well as wheelchair-accessible rest rooms. It is open every day year-round except on Thanksgiving, Christmas, and New Year's

Day. Just behind the visitor center is a family home display with a forked-stick Navajo hogan and a sweat lodge.

The Aspen Forest Overlook Trail branches off the Sandal Trail 400 feet from the visitor center and descends 300 feet to view an ancient, ice-age aspen and fir forest. You cannot see any ruins from this trail.

Next to the visitor center is a Navajo-owned and -operated gift shop, Ledge House (928–672–2404), selling Native American arts and crafts. Here you can find Navajo jewelry, rugs, and folk art, Hopi overlay jewelry, Acoma seed jars, and Zuni carvings and jewelry.

Navajo National Monument is administered by the National Park Service. For more information, you may contact the superintendent of the site at HC-71 Box 3, Tonalea, AZ 86044-9704; (928) 672-2700; www.nps.gov/nava.

KAYENTA

Kayenta, 15 miles northeast of the turnoff of Navajo National Monument on U.S. Highway 160, is the Arizona gateway to Monument Valley, 25 miles to the north on U.S. Highway 163. Both Black Mesa Mine and Kayenta Mine are located near here, and thus the Peabody Coal Company has been a major employer. Today, however, things are changing. In 1985, after several years of effort on the part of Kayenta business leaders frustrated by the loss of opportunities for economic development because of bureaucratic red tape, the Navajo Nation Tribal Council approved the five-year Kayenta Township Pilot Project, a self-governance program unprecedented in the Navajo Nation since the institution of the Tribal Council in 1923. According to this program, a chapter president and vice president are elected to represent Kayenta's 6,500 people, and Kayenta sends one delegate to the Navajo Nation Tribal Council in Window Rock. The township was authorized to pass local ordinances and to impose and collect a sales tax. Kayenta is the first community in Navajoland, and perhaps the first Native American community in the country, with this power.

During the summer, expect high temperatures in the high 80s and lows in the mid 50s. In winter, highs are in the 50s and lows in the 20s. As always on the Colorado Plateau, the best way to keep warm (or cool) is to bring clothing that can be worn in layers. The difference between day and night temperatures is usually 20 to 30 degrees.

Accommodations

PRICE CODE

The following price code is for two adults during the high season, generally between Memorial Day and Labor Day. The codes do not include taxes and other fees.

$	Less than $75
$$	$76 to $125
$$$	$126 to $175
$$$$	$176 to $225
$$$$$	More than $225

Anasazi Inn $$$
U.S. Highway 160, Tsegi
(928) 697-3793
The Anasazi Inn is 10 miles west of Kayenta. The motel has 56 small, basic rooms with coffeemakers, cable TV, hair dryers, irons and ironing boards, but no phones. The coffee shop serves breakfast, lunch, and dinner and is open 24 hours a day in the summer season from April to mid-October. A public phone can be found just outside. Children under six stay free at the motel. The office has a small gift shop with tourist necessities, snacks, and T-shirts. Pets stay for an additional $10 nonrefundable fee. Some rooms are nonsmoking, and some are wheelchair accessible. All major credit cards are accepted; personal checks are not. The Anasazi Inn is the closest motel to Navajo National Monument.

Best Western Wetherill Inn $$$
1.5 miles north of the intersection with U.S. Highway 160 and U.S. Highway 163, Kayenta
(928) 697-3231
You'll find TVs, coffeemakers, phones, irons, ironing boards, and alarm clocks in each of this motel's 54 rooms; and the indoor swimming pool is open year-round. Smoking and nonsmoking rooms are available, but wheelchair-accessible rooms are not. A gift shop in the lobby offers Navajo jewelry and rugs, a large selection of concho belts, Zuni jewelry, books, cassettes, and CDs. All major credit cards and traveler's checks are accepted. The Golden Sands Restaurant is adjacent.

Hampton Inn $$$
U.S. Highway 160 at the west end of town, Kayenta
(928) 697-3170

Navajo-owned and -operated, this three-story, adobe-style hotel has 73 rooms, each with one king or two double beds. A large, comfortable lobby with Southwest-style furniture is separated by a central fireplace from the dining area, where you'll enjoy a free continental breakfast of danish pastries, fruit, cereal, oatmeal, waffles, coffee, and juice. The pleasant, spacious smoking and nonsmoking rooms have coffeemakers, cable TV, phones, computer dataports, hair dryers, clock radios, irons, and ironing boards. Standard rooms have a recliner, and king studios have a pull-out couch for extra people. Children under 18 stay for free and there is a small charge for more than two adults in a room. Four first-floor handicapped rooms are available, two of which have roll-in showers. An outside heated pool is open from May through October, and a two-and-a-half-acre Navajo cultural center including exhibits and displays adjoins the hotel grounds. Major credit cards and traveler's checks are accepted; pets are allowed.

Holiday Inn $$$$$
Intersection of U.S. Highway 160 and U.S. Highway 163, Kayenta
(928) 697-3221
A comfortable reception area greets you at this 163-room, two-story motel operated by Ocean Properties, Inc. Children under 12 stay and eat for free. There is an additional charge for more than two adults in a room. The motel features well-appointed rooms with cable TV, in-room movies, coffeemakers, irons, ironing boards, and hair dryers. An outdoor swimming pool and a fitness room with cardiovascular and weight-training equipment will help get you in shape for horseback riding in Monument Valley. Some rooms are wheelchair accessible. Credit cards and traveler's checks are accepted; pets are not allowed. In the lobby of the motel is the Little Mesa Gift Shop, offering authentic Native American jewelry and souvenir items. Be sure to ask which items are handmade and which are machine produced. The Wagon Wheel Restaurant provides room service.

Restaurants

The price codes below represent average prices for dinner for two, excluding tax, gratuity, and drinks.

$	Less than $20
$$	$21 to $35
$$$	$36 to $60
$$$$	More than $60

Amigo Café $
U.S. Highway 163, a quarter mile north of the intersection with U.S. Highway 160, Kayenta
(928) 697-8448
Don't let the shabby exterior of this place fool you—it is very nice inside and serves the best Mexican food around. Their most popular entrees are the combo plate, chimichangas, and the "largest Navajo taco on the reservation." This restaurant is locally owned and the dishes are all made from scratch. Open-air dining is available on the patio in good weather. Open Monday through Saturday for breakfast, lunch, and dinner, the Amigo Café takes major credit cards and traveler's checks, but not personal checks. The restaurant is wheelchair accessible, though the parking lot is gravel. The rest rooms are not accessible. This casual eatery does not accept reservations.

Blue Coffee Pot Restaurant $
On U.S. Highway 160 just west of the intersection with U.S. Highway 163, Kayenta
(928) 697-3396
If you want to find the best place in town to eat as far as the locals are concerned, head for the Blue Coffee Pot Restaurant for lunch. Here you can choose between a Navajo taco with chili, meat, beans, lettuce, tomatoes, and sour cream; and Navajo mutton strips, which are fried mutton strips rolled in a tortilla and served with potato salad. Or try the cold beef and fry bread sandwich, also served with potato salad. On the dinner menu, you'll find steak, roast beef, pork chops, enchi-

Shonto Trading Post

If you're eager for a small adventure, take Arizona Highway 98 north off U.S. Highway 160 toward Shonto. Six miles down the road, turn right at the sign for Shonto. Go 4 more miles, turn right at the sign for Shonto Trading Post, and get ready for a hair-raising, sharply vertical drive down a gravel road and across Shonto Wash, where the trading post, established in 1919, is located. The cottonwoods and palo verde trees at the bottom of the wash are beautiful, and Shonto gives you a sense of why communities were (and are) located where they are. While the trading post is mostly a convenience store, you will also find gasoline, a public phone, and a Laundromat here. Unless you have a four-wheel-drive vehicle and know how to drive over very slick, steep roads, do not attempt this half-mile journey into the canyon in wet weather, as you are likely to end up in the wash in very uncomfortable circumstances.

Shonto Trading Post is open six days a week with shorter hours on Saturday. It is closed Sunday. The phone number is (928) 672-2320.

---

ladas, tacos, and barbecue ribs. Daily specials are offered for lunch and dinner. The restaurant is an octagon-shaped building, with casual tables and booths. Several of the walls are glassed, creating a particularly cheerful atmosphere during the day. The restaurant is open for breakfast, lunch, and dinner on weekdays. Reservations are not accepted. The building is wheelchair accessible. The Blue Coffee Pot accepts only cash.

Golden Sands Restaurant **$$**
U.S. Highway 163, about 1.5 miles north of U.S. Highway 160, on the left, Kayenta
(928) 697-3684
The Golden Sands has been here forever, serving Navajo and American food in a very casual western-theme atmosphere. Frequented mostly by locals, the restaurant serves hot and cold sandwiches, Navajo tacos, soup, roast beef, chicken and trout dinners, and a dinner omelet. Open daily for breakfast, lunch, and dinner, Golden Sands closes in mid-afternoon on weekends. Cash, personal checks, or traveler's checks are accepted; credit cards are not.

Reuben Heflin Restaurant at
the Hampton Inn **$$**
U.S. Highway 160 at the west end of town, Kayenta
(928) 697-3170
Located in the lobby of the hotel, the very pleasant Reuben Heflin Restaurant is open for lunch and dinner, serving a range of items from Southwest specialties to New York cheesecake. Specialties include black bean soup (served with Navajo fry bread), the Mazalon Club Sandwich (ham, turkey, bacon, lettuce, and tomato rolled in a warm flour tortilla and served with nachos and fire-roasted salsa), and the grilled T-bone steak. They also offer other sandwiches, appetizers, and salads, as well as other steak, chicken, and trout dinners. An outdoor

The Golden Sands in Kayenta is filled with locals eating Navajo tacos and other fabulous dishes. TODD R. BERGER

patio is open for dining when the weather permits. This hotel complex is the newest in Kayenta and is Navajo-owned and -operated. Credit cards and traveler's checks are accepted; personal checks are not. The restaurant is wheelchair accessible. Open daily for dinner.

Wagon Wheel Restaurant at Holiday Inn $$$
**Intersection of U.S. Highway 160 and U.S. Highway 163, Kayenta
(928) 697-3221**

This restaurant offers full menus for breakfast, lunch, and dinner, as well as a breakfast buffet bar and a nonalcoholic beer and wine selection. Decorated in mission style, it is a comfortable, casual place to dine, and you will see many foreign tourists here. The waitresses wear traditional long velvet Navajo skirts with vests, and they are invariably friendly and pleasant. For breakfast, the menu ranges from biscuits to griddle items to egg dishes.

Getting ready for a day of strenuous sightseeing, you'll appreciate the good strong coffee. Lunch and dinner offerings include appetizers, sandwiches, steaks, and a well-stocked salad bar. You can pay with cash or credit cards, but personal checks are not accepted. If you're staying at the Holiday Inn, kids under 12 eat free. The Holiday Inn complex is wheelchair accessible.

Shopping

Historic Kayenta Trading Post
**U.S. Highway 163, Kayenta
(928) 697-3541**

Located just past the Wetherill Inn on the northern edge of Kayenta, this store is worth a stop just to see an example of the evolution of trading posts. Here, as you would expect, you can buy groceries, fresh meat and produce, auto supplies, axes, shovels, oats for your horse, paper goods, and coffee. What you might not expect is a Radio Shack—you can also buy a car stereo, order a computer, and sign up for Internet access and cellular phone service! A small selection of Native American arts and crafts is next to the Western Union desk, where you can also buy a hunting license and check out the community bulletin board. There is a public phone out front and rest rooms in the back. The trading post is open seven days a week.

Kayenta Trading Company at the Hampton Inn
U.S. Highway 160 at the west end of town, Kayenta
(928) 697-3170
This gift shop in the lobby of the Hampton Inn is packed full of unique and interesting items, some of which you won't see anywhere else. The paintings and assemblages by 85-year-old Navajo elder Mammie Deschillie are charming and unusual—most Navajo folk art is expressed in painted wood carvings, of which this shop also has a particularly good selection. The store carries carvings by Carlos Begay, whose vibrant paintings are very well known in northern Arizona. Here you'll also find southwestern-style jackets, skirts, shirts, coats, and shawls. Fine-quality Navajo jewelry and concho belts, Hopi and Acoma pottery, handwoven baskets, and Zuni carvings are for sale. And there is no shortage of the books, guides, tapes, and souvenir keepsakes you would expect to see in a shop geared for tourists. Open daily, Kayenta Trading Company accepts credit cards and traveler's checks, but no personal checks.

Navajo Arts & Crafts Enterprise
U.S. Highway 160 just north of the junction with U.S. Highway 163, Kayenta
(928) 697-8611
The Navajo Arts & Crafts Enterprise was established by the Navajo Nation in 1941 to promote traditional Navajo arts and crafts. The Enterprise's four shops offer high-quality, genuine Navajo arts—rugs, silver and turquoise jewelry, folk art carvings, sandpaintings, original watercolors and pottery, as well as Pendleton items, weaving and jewelry-making supplies, and T-shirts. You'll also find a collection of cassettes and CDs by Native American artists. This store is open daily. Traveler's checks, credit cards, and personal checks are welcome. Navajo Arts & Crafts Enterprise has three other stores—in Window Rock, Cameron, and Chinle.

MONUMENT VALLEY

Monument Valley is a place you will know by heart even if you have never been there. The reason for this strange familiarity is not past-life regression or telepathic powers. It is because Monument Valley has been the backdrop for dozens of Hollywood movies, from *The Vanishing American* of 1925 to *WindTalkers* in 2001. The director John Ford and the actor John Wayne made Monument Valley the very epitome of a western landscape with a long string of westerns shot here, including *Stagecoach* in 1939, *She Wore a Yellow Ribbon* in 1949, and *The Searchers* in 1956. The names of other movies shot entirely or in part at Monument Valley read like a list of Hollywood's hundred best: *How the West Was Won* (1962), *2001: A Space Odyssey* (1968), *Easy Rider* (1969), *The Legend of the Lone Ranger* (1981), *National Lampoon's Vacation* (1983), *Back to the Future III* (1990), *Thelma and Louise* (1990), *Forrest Gump* (1993), *Waiting to Exhale* (1995), *Mission: Impossible 2* (2000), and *Vertical Limits* (2000). This list is only partial: Many lesser known flicks were also shot here.

Well before you arrive at the tribal park, you will see why so many Hollywood directors packed up cast and crew and headed for this remote corner of the Navajo Nation. As you drive on U.S. Highway 163 north from Kayenta or south from Mexican Hat, you will soon see long expanses of red desert punctuated by

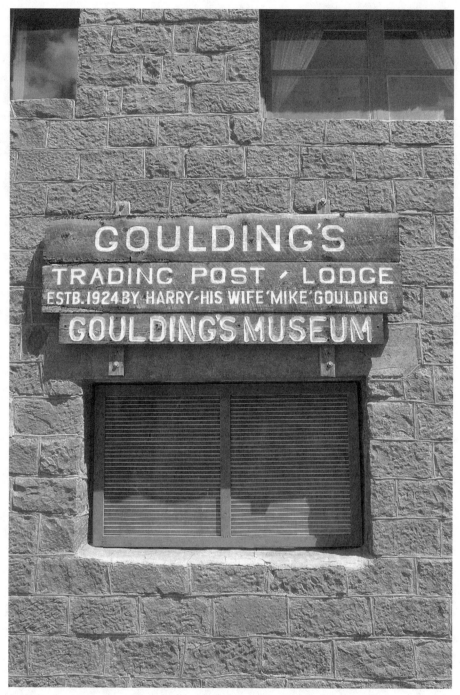

Goulding's Lodge, a few miles west of Monument Valley Tribal Park, offers the only motel accommodations and services for miles. TODD R. BERGER

massive, rugged rock spires, buttes, mesas, and pinnacles. The rock towers look like half-melted chili-powder popsicles rammed into the desert sand. And the formations stretch across the horizon like gigantic soldiers moving into battle. When you first see Monument Valley for yourself, you may well be tempted to pick up your cell phone and start lining up funding for your own Hollywood production, so perfectly suited is this landscape for celluloid.

The rock formations seen today are the result of long-ago flooding and uplifts. Some 70 million years ago, the land in the Four Corners region began to rise. This uplift led to the formation of the Rocky Mountains, among other western icons. In the arid Monument Valley area, the earth was primarily made of sandstones and shales. Periodic floodwaters rushed through the valley, carrying away the surrounding sediment and leaving the harder pinnacles. Today, some of these rock formations rise more than 1,000 feet above the red sand floor.

Monument Valley straddles the Utah-Arizona border, stretching some 60 miles in length and 40 miles in width. Monument Valley Tribal Park, the section of this vast, fantastical region that is open for public visitation, is 23 miles north of Kayenta off U.S. 163.

Accommodations

PRICE CODE

The following price code is for two adults during the high season, generally between Memorial Day and Labor Day. The codes do not include taxes and other fees.

$	Less than $75
$$	$76 to $125
$$$	$126 to $175
$$$$	$176 to $225
$$$$$	More than $225

Country of Many Hogan Bed and Breakfast $$
U.S. Highway 163, south of Monument Valley Tribal Park
(928) 283-4125

Located 10 miles south of Monument Valley Tribal Park, Country of Many Hogan offers a lodging experience you won't find in Jacksonville, Duluth, or even Phoenix. The two "rooms" of this bed-and-breakfast consist of traditional Navajo hogans—round, hemispherical structures made of mud held in place by a juniper-log frame. Despite the bed-and-breakfast moniker, there are no beds: Bring your own sleeping bag or rent one at the B&B. Perhaps not quite intimate, groups of up to 30 people can spread out the bedroll in these hogans. For a small extra fee, the owner will cook up Navajo tacos for dinner, but homemade breakfast is included in the per-person rate. The host stresses that people are welcome to stay as long as they wish and may bring and cook their own food, just as visitors would if they were camping. The proprietors also offer horse, jeep, and hiking tours of Monument Valley.

Goulding's Lodge $$$$
Indian Route 42, Monument Valley, Utah
(435) 727-3231
www.gouldings.com

Located just across the Utah border a few miles northwest of Monument Valley Tribal Park, Goulding's Lodge, as well as the company's museum and trading post, campground, private airport, Stagecoach Dining Room, Arts & Crafts gift store, gas station, convenience store, theater, Laundromat, and car wash, provides the only services for miles in any direction. The closest motel to Monument Valley Tribal Park, Goulding's offers 62 rooms with private balconies, western movie rentals (every room has a VCR), coffeemakers, hair dryers, and views of Monument Valley (the part outside the tribal park). The lodge also features an indoor pool. If you want to stay close to the

Navajo Jewelry

Navajos began to make jewelry around the time of the Long Walk in the mid-1860s. Whether they learned jewelry making at Fort Sumner or before their incarceration is not clear, but Atsidi Sam (Old Smith) is known to have been one of the first Navajos to learn metalworking. He probably learned from one of the itinerant Mexican silversmiths who traveled among Navajos trading silverwork for Navajo livestock. In the late 1800s, John Lorenzo Hubbell hired Mexican smiths to teach silversmithing to Navajos; the trader also provided some of the silver coins that were melted down and fashioned into jewelry.

When the railroad was built and the Fred Harvey Company started encouraging tourism in the Southwest in the early 20th century, a new market for jewelry opened up, but most of this "Route 66" jewelry was of inferior quality, both in material and workmanship. Much of it was mass-produced and machine stamped.

In 1941 the U.S. government established the Navajo Arts and Crafts Guild to promote the manufacture and sale of high-quality, Navajo-made jewelry. After World War II, the Navajo Tribe took over the guild. Today, the guild, still operated by the tribe, is known as the Navajo Arts & Crafts Enterprise, with Arizona outlets in Cameron, Kayenta, Window Rock, and Chinle.

Today, some fine jewelers use the lost-wax method of casting, but most use the more traditional tufa or stonecast method. Navajo jewelers also make stamped jewelry using dies and tools they have themselves created. This stamped method of silver decorating had been developed by observing the way Mexican leatherworkers stamped designs on saddles and bridles.

Channel inlay and mosaic inlay (in which there is no metal between the stones) are popular, as is fabrication, in which pieces of silver are soldered together. Navajos also create squash blossom necklaces in which small turquoise stones are set in individual settings. This kind of work resembles Zuni petit point.

park and don't want to pitch a tent, Goulding's Lodge is a good choice.

Campgrounds

Goulding's Campground
Indian Route 42, Monument Valley, Utah
(435) 727-3231
www.gouldings.com
Goulding's Campground is part of the Goulding's Lodge complex a few miles west of Monument Valley Tribal Park. The campground has RV sites with hookups as well as tent sites, which will run you $16 for a tent site and $26 for an RV site. Staying at the campground allows you access to the lodge's indoor pool. You can also wash your duds at the Laundromat, shop at the grocery store or gift shop, and clean the red dust off your body in the hot showers. Goulding's will charge you an extra $3.00

Jewelry with a bumpy surface is probably done using a granulation or granule fusion technique in which tiny pieces of metal are fused onto the piece without solder. Overlay, etching, appliqué, and engraving are other techniques you will see.

Authentic Navajo jewelry uses sterling silver and most items will be marked as such. You will also see pieces for sale made of "German silver" and "Denver silver," both made-up terms describing a mixture of nickel, zinc, and copper containing no silver at all.

Today, much Navajo jewelry includes gemstones such as turquoise, diamonds, malachite, coral, lapis lazuli, and opal. Turquoise is a traditional favorite in Navajo jewelry. A stone's color, texture, and design indicate what mine it came from. Natural turquoise is becoming harder to find and more expensive since many U.S. mines have closed in the last few decades. Most turquoise today is artificially treated. Stabilized turquoise is a lesser-grade stone to which plastic resin has been added under high pressure to improve its color and strength. Stabilized turquoise is difficult to distinguish from the natural stone. Reconstituted turquoise is made from chips of stone that have been glued and subjected to high pressure. Its value is less than that of stabilized turquoise. Poor-quality stones can be temporarily improved in appearance by being treated with wax, oil, or polish, but such stones will revert to their previous whitish color within a few weeks. Plastic turquoise "stones" are used in some jewelry.

If you're interested in buying high-quality Navajo jewelry, look in galleries, museums, guilds, and reputable shops to accustom your eye to what fine jewelry looks like. Ask the proprietor to tell you what kinds of stones are incorporated in the pieces that appeal to you. You can also find very good pieces at craft fairs where artists sell their own work.

for every person over the first two. The sites here are exposed to the full force of the sun, so get a move on early in the day.

Mitten View Campground
Monument Valley Tribal Park
(435) 727-5874

This 99-site campground within Monument Valley Tribal Park will set you back a modest $10.00 per site ($5.00 per site during the winter). The campground does not accept reservations for individual sites; all sites are first-come, first-served. The campground does not have RV hookups. Campsites include a picnic table, fire pit with grill, ramada, and trash barrel. The campground has rest rooms, coin-operated showers, and a dump station. The campground is exposed to the full force of the sun, so during summer mornings you will likely not want to linger in your tent reading a Tony Hillerman novel.

Monument Valley Tribal Park is like no other place on Earth. TODD R. BERGER

Monument Valley Tribal Park

You could pay the $5.00-per-person entrance fee (children seven and under get in free) and feel quite satisfied about your Monument Valley experience by gawking at the pinnacles from the veranda attached to the visitor center (435-727-5874). But you will really get in the thick of things if you get back in your car and drive the 17-mile scenic road through the tribal park. The road is not paved, and it is imperative you drive slowly along the route, but the road is easily passable in a passenger car unless the weather is remarkably foul, a rarity at Monument Valley.

The road loops around, slides in between, and rubs up against some of the most beautiful rock formations on earth. The first buttes you will see from the visitor center area are the East and West Mitten Buttes, pinnacles invariably featured on posters and book covers showing Monument Valley due to their distinctive, hand-warmer shape. There are multiple turnouts along the road for you to hop out and take pictures, and branches of the road dead-end at viewpoints that will leave you breathless. Stick to the road or the viewpoints during your journey through Monument Valley, as freelance hiking or, God forbid, *driving* off the roads is not allowed. However, you can hire a Navajo guide at the visitor center to take you into the backcountry (see the Tours section in the following pages for more information).

Tours

While you can drive the scenic road in your own vehicle, pamphlet or tour book in hand, there's a lot to be said for taking a tour with a Navajo guide. For example, one guide explained that latecomers to this sacred valley bestowed names upon these spectacular rock formations. The names do not convey the meaning or spiritual importance of this place to the people who have lived here for hundreds of years. He said that he had been guiding tours for more than a decade, each time thinking and learning about the significance of Monument Valley. To him, the Mittens and Merrick Butte (another rock formation) represent a human. Merrick Butte is the person's face. The Mittens are his arms reaching out for a hug. Another advantage of taking a tour is that more of the valley is open to tourists with guides than to those exploring on their own.

Several guides for jeep tours, horseback riding, and hiking have booths in the parking lot at the visitor center. If you haven't reserved your tour in advance (reservations are recommended during the summer and for longer tours), prices at the parking lot booths for shorter excursions seem to depend partly on how busy things are that day. You may be able to negotiate. Remember that gratuities are not included in the price of any of the tours.

Black's Hiking, Jeep Tours, and Trail Ride
Mexican Hat, Utah
(435) 739-4226
Roy Black's guided tours originate at the visitor center. The one-hour vehicle tour does the 17-mile loop, and the two-hour tour takes you on the 28-mile loop to some restricted areas. Sunrise and sunset tours, as well as half-day and full-day tours, are also available.

You might also want to try a day hike to Hunt's Mesa or Mitchell Mesa, an overnight hike to Hunt's Mesa and Douglas Mesa, or a trail ride of one-half to seven hours. Children are welcome on trail rides, but they must be over 4 feet tall and able to ride their own horse. Bus groups are welcome. Credit cards and personal checks are accepted.

Crawley's Monument Valley Tours
Kayenta
(928) 697-3463
www.crawleytours.com
Bill Crawley has had more than 40 years'

experience providing Navajo-guided half-day, full-day, and sunset tours of Monument Valley. Tours leave from Kayenta or your guide can meet your tour bus or airplane at any nearby location. A morning tour of the valley leaves at 8:30 A.M. and an afternoon tour leaves at 2:30 P.M. The sunset tour leaves three-and-a-half hours before sunset. Other tours leave throughout the day, and private tours leave at your convenience.

You'll enjoy your trip in comfortable backcountry vehicles, ranging from 8-passenger vans to 29-passenger mini-buses. Crawley's Navajo guides are well versed in Navajo culture, as well as in geological and historical information. All tours make numerous photo stops and even amateurs are assured great pictures. You may also arrange to visit a hogan and see a weaving demonstration.

The company can provide lunch; special diets require 24 hours' notice. No wheelchair facilities are available. There is no minimum age, but parents must provide a car seat if the child requires one, and children of all ages are charged at the regular rate. Reservations may be made a day ahead of time, but shorter notice is fine. No deposit is required. Crawley's Monument Valley Tours accepts cash, traveler's checks, and personal checks drawn on U.S. banks. Inquire about group rates.

This company also offers custom adventure tours to Hunt's Mesa on the southern side of Monument Valley and to Mystery Valley, where travelers will see magnificent natural rock arches, such as Spiderweb Arch, and ancestral Puebloan ruins dating back nearly a thousand years. Four-by-four safaris with overnight camping (gear and equipment provided) include guides who will do all the cooking.

Monument Valley Horseback Trailrides and River Runner
Monument Valley, Utah
(435) 683-2327
www.cas-biz.com/valleyhorseback
This tour company offers a 90-minute horseback ride to the Mittens, a Full

Navajo Code Talkers

The Navajo Code Talkers were instrumental in winning World War II for the Allies. In the spring of 1942, just a few months after Pearl Harbor, a recruiter for the U.S. Marine Corps visited Window Rock. He was looking for young Navajo men to join the armed services. Twenty-nine young men and boys, some of whom exaggerated their ages to enlist, answered their country's call.

During World War I, the Navajo language had been used as a code, and the idea was to try the same strategy for encoding critical military messages during World War II. However, there was some fear that the enemy would be able to figure out what language was being used. So instead, the Navajo Code Talkers, in a military project created by Maj. Gen. Clayton B. Vogel, Amphibious Force, Pacific Fleet, and Commandant Thomas Holcomb, U.S. Marine Corps, developed a code based on the Navajo language. The entire code was committed to memory by the young Navajo soldiers. These soldiers would then code, transmit, and decode the messages.

More than 400 Navajo Code Talkers saw military action in the Pacific at Bougainville, New Britain, Kwajalein, Saipan, Guam, Peleliu, Okinawa, and Iwo Jima. The invasion of Iwo Jima was directed entirely by orders communicated by the Navajo Code Talkers. In two days, they transmitted more than 800 messages without one error. The Code Talkers, more than any other single group, are credited with the success of this mission.

Some names of the young men who served as Code Talkers are Merrill Sandoval, Dan Akee, Johnny Alfred, John Scott, Mike King, Peter MacDonald (who would later serve as president of the Navajo Nation), Martin Napa, William McCabe, Preston Toledo, Harold Y. Foster, Carl N. Gorman (father of the well-known artist R. C. Gorman), Eugene Roanhorse Crawford, and Mike Kiyaani.

No Code Talker was ever captured by the enemy, but they were sometimes mistaken for the enemy by U.S. troops because of their physical characteristics. The Marine Corps assigned white bodyguards to protect them.

For more than 20 years, the contribution of the Navajo Code Talkers went unheralded by the free world that owed them so much. In 1969, the information about them was declassified and in 1981, President Ronald Reagan signed a Certificate of Appreciation for their work. August 14, 1982, was declared National Code Talkers Day.

Today, Navajo Code Talkers proudly march in Veterans Day, Memorial Day, and Fourth of July parades and are honored guests at other events conducted by the Navajo Nation.

The Burger King on U.S. Highway 160 just west of the intersection of U.S. 160 and U.S. Highway 163 in Kayenta (928–697-3534 has an extensive exhibit about the Navajo Code Talkers, including World War II memorabilia, news accounts, and a list of the approximately 400 Code Talkers who served during World War II, 12 of whom were killed in action.

Moonlight Trailride (90 minutes when there is a full moon), Magnificent Sunrise and Sunset Tours by special arrangement, and an All Day Tour lasting six to seven hours. Custom trips for 5 to 20 riders during the summer include a two- to three-hour ride to Saddle Rock and an overnight camping experience (gear, breakfast, and dinner included). The stable is located one-half mile north of the visitor center. The operation also has a booth in the visitor center parking lot.

Roland's Navajoland Tours
One-half mile on the right going north on U.S. Highway 163, Kayenta
(928) 697-3524, (800) 368-2785
Navajo-owned and -operated, Roland's Navajoland Tours offers one- to four-hour tours in open-air 4x4 vehicles or buses. The shortest tour includes Mitten View, Merrick Butte, Elephant Butte, Camel Butte, Raingod Mesa, John Ford Point, and North Window. The two-hour tour adds Moccasin Arch, Big Hogan, Ear of the Wind, Echo Cave Ruins, Thunderbird Mesa, Profile of Navajo, and various petroglyph sites. In three hours you can also see Sam's Eye, and on a four-hour tour you'll be treated to a Navajo rug-weaving demonstration, a visit to a traditional hogan, and an afternoon or evening cookout including steak, beans, corn on the cob, salad, fry bread, juice, and coffee, or, if you prefer, Navajo tacos and Navajo beef sandwiches. For the four-hour tour only, there is a 15-passenger minimum. Roland can also take you on private, custom half-day, whole-day, sunset, sunrise, and overnight camping tours. Special tours for photographers and hiking tours (four-person minimum) are also available. Children under five years old travel free. Cash and traveler's checks, but not credit cards, are accepted.

Roland's has a small bed-and-breakfast on the premises. Four wheelchair-accessible rooms with queen beds are available, or you can spend the night in a tepee! Rates are charged per person for the rooms and per tepee. Both options

include a continental breakfast with cereal, juice, toast, pastry, coffee, and milk. Walk-ins are welcome for both the tours and the bed-and-breakfast, but reservations are recommended in the summer.

Sacred Monument Tours
Monument Valley, Utah
(435) 727-3218
www.monumentvalley.net
Professional guides will take you or your group through Tsebii Nidzisgai or "the valley within the rocks" in a Jeep Wrangler for a one-hour to an overnight tour. Jeep tours, which leave all day from the visitor center, take you along the 17-mile loop road, and into the backcountry to see natural arches, ancestral Puebloan ruins, and petroglyphs, or to Mystery Valley, depending on how much time you have. On the longer tours, you'll have time to explore small side canyons and take short hikes. The Red Earth Tour is three hours in the late afternoon or early morning, particularly good times for photography. Teardrop Drive is a two-hour adventure during which you'll visit ancestral Puebloan ruins and an ancient lookout over Mystery Valley. The 17-mile Loop Tour stops at five scenic points and a hogan. The Mystery Valley Tour takes three hours and includes walking trails to ruins, petroglyphs, and arches. Bring your camera, sunglasses, sandwiches, and cool drinks, and don't forget plenty of water and sunscreen.

One of the best ways to understand this land is to hike it. Sacred Monument Tours offers the Teardrop Trail Walk (two-and-a-half hours), the Hunt's Mesa Trek (a strenuous four-hour hike to the top of Hunt's Mesa, overnight camping, and a four-hour sunrise hike back), and the Mitchell Mesa Day Hike (four-and-a-half hours), a selection of treks for anyone with the time and stamina to see Monument Valley the way its first inhabitants did. The serious adventurer will choose the Navajo Mountain Expedition, a six-day, 65-mile guided trek to the base of Navajo Mountain, or Naatsis'aan. A shuttle will take you back to Kayenta.

Sacred Monument Tours also offers trail rides ranging from one hour to overnight. The Mitten Tour is two hours; The Mystery Valley Trail Ride is an all-day adventure; and the Overnight Trail Ride is a six-hour tour of Monument Valley, a stay in a traditional hogan, dinner, breakfast, and storytelling. Sleeping bags and other necessities are provided.

Credit cards, traveler's checks, and cash are accepted. You may make your reservations ahead of time for the longer tours, including private educational tours; for shorter trips, stop at the yellow booth in the parking lot at the visitor center. Group rates are available.

CANYON DE CHELLY

You come to these sandstone canyon-lands early in the third millennium A.D., but you might have come at the beginning of the fifth millennium B.C. Then you would not have traveled by car, or bus, or plane, or even by horseback, but on foot. You would not have stopped at a motel for the night, but you would have constructed a temporary shelter of brush for a night or a few nights. You would not have gone out to breakfast at the Holiday Inn, but you would have known this 20-mile canyon so well that finding a breakfast of nuts or berries would have been easy.

Even if you had come here 7,000 years ago, though, this magnificent canyon would have looked pretty much the way it does today, with its sheer sandstone cliff walls rising from 30 feet at the west end of the canyon to 1,000 feet at the east end. Chinle (CHIN lee) Wash, part of the drainage system of the Chuska Mountains to the east, would have run in

the winter and spring and during summer monsoon rains. Rock overhangs would have provided shelter from winter rain, wind, snow, and summer sun.

The sandstone rock of these canyons formed during the age of the dinosaurs as flat-lying wind-deposited layers of sand. These layers rose as part of the Defiance anticlime two to three million years ago. The meandering streams draining the Chuska Mountains flowed west, cutting Canyon de Chelly (d'SHAY), Canyon del Muerto, and the other canyons of this system as the land rose.

The caprock, along which you drive on the rim drives (described in the Exploring the Canyons section), is Shinarump Conglomerate—sand and pebbles deposited by streams during Triassic times (205 to 240 million years ago). In the conglomerate, small potholes collect rainwater and tiny plants and animals grow for a few hours or a few days. These living forms create an acidic environment and that acid eats away at the calcium carbonate that holds the conglomerate together. Desert winds then blow away small grains of sand, eventually leaving a pebbly surface.

Below the conglomerate is the peach-colored rock known as the de Chelly sandstone, which formed in Permian times 200 million years ago. Over thousands of millennia, moisture collected in the recesses in the sandstone and weakened the rock walls during alternate periods of freezing and warming. Slabs and sheets of the rock wall fell away (and continue to fall). Canyon de Chelly sandstone is dense, and it erodes to form large, arching alcoves. In time these recesses became deep enough for people to construct the cliff dwellings you see here.

The dark stains on the sandstone walls are formed by manganese and iron oxides. For many centuries, inhabitants of these canyons used smaller rocks to peck through this desert varnish and create the rock art known as petroglyphs.

The early people who came here were hunters and gatherers. They probably made their way through the canyons at certain times of year, collecting useful plants and hunting rabbit, deer, antelope, and some larger mammals. There is no evidence that they lived here on a permanent basis, or that they took advantage of the rock alcoves for more than a few nights' shelter.

During the Archaic Period, which lasted from about 2500 to 200 B.C., small groups of people settled here for longer periods of time, probably for a season or so. They hunted animals and gathered plants on both the canyon floors and the canyon rims. The steep trails they used to get from the bottom of the canyon to the rim can still be seen. The earliest petroglyphs date from this period.

The period from about 200 B.C. to A.D. 750 in this area is called the Basketmaker Period. During this time people made important changes in the way they used the canyon. These were the people who learned to farm the canyon floors and upland mesas, growing corn, which came from the south, as well as beans and squash. Probably these people lived in extended family groups and were able to produce surplus food, necessitating the invention of some way to store that food so that rodents and insects could not contaminate it. They also collected wild plants and hunted rodents, deer, and antelope. Toward the end of the Basketmaker Period, around A.D. 600, these ancient Puebloan people began to make ceramic pots for cooking, food storage, and carrying water, and they built pit houses and storage rooms in the canyon's rock shelters. The earliest circular structures, which may have been used for public ceremonies involving several settlements, also date from this period.

Archaeologists date the Pueblo Period from A.D. 750 to 1300, and in Canyon de Chelly, this period is well documented. The ancestral Puebloan people began to build larger aboveground masonry villages and the use of the rock shelters declined somewhat from about A.D. 1000 to 1250. Around the middle of the 13th century, though, the construction of cliff dwellings

became extremely important. Growing populations and environmental pressures, including climatic changes and severe droughts, may have impelled the people to devise or import new ways to organize their lives and new building technologies. Social organization and religious practices may have become even more complex during this period.

But by the beginning of the 14th century, the cliff dwellings of Canyon de Chelly—in fact, the villages of most of northeastern Arizona—were abandoned. Whether climatic changes, disease, conflict among villages, or religious and philosophical ideas were the cause, the ancient peoples of northeastern Arizona moved south and west to establish the pueblo villages along the Little Colorado River and on Black Mesa. For four centuries, no one made a permanent home in these canyons. In the mid-1700s the Navajo arrived from the north and the east, pushed from the Four Corners area by the Spanish. The Navajo farmed the canyon floor, growing corn, peaches, and other crops, and raised horses and sheep. By the late 1700s, though, Canyon de Chelly had become one of the battlegrounds of the struggle between the Navajo and the Spanish colonists, aided by other Native American tribes.

Canyon de Chelly (a name derived from the Spanish corruption of the Navajo word *Tsegi,* pronounced "SAY-ih") became a refuge for Navajo and others fleeing Spanish, then Mexican, and finally American, raiding parties. The complex of smaller canyons provided defensible hiding places that could be stocked with food and water.

But by the late 1850s, the United States had declared war on the Navajo people. In 1862, Brigadier General Carleton moved against the Navajo, demanding that they surrender and move to Fort Sumner in New Mexico. His scorched-earth policy brought widespread hunger and hardship. In the winter of 1863–64 Kit Carson invaded the eastern end of Canyon de Chelly and

CLOSE-UP

The Hogan

As you explore Canyon de Chelly or drive across the Navajo Reservation, you will undoubtedly see many examples of the traditional Navajo house, the hogan. In Navajo, the *hooghan* is "the home place."

There are several types of hogans; all are one-room, more or less circular buildings. They are heated by a stove or fireplace in the center. A stovepipe or a hole in the center of the roof lets smoke out of the hogan. Hogans have one door, facing east, and no windows.

The styles of hogans were given to the Navajo by Talking God when First Man and First Woman emerged into this world. The hogan itself is more than a place to live—it is a symbolic map of the universe, and each detail of its construction is specified. Every element is an analog to some feature or aspect of the world outside the hogan.

The original hogan was the forked-pole style, which Talking God fashioned from forked poles made of white shell, turquoise, abalone, and obsidian. In this style, three of the four main poles are forked and these interlock to make the framework to support the entry, which is the east pole. Then the vertical sides, made of poles that lean inward, are added, forming a conical structure, which is then covered with damp earth. This is the "male" hogan.

Talking God also gave the Navajo the "female" hogan, a round structure made by stacking logs horizontally in a pattern that diminishes as it rises, forming a building that is almost a hemisphere, chinked with bark and covered with damp earth to keep out wind, snow, and rain. By the late 1800s, another form evolved because steel axes made it possible to notch the logs and make a building with vertical sides and a domed roof. Often these hogans are six- or eight-sided structures.

Hogans were traditionally made of juniper logs, but now they are also made from stone masonry, cinderblock, two-by-fours, and other materials, depending on what is available.

Each hogan is usually home to one family, and hogans may be grouped together to form homesteads based on matrilineal relationships. The family's possessions are stored along the walls, and bedding is put away each day to create an open area in the center of the hogan.

Even when a family lives in a western-style home, they may build a hogan for ceremonial purposes, such as births, weddings, girls' initiations, and healing. During

moved westward toward the canyon mouth, pushing the cold and hungry Navajo ahead of him. Carson took 200 prisoners and came back the next spring to destroy the remaining Navajo hogans, crops, and sheep. In the winter and early spring of 1864, the U.S. government forced more than 9,000 Navajos to walk 300 miles from Fort Wingate and Fort Defiance to the banks of the Pecos River, known as Bosque Redondo. Many died on the Long Walk, and those too weak to

Traditional mud-and-timber hogans are few on the Navajo Reservation, but some, such as this one on display near the visitor center at Navajo National Monument, still exist to educate visitors about Navajo traditions. TODD R. BERGER

a healing ceremony, which may last for several days, men sit on the south side of the hogan, women on the north, and the healer on the west side. When a death occurs in a hogan, especially an unexpected death, the body is removed through a hole made in the wall, and the hogan is then abandoned or burned.

As a visitor to Navajoland, remember that hogans are private family living quarters, so you should not disturb the residents or take photographs.

continue were killed or simply left to perish on the trail. For four years, the Navajo suffered from starvation, cold, disease, loneliness, and demoralization until finally the U.S. government decided that the "experiment" to turn the Navajo into pueblo villagers had failed and was costing too much money. In 1868, the Navajos negotiated a treaty with the United States that allowed the 4,000 survivors of the Long Walk and subsequent imprisonment to return to a small part of their homeland. Barboncito, a Navajo leader from Canyon de Chelly, was instrumental in negotiating the treaty and in convincing the government that the Navajo should be sent home, not to other reservations in Oklahoma and Florida. The boundaries of the 1868 Navajo Reservation were drawn with Canyon de Chelly at its center.

After the Navajos returned from Fort Sumner, government food distribution centers evolved into trading posts, which became important influences in Navajo life. The Navajo exchanged rugs, jewelry, and other crafts for food staples and iron tools. Two trading posts were established near Canyon de Chelly by Lorenzo Hubbell. Camille Garcia's trading post, established in the early 1900s, lasted until the 1960s and is now represented by the restaurant and shop at the Holiday Inn in Chinle. Samuel Day's trading post, built in 1896, is now part of the Thunderbird Lodge complex.

Today, Navajo families continue to farm and raise sheep and horses in this spectacular canyon with its rich history that has such a tremendous physical and spiritual influence on the Navajo people.

In 1931, President Herbert Hoover created the 84,000-acre Canyon de Chelly National Monument. Owned by the Navajo Nation but managed by the National Park Service, Canyon de Chelly National Monument is one of the few national monuments that does not charge visitors an entrance fee.

The town of Chinle, just outside the western end of the canyon, is a Navajo Nation chapter that sends three delegates to the Navajo Nation Tribal Council. Chinle Agency is one of the five Bureau of Indian Affairs jurisdictions for the Navajo Reservation. Chinle is considered one of the major growth centers for the Navajo, and one area of likely development is increased tourism. Like the rest of Apache County, Chinle is a designated Enterprise Zone.

Temperatures during the winter average around 50 degrees Fahrenheit during the day and in the low 20s at night. During the summer, highs are in the high 80s and lows in the 50s.

You'll find a large array of convenience stores, gas stations, grocery stores, and Laundromats in this town, which has a population of about 8,500. The Tseyi' Shopping Center on U.S. Highway 191 has a Wells Fargo bank, a Bashas' supermarket, a U.S. post office, a pizza joint, and a general store. You'll have no trouble finding fast-food restaurants along U.S. 191.

The Chinle area is served by two weekly newspapers, *The Navajo Times* and the *Navajo-Hopi Observer,* two radio stations, and cable TV.

Diné College is 24 miles east in Tsaile. The phone number of this two-year tribal community college is (928) 674-3319. Both the community college and Northern Arizona University in Flagstaff offer college courses in Chinle.

The Navajo Police Department in Chinle can be reached at 911 in emergencies or at (928) 674-2111 for nonemergency situations. If you need help, you can also call the park rangers at (928) 674-5500, ext. 270. After hours only, call them at (928) 674-5523/5524. The hospital's phone number is (928) 674-7001.

You can reach Chinle by taking U.S. Highway 191 south from Monument Valley. You can also take Arizona Highway 264 out of Tuba City and drive east across the Hopi Reservation. If you're coming directly from Flagstaff, go east on Route 66 (U.S. Highway 89 north) past the Flagstaff Mall and turn right onto the Townsend-Winona Road. About 8 miles down the road, turn left at the sign for Leupp (pronounced "loop"), which puts you on Indian Route 15. Take Indian Route 15 (which becomes U.S. 191) north until you reach Chinle at the intersection of U.S. 191 and Indian Route 7. Here you will see signs for Canyon de Chelly National Monument, Thunderbird Lodge, and the Holiday Inn.

The National Park Service Visitor Center is open year-round. For more information about Canyon de Chelly, contact the national moument at (928) 674-5500 or www.nps.gov/cach.

Accommodations

PRICE CODE

The following price code is for two adults during the high season, generally between Memorial Day and Labor Day. The codes do not include taxes and other fees.

$	**Less than $75**
$$	**$76 to $125**
$$$	**$126 to $175**
$$$$	**$176 to $225**
$$$$$	**More than $225**

Best Western–Canyon de Chelly Inn $$$
Indian Route 7, Chinle
(938) 674-5875
www.canyondechelly.com
Located three miles west of the visitor center, this 106-room inn has an indoor heated pool and both smoking and nonsmoking rooms. Expect to pay an extra charge for more than two adults; children under 12 stay free. Some rooms are wheelchair accessible. The rooms have TVs, coffeemakers, phones, and hair dryers. From 10 P.M. to 6 A.M. security patrols check the parking lots as this is a place vendors often stay. Major credit cards are accepted, but pets are not. The motel lobby has a small gift shop with tourist items and some Navajo weavings and jewelry. If you are not certain whether an item is authentic Indian-made work, be sure to ask.

Holiday Inn—Canyon de Chelly $$$
Indain Route 7, Chinle
(928) 674-5000
www.holiday-inn.com/chinle-garcia
Located 2 miles from the intersection of U.S. Highway 191 and Indian Route 7, this is the newest and nicest motel in Chinle, with pleasant landscaping and well-maintained grounds. Built in 1992, the motel has 108 rooms with TVs, phones, irons and ironing boards, hair dryers, and coffeemakers. The outdoor heated pool is open from May through October, depending on the weather. Smoking and nonsmoking rooms are available, and some rooms are wheelchair accessible. The hotel is part of the complex that includes Garcia's Restaurant and a gift shop where you can also book private and group jeep tours, making it a convenient refuge from a day of strenuous horseback riding, jeep touring, hiking, or driving. The staff is invariably helpful. Single and double rooms go for the same price and children under 19 stay free. There is an extra charge for more than two adults in a room. Pets are not allowed.

Thunderbird Lodge $$$$
South Rim Drive, Chinle
(928) 674-5841, (800) 679-2473
www.tbirdlodge.com
Located just 0.5 mile south of the visitor center, Thunderbird Lodge is part of the Canyon de Chelly National Monument complex run by the park service, and the only lodging within the national monument itself. The cafeteria, started when Samuel Day's trading post went out of business, was the first building, and over the succeeding 70 years groups of motel rooms have been added in this bucolic setting shaded by huge cottonwood trees. All 73 rooms are in single-story buildings, and they all have small porches. The rooms have mission-style decor, color TVs, air-conditioning, and phones. The lodge is completely nonsmoking, pets are not allowed, and each person in the room after the first (including children) incurs a small additional charge. Credit cards are accepted, and some rooms are wheelchair accessible. Reservations are strongly suggested, especially from May through October.

Campgrounds

Cottonwood Campground
Canyon de Chelly National Monument, Chinle
(928) 674-5501

Hubbell Trading Post National Historic Site

On your way to or from Canyon de Chelly, make sure to take an hour or two to stop at the Hubbell Trading Post National Historic Site in Ganado.

Trading posts had a significant influence on the life of the Navajos after they returned from Fort Sumner in 1868. Often started as distribution sites for the food promised by the United States to the tribes to help them as they reestablished their fields, orchards, and herds, trading posts eventually became important meeting places for families who lived in small extended family groups; shopping centers to obtain staple foods, tools, fabrics, and other manufactured goods; and venues for selling arts and crafts to traders who sold them to tourists.

John Lorenzo Hubbell, son of a Connecticut Yankee father and a Spanish mother, started trading in Ganado in 1876. Pictures of the exterior of the trading post from the turn of the 20th century show pretty much the same building you can see today: sandstone masonry with vigas (poles used as horizontal roof supports, often seen in Santa Fe–style houses).

The inside of the building is not much changed either. The main room holds trade goods, which now include sodas and snacks as well as fabric, saddles, tools, Minnetonka moccasins, Pendleton blankets, and Blue Bird flour. Farther inside to the left is the rug room, with superb examples of many traditional and modern patterns. You will be encouraged to spread out the rugs you like on the floor. Among these might be a red, white, tan, and black geometric Ganado Red, a style that Hubbell helped to encourage Navajo women to weave because he thought it was a style tourists would be likely to buy—and he was right. Most rugs will have a card that tells the artist's name, the area from which she comes,

---

Cottonwood Campground is maintained by the National Park Service and is just southwest of the visitor center next to Thunderbird Lodge. Except for groups of 15 to 50 tent campers, no reservations are accepted and sites are allotted on a first-come, first-served basis year-round, so arrive early in the summer. The campground welcomes both tents and RVs. Ninety-six sites are available with rest rooms. There is a dump station with water, but no showers or hookups are available. There is no fee to camp here.

Spider Rock RV Park
South Rim Drive, Chinle
(928) 674-8261, (877) 910-CAMP
home.earthlink.net/spiderrock
Located 10 miles east of the visitor center on South Rim Drive, this campground is run by the Navajo. Sites run $10 for tents and $15 for RVs. The campground also has two hogans available to guests. The smaller hogan can house up to three people and runs $25 per night; the larger hogan sleeps up to 11 people, and the price depends on the number of guests. No

and the price of the rug. A photograph of the weaver might also be attached. Ask the salesperson to help you identify the differences among the rugs, and to find out if there is any leeway in the marked price. (There probably is.)

The middle room has jewelry (including some incredible concho belts), fine Hopi kachina carvings, pottery, basketry, and the usual tourist souvenirs. The trading post carries items from many Southwest tribes, including Navajo, Hopi, Zuni, Acoma, Tohono O'odham, and Apache.

The Hubbell Trading Post National Historic Site also includes a visitor center that is open seven days a week year-round except January 1, Thanksgiving, and December 25. The National Park Service staff are friendly and helpful, and weavers or other artists may be giving demonstrations. Photos may be allowed, but ask first. The visitor center is a good place to shop for books, tapes, and maps.

Tours of the Hubbell home behind the trading post are offered daily, conducted by park rangers, or you can get a booklet for a self-guided tour. The Hubbell Homestead also includes a barn, a warehouse, a guest hogan, and a chicken coop, all of which are open to the public. You can find public rest rooms, a drinking fountain, and picnic tables near the visitor center. No camping facilities or motels are available in Ganado, but Chinle is not far away.

To get to the trading post from Chinle, take U.S. Highway 191 south and turn east toward Ganado at the intersection with Arizona Highway 264. Coming from the Hopi Reservation, you'll be on AZ 264, so just continue past U.S. 191 about 5 miles. From Flagstaff, you will be on U.S. 191 north. Turn east at the junction with AZ 264. Signs clearly direct you to the trading post, just across the Ganado Wash.

For more information on this historic site, contact the Hubbell Trading Post Historic Site, P.O. Box 150, Ganado, AZ 86505-0150. Or call (928) 755-3475. You can also visit the Web site at www.nps.gov/hutr.

water or electricity are available here, but you can buy bottled water and lanterns. The Chapter House in Chinle has showers that you may use for a fee.

Restaurants

PRICE CODE

The price codes below represent average prices for dinner for two, excluding tax, gratuity, and drinks.

$	Less than $20
$$	$21 to $35
$$$	$36 to $60
$$$$	More than $60

Garcia's Restaurant $$
Indian Route 7, Chinle
(928) 674-5000
www.holiday-inn.com/chinle-garcia
Located at the Holiday Inn–Canyon de Chelly, just 2 miles from the intersection with U.S. Highway 191, this casual restaurant in a mission-style building offers a

pleasant dining experience with good service, whether you're here for breakfast, lunch, or dinner. Classic cookery with a southwestern flair describes the menu here. The produce, meat, and fish are always fresh and top quality. For lunch, salads, burgers, sandwiches, and local specialties are offered, and the Veggie Quesadilla is very good. The whole wheat tortillas were full of fresh vegetables and low-fat cheese. The lunch serving was enough for two meals. At dinner, sirloin steaks, ribs, chicken, salads, and burgers make for a varied menu. Because the restaurant is on the Navajo Reservation, no alcoholic beverages are served, though there is a selection of nonalcoholic beers and wines. The restaurant is open daily year-round, is wheelchair accessible, and accepts major credit cards. Reservations are recommended for dinner. There is plenty of parking in the motel parking lot.

Junction Restaurant $$
Indian Route 7, Chinle
(928) 674-8443

This is a popular stop for tour bus groups, serving such favorites as Navajo sandwiches made with shredded beef, Navajo beef stew and fry bread, Navajo tacos, steaks, salads, and sandwiches. The restaurant is open for breakfast, lunch, and dinner seven days a week. Reservations are not needed, except for large groups. The Junction also offers set menus for tour groups. Major credit cards are accepted, and the restaurant is wheelchair accessible.

Thunderbird Cafeteria $
South Rim Drive, Chinle
(928) 674-5841, (800) 679-2473
www.tbirdlodge.com

Located 0.5 mile south of the visitor center on South Rim Drive, this cafeteria offers simple breakfasts, burgers, chili dogs, fish and fries, fresh fruit, and salads.

The central part of this building was constructed in 1896 by Samuel Day as a trading post. One important function of trading posts at the turn of the 20th century was that they pawned jewelry for

people when they needed cash. Day's large vault, where he stored these valuable items, is now a picture gallery. The trading post closed in 1969 and the building was later converted to a restaurant and expanded. Open daily for breakfast, lunch, and dinner from very early in the morning into the evening. Large comfortable booths, varied artwork on the walls, and friendly staff more or less compensate for the unexciting food. Some of the wall displays are contemporary Navajo weavings, reconstructions of hunting weapons and other tools, and genuine antiques, and all of it is for sale. The cafeteria accepts major credit cards, but no personal checks. It is wheelchair accessible, and of course, it is the most convenient restaurant if you are staying at Thunderbird Lodge or booking one of their motorized tours of the canyon.

Shopping

Holiday Inn—Canyon de Chelly Gift Shop
Indian Route 7, Chinle
(928) 674-5000
www.holiday-inn.com/chinle-garcia

In addition to a great selection of T-shirts (some of which have designs not seen elsewhere), Tony Hillerman novels, snacks, tourist pottery, Pendleton items, and other souvenirs, this gift shop, just 2 miles from the intersection of U.S. Highway 191 and Indian Route 7, carries a lot of jewelry. Most of the jewelry is Navajo, but some is Zuni and Hopi. The buyer here features the work of well-known artists. Ask for help when selecting your jewelry, pottery, and kachina carving purchases to ascertain whether what you are considering is Native American made (and in the case of kachinas especially, by what tribe), what kind of metal is used, and what stones are incorporated in the piece. Ask the salesperson to help you distinguish between handmade, traditionally fired pots and hand-painted greenware. This shop is also a good place to book group and private jeep tours of the canyon. The shop is open daily but closes in December for the off-season and reopens in March. Credit cards are accepted.

Navajo Arts & Crafts Enterprise
Intersection of U.S. Highway 191 and
Indian Route 7, Chinle
(928) 674-5338

Established by the Navajo Nation in 1941 to promote traditional Navajo arts and crafts, the Navajo Arts & Crafts Enterprise offers high-quality, genuine Navajo arts—rugs, silver and turquoise jewelry, sand-paintings, and pottery, as well as Pendleton blankets, backpacks, pillows, purses, yarn, moccasins, and T-shirts. For the music lover, an extensive collection of cassettes and CDs by Native American artists makes the stop worthwhile. Among the books offered are some out-of-print scholarly texts and anthropological studies reprinted by the University of Arizona's Arizona Books on Request.

Navajo Arts & Crafts Enterprise has three other stores, in Cameron, Kayenta, and Window Rock. Open daily.

Thunderbird Lodge Gift Shop
South Rim Drive, Chinle
(928) 674-5841, (800) 679-2473
www.tbirdlodge.com

From beautiful Navajo weavings to the dyed weft yarn and neutral warp yarn from which they are woven, this shop—located just 0.5 mile south of the visitor center on South Rim Drive—offers a wonderful selection of rugs, Zuni and Navajo jewelry, pottery, and souvenir items, such as T-shirts, books, maps, moccasins, and tapes and CDs. The good Navajo rugs and the Hopi kachina carvings have a room of their own (which they share with some charming Navajo folk art), and the strictly tourist items are separated from the handmade Native American items and clearly labeled to avoid any confusion about what you are buying. The shop also offers sandpaintings and reconstructions of early weapons, shields, and other interesting items. If you're touring the canyon by jeep, truck, or horseback, be sure to stop here

to pick up a hat, sunscreen, and water if you've forgotten them. Open daily year-round, the shop accepts major credit cards and personal checks with identification. In the front of the shop is the counter where you can book the canyon tours offered at Thunderbird Lodge.

EXPLORING THE CANYONS

You may explore the park's canyons by driving along the south or north rim, hiking down White House Trail, taking a horseback or jeep tour, or hiking into the canyons. All activities except the rim drives and the White House Trail hike require that you be escorted by an authorized Navajo or National Park Service guide.

The Rim Drives

Both rim drives start from the National Park Service Visitor Center. The center, open year-round, has a small museum, offers an extensive collection of books for sale, and shows a 22-minute video, *Canyon Voices,* to introduce you to the canyons. Ask here about ranger-led activities such as Hogan Talks, Campfire Programs, and other special programs.

The rim drives are spectacular at any time of day. The colors of the sandstone walls of the canyons change as the sunlight hits them from different angles.

THE SOUTH RIM DRIVE

The South Rim Drive takes you along the southern rim of Canyon de Chelly. The drive is approximately 37 miles round-trip and offers seven overlooks, three of which are wheelchair accessible. The drive is at an elevation of 5,500 feet at the visitor center and rises to about 7,000 feet at Spider Rock Overlook.

At Tunnel Canyon Overlook, the canyon walls are 275 feet high. A sign will alert you not to proceed farther without a guide. This overlook is wheelchair accessible.

From Tsegi Overlook, you can see some of the Navajo agricultural lands at the bottom of the canyon, which are farmed during the summer months. Horses and sheep graze here as well. If you look across the road, you will see sand dunes. Millions of years ago, the De Chelly Sandstone formed from dunes like these.

Traveling east to Junction Overlook, you can see First Ruin across the canyon to your left. This small ruin was occupied about a thousand years ago. Looking straight ahead across the canyon, you can see Junction Ruin where Canyon de Chelly and Canyon del Muerto meet. You will notice that most of the cliff dwellings are on the north side of the canyon, offering a southern (and therefore sunnier and warmer) exposure during the winter months. Junction Ruin is also small, consisting of 15 rooms and one kiva.

White House Overlook is a "must" stop. White House Ruin once was home to more than a dozen families, with cliff dwellings in the canyon wall and pueblo buildings on the canyon floor. At the height of its occupancy about 800 years ago, this ruin probably had 80 rooms and four kivas, though only about 60 rooms remain. You can hike to White House Ruin beginning about 150 yards to the right of the rim. The trail is 2.5 miles round-trip and drops about 550 feet to the canyon floor. This is a moderately difficult hike, and plenty of water, good hiking shoes, sunscreen, and a hat are absolutely required. Plan on spending about two hours on this trail. Pit toilets are available at the bottom of the canyon. Temperatures may be extreme during the summer and the winter. You are requested not to disturb any of the natural or archaeological features you may encounter, and not to bother the Navajos for whom this canyon is home. Pets are not allowed on the trail. The overlook, but not the trail, is wheelchair accessible.

Sliding House sits on a narrow ledge across from the overlook. Retaining walls kept the houses from sliding down into the canyon below. This ruin of about 50 rooms and three kivas was built and occupied from the beginning of the 10th century to the middle of the 13th century.

Face Rock Overlook has a viewfinder through which you can see four small ruins. Look to the far right to see Face Rock, which tells Spider Woman the names of naughty children.

Spider Rock Overlook is the highest point on South Rim Drive at about 7,000 feet. The canyon floor is 1,000 feet below. The 800-foot sandstone spire at the meeting of Canyon de Chelly and Monument Canyon is Spider Rock, the home of Spider Woman, who taught Navajo women how to weave. Black Rock, just to the left of and a little above Spider Rock, is a volcanic plug, the core of an ancient volcano about 70 million years old. The Chuska Mountains are on the horizon.

Return to the visitor center along the same road that you followed to get here.

THE NORTH RIM DRIVE

This drive takes you along the north rim of Canyon del Muerto. There are four overlooks, none of which are wheelchair accessible. The 35-mile round-trip from the visitor center will take you about two hours.

Some 900 years ago, the ancestral Puebloan people built Ledge Ruin 100 feet above the canyon floor. No archaeological excavations have been done here, but surface remains of ceramics suggest that this site of at least 29 rooms and two kivas was occupied from about A.D. 1050 to 1275. From this overlook you can also see Round Corner Ruin on your left high above the floor of the canyon. It appears to be a single kiva connected to Ledge Ruin by a toe-and-handhold trail, but its purpose and the reason for its location remain a mystery.

From Antelope House Ruin Overlook, you can see Antelope House on the left and Navajo Fortress on the right. The first ruin is named for an extraordinary painting of a pronghorn to the left of the ruin, which may date to the mid-19th century and may have been done by a renowned Navajo artist named Dibe Yazhi. A pit house under the surface construction here dates back to A.D. 700, and the site has been occupied more or less continuously since then. A 12th-century circular central plaza distinguishes this from other known sites in the area. The ruin also has circular kivas and a multistory pueblo of at least 80 rooms. Like so many other sites in this region, Antelope House was abandoned near the end of the 13th century.

A high redstone butte across the canyon, Navajo Fortress, provided a defensible position for the Navajo defending themselves from Spanish, American, and other Native American enemies beginning around the end of the 18th century. Log poles, which were pulled up behind the refugees, provided the only access to the butte. Navajo Fortress provided temporary refuge for the Navajos during the Americans' slash-and-burn attack on the people in the mid-1860s. But eventually most of the Navajos who sought refuge here surrendered for lack of food, water, and shelter and were forced on the Long Walk to Bosque Redondo, where they were imprisoned until the Treaty of 1868 allowed them to return to their homeland.

Mummy Cave Ruin is one of the largest ancestral Puebloan ruins in Canyon del Muerto. In Navajo, its name means "house under the rock," and archaeological research indicates that this site was occupied from about A.D. 300 to 1300. The eastern cave contains about fifty rooms and four kivas, while the western cave has about twenty rooms. The most recent architecture here is in the Mesa Verde style, and scientists speculate that these seven rooms and a three-story fortress were built by refugees or migrants from Mesa Verde in what is now Colorado. It was probably the last site occupied before the abandonment of the canyon in the late 13th century.

The name Massacre Cave suggests a terrible history, and that is in fact what happened here. Antonio de Narbona led a military force into Canyon de Chelly in 1805 to force the Navajos to accept Span-

ish settlement on Navajo land. When he arrived, most of the men were out hunting. The women, children, and elders saw the soldiers coming and took refuge in a cave high on the canyon wall, but Narbona's troops attacked from the rim and the bullets ricocheted off the walls of the cave, killing 115 women, children, and elderly people. Almost three dozen more were captured.

Yucca Cave Viewpoint allows you to see a small site probably occupied by late Basketmaker and early ancestral Puebloan peoples.

While experiencing the canyons from the rim, there are a few important things to remember. The first is that the canyons are sheer vertical walls as much as 1,000 feet deep. Stay on established trails and remember that the walls at the overlooks are there for your protection. Keep control of your children and pets. A fall from the rim would cause serious injury and quite possibly death.

Keep your eyes open for snakes and stinging insects. Look before you step or put your hands on the rocks and don't put your hands anywhere you cannot see into. Cultural artifacts, natural features, animals, and plants are all protected by federal and Navajo law. Do not remove or disturb anything.

Hiking Tours

Canyon Hiking Service
South Rim Drive, Chinle
(928) 674-1767
This service offers various hiking options, including nighttime hikes into the canyon. You can find them 0.25 mile north of Thunderbird Lodge.

Tsegi Guide Association
Chinle
(928) 674-5500
At the visitor center at the entrance to the national monument, you can hire a guide for a minimum three-hour hike of the

canyon or an overnight camping excursion. You can make your plans when you arrive, but for large groups and for overnight hiking/camping trips, you should call in advance. Remember that except for White House Ruin Trail, unescorted hiking in the canyon is forbidden. Each guide can take up to 15 people. A park ranger at the visitor center will help you get the necessary permit.

Horseback Tours

Two companies, one at either end of Canyon de Chelly, offer guided horseback tours.

Justin's Horse Rental
At the intersection of South Rim Drive and North Rim Drive at the mouth of Canyon de Chelly, Chinle
(928) 674-5678
Justin's Horse Rental is located at the mouth of the canyon; you will see signs on your way to Thunderbird Lodge. The tours start at the shallow end of the canyon and as you go farther, the canyon walls become higher. Riding in the spring may take you along Chinle Wash when there is water running. In the summer, the canyon bottom will be sandy and your guide may let you run the horses!

Visitors pay both for the horse they are renting and for the services of a guide, who must be hired to escort you (partly to protect the canyon and the people who live there, and partly to protect you from hazards such as quicksand). Horses and guide must be reserved for a minimum of two hours, and a guide can be responsible for only six riders. Larger groups need additional guides. The shortest ride (two to two-and-a-half hours round-trip) takes you to Antelope House. The longest one-day ride is eight to nine hours and takes you to Mummy Cave. This is a one-way ride; the horses are trailered and you drive the other way. Rides of in-between lengths are available, and overnights can be arranged. The company

provides horses, guides, dinner, and breakfast. You bring your own sleeping bags, tents, and lunch.

For the spring and summer months, you need to make your reservations here one to two months in advance. It's slower during the winter, but reservations are still a good idea. You should call a few days before your reserved trip to confirm. Only cash and traveler's checks are accepted, and remember to tip your guide.

Totsonii Ranch
South Rim Drive, Chinle
(928) 755-6209
At the other end of Canyon de Chelly, 1.25 miles beyond the end of the pavement of the South Rim Drive, you'll find Totsonii Ranch.

The ranch's rides start at the deep end of the canyon, and the descent from the rim to the canyon floor is along a narrow, rocky, steep trail. You can always get off and walk your horse down the steepest parts, and it's good to remind yourself that the horse wants to fall even less than you do, and it has made this trip dozens if not hundreds of times.

Once you reach the bottom of the canyon, you are very close to Spider Rock, which is even more magnificent from the bottom of the canyon than from the rim. Your guide will point out petroglyphs and other interesting features. Feel free to ask questions, as guides are happy to share aspects of Navajo history and culture. Reservations are strongly recommended, and tipping is appreciated.

Motorized Tours

Canyon de Chelly Unimog Tours
Chinle
(928) 674-1044,
(928) 674-5433 (reservations)
Canyon de Chelly Unimog Tours is the only Navajo-owned motorized tour company at Canyon de Chelly. Leon Skyhorse Thomas is an authorized guide who will

take you on a half-day tour to Antelope House Ruin and White House Ruin in an open, four-wheel-drive vehicle. Other sites on this tour include Kokopelli Cave, Petroglyph Rock, First Ruin, Junction Ruin, Ceremonial Cave, and Ledge Ruin. The three-hour tours leave in the morning and the afternoon from the Holiday Inn parking lot, and they are limited to 12 passengers each. Children 12 and under get special rates, and babies under one year of age must have car seats. The company also offers private jeep tours. You can arrange your tour through the gift shop at the Holiday Inn or you can contact the company directly.

**Thunderbird Lodge Canyon Tours
South Rim Drive, Chinle
(928) 674-5841, (800) 679-2473**
Thunderbird Lodge, operated by the National Park Service, offers all-day, half-day, and private tours with experienced Navajo guides. Their 6x6 open-air jeeps hold up to 24 passengers. The all-day tour

is a 60-mile round-trip through Canyon del Muerto to Mummy Cave and through Canyon de Chelly to Spider Rock. The tour leaves Thunderbird Lodge at 9:00 A.M. and returns at about 5:00 P.M. (Remember that the Navajo Reservation observes daylight savings time from April through October.) Lunch is provided. This tour operates from spring, when the water in the canyons is sufficiently low, into the late fall, depending on the weather.

The half-day tour lasts about three-and-a-half hours and takes you into the lower parts of Canyon de Chelly and Canyon del Muerto. Tours leave the lodge at 9:00 A.M. and 2:00 P.M. during the spring through fall season. In the winter (November through March), plan to leave at 9:00 A.M. or 1:00 P.M..

Private tours are also available. You may buy your tickets for these tours at the gift shop at Thunderbird Lodge, or you may make your reservations in advance (particularly recommended for private tours).

HOPI RESERVATION

The Hopi Reservation in northeastern Arizona today occupies about 1.5 million acres, a small portion of the Hopis' ancestral homeland. More than 11,000 Hopis, divided into 34clans, now live on and around three sandstone mesas rising hundreds of feet above the plateau floor at elevations of 5,000 to 6,000 feet. Second Mesa is about 90 miles northeast of Flagstaff.

The twelve Hopi villages are built on First, Second, and Third Mesas (named from east to west) and the lands surrounding them, with Moenkopi—culturally and historically part of Third Mesa—just across Moenkopi Wash from Tuba City.

Hopi is a Uto-Aztecan language. Still spoken exclusively by many elders, the language is being aggressively preserved by the Hopi through language classes for students and the publication of a Hopi dictionary in 1998 by the University of Arizona Press.

HISTORY

The Hopi people, according to their own accounts, came into this, the Fourth World, from below ground, climbing up through a *sipapu* somewhere in Grand Canyon at some time in the past. The Fourth World, like those before it, will end catastrophically, but how much we will suffer when the Fourth World is destroyed will be determined by how we behave now.

The Hopi are the descendents of the Hisatsenom, who lived on the Colorado Plateau more than a millennium ago. The term *Hisatsenom* refers to the ancestral Puebloan people, or the Anasazi. They were the builders of many of the pueblo and cliff dweller monuments whose remains we see today, such as those at Mesa Verde in Colorado, Canyon de Chelly in Arizona, and Chaco Canyon in New Mexico. The earliest Hopi villages on the mesas are contemporary with some of these ancestral cliff dwellings.

Hopi history recalls that only after the people completed their migrations in the four directions were they allowed by Massau, the caretaker of this world, to settle on the three mesas they now inhabit. They were given three things: a gourd of water, a planting stick, and an ear of corn with which to survive. In return, the Hopis agreed to act as stewards of this sacred land. An account of the founding of the Hopi villages and the different clans and ceremonies associated with them is detailed in *Truth of a Hopi: Stories Relating to the Origin, Myths and Clan Histories of the Hopi* by Edmund Nequatewa. Hopi is a matrilineal society organized by clans. A person's clan membership prescribes his or her obligations within the society.

In such arid country (only about 10 inches of rain fall a year), the Hopi became highly skilled dry farmers and developed a ceremonial cycle tied to the land on which they lived and thrived. Today, they grow corn, fruit trees, squash, beans, melons, and gourds. They are also fine artists, making overlay silver jewelry, decorated coiled pots, kachina carvings (called *katsina* by some Hopi artists and vendors), and weavings of unsurpassed quality. Hopis today are also educators, environmentalists, doctors, lawyers, geologists, hydrologists, historians, and members of many other professions.

The first European record of contact with the Hopi documents the visits of Pedro de Tovar and Fray Juan Padilla, members of Francesco Vázquez de Coronado's expedition in 1540. The Hopi, however, knew about the Spanish before this time. Information, as well as material culture, followed the trade routes from as far south as Central America. And Hopi prophecy told of a *bahana,* a white brother, who would come to them from the east as a savior.

But the Spanish had come instead in search of the mythical seven golden cities of Cibola. They called the Hopi "Tusayan," and believed that they were a hostile and warlike tribe. Coronado sent 20 soldiers with Tovar and Padilla to "explore" the Hopi mesas. This group probably visited the village of Awat'ovi, but their records do not show if they went to any of the other Hopi villages.

Soon thereafter a party led by Garcia Lopez de Cárdenas was sent from Zuni Pueblo in the south to find a great river in the vicinity of Hopi (presumably the Colorado River). He reported that the Hopi were ruled by an assembly of old men and that their priests told the people how to live. He estimated that Zuni and Hopi together had a population of 3,000 to 4,000 people, counting only adult males. Based on that estimate, there may have been about 8,000 Hopi in the middle of the 16th century.

In 1598, the Spanish sent Don Juan de Onate to "conquer" the Hopi for the Spanish crown, but the Hopi did not then, or ever, submit to any outside authority.

The Hopis received from the Spanish horses, sheep, burros, and cattle, as well as some Old World fruits and vegetables. The addition of foods high in animal fat to the diet of a mostly vegetarian people has taken its toll—diabetes is a serious health threat among the Hopi, as it is among other Native American tribes.

During the Pueblo Revolt of 1680, the Hopi joined the Rio Grande pueblo tribes and rose up against the Spanish, destroying churches and killing several priests. It was after the Pueblo Revolt that the villages of First and Second Mesa moved to the mesa tops to defend themselves against further Spanish invasions.

Pueblo tribes in what is now New Mexico were reconquered in 1692 and the Spanish visited Awat'ovi, Walpi, Mishong-

On the Hopi mesas, the average daytime temperatures in the winter are in the mid 40s; overnight lows average about 18 degrees Fahrenheit. In the summer, daytime temperatures are in the mid to high 80s, and nighttime lows are in the low 50s. Spring and fall temperatures are cool to warm during the day and cool to cold at night.

novi, and Shongopavi, but Spain never gained military dominance over the Hopi, in part because of the Hopis' ability to negotiate without surrendering to foreigners. Awat'ovi on Antelope Mesa was the only Hopi village to tolerate missionaries, who first arrived in the region in the late 16th century. The village was destroyed in the early 18th century by Hopis from other villages in protest.

The Hopi sent diplomats, as representatives of their sovereign nation, to offer to make a peace treaty with the Spanish, but Spain summarily rejected the offer.

Attempts by the Spanish to conquer Walpi in 1716 and 1724 failed. Missionaries tried unsuccessfully to convert residents of the six Hopi villages—Walpi, Oraibi, Mishongnovi and Shongopavi, Shipaulovi and Tewa—in 1744 and 1745. The last two villages had been founded after the 1680 Pueblo Revolt.

The Hopi were under the authority of Mexico from 1821 to 1846, but the Mexican government never attempted to govern villages so far away from their base of power. They did, however, raid Hopi villages to capture children, who were sold as servants for rich Mexican families.

During the Spanish and Mexican periods, the Hopi were continually threatened by other tribes, particularly the Navajo, who had migrated from the north and east. These seminomadic herders needed grazing land for their animals—the same land that the agricultural Hopi needed for farming. The Hopis sought help from the Mexican government to protect their

Visiting the Hopi Reservation

Most villages have an office where you should check in when you arrive to find out if visitors are welcome at that time.

Disruption of shrines or removal of any artifacts is strictly prohibited, and all archaeological sites are protected by federal and Hopi law.

Overnight camping is limited to two nights at designated campgrounds only. Non-Hopis must have the permission of the village leader to stay in the village for any length of time.

Photographing, sketching, painting, and video and audio recording in the villages are never allowed.

Most ceremonial dances are closed to non-Indians. Social dances and Butterfly Dances held from late August through November, mostly on weekends, are often open to visitors. Precise dates are not known until a few weeks in advance. If you are not sure whether non-Hopis are welcome at a dance or ceremonial, ask. Should you be privileged to be invited to a ceremonial dance, you need to remember that you are a guest and are expected to behave appropriately and sensibly. You should wear neat clothing. Women are asked to wear clothing that completely covers them, and men should wear pants and shirts. Hats and umbrellas are discouraged. You should not discuss the event while it is happening, nor should you follow the dancers when they leave the plaza. Choose a place from which to observe—and stay there; do not move around the plaza or the village. As a guest, you are also expected to contribute to the event with positive thoughts and prayers to strengthen and benefit all the forms and things in the world.

No alcohol or illegal drugs are permitted on the Hopi Reservation.

lands, but Mexico was either not willing or not able to provide that help.

The first Anglo-American visitors to the Hopi arrived in the 1820s. They included Bill Williams (see the chapter on Williams), who may have lived among the Hopi, though no written record of this exists. However, a party of trappers from Rocky Mountain Fur Company did invade the gardens at Oraibi in 1834, massacring 15 to 20 Hopis who objected to this raid.

The 1848 Treaty of Guadalupe de Hidalgo ceded the Southwest from Mexico to the United States at the end of the Mexican War. This treaty is an important document in Hopi history because it recognized the Hopi and other pueblo tribes as citizens with full rights. The pueblo tribes, with sophisticated systems of government, agriculture, arts and crafts, and complex religious beliefs, were distinguished from the warring tribes of the Southwest. The treaty also demarcated a specific Hopi land base and promised to protect the Hopi from the Navajo who were encroaching on Hopi land.

The first meeting between the Hopi and the U.S. government occurred in 1850 when some Hopis visited the Superintendent of Indian Affairs James S. Calhoun in Santa Fe, New Mexico, to try to determine the government's intentions toward them and to ask for military protection against the Navajo. In 1852, the Hopi initiated contact with President Millard Fillmore via a messenger who carried ritual objects as gifts. The Hopi offered friendship and communication. Oral histories also recall that in the early 1850s another smallpox epidemic caused widespread death. The epidemic was followed by a severe drought. The population of Oraibi was reduced to 200.

In 1858 Mormon missionaries, who believed American Indians to be Lamanites, one of the lost tribes of Israel, arrived on Hopi. Mormons apparently treated Hopis with more respect than other Anglo-Americans, and the Hopi distinguished them by calling the Mormons by a different name from the one that referred to all other Anglo-Americans. The Mormons left four missionaries, but they stayed only a few weeks. Other Mormon missionaries came, and in 1862 some Hopis went to Salt Lake City and met with Brigham Young.

The ongoing conflict with the Navajo ended for a brief period in the mid-1860s when thousands of Navajo were forced on the Long Walk, which they still remember vividly today, and imprisoned at Bosque Redondo, New Mexico, until 1868. The decade also brought famine and another smallpox epidemic to the Hopi.

The 1868 Navajo treaty with the federal government allowed them to return to northwestern New Mexico and northeastern Arizona to live on a 3.5-million-acre reservation there. The Navajos, however, moved westward, again intruding on land to which the Hopi had ancestral claims.

Tuuvi, a Hopi from Oraibi, and his wife, Katsinmana, visited Utah around 1870 and converted to Mormonism. Tuuvi welcomed Mormon settlement of the Moenkopi area west of Third Mesa in 1875 as a means to protect the Hopi from enemy incursions. A year later the Mormons moved a little farther west and founded Tuba City. Not many Hopis converted to the Mormon faith, however, and Tuuvi was treated as an outcast. In 1903 the U.S. government forced the Anglo Mormons out of Tuba City, since they had settled on land already allocated to the Native Americans.

In case of emergency, call the Hopi Police Department at (928) 738-5110. The Public Health Service Hospital is in Keams Canyon, (928) 738-2211. Ambulance service and air transport to Phoenix are available.

On December 16, 1882, President Chester Arthur created by executive order a 2.5-million-acre reservation for the "Moqui and other such Indians as the Secretary of the Interior saw fit to settle thereon." This may have discouraged some Anglo settlement in the area, but it had no effect on other tribes encroaching on Hopi land.

The Navajos continued to occupy lands outside the original boundaries of their 1868 reservation, and the federal government expanded the area allotted to the Navajos 14 times between 1868 and 1934. This expansion of Navajo lands decreased the Hopi land base.

The federal government built a school at Keams Canyon in 1887, and the late 19th century saw increasing pressure on the Hopi to let the federal government educate their children. Some parents and 30 Hopi religious leaders were captured and imprisoned at Alcatraz for keeping their children at home. They did not accept the U.S. mandate to send their children to government schools—they wanted to educate Hopi children themselves in order to keep the Hopi way of life vibrant. More government day schools were built, and military force was used by the government to make the children of more traditional families attend the schools.

Despite their exemption from military service because of their pacifist religious beliefs, many young Hopi men joined the armed services because they saw it as an opportunity to learn a vocation. During World War I, one-tenth of the Hopi Tribe served in the army, but it was not until 1924 that Congress declared Hopis to be citizens of the United States, and not until mid-century that they were allowed to vote in the state of Arizona.

In 1935, the U.S. government mandated a tribal government on Hopi to act as one body for the Hopi villages, which prior to this time had been largely autonomous. The government needed a body that it could authorize to sign leases for the mining of valuable minerals on Hopi lands and was not worried that only a minority of Hopis voted to accept the new Tribal Council. Disagreement as to what legitimate authority the Tribal Council wields on Hopi continues to this day.

In 1958, the attorney for the Hopi Tribal Council helped craft a bill to clarify the language in the 1882 executive order that established a reservation for the "Moqui and other such Indians as the Secretary of the Interior saw fit to settle thereon." The bill was passed and Congress thereby authorized the creation of a three-judge panel to determine who those "other such Indians" were and what interest they had in the land set aside by the executive order. John Boyden argued on behalf of the Hopi that all of the 1882 reservation should belong to the Hopi Tribe, while attorneys for the Navajo Tribe argued that they were the other Indians referred to in the executive order. Why else had the government built roads and schools for the Navajos on that land?

In the 1960s, Hopi coal and water resources were leased to a mining company. The mining leases generate income that supports the Tribal Council, which determines how the money will be spent in the villages. The Navajos also signed leases for the mining of coal on the part of Black Mesa they owned.

The dispute over land between the Navajo and Hopi continued and a Federal Court in 1962 ruled that because the Secretary of the Interior had not acted to remove Navajos from Hopi lands, the Navajo had acquired squatter rights to that land, which constituted nearly one-half of the 1882 Hopi Reservation. Hopi and Navajo were to share this land, almost one million acres, which became known as the Joint Use Area.

By 1974, it became clear that the 1962 solution was not working, and Congress determined that the Joint Use Area would have to be partitioned—part would be given to the Navajo for their exclusive use and part to the Hopi. Hopis living on land allotted to the Navajo would have to move, as would Navajos living on land assigned to the Hopi. As part of the 1974 settlement, the Navajo were allotted a quarter million acres to relocate those who would have to move. In 1980, Congress allotted an additional 150,000 acres for Navajo relocatees.

The 26 Hopi families living on Navajo land moved, and many Navajo families moved off the Hopi land. However, further court cases ensued when the Navajos challenged the settlement act on religious grounds. Proposed settlements, which would have had the Hopi agree to cede land in exchange for monetary payment, were rejected by the Hopi, who had already lost half of their 1882 reservation. After many proposals and counterproposals, the Hopi Tribal Council offered an Accommodation Agreement to the Navajo families who remained on Hopi land and refused to move.

Under the Accommodation Agreement, Navajo families who signed the agreement were given a 75-year lease, which allows them to remain on Hopi land under the jurisdiction of the Hopi Tribe. Most of the Navajo families remaining on the Hopi Partitioned Lands either signed the agreement or moved prior to the February 1, 2000, deadline. The Hopi received reparations from the federal government, part of which they used to purchase ranches near the reservation as a way of regaining some of their Tutsqua, or ancient homeland.

The dispute over tribal land in northern Arizona has long been of concern to the United States. In 1998, a Special Rapporteur from the UN visited the Hopi Partitioned Lands to talk to the Navajos who refused to move or sign the Accommodation Agreement. A Hopi delegation who wanted to talk to the UN representative was refused access to him by some of the "supporters" of the Navajos. In the summer of 2000, a Hopi delegation went to the United Nations to present their perspective and concerns.

HOPI CEREMONIES AND TRIBAL GOVERNMENT

Hopis observe a complex ceremonial calendar divided into two parts: a secular year and a religious year. The secular calendar begins at the end of the purification rituals commonly known as the Bean Dance and usually continues through the end of September. Religious activities generally take place from November through the end of December. The calendar has never been accurately understood or described by non-Hopis.

Many religious activities are carried out in the kivas, ceremonial rooms accessed by a ladder leading down into the kiva from its roof. Ancient kivas can be seen at Chaco Canyon, but kivas in the villages are not open to the public. Each village has its own schedule of religious ceremonies. Ceremonial dances are held in the village's plaza. These are usually closed to outsiders, but tourists may enjoy the Butterfly or social dances held in the late summer and early fall. Usually the date for a particular dance is announced only a few weeks or days before the event.

Kachinas, of which there are perhaps 400 (though some of these no longer dance in the village ceremonies), are supernatural beings. They are represented by masked dancers when they live in the villages between Powamu and Home Dance. They are also depicted by wood carvings that are available for visitors to purchase.

The Hopi Tribe is governed by an elected chairman, vice chairman, and tribal council.

GETTING AROUND THE HOPI RESERVATION

The listings in this chapter go from east to west, which makes sense if you leave the South Rim of Grand Canyon and take Arizona Highway 64 to Cameron, then on to Tuba City. From there you travel north to Kayenta and Monument Valley, and then south to Canyon de Chelly and the Hopi Reservation. However, you can also take Arizona Highway 264 out of Tuba City and go across the Hopi Reservation from west to east, then head for Canyon de Chelly and do the loop back to Tuba City. In that case, read the following sections starting at the end.

KEAMS CANYON

Keams Canyon is not a Hopi village, but rather a U.S. government administrative center situated at the mouth of the canyon named after Thomas Keams, who established a trading post there in 1875. The Public Health Service Hospital is here; call (928) 738-2211. Doctors, nurses, and medical technicians are available all day every day.

Keams Canyon Shopping Center
Arizona Highway 264
Located in Keams Canyon on the north side of the road, this shopping center includes a cafe and gallery, a convenience store, a grocery store, a Laundromat, a garage, and a gas station. The motel at Keams Canyon is closed.

The garage does repairs on all domestic and some foreign cars and is open five days a week, though emergency towing and wrecker service are available 24 hours a day seven days a week. You can reach them by calling (928) 738-5555 during regular business hours. The 24-hour tow service can be reached at (928) 738-2298. The Hopi Police Department is also very helpful in case of car emergencies. Their number is

(928) 738–5110. The garage takes credit cards, traveler's checks, and cashiers checks, but no personal checks.

FIRST MESA

First Mesa is 15 miles west of Keams Canyon on Arizona Highway 264. The three villages of Walpi, Sichomovi, and Tewa on top of the mesa are governed by a traditional form of Hopi government of which the Kikmongwi is the head. Leaders of various religious societies help him to govern the villages. If you need more information on First Mesa villages, contact the Community Development Office at (928) 737–2670.

POLACCA

This settlement at the base of First Mesa stretches for about a mile along the highway. If you are planning to visit the top of the mesa and have a large vehicle, such as an RV, plan to park in Polacca. The Polacca M is a convenience store with phones, a Bank of America ATM, but no rest rooms.

TEWA

Tewa is on top of First Mesa and can be accessed by passenger vehicle along a 1-mile, steep paved road; larger vehicles should park in Polacca. The village was settled by refugees from a pueblo town on the Rio Grande in the early 1700s. The refugees were fleeing from the Spanish after an unsuccessful revolt. Hopi leaders allowed them to stay on First Mesa in exchange for protecting the path to the mesa top. The Tewa have their own language and ceremonies.

SICHOMOVI

Sichomovi was built in the mid-1600s by the people of Walpi. It is located in the middle of the mesa top between Tewa and Walpi.

WALPI

First Mesa narrows to 15 feet then widens at the village of Walpi, founded in about A.D. 900. When Pedro de Tovar visited Walpi in 1540, as many as 2,000 Hopis may have lived there.

Walking tours of the villages atop First Mesa begin at Punsi Hall Visitor Center in Sichomovi or at the tourist building at the Walpi parking lot. Tours, which take place during daytime hours every day, are led by a Hopi guide, who will share information on the history, life, and traditions of the Hopi people. There is a nominal fee, and it is a good idea to call in advance for current information. The First Mesa Consolidated Villages Tourism Program can be reached at (928) 737–2262. This is the only Hopi village that offers guided tours.

Visitor guidelines, which apply not only to First Mesa villages but to all Hopi land, forbid photography, sketching, painting, videotaping, or tape recording. Visitors must also be careful not to approach shrines, prayer feathers, or kivas. Unescorted touring of First Mesa is not allowed, and visitors are asked to stay on the trails the guide will show you.

Artists may be selling their kachina carvings and polychrome pottery on First Mesa. Signs around the villages indicate which houses to approach if you're looking for art to buy. Here you may be able to speak with the artist directly about the piece you wish to purchase. It is always fascinating to ask the artist to explain the meaning of the symbolic images on a piece of carving, pottery, or jewelry. When you buy directly from the artist, prices are sometimes negotiable.

SECOND MESA

Arizona Highways 264 and 87 meet at the foot of Second Mesa, 10 miles west of First Mesa. There is a post office at the intersection on the south side of AZ 264. Second Mesa artists are renowned for their kachina carvings, silver overlay jewelry, and coiled baskets.

Second Mesa villages are Shongopavi, Sipaulovi, and Mishongnovi. The Sipaulovi Community Development Office's number is (928) 734-2570. To reach the Mishongnovi Community Development Office call (928) 737-2520. You can reach these villages by driving a short paved road that climbs steeply from the north side of AZ 264, one-half mile west of the intersection with AZ 87, or by the paved road about 0.25 mile east of the Hopi Cultural Center. Mishongnovi is the village to the east. Its people are charged with protection of the Corn Rock Shrine.

Accommodations, Restaurants, and Shops in Second Mesa

ACCOMMODATIONS PRICE CODE

The following price codes are for two adults. The codes do not include taxes and other fees.

$	Less than $60
$$	$61 to $75
$$$	$76 to $100
$$$$	$101 to $125
$$$$$	More than $125

RESTAURANT PRICE CODE

The price codes below represent average prices for dinner for two, excluding tax, gratuity, and drinks.

$	Less than $20
$$	$21 to $35
$$$	$36 to $60
$$$$	More than $60

Alph Secakuku-Hopi Fine Arts
Arizona Highway 264, Second Mesa
(928) 737-2222

Set back on the south side of the road (just east of LKD's Diner), Hopi Fine Arts carries the work of "as many local artists as possible." The owner works directly with the artists, and custom orders are welcome. A special treat is watching a silversmith while he creates some of the fine silver overlay pieces that are for sale. He is on the premises every day. Here you will also find kachina carvings, pottery, baskets, and plaques (flat, plate-size basketry). An item carried here that we have never before seen is a series of three small connected pots. The form is based on items found by the potter, a descendent of Nampeyo, among her grandfather's possessions. The gallery also carries a small selection of Navajo, Santa Domingo, and Zuni jewelry. Open seven days a week including holidays, the shop accepts credit cards and personal checks.

Honani Crafts Gallery
Arizona Highway 264, Second Mesa
(928) 737-2238
Located on the north side of AZ 264, a half mile west of the junction with AZ 87, Honani Crafts Gallery's hallmark item is their spectacular gold-on-silver jewelry. Owned by King Honani, this small gallery welcomes custom orders for items such as wedding rings. Also ask to see the fine inlay jewelry and the gold-on-silver rings with semiprecious stones such as sapphire, green turquoise, and amethyst. The acrylic paintings by artist Bill Dixon are one of a kind. Among the other artists whose work you will find here are Willis Humeyestewa, Phil Sekaquaptewa, Art Honanie, Terrance Lomayestewa, and Hale Kaye. The gallery is open year-round, seven days a week, including holidays.

Hopi Arts & Crafts Silvercraft Cooperative Guild
Just west of the Hopi Cultural Center on Arizona Highway 264, Second Mesa
(928) 734-2463

Hopi Pottery

Hopi pottery has a long and venerable history, dating back at least to the black-on-white pots produced by the ancestral Puebloan people. After the arrival of the Spanish, Hopi pottery declined in quality and the art was nearly lost. In the late 1800s, Nampeyo, a woman from the village of Tewa on First Mesa, revived pottery making by copying the techniques, colors, and designs she found on ancient pots.

Today Hopi pottery is made by quarrying clay from traditional sources and preparing it to the proper consistency by kneading. The potter shapes the base of the vessel by hand and then builds up the form by adding coils of clay around the base and pinching them in place.

Once the bowl or other form is shaped, the potter scrapes it with a gourd rind to get rid of the coil and pinch marks. Then the piece is dried in the sun. When the pot is "leather hard," the potter scrapes the surface again, this time with a pottery shard or something similar to make sure the walls are thin enough and that all of the walls have the same thickness. Then it is hand polished with a small stone. The potter decorates the piece using natural slips and other natural paints applied with a strip of yucca pine or a commercial paintbrush.

Often Hopi pots are decorated in black and red, each color having a brownish tint. The black is made by crushing hematite (a black mineral) and mixing it with the juice of a plant. The red is made from limonite clay, to which a small amount of water is added after the clay has been crushed into dust-size pieces. When the design is dry, the pottery is

This gallery carries Hopi overlay jewelry and other authentic Hopi arts and crafts. At the guild, young silversmiths are trained at no charge by experienced Hopi silversmiths who donate their services, but there is nothing amateurish about the work offered for sale here: money clips, bolos, earrings, pendants, necklaces, and other items. You can also see displays about some of the semiprecious stones used in silverwork, including turquoise, coral, and lapis, as well as some jewelry-making supplies. In addition to selling work by its members, the guild offers its marketing services to artists in all of the Hopi villages. The gallery is open daily.

Hopi Cultural Center Restaurant and Inn
Arizona Highway 264, Second Mesa
(928) 734-2401
Being at the "Center of the Universe," as the Hopi Cultural Center claims to be, must be something like being in the eye of a hurricane because this pueblo-style motel is tranquil and comfortable, not to mention the most convenient for visiting all of the Hopi villages and arts-and-crafts stores. The 33 nonsmoking rooms ($$) have coffeemakers, TVs, and air-conditioners. A $5.00 charge applies for each of more than two adults in a room, and pets require a $50.00 deposit. Major credit cards are accepted. Reservations are mandatory in the summer and recommended the rest of

dried around a fire of sheep dung and juniper wood. When the pots (several are fired together) are ready, a grate is put over the fire and topped with pieces of broken pottery. On this pile, the pots are placed upside down. Shards of broken pottery are placed over the pots, and these pottery pieces are topped with more sheep or goat dung. The whole pile bursts into flame and the pots are fired until the ashes of the fire are nearly cool. Hopi pots are fired in an oxidizing atmosphere, and the temperature of the kiln is usually less than 850 degrees Celsius.

Hopi pottery was traditionally made by women, with the art passed down from mother or grandmother to child, but now some men also make pottery. Most often the pot will be smooth and beige to red in color with rust red and dark brown painted designs, though recently pottery with etched designs and textured surfaces is being made, and some pots may not be painted. You may also encounter decorated white Hopi pots.

Once you have seen some examples of Hopi pottery, you will easily be able to distinguish it from pottery made by other pueblo tribes. The quality of a piece is evaluated by the symmetry and beauty of its form, the consistent thickness of its walls, and the detail, appropriateness, and application of its decoration. Usually potters decorate the pot without any preliminary drawing on the item, and each one is a unique work of art. Executing a fine design without error (for errors cannot be corrected) is a task requiring consummate skill and many years of practice.

the year. Some rooms are wheelchair accessible. The front desk has a selection of T-shirts and books for sale.

Whether you're staying at the motel or just visiting Hopi for the day, you shouldn't miss the restaurant ($) at the Cultural Center. The white stucco, open-beamed interior is furnished with hand-carved chairs, booths, and valances showing traditional Hopi designs, and the establishment is staffed entirely by Hopis. The restaurant serves both American and Hopi dishes. For breakfast, try the *sakwaviqaviki* (blue corn cakes), *piki* (a thin round piece of corn bread rolled into a cylinder), or blue corn fry bread. For lunch or dinner, the *tsili'öngava* (pinto beans and ground beef in a red chili sauce with fry bread) or the *nöqkwivi* (traditional Hopi stew with hominy, lamb, red chilis, and fry bread) are good choices. Or try the Hopi taco, which the friendly staff admits, with a smile, is pretty much the same as a Navajo taco.

If you don't feel like trying something new, you can order from a selection of burgers, salads, and sandwiches, or try one of the weekday specials. The casual restaurant is open year-round seven days a week and you'll probably see as many local people as tourists eating here. It is wheelchair accessible. Reservations are recommended for large groups. Note that while breakfast, lunch, and dinner are served here, the restaurant closes earlier in the evening than you might expect. Call to find out what the hours are at the time of year you will be visiting.

The Cultural Center also has a museum with a well-stocked bookstore and T-shirt inventory. There is a nominal entrance fee for the museum (but not the museum shop).

i

Arizona Highway 264 is paved, but the driveways and parking lots of the shops and galleries are gravel. The Hopi Cultural Center Restaurant and Inn on Second Mesa seems to be the only wheelchair accessible stop on Hopi. It is also the only motel.

Iskasokpu
On the north side of Arizona Highway 264, Second Mesa
(928) 734-9353

Featuring Hopi silver overlay and gold-on-silver jewelry, Navajo and Zuni jewelry, baskets, Hopi-Tewa pots, and kachina carvings, this shop also sells silver jewelry-making supplies. It's open daily. The word *iskasokpu* means "the spring where the coyote burped." The story of the spring's name, according to a handout at the shop is this: A coyote was traveling toward Shongopavi when he came to a spring on the south side of the village. There he found a turtle, which he decided to eat, but the turtle retreated back into its shell every time the coyote tried to take a bite. He gave up and went to the spring for a drink. He saw something very scary in the spring, so he hightailed it out of there. He came to another spring, Gostutbalvi, but the scary thing was there too. Finally he reached the spring just below the shop's location at the edge of the mesa. This time he was so thirsty that he drank from the spring despite the scary thing. He drank a lot of water and let out a huge burp. The coyote did not know that when he had tried to eat the turtle, he had hurt his mouth. The scary thing he kept seeing in the water was only his own reflection. This is how the spring (and later the shop) got its name.

LKD's Diner $
Arizona Highway 264, Second Mesa
(928) 737-2717

For a down-to-earth eating experience in a very casual setting, try this diner, where you are sure to see more locals than tourists. Located between Hopi Fine Arts and the post office on the south side of the road, LKD's Diner is open Monday through Saturday for lunch and dinner. The diner serves burgers, sandwiches, chili beans with fry bread, chicken nuggets, and Hopi tacos and tostadas. There is a rest room (for customers only) and a phone, as well as the post office next door. The diner accepts only cash. Be sure while you're here to visit Hopi Fine Arts, just east of the diner.

Phil & Hil's Emporium $
In Shongopavi Village, off Arizona Highway 264, Second Mesa
(928) 734-9278

This place is off the beaten track and known only to locals. Take the road into Shongopavi. Where the paved road ends and the village really begins, the gravel road forks. In the fork you'll see a new cinderblock building with no windows. Go around to the other side to find the entrance to this tiny restaurant/convenience store. It does a booming business in Hopi tacos and tostadas, hot wings, fries, burgers, pizza, nachos, snowcones, snacks, and ice cream. They do a great take-out business, but there is also a small sit-down counter and a couple of booths if you'd rather eat there. Open for lunch through a late dinner hour, the restaurant is open seven days a week, including holidays. Personal checks are accepted, but credit cards are not. Shongopavi was one of the first villages in the area. For more information about the village, contact the Community Development Office at (928) 734-2262.

Selina's Silver Art & Crafts
South side of Arizona Highway 264, Second Mesa
(928) 734-6695

This shop, owned by Weaver and Alberta Selina, has its own silverworkers who are there on weekdays. Visitors are invited to watch them as they work. The shop specializes in Hopi silver overlay and gold over silver, but also carries pottery, kachina carvings, and some Navajo and Zuni jewelry. The owner sells T-shirts he designed himself. The hours vary, but usually the shop is open seven days a week.

Tsakurshovi
Arizona Highway 264, Second Mesa
(928) 734-2478

One-and-a-half miles east of the Hopi Cultural Center, on the north side of AZ 264, Tsakurshovi is the home of the "Don't Worry, Be Hopi" T-shirt. This tiny shop is crammed with interesting merchandise and staffed by friendly and helpful people who will not only give you directions to where you're going next but will suggest places to go and books to read. Half the shop is devoted to art for visitors to purchase, including a huge selection of traditional-style kachina carvings, jewelry, and many Second and Third Mesa–style baskets. One of the people minding the store was an old-style kachina carver, Wallace Hyeoma. Other carvers whose work is sold here include Bert Tenakhongya, Philbert Honanie, Manuel Chavarria, and Clark Tenakhongya. You're very likely to meet Hopis here because the other half of the store sells ceremonial items for dances such as turtle shells, deer hooves, furs, skins, shell bandoliers, gourds for making rattles, Hopi textiles, and moccasins, as well as cottonwood root for kachina carvings and mineral pigments. It's "the place where all the Hopis shop," according to the staff. You'll also find Plains Indian beadwork, a large selection of Zuni fetishes, and Navajo and Santa Domingo pottery—"a little of everyone's work." Personal, traveler's, and cashier's checks are

> From Second Mesa, you can take a shortcut to Canyon de Chelly. Turn north off Arizona Highway 264 beside the Hopi Cultural Center and head for the Pinon Trading Post, then go 42 miles east. However, 14 miles of the road is not paved, so you should not attempt this route in wet weather.

accepted, but not credit cards. The shop is open seven days a week, except for Thanksgiving and Christmas.

THIRD MESA

KYKOTSMOVI

Founded in the late 1800s near a spring at the base of Third Mesa, Kykotsmovi is now the Headquarters for the Hopi Tribe, P.O. Box 123, Kykotsmovi, AZ 86039; (928) 734-3000. The Office of Public Relations is 1 mile south of Arizona Highway 264. Third Mesa artists are known for kachina carvings, weaving, silver overlay jewelry, and wicker baskets. The number of the Community Development Office for Kykotsmovi is (928) 734-2474.

Calnimptewa Galleria
South side of Arizona Highway 264, Kykotsmovi
(928) 734-2406

Located about 4 miles west of the Kykotsmovi turnoff on the south side of the highway, this gallery is locally owned and is a good place to get information on Cecil Calnimptewa, though you will not find his work here as most of his pieces are spoken for before he even carves them. But you will find a spacious, artful display of silver overlay jewelry, kachina carvings, baskets, pottery, sash belts, and paintings all produced by local artists. The collection also includes some Navajo silver and turquoise jewelry, Navajo rugs, and Zuni jewelry. MasterCard and Visa are accepted, and the shop is open every day in the summer, but closed Sunday in winter.

CLOSE-UP

Hopi Overlay Silver

The Hopi learned silversmithing from their neighbors, the Zuni and the Navajo, about a hundred years ago. At first, they made jewelry primarily for use by other Hopis, and their work was similar to that of their teachers. Therefore, much pre-1940 Hopi silver jewelry was (and is) identified as Navajo.

The silver for early jewelry was derived from coins, which were melted down, formed into ingots, and then hammered into sheets, or the molten silver was cast in molds. Some pieces incorporated turquoise inlay or turquoise stones in settings.

Mary Colton, who, with her husband, founded the Museum of Northern Arizona, was a major influence in the development of Native American arts and crafts throughout the region. In 1939 she wrote a letter to some 20 Hopi silversmiths making some very important points. The first was that even as early as the 1930s, the artwork of the Native peoples of the Southwest was being imitated and machine made by non-Indians. Since buyers were not sufficiently sophisticated to be able to tell the difference between genuine and imitation work, this served to keep the prices of the authentic pieces low. She suggested that Hopi silversmiths have their work stamped by the government's arts-and-crafts board to guarantee its authenticity. Her second point was that Hopi silver was difficult to distinguish from other Indian silver, and Hopis should develop their own distinctive style. And her third point was that the museum would help Hopis design a few pieces to show what she meant by making the work different from that of other tribes.

However, Hopi silversmithing was affected greatly by World War II as many Hopi men served in the armed forces. Since others had to do their work in the villages, few people had time to pursue silver work. After the war, silversmithing

Gentle Rain Designs
South side of Arizona Highway 264, Kykotsmovi
(928) 734-9535

Located approximately one-half mile before Kykotsmovi on the south side of AZ 264, this is a unique shop, first because it supports the nonprofit Hopi Foundation, and second because it offers locally made Native-designed and produced clothing and accessories. Most of the jackets and other items are made of fleece, which is produced from recycled plastic bottles. The jackets come in several styles and lengths with colorful Southwest-style designs. Fleece is also used to make hats, pillows, and purses. In addition, the shop carries a selection of Hopi jewelry, carving, and pottery. The cradle dolls are particularly well-executed with detailed and carefully carved designs. Cradle dolls are flat kachina carvings about 6 inches tall. They are the first kachina carving to be given to little girls. One of the Hopi Foundation's most ambitious projects has been the establishment of a Hopi radio station, which broadcasts Native American and other news all across the reserva-

classes for veterans were set up under the G.I. Bill and many Hopis took the classes. It was in the late 1940s and early 1950s that the style known as Hopi overlay silver jewelry developed. This is the highly sophisticated, superbly designed work that the tourist will see in the shops on Hopi and in galleries around the world.

The Hopi artist begins creating an overlay piece by tracing one of his designs onto a sheet of silver from a template. Then small holes are punched into the parts to be cut out and a tiny saw blade is inserted. The design is very carefully cut out, then the piece of silver with the cutout design is soldered onto a piece of solid silver. After the pieces are joined and cooled, the artist uses chisels to make a texture in the bottom piece of silver where it shows through the cutout design. The bottom piece of silver is trimmed into the shape necessary to make a belt buckle, pendant, concho belt, or bracelet and the piece is hammered into its final shape. The finding is soldered on and the whole piece is blanched in an acid to get rid of any discolorations from heating. Liver of sulfur is put on the interior of the design to oxidize the silver and create the black interior of the cutouts. Finally, the piece is cleaned and polished.

Many Hopi artists now hallmark their jewelry with a stamp on the back with the silversmith's personal mark, which is often related to the artist's clan. Dictionaries of hallmarks are available for the collector. But the problem of imitations still remains. Buyers should examine many pieces of work to develop their ability to discern authentic work from fake, and they should buy only from reputable shops and galleries, or directly from the artist.

tion, mostly in the Hopi language. The station not only provides a much-needed service to elders who speak only Hopi, but also helps youngsters learn the language. The project has been in the works for more than 10 years. Among other projects is the implementation of an educational scholarship fund, the retrieval and return of sacred objects to Hopi villages, the restoration of an ancient clan house, the establishment of a solar electric enterprise to bring electricity to rural homes, the publication of a children's book by local children, and the revival of the traditional art of rock quarrying. Credit cards are accepted at the shop, which is open daily except major holidays.

Kykotsmovi Village Store
In the center of the village, between Indian Route 2 and Arizona Highway 264, Kykotsmovi
(928) 734-2456
You may not think you need to know about a village store, but you do. Here you can get groceries, fresh meat, produce, baby supplies such as formula and diapers, gasoline, basic automotive supplies, and

money orders. You can also send (or receive) money via Western Union, use the rest room, and make a phone call. Major credit cards are accepted. The store is open every day except holidays, which is helpful, because the next closest places for such items are 50 miles in either direction.

OLD ORAIBI

Old Oraibi was for a long time the largest and most important Hopi village, at least according to outsiders. People have lived at Old Oraibi since at least A.D. 1150, making it the oldest continuously inhabited settlement in North America.

In 1906, "Hostiles" (that is, hostile to the federal government) left this village after losing a pushing contest with the "Friendlies." The Hostiles established the village of Hotevilla, 4 miles to the west.

The issue was forcible education of Hopi children by the U.S. government. An Old Oraibi leader, Lololoma, had visited Washington, D.C., and decided that such an education would benefit the children and the Hopis in general. A more conservative group, headed by Lomahongyoma, strongly disagreed. Eventually a group of parents, including Lomahongyoma, were imprisoned at Alcatraz by federal authorities for refusing to send their children to the government school in Keams Canyon. Fifty-three men served 90 days in jail, while their children were forcibly removed to the boarding school.

About 150 of the roughly 450 people who left Old Oraibi went back to the village in 1907, but then left in 1909 to form the village of Bacavi.

A ruin near Old Oraibi is the remains of a church built in 1901 by Mennonite missionary H. R. Voth, who was in Oraibi from 1893 to 1902. He became privy to, and divulged, many Hopi religious secrets. Lightning has struck the church twice, the first time in 1942. No one is allowed to visit the site.

Old Oraibi is 2 miles west of Kykotsmovi. You are requested to park next to Hamana So-o's Arts and Crafts shop and walk through the village to avoid stirring up dust driving your vehicle. The shop has a selection of silver overlay jewelry, kachina carvings, and *dawa* wall plaques, as well as a display of some large storage pots from the 1800s. The shop is open every day, so you can stop here to get information on what is happening in the village. Call the shop at (928) 734-2406.

Picnic areas are located on the north side of AZ 264 just east of Oraibi and just east of Kykotsmovi on Oraibi Wash.

Monongya Gallery
South side of Arizona Highway 264
Old Oraibi
(928) 734-2344
Located on the south side of AZ 264 between Kykotsmovi and Old Oraibi, this is probably the largest gallery on Hopi, so you won't want to miss it. The main room houses a large selection of Hopi arts—silver overlay and gold-on-silver jewelry, kachina carvings, decorated coiled pottery, sash belt weavings, plaques, and painted gourd rattles. The room to the right is reserved for Navajo, Zuni, and Acoma pottery, Navajo and Zuni jewelry, Navajo sandpaintings, Zuni fetishes, and paintings. All of the souvenir items—T-shirts and sweatshirts, Pendleton blankets, jackets, books, mugs, and other items with Hopi and southwestern designs—are in the room to the left. The gallery is open daily except major holidays. Credit cards are accepted.

HOTEVILLA

Hotevilla, founded in 1906 under the leadership of Yokioma after the split from Old Oraibi, is a traditional village known as an agricultural center and has been called the Peach Capital of the World. You will notice the terraced gardens along the mesa slopes. It is also the only village that is totally self-sufficient in terms of energy production, relying on high-tech solar power. The village is west of Old Oraibi on Arizona Highway 264. Check at the Hopi Cultural Center on Second Mesa to find out about late summer and early fall Butterfly and other social dances that you might attend. Contact the Hotevilla Community Development Office at (928) 734-2420.

BACAVI

The founders of Bacavi were also on the losing side of the 1906 split. Some 150 people returned to Old Oraibi after the split, but the situation was untenable, so in 1909 they moved to Bacavi Spring on the opposite side of the highway from Hotevilla. Brian Honyouti—the contemporary leader in Hopi kachina carving, whose work is in collections around the world—lives in Bacavi. His brother Ronald is a well-known carver as well, and his brother Rick creates custom-designed carved furniture with Hopi motifs. For more information, contact the Community Development Office at (928) 734-2404.

MOENKOPI

The two villages Upper Moenkopi and Lower Moenkopi are 2 miles east of Tuba City on Arizona Highway 264. Prehistoric pueblo villages sited here date back before A.D. 1300, when they were abandoned. This village was founded by Mormons in the 1870s. The Mormons constructed a woolen mill in 1879, but the Hopis refused to work there.

The name "Moenkopi" means "The Place of the Running Water," referring to the numerous springs that created the successful farming community that flourished here until recently. Residents have been saying for years that the Peabody Coal Company's removal of water from the Navajo Aquifer to slurry coal to a Laughlin, Nevada, power plant is causing the seeps and springs to dry up. People in Moenkopi, who once drank water from the

The tribal newspaper is **The Hopi Tutuveni,** *which you can find at the Hopi Cultural Center, village stores, and some shops. The address is P.O. Box 123, Kykotsmovi, AZ 86039; (928) 734-3283.*

pristine aquifer underlying the Hopi and the western Navajo Reservations, now are forced to buy bottled water.

The Black Mesa Trust has recently been organized to investigate Black Mesa coal and water operations. The trust argues that the 1983 water model developed by the U.S. Geological Survey to study the Navajo Aquifer and to assess how domestic and Peabody pumping affect the aquifer may have been misapplied and that therefore conclusions drawn from the model are probably incorrect. According to a 1997 report, the coal company is being allowed to pump 4,000 acre-feet of water from an aquifer that recharges at a rate of only 2,500 to 3,500 acre-feet per year.

The group also argues that the U.S. government's Office of Surface Mining, which oversees operations at the Peabody Coal Company's mines on Black Mesa, failed to take into account traditional wisdom (as opposed to western science) to evaluate the effects of pumping water from the 35,000-year-old aquifer.

An October 2000 report by the Natural Resources Defense Council, "Drawdown: Groundwater Mining on Black Mesa," affirms that the Interior Department's Office of Surface Mining Reclamation and Enforcement's own criteria for determining if material damage to the aquifer has occurred have been exceeded. The report is available at www.nrdc.org. For more information about Black Mesa Trust, call (928) 734-9255 or (480) 421-2377. For more information about Moenkopi, contact the Community Development Office at (928) 283-8051.

HOPI RESERVATION TOURS

Left-Handed Hunter Tour Co.
Second Mesa
(928) 734-2567

Left-Handed Hunter Tour Co. is Hopi owned and operated. Gary Tso, a Hopi/ Navajo from Second Mesa, will guide you through ancient villages, introduce you to traditional and contemporary artists, and take you to a spectacular site where you will see more than 15,000 petroglyphs, all the while sharing Hopi history and culture with you. Tso lives on Hopiland, and he is a traditional kachina carver and experienced interpreter of the Hopi culture. Lunch, transportation, and entry fees are part of this all-inclusive package of "private cultural and archaeological tours deep into Hopiland."

PETRIFIED FOREST NATIONAL PARK

L ocated 110 miles east of Flagstaff off Interstate 40, Petrified Forest National Park is an easy day trip from most locations in northern Arizona. The park anchors the southeastern edge of the Painted Desert, a pastel-striated landscape arcing across northeastern Arizona. It is also home to the largest concentration of petrified wood in the world, and examples of the national park's star attraction can be seen throughout the park. The 93,533-acre wilderness area also features archaeological sites, pioneer-era historic structures, a museum, hiking trails, petroglyphs, and wildlife from short-horned lizards to pronghorn.

HISTORY

The decidedly odd and colorful petrified wood of Petrified Forest National Park is a result of a long-ago process that transformed the wood of native trees similar to modern-day pines into stone. The time frame was the late Triassic Period, some 225 million years ago, when the region was a vast plain of swamps and lakes. Flooding washed the tree trunks into the floodplains of the Painted Desert, and, over time, mud, silt, and volcanic ash covered the logs, creating a barrier between the wood and oxygen, which kept the logs from rotting. Groundwater rich in silica slowly seeped into the wood and crystallized, turning the wood into quartz. Later upwarps of the land broke apart the huge rock logs, and the pieces of these ancient trees are what visitors can see today.

Human history in the area that would become Petrified Forest National Park dates back a paltry (in comparison) 2,000 years. The region sits on what has always

been a major trading route following the Puerco River, a route followed by today's Interstate 40. Tribes that inhabited this area include the Mogollon, Sinagua, and ancestral Pueblo, the latter inhabiting the region until around A.D. 1400.

In 1540, the first Spanish explorers traveled through the region, naming the surrounding land *El Desierto Pintado,* the Painted Desert. But the explorers did not linger. It wasn't until 1851 that another non–Native American officially visited the area, when Capt. Lorenzo Sitgreaves of the U.S. Army researched and published reports about petrified wood in the area, the first written record of the area's geologic anomaly. Sitgreaves was followed two years later by the Whipple Expedition, a team of 100 scientists, soldiers, and engineers who visited the region and confirmed the existence of petrified wood in the area that would become Petrified Forest National Park.

Settlers arrived en masse in northern Arizona and the area around the future park in 1883, when the Atlantic and Pacific Railway line was completed across the northern part of the state. The railroad ran through the future park's boundaries. The increased numbers of people in the Southwest posed a grave danger to the petrified wood, as it proved irresistible to souvenir hunters, gem speculators, collectors, and merchants looking to make a killing selling petrified wood. As early as 1899, a published article predicted the elimination or destruction of petrified wood from the region.

The imminent threat drove the desire to protect this land and its natural resources. By 1906, the federal government realized the petrified wood was in danger of disappearing, and President Theodore Roosevelt

Campers heading into the backcountry at Petrified Forest National Park must hike from Kachina Point, near the Painted Desert Inn. TODD R. BERGER

proclaimed the southern portion of the future national park Petrified Forest National Monument. The northern portions of the future park were added to the national monument in 1932. In 1962, the petrified wood finally gained one of the highest levels of federal protection, when the national monument was declared Petrified Forest National Park. Eight years later, Congress further protected the park's resources by declaring 50 percent of the park designated wilderness.

Created to protect the petrified wood in the region, Petrified Forest National Park depends on respectful treatment of the remarkable natural resource inside the park. Those who attempt to steal any petrified wood from the park boundaries are subject to prosecution, fines, and imprisonment. Such criminals are stealing part of America's heritage, destroying the resource that makes this national park remarkable, and eliminating for future generations what you came here to see one small piece at a time. You might think, "This is a tiny rock and looks really cool. I think I'll stick it in my pocket." But some 600,000 people visit this park every year, unfortunately many with similar thoughts. The old mantra applies here: "Be part of the solution, or be part of the problem." Just like Smokey Bear, only you can stop the depletion of petrified wood from this park. It's up to you, and you alone. Legally collected petrified wood can be purchased at gift shops all around the area, so leave the petrified wood in its rightful home and leave this park with a clean conscience.

GETTING TO PETRIFIED FOREST NATIONAL PARK

Petrified Forest National Park can be reached via Interstate 40 from Flagstaff. The park lies 110 miles east of the city, 25 miles beyond the town of Holbrook. There is no commercial airport closer to the park than Flagstaff, but Greyhound serves Holbrook, and Amtrak stops in Winslow,

about 55 miles west of the park, and Gallup, New Mexico, about 70 miles east of the park.

You can also follow U.S. Highway 180 south from Holbrook to the southern entrance to the park, about 20 miles southeast of the town. The road through the park travels due north to rendezvous with I-40 some 27 miles later.

PARK BASICS

Petrified Forest National Park is open daily year-round, except for December 25, although the park sometimes closes when roads are icy in winter. Entrance fees are $10.00 per vehicle, $5.00 per bicyclist, and $5.00 for those arriving somehow on foot. The National Parks Pass, Golden Eagle Passport, Golden Age Passport, and Golden Access Passport are all valid for entrance to the park, and they can be purchased here as well. The park also sells a Petrified Forest National Park Annual Pass for $20.00, allowing admittance to the park at no additional charge for one year.

The park has three visitor centers, one, the **Painted Desert Visitor Center** (928-524-6228), just inside the northern entrance to the park; one, similarly named and located just a mile down the park's main road, **Painted Desert Inn National Historic Landmark** (928-524-6228); and the last the **Rainbow Forest Museum** (928-524-6228) near the southern entrance to the park. All three visitor centers have general park information and a bookstore. The Painted Desert Visitor Center shows a video on the park every half hour, and the Rainbow Forest Museum visitor center includes exhibits on dinosaurs and petrified wood.

Petrified Forest National Park is a high-desert environment, with hot summers and cool winters. During the summer, highs occasionally top 100 degrees Fahrenheit and lows overnight will dip to the 50s. Winter daytime temperatures average in the 40s and 50s, while overnight lows can dip to 0 degrees. Avoid high points and open areas in the desert during the summer monsoon rains, as lightning, flash floods, and high winds can strike the area.

Hungry folks can get satiated at the **Painted Desert Oasis** restaurant next to the Painted Desert Visitor Center and at the snack bar in the Rainbow Forest Museum. The Painted Desert Oasis also has a gas station and gift shop.

For further information about Petrified Forest National Park, call the park at (928) 524-6228 or visit the park on the Web at www.nps.gov/pefo.

ACCOMMODATIONS

There are no lodges inside the park. The Painted Desert Inn National Historic Landmark near the northern entrance is no longer a lodge (although it is well worth visiting for its beautiful architecture, stunning murals, and useful visitor center). All of the following motels and bed-and-breakfasts are in Holbrook, 25 miles west of the park.

PRICE CODE

The following price code is for two adults during the high season, generally between Memorial Day and Labor Day. The codes do not include taxes and other fees.

$	Less than $75
$$	$76 to $125
$$$	$126 to $175
$$$$	$176 to $225
$$$$$	More than $225

Best Western Arizonian Inn $$$
2508 Navajo Boulevard, Holbrook
(928) 524-2611, (877) 280-7300
(reservations only)
This 70-room motel offers comfortable accommodations away from the train tracks that keep people awake at night in this sleepy community. Each room includes a coffeemaker, hair dryer, free

movie channels, and a free continental breakfast. Some rooms have a king-size bed, refrigerator, and microwave. The motel has a heated outdoor pool that is open seasonally, and for those looking for a Grand Slam Breakfast rather than the more modest continental breakfast included with a room, a 24-hour Denny's restaurant is next to the motel.

**Heward House at Holbrook Bed
and Breakfast** $$$
108 Crestview Drive, Holbrook
(928) 524-3411, (877) 740-0452
www.bbonline.com/az/heward
Prices at this B&B will set you back just about the same amount as area motels, so it is certainly worth checking whether rooms are available on your travel dates. The Heward House is a 1930s art deco building on a mesa overlooking Holbrook. Although far from the railroad tracks that run through town and its resident freight trains, the B&B is just off busy I-40. The beautiful house has four guest rooms, a Jacuzzi garden, a game room with pool table and dartboard, an outdoor fireplace, and a large collection of southwestern art decorating the interior. The common rooms include a semi-formal dining room, where guests enjoy the inn's breakfast (in nice weather, breakfast is served on the patio), before-dinner hors d'oeuvres, and post-dinner dessert. The guest rooms include the African-inspired Wildlife Room, with a faux-zebra-skin bedspread and mosquito netting over the bed; the Navajo Room, with a red cedar bed and beautiful Native American artwork; the Cowboy Room, with a lodgepole-pine bed and a sunken bathroom featuring an antique claw-foot tub; and the Western Rose Room, a more subtle, lavender-painted room with floral paintings and a pink-tile bathroom.

Holiday Inn Express $$$
1308 East Navajo Boulevard Holbrook
(928) 524-1466, (800) 465-4329

The 63-room Holiday Inn Express is a clean, simple choice. The motel has an indoor pool and whirlpool, guest laundry facilities, Native American Art Gallery, gift shop, and business services such as photocopying, e-mail and Internet access, fax machines, and printing services. Rooms include four suites, 12 rooms with single king-size beds, and 47 rooms with two double beds. Pets are allowed.

CAMPGROUNDS

There are no maintained campgrounds within Petrified Forest National Park, although dispersed camping is allowed in the park's backcountry (see the following Dispersed Camping section). The closest maintained campgrounds for tents and RVs are in Holbrook.

Holbrook/Petrified Forest KOA
102 Hermosa Drive, Holbrook
(928) 524-6689, (800) 562-3389
(reservations only)
RV and tent sites run $15 per night at this Kampgrounds of America facility. The campground also has small cabins available for $35 per night. The sites are pull-through for vehicles up to 70 feet, and hookups are available. The campground features an outdoor heated pool (open seasonally), a playground, and a game room, as well as a seasonal pancake breakfast and "cowboy cookout." To reach the campground from I-40, take exit 289 5 miles east of Holbrook and 20 miles west of Petrified Forest National Park and follow Arizona Highway 77 1.5 miles south to Hermosa Drive and the campground.

DISPERSED CAMPING

Camping is allowed in the backcountry of Petrified Forest National Park for campers with a free permit, but access to the areas where camping is permitted requires hiking or horseback riding (there are no pull-in sites for cars or RVs). Permits can be obtained at either the Rainbow Forest Museum or Painted Desert Visitor Center, and you must request a permit at least one hour before the visitor center closes. The permits need to be returned to the chosen visitor center after you return, the method the park uses to guarantee visitors return from their foray into the backcountry. Hikers must park in the parking area at Kachina Point near the Painted Desert Inn Visitor Center and follow a 1-mile access road (on foot or horseback), which leads into the backcountry. Camping is permitted in the area north of Lithodendron Wash, an area with no maintained campsites and no trails (given this, it is wise to bring a topographic map of the area and a compass). Campfires and charcoal grills are prohibited, although fuel backpacking stoves are allowed. The family pet cannot accompany you into the backcountry. When visiting the Petrified Forest National Park backcountry, practice zero impact ethics, leaving any camping area cleaner than when you arrived. Choose a campsite that has been previously used if possible. There are no trash barrels, and all garbage must be packed out. As with the rest of the park, it is illegal to remove anything from the backcountry. There are no water sources in the backcountry, so you will need to bring sufficient water: One gallon of water per person per day is recommended.

WHAT TO DO

When arriving at the park from the north (note that you can easily travel this route in reverse, south to north, as well), the **Painted Desert Visitor Center** will be the first place to stop. In addition to housing the only gas and food services for miles, the visitor center has maps, rangers with plenty of advice on where to go and what to see, a bookstore, a gift shop, and rest rooms. The visitor center is a good place to get your bearings, formulate a plan, and refuel your body and your vehicle if needed.

The northern portion of Petrified Forest National Park includes spectacular stretches of the Painted Desert. TODD R. BERGER

About a mile down the road, the **Painted Desert Inn National Historic Landmark** is the next stop. The Spanish-pueblo revival building, which today serves as a visitor center and as administrative offices for the park service, was built between 1937 and 1940. The inn was once owned by the Fred Harvey Company, the famed entrepreneur known for his elegant hotels and restaurants, "Harvey Girls" hostesses, and proximity to some of the West's most beautiful natural areas. The gorgeous structure is built of adobe and petrified wood blocks (quarried outside the then-national monument). The interior Trading Post Room features a skylight painted to resemble ancestral Puebloan pottery and murals by the Hopi artist Fred Kabotie. The Painted Desert Inn Visitor Center within the inn offers park information, a bookstore, a curio shop that sells legally collected petrified wood among other items, Native American artists practicing their crafts, and information on ranger-guided tours.

The **Rim Trail** runs along the edge of the Painted Desert valley within the park. The 1-mile loop trail stretches between Tawa and Kachina Points near the Painted Desert Inn.

The area around the Painted Desert Inn—extending about 10 miles south on the park's main road—shows some of the most spectacular examples of the Painted Desert in the region. The Neapolitan ice cream–like striated layers of rock stretch to the horizon, dazzling visitors. There are multiple pullouts along the road south of the inn, all well positioned for optimal photo taking.

Farther south along the park's main road, the 100-room **Puerco Pueblo** dates from the 13th century. You cannot visit the partially stabilized ruins, but the ruins and petroglyphs are viewable from an overlook along the road.

Continuing south, the park's famous **Newspaper Rock** looms. The large boulders in the area are covered with petro-glyphs, hence the name. You can take a gander at the petroglyphs using the telescopes at the overlook. Look in particular at the dark boulders directly below the lookout. **Blue Mesa** is nearby, with a loop road running along a petrified wood field sitting among beautiful mesas rising from the Painted Desert. Along the loop road is the trailhead for the 1-mile **Blue Mesa Trail,** a self-guiding loop trail that will take you down among the petrified logs and mesas. The park service rates the trail as moderate in difficulty.

Back on the park's main road, the next stop is the **Jasper Forest Overlook,** with a wonderful view of petrified logs scattered like funny-looking Tootsie Rolls around the multihued landscape.

Farther south, the **Crystal Forest Trailhead** accesses a 0.75-mile loop trail that winds through a field of petrified logs. The park service rates this trail as easy. Another trail, the **Long Logs Trail,** is even shorter at 0.5 mile and will lead you into a large field of petrified wood. This trail is also rated as easy, and the trailhead is south of the Crystal Forest Trailhead along the park's main road.

The **Agate House Trail,** south of the Long Logs Trail along the park's main road, is 1.6 miles round-trip. The easy trail leads to a fascinating pueblo constructed in A.D. 1150 of petrified wood.

The final stop in the park is the **Rainbow Forest Museum.** Before stepping inside the building, it is worth checking out the easy **Giant Logs Trail,** a half-mile paved trail with its trailhead at the museum. The trail loops by the largest petrified log within the national park's boundaries.

The museum has exhibits about petrified wood and dinosaurs, which are sure to please the kids. The museum is also a visitor center, with park information, information on ranger-led tours, a bookstore, a snack bar, and a curio shop (across the street from the visitor center) selling legally collected petrified wood and other neat stuff.

The Giant Logs Trail, which begins behind the Rainbow Forest Museum near the southern entrance to the park, winds through a hilly field of petrified logs and smaller chunks of petrified wood. TODD R. BERGER

If you entered the park in the north, and it is time to head home or back to Holbrook, head north on U.S. 180 20 miles to Holbrook and I-40.

NEARBY SITES

Meteor Crater
Exit 233 on Interstate 40
(928) 289-5898
www.meteorcrater.com
Thirty-five miles east of Flagstaff and 75 miles west of Petrified Forest National Park, Meteor Crater is a privately owned site featuring a gigantic crater created by a meteorite that struck the earth 50,000 years ago. The meteorite was some 150 feet in diameter and weighed hundreds of tons, and the crater resulting from the impact is an astounding 550 feet deep,

more than 4,000 feet in diameter, and 2.4 miles around. After impact, pieces of limestone, some the size of small houses, showered onto the crater rim, where they sit today. The meteorite itself was vaporized upon impact.

No longer directly threatened by space objects, Meteor Crater today is a popular attraction with an elaborate visitor center. In 1968, the federal government designated Meteor Crater a National Natural Landmark. It is home to the Museum of Astrogeology, a state-of-the-art facility with interactive displays about the solar system, meteorites, and asteroids.

The Astronaut Hall of Fame commemorates the Mercury, Gemini, and Apollo astronaut crews of the 1960s and 1970s. The hall includes a spacesuit worn by astronaut Charles Duke and an Apollo test capsule that was used for studies and retrieval practice. The hall also features a movie theater showing *Collisions and Impacts,* a film about meteorites and asteroids, every half hour.

Behind the visitor center, four observation viewpoints look out over the crater. The overlooks feature telescopes. If you want to get a more intimate view of the crater and the results of the impact, consider taking one of the daily guided tours, which leave hourly from the visitor center. The tours last about an hour and take you about 0.3 mile along the rim.

Meteor Crater is open daily year round.

SUNSET CRATER, WUPATKI, AND WALNUT CANYON NATIONAL MONUMENTS

Imagine yourself living nearly 1,000 years ago. You are a Native American, a Sinaguan. (This name would be given to you in the 20th century by Harold S. Colton, based on the Spanish phrase for the nearby San Francisco Peaks, *Sierra sin Agua* or "mountains without water.") You live in a village of pit houses dug into the ground and roofed with poles supporting brush. Your ancestors migrated here from the south roughly 400 years ago. This rock-strewn land at the foot of the mountains has been your home for many generations. You make your living by gathering pinyon nuts, hunting squirrels and rabbits, and collecting seeds. You also grow corn, beans, and squash, trying to time your planting to take advantage of the unreliable water cycles of the Colorado Plateau. You build dams across the washes to gather water when the washes run during spring snowmelt and after summer thunderstorms.

One day you begin to feel the ground shudder. You hear a rumbling from far within the earth. Your life is about to change forever.

The Sinagua who lived near Sunset Crater apparently had sufficient warning to move away before the volcano erupted. The remains of their pit houses show that they were abandoned in an orderly way. The Sinagua took with them their stunning redware and brownware pots, the beams so painstakingly cut for roof poles for their houses, and most of the rest of their possessions.

Sunset Crater erupted in the winter of A.D. 1064-65, spewing black cinders, deadly gases, acid rain, and forest fires across hundreds of square miles of the eastern part of the San Francisco Volcanic Field. Archaeologists know that the area was inhabited before the volcano erupted because they have found a pit house covered by a layer of cinders. The volcano erupted sporadically for 200 years, but a few decades after the first eruption, the Sinagua returned to a vastly different landscape from the one they had left.

Colton theorized that the layer of volcanic cinders and ash acted as a mulch that held in water, so the land was now richer and easier to farm. He argued that many peoples, learning of this new and better farmland, came from miles away. The ancestral Puebloan people came from the north and the Cohonina from the west. With them came new technologies. It was during the decades after the eruption of Sunset Crater that the great pueblo of Wupatki was built. No longer did the Sinagua live in scattered villages of pit houses. They now built multistory, above-ground pueblos similar to those that can be seen on the Hopi Reservation today. Colton guessed that the population grew from 3,000 people before the volcano erupted to 8,000 after people returned to the area.

Wupatki, a pueblo of rooms for living, ceremonial rooms, and even a ball court (showing evidence of contact with peoples far to the south), was a great trading center, one of the many that connected the peoples from south of the Mogollon Rim, perhaps as far south as Central America, to those who lived in the Four Corners area.

The pueblo, ball court, and amphitheater have been partially reconstructed and now, along with outliers such as Wukoki and Lomaki, they make up Wupatki National Monument, located about 18 miles from Sunset Crater. The Sinagua also lived at Walnut Canyon National Monument, just east of Flagstaff, building cliff dwellings and pit houses near their agricultural fields.

SUNSET CRATER NATIONAL MONUMENT

Just one of the more than 600 cinder cones of the San Francisco Volcanic Field, Sunset Crater is the most recent to have been active. It began erupting in the winter of A.D. 1064–65 and continued to explode intermittently for about 200 years, covering the area with cinder cones and lava flows. Volcanic activity around Flagstaff, which began six million years ago, is moving from west to east, so the cinder cones around Williams are older than those east of Flagstaff. The entire volcanic field covers more than 2,200 square miles.

Sunset Crater Volcano National Monument is open year-round except December 25. Drive north from Flagstaff 12 miles on U.S. Highway 89 and turn right onto the Sunset Crater–Wupatki Loop Road. The visitor center is 2 miles farther along the road. The entrance fee of $5.00 per person covers both Sunset Crater and Wupatki National Monuments. Golden Eagle, Golden Age, and Golden Access Passports are accepted, but wheelchair access to Sunset Crater is limited.

The **Lava Flow Nature Trail** is 1.5 miles from the visitor center. This 1-mile self-guided hike takes you past a variety of volcanic formations, which are labeled and described for you.

The **Lenox Crater Trail** is a steep 1-mile trail up a cinder cone. Expect to spend about 30 minutes going up and 15 coming down. Sunset Crater Volcano itself is closed to hikers and climbers. Little vegetation grows on this very young cinder cone, so it is too fragile for hikers (much less all-terrain vehicles).

The Sunset Crater cinder cone rises 1,000 feet above the surrounding land. A cinder cone forms when magma (molten rock and compressed gases) rises from its underground source and explodes from a central vent. The magma cools and falls back to the earth as solid rock, forming a mound, or cone, of cinder.

Lava may also flow from the base of the cone. When this liquid rock is exposed to air, the surface cools more quickly than the interior, producing "aa" (pronounced ah-ah). This is the jagged, sharp rock "field" that you see in the Bonita Lava Flow at Bonito Flow Pullout on the north side of the road near Lenox Crater.

Spatter cones are the smaller cones you see around Sunset Crater. The self-guided tour will also help you recognize other volcanic formations such as squeeze-ups, where partly cooled lava pushed through cracks.

Around A.D. 1250, at the end of Sunset Crater's active period, iron- and sulphur-bearing lava erupted from the central vent. These red and yellow particles fell back onto the top surface of the cone, and they are what give Sunset Crater its distinctive color and its name.

Scientists and archaeologists are still working on two fascinating questions. The first concerns the origin of the San Francisco Volcanic Field. One theory is that this area is on top of a hot spot, an active spot on the earth's surface where the crust is moving over the mantle below. Another hot spot in North America is Yellowstone National Park. The second theory is that the southern Colorado Plateau is being cut into by valley and mountain ranges to the south and the west. This kind of collision can cause volcanic activity.

Another question revolves around the people who lived in the area when the volcano erupted. One theory says that the ash from the volcano acted as a sponge, holding rainwater in and making the area much more fertile. Therefore, people moved here to settle. Another theory argues that above-average rainfall in the area between about A.D. 1050 and 1130 is

You can't hike to the top of Sunset Crater within Sunset Crater National Monument, but there are several pullouts and trails within the monument with nice views of the mountain.
TODD R. BERGER

what led ancient peoples to build communities such as Wupatki and the many hundreds of other ruins in the area.

When you visit Sunset Crater, you will find picnic areas at the visitor center, Lava Flow Trail, and Painted Desert Vista, and vending machines at the visitor center. There are no other services (so make sure you start out with enough gas in your car to see both Sunset Crater and Wupatki National Monument). Bonito Campground is just before the entrance to the monument and is open late March/early April to mid-October, weather permitting. The largest vehicle that can be accommodated is 42 feet long; there are no hookups. For more information on the campground, call (928) 526–0866. Flagstaff has plenty of hotel and motel accommodations, as well as other campgrounds.

For more information, call Sunset Crater Volcano National Monument, (928) 526–0502, or visit the Web site at www.nps.gov/sucr.

WUPATKI NATIONAL MONUMENT

Drive through Sunset National Monument, then through a wilderness area until you reach Wupatki National Monument. The Wupatki Visitor Center is 21 miles from the intersection with U.S. Highway 89. Along this two-lane road, you will see magnificent vistas of the Painted Desert (there is a pullout for picture taking) and you will notice that as the elevation drops, ponderosa pine forest gives way to juniper and pinyon. Cattle graze on these lands. You may also see muledeer, pronghorn, chipmunks, squirrels, red-tailed hawks, and eagles. And the thing that looks like a yardstick flitting across your path is actually a roadrunner.

The Wupatki pueblo is built of red Moenkopi sandstone and Kaibab limestone. The ball court incorporates some black volcanic rock. According to Colton's theory, the ancestral Puebloan people,

the famed builders of Mesa Verde and Chaco Canyon, taught the Sinagua the masonry techniques for the construction of the pueblo. The purpose of the so-called amphitheater has never been satisfactorily explained. The ball court structure resembles known courts for ball games found as far south as Central America. Exactly what game was played there, with what rules, implements, and consequences, remains a mystery.

Evidence that this was a trade center includes archaeological finds of textiles from the Verde Valley 50 miles to the south, turquoise from New Mexico, shells from the Pacific, and copper bells and parrot feathers from Mexico.

According to Colton's "black sand" theory, Wupatki was occupied by Sinagua, ancestral Pueblo, and Cohonina until about A.D. 1220. A severe drought that began in 1150—and the wind's removal of the ash that made the land especially fertile—are perhaps the reasons that the people left Wupatki, which would never again be a permanent residence.

Colton's black sand theory has been challenged by archaeologist Peter Pilles. He argues that Colton overemphasized the importance of the ash from Sunset Crater Volcano on the quality of the land for farming. During the same period that Wupatki was built and occupied, the area experienced unusually high rainfall. The rainfall, according to Pilles, may have been a more important factor than the volcanic ash in enticing people to move to the area. Another group, the Hohokam, may also have lived in the area. If so, they may have been the people to bring ball courts, clay figurines, and shell ornaments to the region. Pilles also maintains that the masonry techniques used at Wupatki were known to the Sinagua before the ancestral Pueblo arrived.

The ancestral Puebloan people are best known for the fabulous cliff dwellings they constructed at Mesa Verde (in Colorado) and Canyon de Chelly (in northeastern Arizona), as well as the incredibly

Entering Wupatki National Monument from the south along the road from Sunset Crater National Monument. TODD R. BERGER

rich pueblo complex in New Mexico known as Chaco Canyon, but these are only a few of the places they lived on the Colorado Plateau. As early as A.D. 400, they lived in pit houses on Black Mesa, around Navajo Mountain, and in the Tsegi Canyon area. Ancestral Puebloan sites all across the Colorado Plateau show evidence of having been inhabited, abandoned, and reoccupied over hundreds of years. When the Indian reservations were created by the U.S. government, the indigenous peoples of the Colorado Plateau were denied access to the lands on which their ancestors had thrived for hundreds of years.

The origins of the ancestral Puebloan people, known also for their black-on-white decorated pottery, are unclear, but archaeologists do know that they emerged as a distinct culture in the first or second century A.D. Their technology included domesticated plants, the digging stick,

grinding stones, and storage rooms, all of which are shared by contemporary Hopi.

Also like today's traditional Hopi farmers, the people of the ancestral Puebloan culture dry-farmed, taking full advantage of the moisture provided by snowmelt and the July-to-September monsoon rains that soak this area with spectacular afternoon thunderstorms during the late summer. Their primary domesticated plant was maize, or corn, first domesticated in Mexico. They also grew beans and squash. Beans, squash, and corn are the Three Sisters of the traditional Hopi diet.

The ancestral Puebloan people did not rely entirely on farming for their living. They gathered pinyon pine nuts, the fibers of the banana yucca, and the fruit of the prickly pear, and they hunted jackrabbits, prairie dogs, and deer. They also used indigenous plants for many other purposes such as basketmaking and medicine. The addition of the bow and arrow

Federal Recreation Passport Program

If you are planning to visit several national parks (such as Grand Canyon), national monuments (such as Sunset Crater) and historic sites (such as Hubbell Trading Post), you will probably save money by purchasing a Golden Eagle Passport.

The passport admits the passport owner and any accompanying passengers in a private vehicle to most national parks, monuments, historic sites, recreation areas, and national wildlife refuges that charge an entrance fee. The passport is good for one year and provides unlimited entries to the fee areas.

Golden Eagle Passports cost $50 and may be purchased at any federal area where fees are charged. This passport does not cover use fees (fees for camping, swimming, boating, parking, and so on).

An even better option for U.S. citizens or permanent residents age 62 or over is the Golden Age Passport, a lifetime pass to most national parks, monuments, historic sites, recreation areas, and national wildlife refuges. This passport must be purchased in person at any federal area where a fee is charged, and you must show proof of age (a driver's license, a birth certificate, or similar document). A one-time $10 processing fee will allow the passport signee and any accompanying passengers in a private vehicle unlimited access. The Golden Age Passport also gives the holder a 50 percent reduction for some use fees.

Golden Access Passports are available to people who are blind or permanently disabled. In addition to entrance fees, this passport provides a 50% discount on federal use fees. The Golden Access Passport must be obtained in person at any federal area where a fee is charged. You will be required to show proof of U.S. citizenship or permanent residence status and proof of medically determined eligibility.

The National Park Service also offers a $25 Local Passport, allowing entrance to the three Flagstaff-area national monuments (Sunset Crater, Wupatki, and Walnut Canyon) for one year. You can buy this pass at any of the three monuments, or at the National Park Service Flagstaff Area office at 6400 North Highway 89 in Flagstaff; (928) 526-1157.

For more information on the Federal Recreation Passport Program, write the National Park Service Office of Public Inquiries, Room 1013, U.S. Department of the Interior, 1849 C Street NW, P.O. Box 37127, Washington, D.C. 20013-7127. Or write to a regional office of the forest service. The address of the office for the Southwestern Region is Federal Building, 517 Gold Avenue SW, Albuquerque, NM 87102.

to replace the spear or atlatl for hunting and the development of pottery around A.D. 500 contributed to the ability of these people to build and settle in pueblo villages or cliff dwellings. They began building such structures around A.D. 700 and this building technology culminated in the construction at Chaco Canyon from about A.D. 900 to 1130 and the cliff dwellings of Mesa Verde, Keet Seel, and Betatakin

The surrounding desert seen through a window in Wukoki Pueblo, Wupatki National Monument.
TODD R. BERGER

around A.D. 1200. By the late 13th century, all of these sites had been abandoned.

For many years, archaeologists believed that the ancestral Puebloan people simply "disappeared." But they did not disappear. They moved—to northern New Mexico and central Arizona, to the upper Rio Grande, Pecos, and Little Colorado River regions. The mesas where the Hopi now live are a mere 60 miles from Wupatki. The Hopi, the Zuni, and the peoples of the Rio Grande pueblos are descendants of the ancestral Puebloan cultures.

For two reasons—because it is an archaeological site protected by the U.S. government and because it is an important site in the religious life of contemporary Native Americans—tourists should think of themselves as invited guests when they visit this and other archaeological sites on the Colorado Plateau. Staying on established trails is important to protect the sites from damage. Sitting or walking on walls damages them, and taking or moving items such as rocks, fossils, animals, plants, or pottery destroys the archaeological record. Needless to say, graffiti scribed or painted on rocks degrades the site. All of these activities are against the law and are punishable by fines.

The **Wupatki Trail** is one-half mile round-trip and will allow you to see the main pueblo, the ball court, and the amphitheater. You can also view the entire complex from the overlook just a few feet from the visitor center.

Lomaki Trail is also a half mile long, and gives views of several other ancient pueblos. There are also trails at Wukoki, Citadel, and Nalakihu. The **Doney Mountain Trail** takes you from the picnic area to the top of the mountain for unparalleled views of the whole region. Wupatki Trail is wheelchair accessible to the overlook, and wheelchair-accessible rest rooms can be found at Doney Mountain picnic area and Lomaki. Hiking is restricted to signed trails, and the backcountry of this national monument is closed to hikers to protect the fragile ecosystem and ruins.

Wupatki National Monument is open year-round except December 25. Generally the hours are from dawn to dusk. The road through Sunset Crater and Wupatki is a loop, and if you follow the loop all the way around you will end up farther north on U.S. Highway 89, well on your way to Cameron. (You can also enter Wupatki National Monument from this northern entrance and loop south to Sunset Crater National Monument.)

At Wupatki you will find picnic areas, as well as vending machines for snacks and drinks at the visitor center, but there are no other services, such as gas, and no food that could be considered lunch.

The closest camping is at Bonito Campground across from the Sunset Crater National Monument Visitor Center. Flagstaff has other campgrounds, as well as many motels and hotels.

For more information, contact Wupatki National Monument, (928) 679-2365; www.nps.gov/wupa.

WALNUT CANYON NATIONAL MONUMENT

The third Flagstaff-area national monument, Walnut Canyon, sits 7.5 miles east of Flagstaff off Interstate 40. Walnut Canyon has cliff dwellings that were also home to the Sinagua, who lived at Walnut Canyon until A.D. 1300. The northern side of Walnut Canyon and the rim areas provided the best areas for farming, particularly of corn, which made up the bulk of the Sinaguan diet. The Sinagua built cliff dwellings and pit houses near their agricultural fields.

There are two paved trails within the national monument. The **Island Trail** descends to the canyon floor along an 0.9-mile loop trail, passing by 25 cliff dwelling rooms. For a close-up view of the rim structures and beautiful views of the canyon, take the 0.7-mile **Rim Trail.** The interior of the monument is not open to hikers, but you can visit other areas by

Dozens of ruins line the canyon walls at Walnut Canyon National Monument. For an up-close look, walk the strenuous-but-rewarding Island Trail (the trailhead is behind the visitor center), which passes right by numerous ruins in varying states of decay. TODD R. BERGER

participating in one of two ranger-guided backcountry hikes, offered on Saturday, Sunday, and Tuesday between Memorial Day and Labor Day. Reservations are required; call (928) 526-3367 for more information.

The visitor center is 3 miles from the exit off I-40. The visitor center complex includes an information desk, a Western National Parks and Monuments bookstore, rest rooms, exhibits, a picnic area, and a panoramic view of Walnut Canyon. Both the Island Trail and the Rim Trail begin at the visitor center.

For more information about Walnut Canyon National Monument, call the visitor center at (928) 526-3367, or visit the monument on the Web at www.nps.gov/waca.

MEDIA 📺

NEWSPAPERS

Arizona Daily Sun
1751 South Thompson Street, Flagstaff
(928) 774-4545
www.azdailysun.com
Flagstaff's daily newspaper, the *Arizona Daily Sun,* is available for sale or by subscription throughout northern Arizona. The paper includes local, state, national, and international news; sports coverage with an emphasis on Northern Arizona University teams and prep sports throughout the region; classified advertising including job listings and real estate for sale in Flagstaff and surrounding areas; an Arts & Living section; community events; and an Outdoors section. The paper prints a special Wednesday edition for the Navajo and Hopi Reservations, and a Wednesday Extra for Flagstaff.

Arizona Republic
200 East Van Buren Street, Phoenix
(602) 444-000, (800) 332-6733
www.azcentral.com/arizonarepublic
The *Arizona Republic* has the widest circulation in the state, and the paper is available for sale or by subscription throughout northern Arizona. The newspaper is a major metropolitan daily with coverage of domestic and international news, state news, local (Phoenix-area) news, sports, Arts & Entertainment and "Arizona Living," a Travel section (on Sunday), Phoenix and out-of-state real estate listings, and extensive classified advertising. Throughout most of the northern part of the state, the *Republic* is the best newspaper for current news.

Flagstaff Live!
111 West Birch, Flagstaff
(928) 779-1877
www.flaglive.com
Flagstaff's arts and entertainment weekly (published on Thursday) is the best source for weekly listings of live music performances, art exhibits, community events, and the performing arts. The free newspaper is available at many locations (look particularly in bars and coffeehouses) throughout Flagstaff and Sedona.

The *Guide*
Grand Canyon National Park
(928) 638-7888
www.nps.gov/grca
The National Park Service at Grand Canyon, in cooperation with the Grand Canyon Association, publishes the free *Guide* quarterly for Grand Canyon National Park's South Rim and annually for the park's North Rim, with information on ranger programs, visitor centers, sunrise and sunset times, Kolb Studio art exhibits, day hikes, seasonal news, lodging, restaurants, other services, and a map of Grand Canyon Village and its shuttle bus system. The *Guide* is handed out to visitors as they enter the park, and you can also find copies at Canyon View Information Plaza and all Grand Canyon Association bookstores (Kolb Studio, Yavapai Observation Station, Books & More at Canyon View Information Plaza, Tusayan Ruin and Museum, Desert View, and the North Rim).

Navajo-Hopi Observer
417 West Santa Fe Avenue, Flagstaff
(928) 226-9696, (877) 627-3787
www.navajohopiobserver.com
The weekly (published on Wednesday) *Navajo-Hopi Observer* covers news relevant to the Navajo and Hopi Reservations, sports, community events, classified advertising, and weather. The newspaper is widely available in Flagstaff, on the Navajo and Hopi Reservations, and in surrounding communities.

Navajo Times
Highway 264 at Route 12, Window Rock
(928) 871-7461
www.thenavajotimes.com
Published weekly (every Thursday), "the Newspaper of the Navajo People" includes current events, Navajo Nation capital reports, Native American news, culture, opinion, education, community events, sports, job announcements, and classified advertising. The newspaper is widely available on the Navajo Indian Reservation and in surrounding northern Arizona communities.

Red Rock News
Sedona
(928) 282-6888
www.redrocknews.com
Sedona's biweekly newspaper is printed every Wednesday and Friday. Widely available in the Sedona area and by subscription throughout northern Arizona, the paper covers local news, forest service activities, community events, arts, and other happenings around Sedona, and includes real estate listings for Sedona and surrounding communities.

Williams-Grand Canyon News
118 South Third Street, Williams
(928) 635-4426, (800) 408-4726
www.grandcanyonnews.com
The *Williams–Grand Canyon News* is a weekly (published on Wednesday) covering news, community events, education, the Ranger Report, classified advertising, and sports for the Williams and Grand Canyon areas. The Ranger Report, an incident-by-incident account of events involving rangers in and around Grand Canyon National Park, is particularly intriguing to visitors, with briefs describing inner-canyon rescues, heat-related medical emergencies (these dominate the report during the summer months despite extensive park service warnings to take precautions and avoid dangerous activities), other medical emergencies and minor injuries, dispute resolutions, and petty

(most of the time) criminal activity such as the theft of bikes. In a rather refreshing way, the petty criminal activity is usually resolved, as the return or recovery of stolen items is often noted a few lines down in the Ranger Report. The newspaper is for sale at retail outlets and in newspaper boxes along the Williams–to–Grand Canyon corridor, and is available by subscription throughout northern Arizona.

MAGAZINES AND NEWSLETTERS

Arizona Highways
2039 West Lewis Avenue, Phoenix
(602) 712-2200, (800) 543-5432
www.arizonahighways.com
Although based in Phoenix and with coverage of the entire state, *Arizona Highways* is the best magazine featuring northern Arizona natural areas and historic sites. The quality of the photography will make your eyes pop, and the stories on everything from hiking in the San Francisco Peaks to monsoon season at Grand Canyon to visiting the Hubbell Trading Post National Historic Site will engross you. The magazine is widely available at newsstands and retail outlets throughout northern Arizona, and by subscription everywhere else.

Canyon Views/Nature Notes
Grand Canyon Association
1 Tonto Street, Grand Canyon Village
(928) 638-2481
www.grandcanyon.org
Canyon Views and *Nature Notes* are available to members of the Grand Canyon Association. *Canyon Views,* the association's member newsletter, is published quarterly and features articles about events in Grand Canyon National Park; art exhibits; interviews with artists, photographers, and authors; natural history; and Grand Canyon Association activities to benefit the park. *Nature Notes,* produced by the National Park Service at Grand

The Grand Canyon Association, which publishes Canyon Views, offers publications, member services, and books on many subjects at several bookstores in the park, including Books & More at Canyon View Information Plaza. TODD R. BERGER

Canyon and published twice a year with *Canyon Views,* contains natural history articles on everything from California condors to the Vishnu schist.

Plateau Journal
Museum of Northern Arizona
3101 North Fort Valley Road, Flagstaff
(928) 774-5211, ext. 240
Plateau Journal is published twice a year by the Museum of Northern Arizona. The large-format magazine features stunning photography and in-depth articles on the Colorado Plateau (especially northern Arizona) natural areas, historic sites, art, and much more. The magazine is available at the museum, in some retail outlets in the region, at Grand Canyon Association bookstores at Grand Canyon National Park, by subscription, and as a membership premium from both the Museum of Northern Arizona and the Grand Canyon Association. You can purchase back issues of the magazine on-line from the Grand Canyon Association at www.grand canyon.org/bookstore (search using the keywords "Plateau Journal").

TELEVISION STATIONS

KAET-TV 8 (PBS)
Arizona State University, Tempe
(480) 965-3506
www.kaet.asu.edu
Based in the Phoenix metropolitan region on the campus of ASU, KAET is available by broadcast, via satellite, and on cable systems throughout much of northern Arizona. The station is the area's PBS affiliate.

KFTH-TV 13 (TeleFutura)
2158 North Fourth Street, Flagstaff
(928) 526-1396
Channel 13 is the Flagstaff Spanish-language TeleFutura affiliate.

KNAZ-TV 2 (NBC)
2201 North Vickey, Flagstaff
(928) 526-2232

KNAZ is Flagstaff's NBC affiliate, with local news and national programming available by broadcast, via satellite, and on local cable systems.

KNXV-TV 15 (ABC)
515 North 44th Street, Phoenix
(602) 273-1500
www.knxv.com
KNXV, although based in Phoenix, is northern Arizona's ABC affiliate. The station can be picked up with an antenna in some areas, and is available on satellite and cable broadcasts throughout the region. Although not perfect, the local news of Channel 15 is widely regarded as the least sensationalistic of the commercial network stations broadcasting out of Phoenix, a refreshing information source in a sea of "If It Bleeds, It Leads" broadcast stations.

KPHO-TV 5 (CBS)
4016 North Black Canyon Highway, Phoenix
(602) 264-1000
www.kpho.com
Channel 5, based in Phoenix, broadcasts CBS programming and local news to northern Arizona. The station can be picked up with an antenna in some areas, and is available on cable and satellite systems in most other areas.

KPNX-TV 12 (NBC)
1101 North Central Avenue, Phoenix
(602) 257-1212
www.azcentral.com/12news
Channel 12, based in Phoenix, broadcasts NBC programming and local news to northern Arizona.

KSAZ-TV 10 (Fox)
511 West Adams, Phoenix
(602) 257-1234
www.fox10phoenix.com
Channel 10, the Phoenix Fox affiliate, can be picked up in parts of northern Arizona via television antenna and watched on cable or satellite in most of the rest of the region.

KTVK-TV 3 (Independent)
100 North San Francisco Street, Flagstaff
(928) 773-9136
KTVK is a Phoenix-based independent station with a satellite bureau in Flagstaff. Channel 3 can be picked up through the airwaves in parts of northern Arizona, and by satellite and cable in most other areas.

KTVW-TV 6 (Univision)
2158 North Fourth Street, Flagstaff
(928) 527-1300
Channel 6 is the Spanish-language Univision affiliate in Flagstaff.

KUTP-TV 45 (UPN)
511 West Adams, Phoenix
(602) 257-1234
www.kutp.com
The Phoenix-based UPN affiliate can be picked up in Flagstaff and is available by satellite and cable services throughout much of northern Arizona.

RADIO STATIONS

KAFF 930 AM and 92.9 FM
1117 West Route 66, Flagstaff
(928) 774-5231
www.kaff.com
KAFF plays classic country music from stars such as Johnny Cash, Patsy Cline, Loretta Lynn, Waylon Jennings, and George Jones. You can also tune into the station for such nationally syndicated programs as ABC News, Rush Limbaugh, and Paul Harvey.

KFLX 105.1 FM
112 East Route 66, Flagstaff
(928) 779-1177
www.kflx.com
KFLX "The New Eagle" plays alternative rock hits from groups such as the Dave Matthews Band, U2, Train, Lenny Kravitz, and Creed.

KMGN 93.9 FM
1117 West Route 66, Flagstaff
(928) 774-5231
www.kmgn.com
Specializing in classic rock, KMGN plays artists such as the Beatles, David Lee Roth, ZZ Top, Steely Dan, Aerosmith, and Lynyrd Skynyrd.

KNAU 88.7 FM
Northern Arizona Public Radio
Flagstaff
(928) 523-5628, (800) 523-5628
www.knauradio.org
KNAU's sister frequencies across northern Arizona broadcast National Public Radio programming, local news, and classical music. The primary frequency in Flagstaff is 88.7 FM, but the broadcast is also relayed on transmitters at Grand Canyon Village (90.3 FM), Page (91.7 FM), the Navajo and Hopi Reservations (88.1 FM), and several other northern and central Arizona communities.

KOLT 107.5 FM
112 East Route 66, Flagstaff
(928) 779-1177
www.koltcountry.com
KOLT Country broadcasts country music hits by stars such as the Dixie Chicks, Garth Brooks, Reba McIntyre, and Shania Twain.

KSGC 92.1 FM
Tusayan
(928) 638-9552
KSGC broadcasts contemporary top-40 rock hits to listeners in and around Grand Canyon Village.

KVNA 600 AM
2690 East Huntington Drive, Flagstaff
(928) 526-2700
www.radioflagstaff.com/am600/am600.htm
KVNA on the AM dial broadcasts news, talk, and sports, including nationally syndi-

cated programs like The Radio Factor with
Bill O'Reilly, Dr. Laura Schlessinger, and
ESPN Radio.

KVNA 97.5 FM
2690 East Huntington Drive, Flagstaff
(928) 526-2700
www.radioflagstaff.com/Sunny/sunny.htm
KVNA's FM station, Sunny 97, broadcasts
easy-to-digest smooth rock hits from
artists such as Sheryl Crow, Natalie
Imbruglia, Jewel, the Calling, and John
Mayer.

KWMX 96.7 FM
112 East Route 66, Flagstaff
(928) 779-1177
www.coololdies.com

KWMX plays oldies from the Beatles, Elvis,
and a whole lot more. The station is also
the home of Arizona State Football
broadcasts to northern Arizona.

KZGL 95.9 FM and 101.7 FM
2690 East Huntington Drive, Flagstaff
(928) 526-2700
www.radioflagstaff.com/kzgl/ZHome.htm
KZGL plays harder-edged rock from alt-
metal groups like Limp Bizkit, Metallica,
Type O Negative, Staind, Revis, Radio-
head, and Marilyn Manson.

INDEX

ABOUT THE AUTHORS

TODD R. BERGER

Todd R. Berger is the managing editor of the Grand Canyon Association and a freelance writer, editor, and photographer based in Grand Canyon National Park. His work has been published in *Arizona Highways, Lighthouse Digest, Williams–Grand Canyon News, Plateau Journal,* and *Canyon Views.* He is the editor of 11 anthologies on subjects ranging from golden retrievers to loons, and the editor of dozens of books on wildlife and the natural world, including various aspects of Grand Canyon National Park. A former resident of Minnesota, he is the author of *Lighthouses of the Great Lakes* and a co-author of the *Insiders' Guide to the Twin Cities* (fourth edition), published by The Globe Pequot Press .

An avid hiker, bicyclist, and canoeist, Todd Berger has logged hundreds of miles on the trails of Grand Canyon National Park, along the waterways of Minnesota's Boundary Waters Canoe Area Wilderness, along the Kickapoo River and among the isles of Apostle Islands National Lakeshore in Wisconsin, and in other northern Arizona natural areas He also works as a volunteer Preventive Search and Rescue (PSAR) ranger at Grand Canyon National Park and sits on the board of the Grand Canyon Community Library. In the process of updating the *Insiders' Guide to Grand Canyon and Northern Arizona,* he traveled thosands of miles across northern Arizona.

Todd R. Berger. BONNIE PLATT

TANYA H. LEE

Writer and artist Tanya H. Lee first visited the enchanted land of the Colorado Plateau two decades ago. A few years later, she and her husband, Garret Rosenblatt, bought some land east of Flagstaff, built a house, and relocated from Cambridge, Massachusetts. A barn, two horses, and innumerable cats later, she is still exploring the many facets—geological, historical, and cultural—of this unique area.

Tanya Lee has been a freelance writer and artist for many years. Her job as managing editor of the *Navajo-Hopi Observer* allowed her to pursue her long-standing interest in the Native cultures of northern Arizona and Grand Canyon. She has traveled widely on the Navajo and Hopi Reservations and developed a working knowledge of the peoples' histories and current concerns.

KERRI QUINN

Kerri Quinn was born in New York City and lived on the East Coast until the age of 20. She had always been intrigued by the landscape and people of the West and moved to Phoenix. After spending a few years traveling around the Southwest and through Montana and Wyoming, she came to Flagstaff to finish her degree in English and Spanish at Northern Arizona University. Following a period of studies in Spain, Kerri Quinn returned to Flagstaff, where she has worked as a Spanish teacher, a marketing coordinator for a local publishing company, and a freelance writer for *Flagstaff Live!, SWEAT Magazine,* and *Arizona Daily Sun.*

Grand Canyon - South Rim
Apache Stables - 928-638-2891
Canyon Dave -

? Lava River Cave Hwy 180

Thunderbird Lodge Canyon Tour - Canyon de Chelle